Transatlantic Crossings

D0956497

Rethinking British Cinema

Series Editor: Professor Pam Cook, University of Southampton

This series is dedicated to innovative approaches to British cinema. It expands the parameters of debate, shedding new light on areas such as gender and sexuality, audiences, ethnicity, stars, visual style, genre, music and sound. Moving beyond narrow definitions of national cinema, the series celebrates the richness and diversity of British film culture.

Published titles in the series:
The Beatles Movies, by Bob Neaverson
Dissolving Views, edited by Andrew Higson
Gainsborough Pictures, edited by Pam Cook
Searching for Stars, by Geoffrey Macnab
Women in British Cinema, by Sue Harper

Also of interest from Continuum:
British Cinema and the Second World War, by Robert Murphy
Stars and Stardom in French Cinema, by Ginette Vincendeau
Black in the British Frame, 2nd Edition, by Stephen Bourne
Alice Guy Blaché: Lost Visionary of the Cinema, by Alison McMahan
Cinema's Illusions, Opera's Allure: The Operatic Impulse in Film,
   by David Schroeder
The Guerilla Film Maker's Handbook, 2nd Edition,
   by Chris Jones and Genevieve Jolliffe
Gaslight Melodrama, by Guy Barefoot
Cinema and the Second Sex, by Carrie Tarr with Brigitte Rollet
Popular Cinemas of Europe, by Dimitris Eleftheriotis
Italian Cinema, 3rd Edition, by Peter Bondanella
The Power of Film Propaganda, by Nicholas Reeves

Transatlantic Crossings

British Feature Films in the United States

Sarah Street

CONTINUUM

New York • London

The Continuum International Publishing Group Inc
370 Lexington Avenue, New York, NY 10017

The Continuum International Publishing Group Ltd
The Tower Building, 11 York Road, London SE1 7NX

Copyright © 2002 by Sarah Street

All rights reserved. No part of this publication may be reproduced or transmitted in any form or by any means, electronic or mechanical, including photocopying, recording, or any information storage or retrieval system, without permission in writing from the publishers or their appointed agents.

Printed in the United States of America

Library of Congress Cataloging-in-Publication Data
Street, Sarah.
    Transatlantic crossings : British feature films in the USA / Sarah
  Street.
       p. cm. — (Rethinking British cinema)
  Includes bibliographical references and index.
    ISBN 0-8264-1395-1 (alk. paper) — ISBN 0-8264-1396-X (pb. alk. paper)

    1. Motion pictures. British—United States. 2. Motion pictures—Great
  Britain—History. I. Title. II. Series.
    PN1993.5.G7 S76 2002
    791.43'75'0941—dc21
                             2002067650

For Jill Forbes

Contents

List of Illustrations

Cover still: Richard Dix in *The Tunnel/Transatlantic Tunnel* (Maurice Elvey, 1935); copyright, Carlton International.

Stills

Posters and Press Books

Note: All stills courtesy of the British Film Institute: Stills, Posters and Designs; Plates 22–29, courtesy of University of Southern California.

List of Tables

Acknowledgements

Many people have helped towards the completion of this book. In the United Kingdom, thanks are due to Janet Moat at the British Film Institute; the staff at the John Rylands Library, Manchester and at the Bodleian Library, Oxford. In the United States, I was assisted in particular by Barbara Hall at the Margaret Herrick Library, Los Angeles, and by Ned Comstock at the University of Southern California, who both helped me locate key materials which have proved to be extremely important for my research. Barbara Diamond kindly gave her permission to reprint *Hollywood Jabberwocky*. I would like to thank the Leverhulme Trust, the British Academy and the University of Bristol for providing me with research grants which made the initial research and final writing up of this book possible. Along the way I have benefited from the assistance of colleagues and friends who have helped me grapple with what at times seemed like an impossible task. Pam Cook, series editor for 'Re-thinking British Cinema' has been a kind, supportive and helpful editor. Sue Simkin, my companion on many transatlantic crossings, assisted me on my archival trails and was always there with helpful advice and comments. Brian Harvey undertook some useful supplementary research in the New York Public Library. I am also grateful to Mike Walsh who shared his researches into the United Artists' financial ledgers; he also provided useful comments on my chapter on Korda and United Artists. Andrew Higson read the chapter on silent cinema and offered some extremely constructive suggestions. Barbara Wilinsky Selznick discussed the art market with me when she was revising her doctoral dissertation for publication. I also had some very stimulating discussions about *Black Narcissus* with Priya Jaikumar. Other people who have shared their knowledge and been enthusiastic about the project include John Sedgwick, Mark Glancy and Steve Neale. As usual, Ian Conrich was extremely helpful in locating obscure films and articles. Finally, I would like to thank some key people who gave invaluable support at different times: Tony Aldgate, Sue Harper, Janet Thumim and the late Jill Forbes, to whom I dedicate this book.

Hollywood Jabberwocky

'Twas ciros, and the cinelords
Were lollyparsing with their babes:
All goldwyns were acadawards
But demille rules the nabes.

'Beware the Jarthurank, my lad!
The lion's claw, the eagle's wing!
And when U-I his pix, be glad
That DOS dos everything!'

He took his johnston code in hand:
Long time the ranksome foe he sought –
So rested he by the schary tree,
And stood awhile in thought.

And as in quota-quotes he stood,
The Jarthurank, of happy breed,
Came boulting through the korda wood
And carolled on his reed!

For sin! For shame! On cleavaged dame
The censor shears went flicker-flack!
He scarred the Bard, and coward marred
Went galluppolling back.

'And hast thou haysed the Jarthurank?
Come to my arms, my breenish boy!
O date and day! Elate! L.A.!'
He xenophobed with joy.

'T'was ciros, and the cinelords
Were lollyparsing with their babes:
All goldwyns were acadawards
But demille rules the nabes.

—I. A. L. Diamond
First published in *The Screenwriter*, vol. 3, no. 1, June 1947: 22

Introduction

I. A. L. Diamond's *Hollywood Jabberwocky* conveys something of the perilous journey experienced by British films when they crossed the Atlantic.[1] When J. Arthur Rank launched a major campaign for the exhibition of British films in the 1940s, they had to contend with serious obstacles, including the rigours of the censorship system and the wrath of the 'cinelords' who forbade entry into their kingdom. While exportation appeared to be a gamble, it was one Rank was prepared to take with varying, occasionally spectacular results. Like many producers before and after him, he found the prospect of British films being screened all over the United States to be an irresistible but somewhat unpredictable one. Just as travel leads to new encounters and experiences and often a re-evaluation of self, the British films that made the transatlantic crossing were similarly exposed to new contexts of reception. They did not become 'new' texts, but they were subject to interpretations that privileged American sensibilities and experiences.

Few studies have considered the history of British films in the United States.[2] It has been assumed that British films made little headway, largely because of Hollywood's domination of the home market. In Britain, film exports have been associated with profligacy, big budgets, empty 'internationalism' and a misguided pursuit of Hollywood-style reputation and profits. Commentators have argued that exports are inappropriate for a struggling national film industry that does not command the attention of its own audiences, let alone those overseas.[3] But American audiences did see British films; they were reviewed by critics, and, along with other European films, made an impact on film culture. While the opportunities for extensive distribution and exhibition were limited, many British films were popular with metropolitan audiences, occasionally 'crossing over' to wider circulation in 'the nabes' and beyond.[4] 'Transatlantic Crossings' is intended to convey the essence of the cross-cultural reception of these films: my research has been concerned with patterns of economic negotiation and cultural exchange. The case of Britain and the United

States is interesting because of the assumed 'special relationship' between the two countries – at times distant while on other occasions a close bond – implying that a shared transnational identity might exist, to be understood and absorbed by audiences in both countries.

Michael Walsh has discussed questions of national transferability with reference to the various options that were available to film producers just after the First World War (Walsh, 1997: 3–17). Hollywood appeared to offer a model of a successful international film industry that exemplified 'universal' standards, resulting in a dominant critical appreciation for particular attributes, such as classical Hollywood narration, that were seen to provide qualitative pointers to international acceptance. Producers learned from Hollywood that successful exportation depended on presenting a combination of 'local' representations with 'international' elements, something that was a little different but not alienating or incomprehensible to overseas audiences. Some films which were exported successfully therefore contained references that could be described as 'nationally specific' but which also proved to be 'transferable', exemplifying the aim of many producers to make films that would be successful at home and abroad. Arguments based on an uncritical acceptance of Hollywood's superiority invariably concealed the economic underpinnings of that success, resulting in a discourse that associated Hollywood with 'universal' standards, technical and thematic modernity. This observation is crucial because it reveals the extent to which claims that foreign films were 'inferior' were inextricably related to Hollywood's defence of its own hegemonic position. In this analysis films therefore respond to 'imperatives of international competition rather than simply "reflect" a national identity' (Walsh, 1997: 4).

The research presented in this book provides ample evidence for the validity of this claim, as many British films were subject to differing contexts of reception in the United States, not least in economic terms. While some films could be said to have been popular, to a great extent this depended on economic questions such as advertising policy, distribution strategy, access to cinemas, and rate of return to the producer. What is clear is that when British films were given a chance many were successful despite their apparent 'Britishness': they demonstrated qualities that were appreciated for their difference but at the same time were comprehensible. They were also incorporated into contemporary American concerns or were presented to audiences in such a way that reduced their difference to acceptable levels. What emerges is a model of exportability that depends as much on the film itself as on the way it was presented for consumption. This supports the weight given in this book to extraneous, intertextual sources, including posters and press books as well as film reviews (see discussion later in this chapter).

A study of film exports raises important questions about the economics of the film industry and about the effects of cross-cultural reception. Are exports a viable economic strategy? What are the problems and rewards? How is the impact of British films abroad different from their reception in the home market? Do films have to be made differently if they are to have any chance abroad? The neglect of how films are received abroad is in part explained by an over-concentration on the indigenous address of national cinemas. It has been assumed that a national film industry's primary concern is to reflect experiences which are of relevance to those within that culture. The trend in studies of national cinemas has therefore been to concentrate on 'the indigenous' rather than 'the exportable'. Increasingly, however, 'the national' is considered to be a concept that is unstable and fluid. Hjort and Mackenzie (2000) have demonstrated how studying national cinemas has become complicated by terms such as 'globalization', 'hybridity', 'transnationalism' and 'cosmopolitanism'. Analyzing a national cinema is less about looking for a set of shared values and assumptions across a range of films and more about appreciating how, for example, films engage Britain as a heterogeneous country with many different and often conflicting identities.

The appreciation of what Andrew Higson has termed 'the instability of the national' helps to promote a greater sense of films in cross-cultural contexts:

> The debates about national cinema need to take greater account of the diversity of reception, the recognition that the meanings an audience reads into a film are heavily dependent on the cultural context in which they watch it. The movement of films across borders may introduce exotic elements to the 'indigenous' culture. One response to this is an anxious concern about the effects of cultural imperialism, a concern that the local culture will be infected, even destroyed by the foreign invader. A contrary response is that the introduction of exotic elements may well have a liberating or democratising effect on the local culture, expanding the cultural repertoire. A third possibility is that the foreign commodity will not be treated as exotic by the local audience, but will be interpreted according to an 'indigenous' frame of reference; that is, it will be metaphorically translated into a local idiom. (Higson, 2000: 68–9)

The experience of British films in America provides examples of all three of Higson's responses. First, the way films were reviewed often betrayed a defensive attitude towards foreign films. While grounds for charges of cultural imperialism were hardly evident, an analysis of American critical reactions to films made in Europe reveals that Hollywood's domination was never taken for granted. The appearance of British, French, German and Soviet films in the

1920s, for example, presented critics and audiences with different models of cinema, models that deviated from but sometimes connected with contemporary Hollywood film-making. A defensive critical discourse, articulated in reviews and other commentary, produced a set of assumptions based on Hollywood cinema as the epitome of film style and entertainment. By contrast, foreign films were frequently considered to be deficient, lagging behind Hollywood in terms of technique, star quality or narrational sophistication. They were welcomed, however, by the art market which became established in the 1920s. Later, in the 1950s, reports on the continued growth of the art market also revealed that Hollywood was seriously concerned that its own hegemony might be threatened by films which encouraged audiences to acquire different, more exotic tastes. While many British films were shown in art cinemas they occupied a somewhat uneasy position both formally and in terms of critical positioning between other European films and Hollywood cinema.

Not all responses were negative, providing evidence for Higson's second category concerning the impact of foreign films on 'local' culture. Indeed, many British films were welcomed for expanding the 'cultural repertoire'. *Henry V* (US release 1946), *Hamlet* (1948) and Ealing comedies were appreciated for their 'class', educative qualities and comedic sophistication. More recently, *Trainspotting* (1996) was applauded as a fresh and dynamic relief after a summer of turgid, uninspiring blockbusters.

The third category, of films being interpreted according to an 'indigenous' frame of reference, also applied to British films. Examples discussed in this book include *The Private Life of Henry VIII* (1933) and its relation to New Deal philosophy; the relevance of Hammer horror films to American society at the end of the 1950s and Anglo-American preoccupations of James Bond films. British films were often compared to American, as well as with other British films which had made an impact. Identifying 'text pairings', examples of intertextual referencing in reviews and in publicity, suggests the extent to which films were interpreted with particular frames of reference in mind. These were not always confined to British culture, again complicating the idea that cross-cultural reception is one-dimensional.

Studying the distribution and exhibition of British films abroad is not an easy task. We need to know what was successful, assessed by critical reviews, box-office figures and rental grosses. This book draws on many different sources to assess how British films rated in economic and cultural terms. These include critical reviews from a variety of trade papers, newspapers and journals, together with film publicity, press books and posters. Many British films that were applauded by the critics made little impression at the box-office, and vice-versa. Accounting for disparities between critical and popular appreciation presents a methodological challenge, particularly in the absence of detailed audience surveys. The method I have adopted has been inspired by Janet Staiger's (1992) 'historical materialist' approach, which analyses a film's contemporary reception with the assistance of key documents and by the work of Barbara Klinger on the importance of examining a film's 'discursive surround' in reception studies (1997: 113–28). In his study of the impact of British television in the United States, Jeffrey Miller (2000) has also adopted the approach of considering the text-audience relationship as a historically specific yet dynamic process. The result is familiarity with a range of interpretive contexts which can be assessed according to contemporary frames of reference.

Reviews are insightful in gauging a film's place in the overall corpus and in conveying a sense of shifting standards of critical appreciation. In America a broad spectrum of critical opinion can be assessed with reference to publications as varied as *Variety* and *Motion Picture Herald,* which reviewed films from the perspective of box-office potential, and the *New York Times,* which was more concerned about the development of film art. Reading reviews over many years builds up an impression of how British films were perceived within a comparative framework of judgement. As previously noted, many reviewers gave advice to British producers on how to improve the chances of their films at the US box-office, often making detailed comments on style, technique, stars, acting and theme. British films were often compared to Hollywood's and also to European films, resulting in a commentary that concentrated on what they were not, rather than according to other standards. The result is a discourse that positions British films as occupying an ambivalent terrain: on the one hand similar to Hollywood but on the other as different, but not so different as to qualify as *avant garde.* The tensions created by this awkward, intermediate positioning, surface in reviews. In so doing they communicate a sense of the parameters of contemporary critical reception, with all its inherent contradictions and preoccupations.

As for box-office figures, these are often difficult to obtain for the earlier period, but they are a concrete indication of a film's popularity, particularly when analysed in a comparative context. On the other hand, without information about a film's production costs or the deal struck between the producer and distributor, they can be misleading. Popularity and profitability are not necessarily the same thing. For example, while Rank's *Caesar and Cleopatra* (1948) obtained an impressive number of bookings and was a box-office success, because the film had a high budget and the deal favoured United Artists, its American distributor, it was not particularly profitable for Rank. When available, figures obtained from the corporate records of film studios are extremely useful. The rental grosses of films distributed by United Artists, for example, reveal the place of British films in that company's overall financial strategy. Somewhat ironically, many documents produced by British film companies reside in the records of American companies. The archives of United Artists and Universal have proved to be particularly useful in researching relations between British and American film operations.

Other sources that have been important are publicity materials such as press books and posters. These indicate how British films were intended to be appreciated by American audiences: how they were 'pitched' by distributors for American consumption and which 'codes of assimilation' were identified as 'transferable'. Conditions that were specific to British films influenced the nature of publicity campaigns. Distributors feared that since American audiences were for the most part unfamiliar with British stars, film posters would have to attract patrons very much on the promise of the film itself. Posters therefore tended to concentrate on communicating exciting and appealing 'narrative images', conveying a vivid sense of the thrilling experiences delivered by a picture. By contrast, British advertising campaigns tended to be more restrained. Attention given to presentation for the American market is therefore a way of assessing the impact of a film in a new cultural context. Like reviews, the posters and press books act as 'cues' to what was highlighted as of specific interest to American audiences. American advertising campaigns also made much more of promotional activities, 'showmanship' stunts that would make up for the fact that many British stars were unknown in the United States.

The careers of British films can therefore be assessed according to varying standards of success or failure. Critical opinion, box-office receipts, overall profitability and the extent to which British stars gained a reputation are all of relevance but may produce contradictory impressions. The experience of individual films was also influenced by longer-term or endemic factors such as the volatile nature of Anglo-American film relations and wider issues of Anglo-American economic and political collaboration. This book covers a broad chronological period, the 1920s to the 1990s. Assessing the impact of British films over such a long time frame allows for the discernment of trends, the identification of popular films, stars and genres and the shifting patterns of cross-cultural assimilation. Within this overall framework, a number of films are discussed at length, producing case studies which are intended to exemplify particular patterns and which have presented themselves as worthy of detailed analysis. The focus is on films that were comparatively popular, as assessed by rental grosses and box-office figures, or that were marked as 'notable' by reviewers or as controversial in terms of censorship. For every film that did well there were, of course, many that failed to make an impression. These are also considered as a means of distinguishing the factors that eased the path of the 'success stories'. The data presented in the appendices are intended to encourage analysis of other British films which might be identified as significant in future studies of British film exports.

I begin with the 1920s, when Hollywood was challenged by European films which offered audiences cinematic models different from those being developed by the rapidly consolidating 'classical' Hollywood cinema. While European films had been shown in the United States before the First World War, their presence in the 1920s was invested with a particular urgency because of prevailing economic conditions. Somewhat ironically, as Hollywood became more and more aware of the crucial importance of its own export drive, there was a greater sensitivity towards other nations' aspirations to gain a foothold in the United States. International competition was therefore an implicit dynamic behind many pronouncements about cinema during this period. Chapter 1 reveals the extent to which debates about European films, their qualities and perceived deficiencies, were intertwined with contemporary concerns about the need to cater for both a 'mass' audience and a growing art market. The demarcation of particular films for particular audiences was a way of making the presence of foreign films in the United States more acceptable. Indeed, the discernment of different 'taste publics' was a marked feature of discussions about the chances of British films in the US market. While the mass market was intended primarily for films made in Hollywood, foreign films experienced a more enthusiastic welcome in 'little theatre' territory, catered for by independent distributors and exhibitors who were losing ground to the more powerful vertically integrated 'majors'. The separation of economic and cultural contexts was rendered problematic as contemporary reviews betrayed mixed motives about eclecticism in film culture. When compared to US or other European films, British films did not fit easily with prevailing expectations of either classical narrative or art cinema. The location of 'national specificity' was therefore subject to a range of competing interests and ideas. Against this background, Chapter 1 considers the aspirations of several producers and of particular British films, including *Nell Gwyn* (1925), a key precedent for the more celebrated American success of Korda's *The Private Life of Henry VIII*. It demonstrates that in facilitating exportation it was producers, such as Stoll, Balcon, Williams and Wilcox (as producer-director), rather than directors, who were the key players in arranging contracts and making contacts with American distributors. The chapter also examines attempts at Anglo-American cooperation – debates about 'reciprocity' between the two film industries – as a means of defusing an increasingly volatile situation created by the enactment of protective legislation in 1927.

Chapters 2 and 3 deal with the 1930s, a crucial period for British cinema, as the film industry adjusted to protection and the coming of sound. It expanded and consolidated its structure, experienced major successes abroad but was also subject to financial crisis and overextension. Again, it was producers who pursued overseas markets most vigorously. The attempts of Korda, Balcon and Wilcox are examined, illustrating how by the end of the decade several strategies and films had established particular 'models' of acceptance in the United States. The most dominant of these was represented by *The Private Life of Henry VIII*, a film that acquired a controversial reputation when it was an unexpected international success in 1933. A detailed case study of the film's career in the United States proves that it was popular in many locations, not necessarily metropolitan, and that a number of factors conspired to make it particularly susceptible to cross-cultural understanding. The links between Alexander Korda and United Artists are examined in detail, revealing how film company records are an important source of information. They provide an insight into the financial operations of London Film Productions, elucidate elements of contemporary film economics, and reveal the benefits and tensions of Anglo-American collaboration.

This analysis depends not only on identifying box-office success and significant economic variables, but also on a consideration of the films' cross-cultural appeal. I argue, for example, that it is illuminating to consider *The Private Life of Henry VIII* in the context of the New Deal and Korda's 'imperial' films, *Drums/The Drum* (1938) and *The Four Feathers* (1939), in relation to American conceptions of individualism and, drawing on the work of John Fraser (1982), to American appreciation of 'patterns of chivalry'. The prevailing context of Anglo-American political relations was of crucial importance to the reception of these films. This is also explored with reference to *The Ghost Goes West* (1935), a film that deployed an Anglo-American romance as a central narrative strategy. In this film it is suggested that national differences can be overcome by an overriding Anglo-American 'special' relationship: the diegetic world of the film therefore implicitly alludes to contemporary politics. As 'exportable' texts, these films therefore demonstrate how they were integrated into different contexts of exhibition and particular moments of historical reception. During the 1930s some British films self-parodied certain representations of 'Britishness' that make them particularly relevant texts from an Anglo-American perspective. These insights were absorbed into an American cultural context that was both fascinated and repelled by questions of class identity. Reviews of British films frequently reveal an appreciation of their irony and satire. This awareness of national difference invested British films with a sophisticated address which, somewhat ironically, was considered to be highly appropriate for 'highbrow' audiences in New York and other metro-politan centres.

Korda was not the only producer to experience comparative success in the American market in the 1930s. Chapter 3 details attempts by Michael Balcon and Herbert Wilcox to promote British stars, often as an integral aspect of 'star trading' policies: sending British stars to Hollywood and vice versa. This resulted in a somewhat contradictory policy of, on the one hand, aiming to popularise British stars in their own right, while, on the other, trying to entice Hollywood stars to appear in British films. Since a consistent criticism of British films was their lack of stars known to US audiences, many producers aimed to create distinctive personae for British actors and actresses. Jessie Matthews managed to gain a reputation in the United States, starring in a series of 'art deco' musicals she made for Balcon at Gaumont-British. As a star who enjoyed 'crossover' success, her films are considered in relation to Hollywood musicals and their mutual representation of the moderne/art deco style, which epitomized a symbiotic relationship between European and American culture.

The most successful strategy for gaining screentime for British films was via specialised release, aimed at 'niche' markets and often with the aid of a 'roadshow' policy. After discussing relevant developments during the Second World War, Chapter 4 presents case studies of the roadshow releases of *Henry V, Hamlet* and *The Red Shoes* (1948). A roadshow, normally associated with 'prestige' films, involved the distributor renting or leasing theatres in selected locations, undertaking the entire mechanics of exhibition, including advertising and projection. A target audience would be identified and the film's popularity 'built up' from an initially modest exposure in a few key cinemas. The film would then be selectively released so that 'word of mouth' created a climate of expectation elsewhere, culminating in a wider release if the film appeared to demonstrate potential to 'cross over' into a wider market. This strategy proved to be extremely significant in publicizing British films as well as locating them within the art market as it expanded into the 1950s. Documentation located in the archives of United Artists and Universal Studios reveals how these British films were marketed and handled by branch managers all over the United States. It provides a unique insight into promoting British films in areas that were previously resistant, exposing key patterns of regional diversity and the different contexts of reception within the United States. Chapter 4 also highlights the work of J. Arthur Rank in forging links with American companies. This was of crucial importance in establishing a sustained, if at times volatile, presence for British films in the United States.

A significant aspect of the reception of British films involved negotiating the censorship system. Many British films were altered for American exhibition at the direction of the Production Code Administration (PCA). British producers submitted scripts to ensure that their films would be awarded certificates. The records pertaining to British films reveal the extent to which producers were prepared to compromise in order to obtain a US release. Chapter 5 deals with the censorship of British films, mainly in the 1940s when the PCA was extremely powerful but less so in the 1950s when its rulings were increasingly challenged. The chapter includes case studies of particularly controversial films, most notably the censorship of *Black Narcissus* (1947), a film which was cut as a result of action taken by a powerful pressure group, the Catholic Legion of Decency. In this case, the American print was fundamentally different from the British with, as I argue, significant ideological consequences. Acquiescing to the PCA implied that different contexts of reception had to be acknowledged, even if these were determined by norms that were associated with a 'world according to Hollywood' (Vasey, 1997: 3). In this way British films were brought closer to the ideological preoccupations of American cinema, even if on occasion this proved to be an unlikely or uncomfortable combination.

Chapter 6 is concerned with the 1950s, a key decade in terms of British films occupying a place in the expanding art market. Changes in the American film industry, most notably the impact of the divorcement decrees that divested the 'majors' of their cinema chains, benefited British and foreign-language films. As a consequence, there was an increased demand for product, combined with a plethora of independent distribution companies that were prepared to handle 'unusual' films. As demonstrated in previous chapters, prevailing conditions within the American film industry and home market had an impact on the amount of screentime available for foreign films. In the 1950s British films continued to attract 'niche' audiences who responded well to films such as Ealing comedies. While these would appear to relate most obviously to indigenous British concerns, their success proved that big budgets and 'international' themes were not necessarily essential prerequisites for successful exportation. Rather, the themes that appealed related to the films' comedic self-parody of aspects of 'Britishness'. They also relate to contemporary concerns about individualism in a decade when sociologists identified a 'Lonely Crowd' of Americans who had lost their sense of self-identity (Reisman et. al., 1953). Once again, company records provide detail on promoting a range of British films, including Rank productions released by Universal in the early 1950s and two key Hammer horror films, *The Curse of Frankenstein* (1957, released by Warner Brothers) and *Horror of Dracula* (1958, released by Universal). As in the 1920s, British films in this decade occupied an uneasy positioning between foreign language 'art' films, and 'entertainment' films as represented by Hollywood.

In the 1960s, the subject of Chapter 7, the experience of British films is examined against a background of 'internationalism', particularly in terms of production finance. During the 1960s American investment in British films reached an unprecedented level, enabling films registered as 'British' to earn large amounts at the American box-office. While American funding did not play a major part in the initial 'new wave' of social-realist dramas, American reviewers were more enthusiastic than were their British counterparts. Critical appreciation promoted a heightened interest in British cinema and, combined with the existence of economic incentives, resulted in an influx of American capital. Films such as *Tom Jones* (1963), *A Hard Day's Night* (1964) and the James Bond series were extremely popular and profitable, particularly for United Artists, their American financier and distributor. While the focus of this book is not American investment in the British film industry, these films were representative of how Anglo-American collaboration was not necessarily incompatible with the continued representation of themes relating to British experience in British films.[5] As eminently 'transferable' texts, these films show that particular themes and issues, such as class and a satiric view of aspects of British national identity, were appreciated in America as much as in previous decades. The pleasures offered by a film such as *Tom Jones* can be related back to the comedic historical-costume tradition popularised by *Nell Gwyn*. *A Hard Day's Night* can be placed in a youth/cult film category, which in turn influenced later films, particularly *Trainspotting* (1996), a 'text pairing' suggested by American reviews.

Chapter 8, the final chapter, brings the history of British films in America up to date. For this period, information on box-office performance and critical commentary is more readily accessible, but since archival sources are unavailable the period is not covered as extensively as earlier decades. As will be apparent, however, film exports are still considered to be a vital element of film companies' activities. The placement of films in the international marketplace is a reality of contemporary film economics, particularly with the prevailing trend for transnational financing. The success of British films abroad in the 1990s, for example, has promoted debate about the extent to which the structure of the American film industry continues to prevent the successful exhibition of foreign films. Several films, including *Four Weddings and a Funeral* (1994), *Trainspotting, The Full Monty* (1997) and *Elizabeth* (1998), appear to prove the exception to the rule, but there is no doubt that the American market continues to be one of the most difficult to access, particularly now that the reconfigured 'majors' have purchased cinema chains. This book charts how this pattern is a historical one, with similar dilemmas facing British producers in the 1990s to those experienced by Michael Balcon and Herbert Wilcox in the 1920s. While some strategies were more successful than others, it also clear that there is no blueprint for exportability. The 'cinelords' continue to exercise power over their territory, a situation which renders the transatlantic crossing a difficult but at times rewarding journey film-makers will, as they have done in the past, continue to undertake.

Notes

Note on references: Page numbers are indicated for periodical references where possible. If they have been omitted, the source, for example press cuttings files held at the Museum of Modern Art, did not always include page references.

Note on film dates: Year of production is indicated and, where relevant, year of American release.

1. 'Hollywood Jabberwocky' was published in *The Screen Writer,* vol. 3, No. 1, June 1947. I. A. L. Diamond was a Rumanian screenwriter who worked in Hollywood from 1929. He worked on many famous scripts including *Love In the Afternoon* (1957); *Some Like It Hot* (1959) and *The Apartment* (1960). He died in 1988.
2. Existing work consists of Murphy (1983); Macnab (1993); Sedgwick (1996); Street (2000); Swann (2000); and Ryall (2001). For an overview of the theoretical issues involved in studying film exports see Walsh (1997).
3. See for example the study into the enchroachment of American interests in the British film industry undertaken by Klingender and Legg (1937) and comments by Betts (1960: 6). While pertinent to the problems of the British film industry, these books connected the desire to export with increased budgets. It was not however the case that high budgets were solely linked to export policies but rather to rising costs, particularly in the 1930s. Klingender and Legg's study pointed to more fundamental causes of the problems of the British film industry in the 1930s, such as unstable methods of film finance. As argued in this book, successful exportation is not necessarily linked to budget.
4. I. A. L. Diamond has taken the term from *Variety,* the American film-trade paper that used it to refer to 'the neighbourhoods', or outer districts of cities.
5. For a study of the British operations of American companies see Glancy (1999) and Ryall (2001).

The 1920s: British Silent Films in the United States

Before the advent of sound film at the end of the 1920s, the market was, in theory, free of language barriers, conducive to the free exchange of motion pictures and to a culture of internationalism. Yet the experience of European films in the United States during the 1920s shows that this was far from the case. It was a decade when great efforts were made to export European films to the United States and ensure that effective distribution contracts facilitated their careers once they had travelled across the Atlantic. While Hollywood was consolidating its position as the dominant model of world cinema with an increasing reputation as a good business investment, the presence of European films provided spectators with different perspectives, styles, locations and actors. Anthony Guzman has argued that imports from Europe 'decisively influenced American film culture in terms of both the broad acceptance of film as an art form and in the institutionalization of the art film as an alternative to Hollywood film practice' (1993: vi). This chapter examines the British contribution to this trend, the problems facing producers who tried to secure effective distribution for their films in America and evidence of the perception and reception of British films during the 1920s.

The convergence of debates about 'Film Europe' and 'Film America' has been examined from a variety of perspectives in Higson and Maltby (1999). The history of British films in America in the 1920s is intertwined with contemporary pan-European concerns about how to develop robust national film industries which also demonstrated export potential. It is striking how many of the issues which became regular features of debates throughout the century about the suitability of particular films for the American market have their origin in this period. Questions such as which films were best suited for export, which companies should be approached to secure an effective distribution contract and which stars might have transatlantic appeal were debated in trade papers and reviews. Despite experiencing tremendous difficulties in

America, by the end of the decade it was clear that exports were an integral aspect of a dynamic national film industry. As Andrew Higson has commented:

> It is probably fair to say that every company large enough to make an appreciable difference in the formation of pan-European ventures was at the same time looking for an American distributor to provide access to the North American market. Links with American companies were important for the new vertically integrated majors in Britain, since showing American films in the domestic market and gaining access for British films in the American market were both considered vital sources of income (Higson and Maltby, 1999: 289).

Indeed, during the years 1921–28 British producers secured US releases for approximately seventy-nine films, just over double the number of French films imported over the same period and behind only Germany, which had approximately 119 feature films released.[1] How they were received by critics and, as far as we can gauge by audiences, will be discussed later, but it was an achievement for a film industry which had declined to such a low ebb in the mid-1920s that protectionist measures were enacted by the Government (Dickinson and Street, 1985: 5–33). To convey a sense of these figures in relation to British production over the same period, 1921–28, the number of British films trade shown in Britain was 531, a figure which is considerably higher than the number of British films released in the United States.[2] Imports however made up a respectable percentage of the total US market: according to the *Film Daily Year Book,* in 1928 there were 820 features released in the United States, approximately 200 of which were imported.

The British film industry's uphill struggle in Britain and America was exacerbated by prevailing economic conditions. The impact of the First World War had curtailed the advance of European films in the United States, an impression based on figures published in the *Film Daily Year Book* of US film imports: in 1913 Britain exported 2,800,000 feet to the United States whereas in 1925 this figure had fallen to 1,020,000 feet.[3] The American film industry's dramatic consolidation and expansion in the 1920s is well documented, as the feature film became the established exhibition format and the business community put aside its reservations about film investment (Koszarski, 1990: 63–94). Hollywood's vertically integrated structure which ensured domination by the five 'majors', MGM, Paramount, Warners, Fox and RKO, had evolved into a 'mature oligopoly' by the end of the decade. While in the long term the emergence of these monolithic entities made the market extremely difficult to access, European producers who sought American distribution contracts were inadvertently assisted by the struggles within the US exhibition sector as independent distributors and exhibitors fought against being squeezed out of the market. British films were handled by a variety of small companies with intrepid aspirations as indicated by names such as Pioneer, Inter-Ocean and World Wide, distributors who were anxious to secure films in an increasingly competitive market. But they also received attention from larger companies, particularly Paramount, which distributed *Nell Gwyn* (1925) and *Madame Pompadour* (1927) with some success.

Conflict between the emerging majors and independents generated fierce debates in the trade press, especially among small exhibitors who complained about 'block booking', a malpractice which forced cinema owners to buy films produced by the majors in blocks, many of which they had not seen. The *Exhibitors' Herald of Chicago* published a series of articles by Sydney S. Cohen, an exhibitor who linked the practice with an overall decline in film quality: 'The "block booking" system undoubtedly tends to lower the average quality in features thus merchandized and thus unfavourably affect all screen entertainment'.[4] We shall return to the issue of quality and the art market but for now it is important to signal intratrade debates which had a bearing on the experience of British films. While the *Exhibitors' Herald* championed the cause of the small exhibitor, *Variety* tended to represent the larger companies. This impacted how foreign films were reviewed and discussed in both papers, providing a fascinating insight into the connections between film industry politics and contemporary aesthetic judgements. While connections with small exhibitors were of fundamental importance in getting British films shown, it became increasingly clear that to achieve wider exposure it was vital for British companies to seek distribution agreements with the majors. The much-maligned block booking, for example, could have been used as a tactic to persuade exhibitors to give foreign films a chance and then it would be up to them to rent more if audiences demonstrated a taste for them. On the other hand, as the British example shows, after the 1927 Cinematograph Films Act had been passed, British films rented as part of a package could easily be shown at off-peak times or not at all.[5]

In retrospect, these issues can be seen as part of the beginning of a split between the mainstream, major-dominated market and the art cinema movement with its own circuits and links with independents (Guzman, 1993: 19–20 and Gomery, 1992: 172–6). By the end of the 1920s, British films were somewhat caught between the two. For many reviewers they were not considered to be as aesthetically distinctive as *The Cabinet of Dr Caligari* (1919, released in the United States in 1925) or *The Battleship Potemkin* (1925, released in the United States in 1926), films whose notoriety and success helped define the art market. At the other extreme, the majority of British films were unable to compete with Hollywood in the mainstream market. But many producers tried to make links with American companies and put their minds to the problem of how to 'crack' the potentially lucrative US market. I will now discuss some of these efforts in the context of contemporary debate about national identity, stylistic trends and economic necessity.

Stoll Films in America

Sir Oswald Stoll was a frequent commentator on the problems of the British film industry in the 1920s who tried to secure distribution outlets for his company's films in the United States. A cinema owner, Stoll had expanded into production in 1919–20 and established a studio at Cricklewood. Stoll's philosophy for exports was based on difference, and in the early 1920s he made a concerted effort to establish a presence in America. He was convinced that British films should not be cut, altered or re-titled for American consumption so that the American public would not be 'asked to look at something completely emasculated in an unintelligent attempt to make it fit the American market'.[6] Stoll's ambitions led him to establish New York sales offices in 1920, hire American personnel, secure distribution deals with Pathé and small independent renters, and introduce American audiences to British locations and themes in a series of films based on British authors such as Conan Doyle and H. G. Wells. This strategy – of conveying 'Britishness' through adaptations of popular literary genres or of classics by highly regarded British playwrights and novelists – was a common one in contemporary debates about what made films suitable for export. The idea was that the films should demonstrate elements of national specificity rather than conform to the Hollywood model. Stoll's faith in the power of authentic British and European locations was shared by American commentators. When Stoll's *Squandered Lives* was reviewed in *Picture-Play Magazine,* for example, although it was criticized for being technically inferior, admiration was expressed for the interior and exterior settings which were described as 'more interesting than ours and an immense relief after too much Californian scenery'.[7] Similarly, when *The Hound of the Baskervilles,* another Stoll Film Company release, was reviewed by Alison Smith in the same American publication, director Maurice Elvey's use of setting received high praise: 'It is an English film, which makes up for what lacks in photography with the real English setting – these moors are moors indeed and not Hollywood lots'.[8] Finally, *The Bigamist,* a Stoll film distributed by Robertson-Cole, was judged by *Variety* to be remarkable in terms of its scenery. Although the story was considered to be poor, the film was redeemed by 'beautiful scenic settings' (some on location in Nice) and 'splendid' photography.[9]

Stoll's most successful American export was *Sherlock Holmes*, fifteen two-reelers directed by Maurice Elvey and distributed in America by the Alexander Film Corporation in 1921–22. *Variety*'s review commented on how astute the distribution company had been to spot such 'dark horses' which had been a 'very good buy'. The enthusiastic review, however, mentions that the films had been 'dolled up' in 'native sub-title clothes, and here and there snapped up the original action by recutting', a strategy of which Stoll would presumably have disapproved.[10]

While Stoll's efforts were hardly ground-breaking, his experiences in America constitute the most sustained instance of a producer managing to persuade distributors to handle a number of British films before the experiences of Michael Balcon and Herbert Wilcox. According to Guzman's survey Stoll had thirteen features exhibited in 1920–21 as well as the *Sherlock Holmes* films, 1921–22. After just over a year of business, however, Stoll closed his New York office, an indication that his ambitions were not matched by profits which would have facilitated a second 'crack' at the American market. Stoll's overseas activities and well-publicized ambitions created an impression of British films which both assisted and hindered future efforts. On the one hand, a number of good reviews and evidence of the films being released shows exhibitors' willingness to deal with British films, while on the other, as Rachael Low has written: 'In the absence of a film so outstanding that it could turn the tide and create a demand where none had existed before, there was little reason for American cinemas to put on British films' (1971: 78). Stoll's campaign was short and sharp, and without a major success could not be sustained as the British film industry experienced a severe slump in the mid-1920s.[11]

Reports in the *Exhibitors' Herald* reveal that Stoll's comments were increasingly interpreted as anti-American. An article by Ralph F. Stitt, of First National's Foreign Department, summarized Stoll's views in 1924 on the need for a wide variety of motion picture fare which could only be supplied by European pictures so that 'the American public would have a more rounded diet in their amusements, and would not be so surfeited with the sameness that he [Stoll] thinks obtains in American pictures today'.[12] Stoll's views were juxtaposed with an alternative view that American films were special in their ability to generate 'universal appeal'. This point was reiterated in many subsequent responses to the charge that British films were discriminated against in America: if the films were good enough, American exhibitors would show them. By 1927 Stoll's comments had become even more patriotic and unambiguously anti-American. When he visited America, he attacked Hollywood's films as expressive of 'nothing but the monotonous, hectic, small soul of Hollywood itself', contrasting them with British films which he argued were far more advanced.[13] Comments such as this were taken as typical of British producers who had grown bitter as a result of their difficulties in America, an attitude which did much to jeopardize the likelihood of reciprocal trade agreements between the two film industries.

Protection and Reciprocity

After Stoll's American operations had failed, he concentrated on contributing to the debates leading up to the Cinematograph Films Act, 1927, advocating an unsuccessful scheme for a license duty to be paid by British exhibitors to show American films, the proceeds going towards maintaining a supply of British films. Stoll opposed a quota system on the grounds that it would encourage American production in Britain.[14] The debates on the protection of the film industry were indirectly concerned with the question of exports since one of the possible schemes considered by the film trade was known as 'reciprocity'.[15] The President of the Board of Trade, Sir Philip Cunliffe-Lister, was anxious to secure an element of protection for the film industry as part of his desire to institute tariff reform. Once acquainted with the fundamental problems which faced the film industry, he encouraged the film trade to devise a scheme to outlaw booking malpractices and revive production. A Joint Trade Committee representing producers, distributors and exhibitors considered many possible solutions and reciprocity, or coming to an agreement with Hollywood which ensured that British films gained access to the American market, received support from many influential quarters including *The Times,* the *Kinematograph Weekly* and statistician and distributor Simon Rowson. In April 1926 the Joint Trade Committee negotiated with representatives of American renting companies and the proceedings were observed by Colonel Lowry, a representative of the Hays Office. Their discussions involved issues such as American technical advice being given to British producers, as well as assistance with scenario writing and a supply of stars. A plan was devised which included the provisions that every American film rental company should take at least one British feature film a year for every twenty-five American films offered for hire in Britain, and that British producers should receive a third of the gross rental receipts from the exhibition of the films in the United States and Canada.[16] When Ernest W. Fredman, editor of the British trade paper the *Daily Film Renter,* visited New York in October 1926 to discuss the reciprocity issue with Will Hays, a dinner was held in his honour with over 150 representatives of motion picture companies and the trade press also in attendance.[17]

Such expressions of goodwill between the two film industries were promising, but when the final reciprocity plan was sent to America for further examination, no formal reply was received and talks ground to a halt. Consequently, after all the optimism about the negotiations a reciprocity clause was not included in the Films Act (Dickinson and Street, 1985: 24–7). It is likely that the overall anti-American tone of the debates on the protection of the British film industry jeopardized any chance of Anglo-American cooperation. At the same time as the reciprocity negotiations were taking place, the US Department of Commerce established a Motion Picture Division to monitor European legislation which might hamper Hollywood's exports. Simon Rowson did not give up on the principle of reciprocity, however, and advocated it again in 1937 as being of fundamental importance for the revival of the British film industry (Dickinson and Street, 1985: 84).

After Stoll's experiences in America in the early 1920s, British films struggled to gain screentime and, along with other European films, found it increasingly difficult to establish a presence overseas. Cecil Hepworth did particularly badly even though he had established an office in the United States. After *Comin' Thro' the Rye* was trade shown in New York in December 1924 *Variety* predicted its failure: 'As far as the American market is concerned it hasn't a chance', offering slowness, bad photography and period setting as 'enough to condemn it in American eyes'.[18] *Photoplay* declared, 'It is about thirty years behind American films. The story is poor, the settings are poor, the costumes are poor, the acting is worse and the whole thing just gives one a desire to shoot everybody that had a hand in its making'.[19] In 1923–4, however, other British producers were trying, with some success, a new strategy of using American stars such as Betty Compson, Betty Blythe, Mae Marsh and Gertrude McCoy in key roles in British films. This strategy responded to criticism that American audiences did not recognize British stars in a decade when star quality was a key requirement for box-office success (Koszarski, 1990: 259–314). To offset the poor reception of Hepworth's films, two British melodramas achieved an unusual degree of exposure in 1923–4: *Napoleon and Josephine/A Royal Divorce* (Alexander Butler, 1923) and *Woman To Woman* (Graham Cutts, 1923).

Michael Balcon's International Trajectory

Napoleon and Josephine was reported to be strong at the box-office in Washington and did well in smaller theatres.[20] In pursuit of a 'wider vision' for British films, *Woman To Woman* was part of Michael Balcon's international aspirations in the 1920s (Kemp, 1997: 13). Balcon started his long and distinguished career in the British film industry as a distributor, founding Victory Motion Pictures in 1919 with Victor Saville. In 1921 Balcon produced his first film, *The Story of Oil*, a documentary directed by Saville. Two years later he produced *Woman To Woman*, beginning a significant collaborative relationship with Graham Cutts, the director with whom he founded Gainsborough Pictures in 1924. *Woman To Woman* starred Betty Compson who was paid £1,000 a week to leave Hollywood (Balcon, 1969: 15). *Woman To Woman* was distributed in America by independent Lewis J. Selznick and exhibited in Paramount cinemas (Kemp, 1997: 21). The choice of star had been wise: Compson was highly regarded, described in *Picture-Play Magazine* as being 'acclaimed by many directors as the "best bet" in gelatin. . . . In Betty Compson there is combined physical splendour and a fine acting equipment. . . . This actress succeeds remarkably in breathing reality into all of her make-believe people'.[21] Unusually, the première was in New York and the film was greeted with enthusiastic reviews. *Variety* hailed it as the film to reverse the tide of antipathy against British films since 'this assuredly must be an example of the better grade of work over there. It is unquestionably equal to a vast majority of the releases viewed in the first run houses over here and vastly superior to those witnessed in our daily change theatres'.[22] Together with Compson's acting the lighting and lavish interiors were praised. In terms of technique, the film was considered to be in advance of previous offerings, being deficient only in the number of close-ups, the tinting in one cabaret scene and some 'wasted footage'.

The narrative, set in Paris and London, was also considered by *Variety* to constitute a compelling melodrama. Compson plays a dancer in a Monmartre cabaret who falls in love with an English officer when he is on leave in Paris during the First World War. On the eve of their wedding, he is summoned to rejoin his unit and loses his memory when he suffers from shellshock. Five years pass and the dancer, now famous, is working in London, while the officer has married and become a respectable upper-class businessman. His memory returns when he sees the French dancer perform at a show. The French woman has, in the meantime, given birth to their child whom the ex-officer's wife tries to take when she learns the truth. The dancer agrees to perform at a ball at which she dies. Kenton Bamford explains the success of the film in the United States in terms of its departure from many British films of the period, which were over-concerned with patriotism and a fascination with the lives of the upper classes:

> It would appear that when competent British producers and directors, those with a genuine love of the medium, worked with expert performers, the result was film entertainment rather than the false trappings of national identity grafted on to celluloid. (Bamford, 1999: 132)

Woman To Woman instead deals with a cross-class romance which, according to Michael Balcon, 'enjoyed international commercial success' (Balcon, 1969: 15), an observation confirmed by other sources (Low, 1971: 80 and Guzman, 1993: 163). Certainly, box-office reports in *Variety* indicate a respectable screening record.[23] One report from the *Exhibitors' Herald* shows that the film was screened in Los Angeles with the comment that Compson's star presence was an asset in making the film 'appeal to people of all nations'.[24] On the whole, reviews were good with the exception of some sectors of the trade press. Agnes Smith, for example, writing in *Picture-Play Magazine,* a paper which had praised Betty Compson on many previous occasions, was critical of the film: 'Betty Compson's well-known verve is completely lost in one of the soggiest stories of the year. The English producers are getting wise to the stunt of dressing up a picture with cabaret and theatre scenes, but nothing can do much to help a picture in which the heroine is dying of heart failure for three or four reels'.[25] The *New York Times* review similarly commented on Compson's creditable performance but criticized Cutts, observing that his theatre background hampered his direction, particularly in the areas of lighting, use of unmotivated close-ups, lengthy titles and the film displaying 'too much agony and too little real action'.[26]

We shall return to responses to British films in the American press, but for now it can be observed how Balcon's film extended Stoll's approach. This was particularly evident in its British and European settings and opulent style, characteristics which can be associated with the trend for internationalism which was pervasive in the 1920s. American taste for films that displayed elements of European cultural heritage was also evidenced by the success of Ernst Lubitsch's films for Warners and MGM. *Woman To Woman* did not however produce a lasting contract for Balcon since Selznick's company had been in receivership when he struck the original deal. As an expression of confidence in the investment, however, the receivers had been willing to put money into British films and even part-financed Balcon's next film, *The Passionate Adventure* (Balcon, 1969: 18). Nevertheless, Balcon did not make much money from the American distribution of the film, even if its reputation did much to inspire greater confidence in British films (Kemp, 1997: 21).

Balcon continued to seek American support for British films and was offered a contract by Sam Eckman Jnr of MGM for a series of films starring Ivor Novello. The deal was highly unusual in that North and South American revenues to the tune of £30,000 for each film were to be paid to Gainsborough, Balcon's production company. Balcon rejected the deal, fearing that MGM would impose its authority over the productions, preferring instead to collaborate with and recruit American personnel including Charles Lapworth, former editor of *LA Graphic* and London agent for Sam Goldwyn. In 1926 plans were announced for collaboration between Gainsborough and Lee-Bradford, an independent American distribution company, on six films, and Balcon, Lapworth and Gainsborough's financial director went to New York where further business was completed with Lee-Bradford for the distribution of *The Rat, The Pleasure Garden, The Mountain Eagle* and *The Sea Urchin* (Kemp, 1997: 21–7). Balcon was disappointed at being unable to secure distribution through one of the majors and, according to Philip Kemp, was 'hampered by the need to satisfy C. M. Woolf', his British distributor in his talks with American companies, although it is unclear what restrictions had been insisted upon by Woolf (Kemp, 1997: 26). Balcon later wrote that, while Sam Eckman's offer had been generous, he did not accept it because he believed that 'the distribution of British films especially in the UK should be in British hands'.[27] Bradford-Lee did its best to distribute Gainsborough's films in smaller theatres and the films received varying reviews: *Variety* praised Graham Cutts' *The Rat* as 'a masterpiece of sordid realism and animalism', while *The Pleasure Garden*, Hitchcock's first feature film, was considered to be 'foolish', 'illogical' and 'implausible'.[28] It appears that Balcon's aspirations in the United States had been thwarted by a combination of split loyalties (the problems with C. M. Woolf); bad timing (American annoyance at the prospect of protective legislation for the British film industry) and Balcon's own qualms about the nature and extent of Anglo-American cooperation necessary to ensure reciprocity (his rejection of the MGM deal). At the same time Herbert Wilcox, another key figure in the British film industry, was faring better in the United States. Wilcox achieved the greatest American success for any British film in the 1920s with *Nell Gwyn* (1925; US release, 1926).

Herbert Wilcox, *Nell Gwyn* and Dorothy Gish

Herbert Wilcox was a producer and director who sought and obtained American distribution for his films from the start of his long and successful career in the British film industry (Wilcox, 1967: 52–3). A firm believer in the box-office appeal of American stars, his second film, *Flames of Passion* (1922), directed by Graham Cutts, starred Mae Marsh and was sold in the United States (Low, 1971: 133). Indeed, Wilcox had made some headway in America in 1925 when MGM distributed *Chu Chin Chow* (1923), a film directed by Wilcox which had been shot in Germany at the UFA studios and starred Betty Blythe, another American actress. *Variety* praised the film for its spectacular exterior settings shot in Algeria and declared it 'the finest spectacular picture yet produced by a British firm'.[29] Wilcox managed to secure better distribution deals for his films than had Balcon, taking advantage of Famous Players-Lasky's interest in producing in Britain and collaborating with British producers. The deal with Famous Players-Lasky and the Paramount circuit had been facilitated by production executive J. D. Williams, a Canadian who had been a co-founder and head of First National. He was subsequently involved in initiatives to secure an international profile for British films and develop a pan-European film industry (Higson and Maltby, 1999: 276–7). As one of the founding directors of Stoll Picture Productions, Williams had a history of dealings with the British film industry. Later, in 1926, Williams formed British National, bought the world rights to *Nell Gwyn,* and invited Wilcox to join the company. As well as facilitating this important development for British cinema, Williams was a key figure in the establishment of Elstree Studios (Wilcox, 1967: 67–70). It is interesting that by this time Stoll, his former business partner, had become highly suspicious of cooperation with Hollywood and commented that British National's deal with Paramount was 'evidence of a world-wide control of films falling into American hands'.[30] In terms of securing access to the American market, however, the deal was excellent since due to a series of corporate manoeuvres in the mid-1920s Paramount controlled the largest number of theatres in the United States (Gomery, 1986: 28–9).

Nell Gwyn featured Dorothy Gish, an American star who was engaged for a high salary of £1,000 a week (Plate 1). Williams offered Wilcox 50 per cent profit in addition to the entire production cost of £14,000 and signed up Dorothy Gish for three further films with financial backing from Famous Players-Lasky (Low, 1971: 176 and Wilcox, 1967: 67). Gish's trips to Britain were well publicized and the film's release was awaited by the press with keen interest: 'Dorothy Gish travelled to England and made this marvellous production in authentic settings. It will show little Dorothy at a new angle, more fascinating, more beautiful and more appealing than you can imagine'.[31] After being premièred in New York in January 1926, *Nell Gwyn* was shown in Chicago in June and then released selectively in a number of theatres before general release. The première was described as a 'special showing', staged by Broadway impresario Joseph Plunkett and with musical accompaniment in the form of a theme song, 'Nell Gwyn', arranged by Carl Edourde. Prominent figures in the film industry were invited including Sam Goldwyn, Sam and Albert Warner, S. R. Kent (general manager of Paramount) and also the British consul.[32] This example of 'roadshow' exhibition for a British film is significant in that the majority of British films released in subsequent years according to this strategy did far better business than those released indiscriminately in America.[33] A nationwide survey on roadshowing published in the *Exhibitors' Herald* reveals some of the advantages and disadvantages of the practice. On the positive side, films designated for special roadshow treatment were deemed to be of unusual or prestigious quality and capable of attracting new patrons. As an exhibitor in a first-run theatre in Detroit commented, 'Roadshowing creates an interest in pictures by a class of people not normally interested in regular picture houses'. Smaller exhibitors, however, objected to the higher prices often charged for renting roadshow films and having to wait while they were shown at larger theatres. The point was also made that roadshowing created high expectations of a film which were not always satisfied.[34] As demonstrated by the exhibition of *Nell Gwyn*, it could nevertheless assist foreign films and was all the more remarkable an achievement in the context of Anglo-American conflict over the protection issue, 1926–7.

After its première in January 1926 at the Ritz Carlton Hotel, New York, *Nell Gwyn* received an excellent review in *Variety*. The strategy of using a well-known American actress had clearly paid off, since the first paragraph was devoted to the acting talents of Dorothy Gish. The rest of the review is instructive as to which elements were considered to be attractive to American audiences:

> As for *Nell Gwyn* itself and as representative of the advancement of British photoplay production, it simply goes to prove that the English have grasped the idea of sexy stuff and proceeded to undress their players – or, at least, some of their women players – and if not actually undress them, at least give the suggestion of undress. . . . That Nell was the mistress of the king is not left to the imagination, even though it is not expressed in so many words in a sub-title; but the action conveys the story completely. . . . This is the first British picture this reviewer has seen, coming from the British Isles, that seems to have a chance in the best houses in America.[35]

This irreverent brand of comedic 'key-hole' history was, as we shall see, a successful formula in the 1930s with *The Private Life of Henry VIII* (1933) and the sound version of *Nell Gwyn* (1934), starring Anna Neagle. Wilcox's adaptation of the historic events deliberately accentuated 'humour' and 'sex appeal galore' (Wilcox, 1967: 66). *Picture-Play Magazine* praised the film, again focussing on Dorothy Gish's peformance: 'Miss Gish employs her talents as a hoydenish comedienne to the satisfaction of all beholders. . . . It gives us a new conception of the star'.[36] The *New York Times* hailed it as 'a smoothly developed and charming presentation. . . . Whatever may be the shortcomings of English motion picture producers, if they can put together other pictures as simply and with as much dramatic effect . . . they will have no difficulty obtaining a showing for them anywhere'. Nell's charm and vivacity was hailed as one of the film's most positive attributes as well as her being 'equal' to royalty despite her humble origins: 'Majesty never had any terrors for her; she retained her fascination by being herself'.[37] The review in *Variety* makes the additional point that costume pictures were normally a 'hard-sell' but that 'this one seems to have enough of that something in the sex line to overcome the costume handicap', which again makes the film's American experience all the more notable. A survey of exhibitors' generic preferences in the Midwest and Northwest published in the *Exhibitors' Herald* confirms this opinion when costume films were voted the least popular category: 84 per cent of those surveyed put it as their eighth choice.[38] *Moving Picture World*, another trade paper which was biased towards exhibitors, declared the film to be 'by far the best picture that has been brought to this country from England', describing it as a 'fascinating character study' brought to life by Gish in an excellent performance which was enhanced by Wilcox's direction and by the work of American cameraman Roy Overbaugh, considered to be 'on a par with our high class films'.[39] Overbaugh was an experienced cameraman who had worked for Famous Players-Lasky's British production company in the early 1920s. He went on to shoot several British films including *Madame Pompadour* (1928), *Tip Toes* (1928) and *The Return of the Rat* (1929).

Nell Gwyn's success provides evidence for Williams's confidence about the prospects of British films overseas. He believed however that in order to do well they must convey compelling narratives rather than rely on Stoll's faith in physical setting as their major drawing power:

> The Soul of England is in English drama and not in English landscapes. You cannot 'make' a film in the sense of giving it outstanding quality by standing outside and photographing your action in the most beautiful vales of Sussex or Devon or any other country. It is the story that is the soul of your picture. Story is the drama. Drama is the artifice. Exteriors are facts.[40]

Similarly, a report of the New York première in the *Exhibitors' Herald* was full of optimism about the progress of British films: 'In *Nell Gwyn* the spirit of reciprocity seems to have reached a climax. *Nell Gwyn* is nearer to American than any previous English film. . . . The ovation accorded the production was tremendous, and a glowing tribute to the advancement of British productions'.[41] It is interesting that 'advancement' is expressed in terms of similarity to American films rather than qualities which could be identified as specifically British, although Wilcox's direction was given fulsome credit. On the other hand, as one review pointed out, the film's structure was not tightly organized: '*Nell Gwyn* differs from the usual film offering in that it does not follow a certain defined plot or attempt to round out the story at the close'.[42] This is an interesting comment, indicating that the film's similarity to American films was conceived in terms of genre and technical attributes rather than adherence to a classical narrative structure.

The film is not confusing, however. It consists of a number of sequences following Nell's story in a chronological development, introducing the characters as it progresses in its 'character study'. It uses the 'key-hole' history formula which was to be so successful in the 1930s for Alexander Korda with *The Private Life of Henry VIII,* as the second title explains: 'What learned men call "history", the dull records of wars and treaties, often dies, while the simple stories of human love live on forever'. The majority of the close-ups used in the film are reserved for Nell who is shown as vivacious and charming despite her poor surroundings, catching the King's eye outside the Playhouse. Dorothy Gish's affectionate portrayal is indeed a major source of pleasure in the film as she is pitted against the scheming and corrupt Duke of York and the 'dissolute' members of the King's court who shun her as the low-born favourite. Her rival, Lady Castlemaine (Juliette Compton), is made to look ridiculous by Nell when she parodies her on stage, wearing an enormous hat which resembles one worn by Castlemaine to impress the King. In this way the film encourages empathy with Nell, even in her sexual relationship with King Charles, which is tempered with affection and the suggestion of genuine love. At the end of the film, just before the King dies, he asks his brother not to let Nell starve. The ending is ambiguous, leaving audiences unclear as to Nell's fate, unlike Wilcox's sound version of the story (1934) which at the insistence of the Hays Office ended with Nell being punished for her dalliance with royalty (see Chapter 3). In the 1925 version, Nell refuses to take the new King's hand. She walks past him to a bust of Charles II and the title reads: 'My King – forever', implying that her allegiance is pledged only to him. Instead of showing Nell destitute, the 1924 film ends with shots of pensioners and the Chelsea hospital as Nell's enduring legacy to history. With its focus on an 'ordinary' woman who becomes the King's favourite, displays wit and comic talent on the stage and has a moral conscience, *Nell Gwyn* was able to cross cultures and transcend what might on the face of it appear to be specifically British subject matter. As with *Henry VIII,* a strong bond was created between the King and the populace, implying that royalty is neither invincible nor inhuman. Nell is contrasted with the corrupt and hypocritical court, the implication being that in Nell the King appreciated superior qualities. The King acts on her suggestion that the Chelsea palace be made over as a home for ex-soldiers and sailors, referring to her as 'the King's conscience'. In this way the film's American success is understandable, with its appeal to the 'universal' values which critics appreciated in American films.

Reports of the film's career in the United States between 1926 and 1927 confirm the accolades showered on it in these early reports and Wilcox's account of the film as a 'riotous success throughout the world' (Wilcox, 1967: 68). In August 1926, for example, the *Exhibitors' Herald* reported that the film had played in the 'finest theatres' and had been well distributed.[43] The trade paper included a regular 'What the Picture Did For Me' feature which gives an excellent indication of how the film fared in different US locations. *Nell Gwyn* appeared in an additional list of box-office winners for 1927 provided by exhibitors all over America and was named by one exhibitor as one of his theatre's biggest earners. An exhibitor in Nazareth, Pennsylvania, commented that the film was 'a very fine foreign production' while another in Kissimmee, Florida, remarked that the film 'did good business. . . . If Paramount would give us more pictures like this and at the same price I am sure that we would all feel better pleased. Play this one up as it is well worth it'.[44] In the 'box-office ticker' – regular business reports published in the *Exhibitors' Herald* – a film was awarded a percentage rating obtained by dividing a film's average daily gross by the average daily gross of a picture holding the house record to determine its relative box-office value. While the accuracy of this method of calculation is open to criticism, this complicated system resulted in various charts presented in the paper. *Nell Gwyn* featured regularly in 1927, showing at least that the film was widely exhibited.[45] Reports from small theatres nevertheless indicated that foreign films still experienced problems, an exhibitor from Warren, Arkansas, for example, complaining that it was 'not a small town picture'. Another, in Hollyrood, Kansas, warned fellow exhibitors: 'It is a type that will not go in the small towns so watch your step'. There was an interesting exception to this small-town verdict from Eagle River, Wisconsin, where the picture scored a high 80 per cent 'ticker' rating and the exhibitor advised: 'If your people will come in to see a foreign picture, they will stay'.[46] A sense of the film's comparative box-office value can be conveyed by listings from the Million Dollar Theatre in Los Angeles where *Nell Gwyn* took $15,000 on its first day. Top Hollywood films such as *The Gold Rush* earned $17,000 and *The Son of the Sheik* $31,500 on their first days, indicating that *Nell Gwyn*'s performance was more than respectable.[47] Further evidence of the film's successful American career is recorded in *The Film Daily Year Book,* one of Hollywood's major trade manuals, when Dorothy Gish's performance was cited as one of the best of six in April 1926. On the basis of *The Film Daily* reviews, *Nell Gwyn* was also named in the 'Honor Roll' of the best films.[48]

The film's success also reached the attention of the US Department of Commerce, which was monitoring the film situation closely in 1926. C. J. North, Chief of the newly formed Motion Picture Division, wrote to Hugh Butler, Acting Commercial Attaché in London, in February 1926 about the possibility of legislation to protect the British film industry. North cited *Nell Gwyn* as an example of a good British film which could be used as evidence against charges by British producers that their films were discriminated against in America: 'I believe that the fact that Famous Players is going to distribute *Nell Gwyn* in this country, and its favourable reception by the industry and its trade press will help considerably and allay the wholly erroneous impression that British film producers seem to have, namely, that they can not get their pictures shown in America'.[49] Butler replied to North with information about the film's exhibition: 'Mr Graham, of the Famous Players organization, tells me that the film *Nell Gwyn* was not purchased, but was handled on a percentage basis, and that Dorothy Gish's name carried it across as much as anything else. Still it is a fact that a British-made film is showing in the United States successfully'.[50]

Records of such discussions about British films in the Department of Commerce confirm the seriousness with which European protectionism was viewed and the growing recognition that some level of reciprocity was essential for the consolidation of Hollywood's own aggressive export drive. Figures from as early as 1920 reveal that in terms of exports, Britain was Hollywood's best customer.[51] The desire to preserve the *status quo* was acute in 1925–6 since Hollywood obtained 35 per cent of its foreign revenues from Britain (Thompson, 1985: 127). The interdependence of imports and exports was becoming an accepted fact of film industry economics, as indicated by a statement made by Arthur Kelly, Vice-President of Foreign Sales at United Artists, in 1927:

> There is a tendency on the part of all foreign countries to force local production to the front, as well as to find a market in the United States. American distributors will have to meet this competition eventually by releasing a quantity of foreign productions in this country, as they cannot hope to obtain hold of European business unless reciprocal measures are fostered.[52]

As we shall see, in the 1930s United Artists handled many British films in America, a strategy which was already clearly understood as important. The success of *Nell Gwyn* and Dorothy Gish's other films for British National were thus cited as the way forward for British films in the United States. Martin Quigley, editor of the *Exhibitors' Herald,* visited Britain in 1926 and on his return wrote an editorial which praised Wilcox's approach but argued that it was atypical of British producers:

> In being organized by Mr J. D. Williams, an American, on the basis of knowledge of motion pictures gained in the United States, the British National picture firm apparently did not follow what was considered the accepted method of procedure. Hence, one is told frequently in London that the company does not amount to much, that it never will and that talk of the great studio it is building is – just talk. The daily press and the trade press have practically ignored the plans of this company. Even the sale of *Nell Gwyn* to an American company excited more criticism than approval.[53]

Statements such as this indicate the depth of feeling that had developed by 1926 when suspicions had escalated in Britain about the motives of Americans who wanted to 'help' the British film industry. Much of this centred on the fear that American assistance would result in Hollywood taking financial control of the British film industry. Balcon had his reservations about the deal with MGM on these grounds whereas Wilcox had no qualms about using American stars and personnel in order to facilitate the distribution of British films by a major circuit. It is ironic that suspicions about American involvement prejudiced some commentators against the efforts of Wilcox and Williams when their success with *Nell Gwyn* was a clear demonstration of how national specificity need not be compromised by American collaboration. The hardening of Anglo-American film relations at the same time that Wilcox and Williams were experiencing such a notable success for a British film in the United States did not assist them in subsequent deals. In a greater climate of goodwill, had one been instituted, Wilcox and Williams might indeed have taken advantage of a reciprocity scheme.

After *Nell Gwyn,* Wilcox, assisted by Williams, managed to obtain screenings via Famous Players-Lasky in Paramount cinemas for *London* (1926), another Dorothy Gish vehicle. Its critical or box-office performance did not, however, match that of *Nell Gwyn*. Two reports from exhibitors published in the *Exhibitors' Herald* indicate mixed opinion on *London*. While an exhibitor in Akron, Iowa, wrote that the film 'pleased' audiences, and another in Bellaire, Ohio, reported 'we had a lot of favourable comment. It will get by on most any program', others were less impressed, such as an exhibitor from Pierre, South Dakota, who warned other showmen that 'it is poor entertainment and will kill Dorothy Gish if she has to carry many more foreign productions'.[54] Famous Players-Lasky refused to distribute *Tip Toes* (1927), the next Gish film, but Paramount released it after British National had been taken over in 1927 and reorganized into a vertically integrated combine, British International Pictures (BIP), by Scottish renter and exhibitor John Maxwell.

Madame Pompadour (1928), although directed by Herbert Wilcox, was supervised by E. A. Dupont, a highly regarded German director who had been hired by Williams as part of his internationalist strategy.[55] Again starring Dorothy Gish, the film was well reviewed and distributed widely but did not rate highly in the 'box-office ticker' registers. *Variety* nevertheless declared that it was a 'money picture' which appealed because of its exotic theme and 'costume stuff'.[56] The *New York Times* reviewer also commented on its rich sets and costumes but regretted that the narrative lacked tension.[57] Indeed, the film is impressive for its opulent sets and convoluted narrative of court intrigue. Gish plays the part of Pompadour with considerable panache. Although she is hated by Parisians who resent her hold over the King, her character is softened when she falls in love with an artist who does not realize that she is Madame Pompadour. She longs to escape from the King's clutches, but her attempt to leave the court is thwarted. The film's lavish costumes and *mise-en-scène* are used to good effect, for example when the artist first sees Madame Pompadour in a carriage and her face is hidden behind an elaborate masque. Her 'dual' nature, as a scheming figure in the King's court and as a misunderstood, tragic figure who is vulnerable to the King's whims, invests the film with a sophisticated and compelling central performance. In technical terms *Madame Pompadour* is notable for being the first British film to demonstrate the Schüfftan process, a 'special effect' which had already been used in Germany and America.[58]

Wilcox had some success later when Columbia picked up *Dawn* (1928), a film which had been shown in New York by an independent exhibitor and released with some success in art cinemas (Guzman, 1993: 312). In all, it seems that Wilcox's films had performed best in the United States, and that this was in large part due to the success of J. D. Williams in securing contracts with major companies. Despite his valiant efforts for British National, Williams became embroiled in a financial dispute towards the end of 1926, which resulted in him suing the company for wrongful dismissal and arrears of salary (Low, 1971: 186). It is unfortunate that this momentarily disrupted a successful collaboration, but Williams continued his work to advance the cause of British films overseas for BIP, forming World Wide Pictures in 1928 to distribute European films in America (Low, 1971: 188 and Higson and Maltby, 1999: 390–92).[59] Two well-reviewed films directed by Dupont, *Moulin Rouge* (1928) and *Piccadilly* (1929), were distributed by World Wide in America, mainly in art cinemas in large cities. Of the thirty-five British films imported into the United States in 1928, ten were handled by World Wide.[60] Towards the end of the decade BIP's ambitions focussed on pan-European schemes and then, with the coming of sound, on multilingual production (see Higson and Maltby, 1999: 286–94).

British Cinema, Hollywood and the Art-Film Market

While earlier reviews encouraged British films to adopt American techniques, by the end of the decade the art market had formed its own expectations which were based on acceptable departures from the Hollywood model. As the art market became an obvious outlet for European films in the United States, British films, particularly those which were shown by the Film Society in London, might reasonably expect to be compared to French, Soviet and German films. The films that were reaching American screens towards the end of the 1920s – Alfred Hitchcock's *The Case of Jonathan Drew/The Lodger* and *Blackmail*, Anthony Asquith's *Shooting Stars* and Dupont's *Piccadilly* – did not however generate the same degree of excitement in art cinema circuits as European 'classics' such as *Metropolis, The Battleship Potemkin* or *The Last Laugh*. As was often the case with British films, while improvements were commented on in reviews, no definite impression emerges as to what might constitute a 'British' film from an American perspective. Throughout the decade, however, plenty of advice was given by reviewers as to how British producers should improve standards so that their films would be more acceptable to exhibitors and to the public. In the absence of audience surveys, these reviews convey some sense of contemporary standards and expectations. An account of how British films fared in reviews illustrates many of the prevailing attitudes towards film form and confirms the impression that Hollywood's 'classical' style was increasingly understood in terms of very specific expectations regarding length, editing, titling, sets, acting style and the importance of stars. As early as 1920 Martin Quigley complained that 'British pictures as a rule have not as yet attained a standard comparable with that required by the American motion picture public'.[61] The 'standard' was assumed to be set by Hollywood. Thus while Stoll's *The Agony of the Eagles* was described by a *Variety* reviewer in 1922 as a 'magnificent' adaptation, it was also considered 'too tragic in theme and too foreign in treatment for general American audiences. . . . The captions in the English version are verbose and the whole thing is more narrative than active', implying that faster pacing, minimal, succinct titling and 'action' scenes were superior.[62] Some films which were reviewed in London but did not reach American screens were given very different verdicts, for example, *Wonderful Year* (1922), Herbert Wilcox's first production, was described as 'very fine' and Graham Cutts, the director, as 'probably the best and most truly artistic producer in England'. As commented earlier, British scenery was seen as a marker of authenticity, the same film being praised for its photography of 'beautiful lanes and pasture lands'.[63] It is striking that although many British films such as *Wonderful Year* received excellent reviews from *Variety*, a publication not normally well disposed towards foreign films, they were never premièred in New York. In 1922, for instance, *Variety* reviewed twenty-two British films but only four were recorded as being screened in New York – *Sherlock Holmes*, *The Bigamist*, *A Woman of No Importance* and *The Money Monster*. The first two have already been discussed and were relatively successful. *A Woman of No Importance* was produced by Ideal Films and starred Fay Compton. According to the review it played well in New York: 'Altogether the picture will have an excellent appeal here and is a fortunate introduction of the better class British production in this market'.[64] *The Money Monster* was praised for its 'pantomime' acting style which the reviewer considered to be more effective than the style of American actors who were taught to 'register' on screen, an interesting comment indicating the reviewer's appreciation of film acting which alluded to popular theatre rather than to styles which were being developed for the screen. The direction, however, was considered to be 'inferior'.[65] British films were often reprimanded for their length and for poor continuity. The *Variety* reviewer of *The Luck of the Navy* (1927) wrote: 'It is hard to believe this film runs 110 minutes. It seemed years. Not alone in time, either. Technique, story, continuity, appeared to belong to a dim and distant era'.[66]

It was primarily in the area of film technique that British films were most often accused of being deficient. Even *Nell Gwyn*, the most successful British film on American screens in the 1920s, was criticized in the occasional review as being technically anachronistic: 'The lighting was incomprehensibly monotonous. . . . The cameraman must have been suffering from the gout, for he seemed loath to change his position from that corresponding with the front row of the orchestra stalls. Ordinary primary grade close-ups were the only variant. Given photography of a less primitive nature, Miss Gish's work would have been immeasurably enhanced'.[67] This comment conflicts with other reviews which praised the work of the American cameraman Roy Overbaugh, illustrating how reviews often relied on standard criticisms based on assumptions about British films being technically backward. Two of the most highly regarded British films of the late silent period, *Shooting Stars* and *The Case of Jonathan Drew/The Lodger*, had a very poor critical reception outside New York. *Variety* was merciless about *Shooting Stars*, describing it as 'a disgrace to the film industry of any country' interpreting the film, with its story of love and rivalry among film actors, as an irreverent critique of the profession with 'a rather involved story well worked out until its finish'.[68] The review of *The Case of Jonathan Drew/The Lodger*, written after its screening at the Fifth Avenue Playhouse, New York (an art cinema), is no better:

> Here's a story idea that, adequately carried out, would have knocked the 'art' fans for a row of ecstatic exclamations. But the English producers couldn't make the grade. They took a smashing theme, gummed it up with cheap and shoddy catering to the lowest taste of what they supposed to be their public, and then further smeared it with acting and photography that belongs in the American studio of ten years ago. . . . The Germans might have made a fine, bitter social satire out of the material for supercilious high brows to rave over. Here it has been turned into a trashy commercial film worthless for the 'art' audiences and for the generality of American fans alike.[69]

Reviews such as this contrast somewhat with the *New York Times* which championed the art film but conceived it as distinct from mainstream drama. Thus *Shooting Stars* was admired for its ingenuity but criticized for lapsing into melodrama. While the opening of *The Case of Jonathan Drew/The Lodger* was viewed as 'excellent', its melodramatic middle and closure were described as 'mediocre' and 'deplorable'.[70] These comments allude to the problematic status of British films in the art market. Even Ivor Novello's acting, which had been appreciated by American reviewers and audiences in several films (discussed later) was criticized as 'unbelievably stilted'. Hitchcock's much-publicized debt to German cinema was dismissed as 'trick shots borrowed from the German technique', and the love-interest described as 'little slants of sex kick lifted from the American studio with that brutal crassness that only the Briton is capable of in his most earnest moments'. Such criticism was not entirely confined to British films. Murnau's *Sunrise*, for example, filmed in Hollywood as part of Fox's strategy to corner the market for 'quality' pictures towards the end of the 1920s, was another film which combined Hollywood narrative conventions with European techniques and sensibilities. Reviewers and audiences were puzzled by the film because it did not appear to fit into the categories of either mainstream Hollywood or art cinema.[71] Similarly, while for the most part demonstrating elements of classical narrative form, *The Case of Jonathan Drew/The Lodger* contained elements which exceeded the normal requirements of continuity editing, and these were singled out as jarring. An example of this is the montage sequence when the news of the latest murder in London is heard by the immediate crowds and is transmitted across the airwaves and reported in the newspapers. While important in establishing the theme of communication, and also in demonstrating a modernist fascination with technology, this sequence was criticized for being too long and laborious in communicating a simple piece of narrative information.[72] Such comments indicate the extent to which critics utilized clear distinctions between popular and art cinema and, particularly in the trade press, how distinct audiences were being identified as the primary patrons for both types of cinema. In view of this initial negative reception, it is interesting and perhaps ironic that *The Lodger* eventually became accepted as an art film in America as evidence of Hitchcock's affinity with Expressionism and as part of his early auteurist trajectory.[73]

British Stars: The Case of Ivor Novello

Although European stars went to Hollywood and a culture of internationalism existed to some extent, British stars failed to rival Hollywood's or experience the popularity of an émigré such as Polish star Pola Negri. Negri was imported by Adolph Zukor at Famous Players-Lasky in 1922 after gaining a reputation in Berlin cabaret and German cinema and scored a notable box-office hit in America with *The Passion* in 1921.[74] By contrast, the most successful British films tended to feature stars such as Betty Compson or Dorothy Gish, with whom audiences were already familiar from American films. One British star who did make a small impact in the United States, however, was Welsh-born Ivor Novello, whose experiences as an actor in Hollywood and as a star of British films provide a useful focus for a discussion about American perceptions of British cinema, issues of stardom and national identity.

Novello was well known as a popular songwriter before he became a film actor. His first film roles were for French director Louis Mercanton in *L'Appel du Sang/The Call of the Blood* (1919) and *Miarka, Fille de L'Ourse/Miarka: Daughter of the Bear* (1920). His first British films were made in quick succession: *Carnival* (Alliance, directed by Harley Knoles, 1922), followed by *The Bohemian Girl* (Alliance, directed by Harley Knoles, 1922) and *The Man Without Desire* (Atlas Biocraft, directed by Adrian Brunel, 1923).[75] Knoles was keen to obtain American screenings for *Carnival* and went to America in 1921 where the film was handled by United Artists. *Carnival* was a box-office success in Britain where Novello was fast becoming a major star who was often compared to Valentino for his handsome, dark looks (Low, 1971: 146).[76] *Carnival* was a lavish adaptation of a stage play, also starring British actor Matheson Lang and with carnival scenes shot on location in Venice. Agnes Smith's review in *Picture-Play Magazine* was highly favourable: 'It reeks with Old World splendor, and the Venetian scenes are particularly fine. If you want to be strictly up to date in your film entertainment you can't afford to miss it.

It is more of a treat to the eyes than any scenic picture you ever saw'.[77] *Variety* was also enthusiastic: 'American producers would do well to view this picture for plot and acting; both are splendid, but the photography is rather poor. . . . Novello, playing Andrea, is the best-looking villain ever on the screen, any-where'.[78] The film was shown in New York and Chicago, but this did not result in nationwide bookings. Novello's next film, *The Bohemian Girl*, was distributed by the American Releasing Corporation after being screened in New York in February 1923. Accompanying Novello, the film starred Gladys Cooper, C. Aubrey Smith and celebrated stage acrtress Ellen Terry. Once again *Variety* was full of praise: 'Should be a sure-fire drawing card as a regular release', but there is little evidence to suggest that the film was released widely.[79] The *New York Times* compared Novello to Ramon Novarro and Richard Barthelmess.[80] Such opinions were important because they meant that when Novello went to the United States in 1923 to publicize the film with Gladys Cooper he was known by some, and attracted considerable publicity when he took up an offer to star in a film for celebrated Hollywood director D. W. Griffith.

Griffith had noticed Novello at the Savoy when he visited London for the opening of *Orphans of the Storm*. Griffith was attracted by Novello's photogenic qualities and his resemblance to Richard Barthelmass, an actor Griffith admired and had used in films such as *Broken Blossoms* (Harding, 1997: 51 and Schickel, 1984: 477). After being introduced to Novello by a drama critic Griffith arranged a further interview. The result was an offer to star along with Mae Marsh in *The White Rose,* a melodrama about a divinity student who falls in love with a young woman while on his travels. He abandons her but finally accepts responsibility for her and their unborn child. Novello's American visit received much publicity both in Britain and America. While the British press concentrated on his welcome by fans in 'the bohemian quarters of New York' and described the film's extensive southern locations which included Mississipi, New Orleans, Alabama and Georgia, there was also comment that as a British star, Novello was 'unspoilt' by Hollywood and even a little homesick for England. As with many subsequent reports on British stars in Hollywood, British commentators were convinced that their experiences were potentially dangerous. Hollywood was perceived to be full of vice and temptation, a far cry from the supposedly more sheltered lives led by film stars in Britain. On the other hand, American reports concentrated on the link with Griffith and on Novello's exotic persona which did not exude a particularly British national identity. *Picture-Play Magazine* described him as a 'Griffith find' with an Italian accent and his Latinate looks and foreign-sounding name even caused confusion as to whether he was Swedish or Russian.[81]

When *The White Rose* opened in the Spring of 1923, Novello became the focus of even more comment. *Variety*'s reviewer approved of Griffith's casting, observing that Novello played 'effectively' and that 'his work displays the expertness of the direction'.[82] The New York press was particularly enthusiastic, recommending that he should stay in America and continue to work for Griffith.[83] In Washington his resemblance to Valentino was noted, and Novello was even tipped as his successor as America's most popular male actor: 'Ivor has everything earlier sheiks had, and more. He is Grecian in form and features and fortunate enough to be taller and slimmer than Valentino'.[84] The film performed reasonably well at the box-office, but despite having optioned him for further roles, Griffith did not renew his contract. According to Griffith's biographer, he was disappointed with Novello's performance in *The White Rose* and described the film rather dismissively as a 'pot-boiler'.[85] Novello later criticized his role in the film as 'a sanctimonious clergyman utterly devoid of humour' and felt that an opportunity had been lost to make a successful career in Hollywood, especially since his previous films had given him favourable exposure.[86] A bitter Novello sued Griffith and returned to Britain to work for Gainsborough Pictures in his most celebrated roles in films directed by Graham Cutts and Alfred Hitchcock. American interest continued, however, when Sam Eckman proposed the deal with MGM on the strength of seeing Novello in *The Rat,* a contract which, as we have seen, was rejected by Balcon. Novello's experience with Griffith shows that even when employed by American directors, British actors were vulnerable. Nevertheless, it also reveals that praise from critics did not necessarily depend on an American connection, as confirmed by the many positive responses to his early British films.

British Film Exports at the End of the Silent Period

Many factors influenced British producers' attempts to exhibit their films in America during the 1920s. As we have seen, they were at the mercy of American distributors, many of which did not have the industrial muscle to market foreign productions effectively. As the drive towards vertical integration accelerated, it became more and more important to make links with the larger companies which controlled 'key' theatres and hired films on a percentage basis. Not all producers, however, shared the same opinion of the necessity for Anglo-American collaboration. While Balcon was cautious about tantalizing offers which promised to assist British production but also implied American domination, Wilcox was enthusiastic about using American stars in his films and securing deals with the most powerful companies. Both views reflected opinion in the United Kingdom, which was divided on the issue of independence. The debates on the protection of the film industry provided a forum on the one hand for advocates of a film industry which was unashamedly British, even if its characteristics were largely unspecified, and on the other for those who wanted reciprocity to be a key element in any statutory provision. As the remarkable distribution and exhibition of *Nell Gwyn* shows, Wilcox's and Williams's strategy was effective – and realistic – and the film's status as British was never questioned.

Expectations of what a British film was understood to be and how it might develop can be gauged from reviews and commentary. As we have seen, Oswald Stoll was a firm believer in the use of British and European locations as a distinctive marker of British/European identity, a strategy which was applauded by some critics but did not lead to sustained success. When Edward Godal, president of the British and Colonial Film Corporation, gave an address to members of the Associated Motion Picture Advertisers in New York in 1920, he predicted that in ten years London would be the recognised centre of film production because 'Europe surpasses any other area in diversity of "locations" and of local atmosphere'.[87] While reviewers often appreciated seeing British locations and distinguished them from substitutes created on Hollywood lots, they were clearly not enough to carry what was otherwise understood as an inferior picture in terms of technique. The poor reception of Hepworth's *Comin' Thro' the Rye* is a case in point of a director whose films depended on pictorial representation, long takes and minimal use of close-ups, a stylistic approach which was opposed to the classical Hollywood model which was gaining ground in the 1920s. By contrast, the British films which did best in the United States were lavish 'spectaculars', European co-productions or, like *Nell Gwyn,* comedic interpretations of British history featuring well-known American stars. Despite Dorothy Gish's nationality, reviews of *Nell Gwyn* mentioned the British context and the fact that the film was an example of the latest from British studios.[88] Many producers were anxious to adopt Hollywood's production methods in the hope that British films would improve their technical standards yet retain some sense of national identity by, for example, being based on the work of British authors.[89] The question of national distinction became more acute as German and Soviet films demonstrated that, for the rapidly growing 'little theatre' movement, difference was a key rather than a barrier to success. British films were left occupying uncertain territory and, in the absence of an obvious link to the *avant-garde,* could not avoid repeated comparison with classical narrative cinema. The reception of *The Case of Jonathan Drew/The Lodger* reveals the extent to which critics and audiences were intolerant of films which incorporated both experimental and classical styles. *Nell Gwyn* shows, however, that in certain cases British films which were not entirely classical in their form were tolerated and, in this case, well reviewed and exhibited.

At an industrial level, the quest for reciprocity was also fraught with difficulties. In the early 1920s many producers were optimistic about the exchange of films as a means of enhancing Anglo-American understanding.[90] As the decade progressed, many American commentators viewed statutory protection of the film industry as contrary to the spirit of the reciprocal agreements which had been planned by several British and American companies. Even before the protectionist debates intensified, however, as comments in the American trade press reveal, British films were not considered to be equal to American, and were therefore assumed to be junior partners in reciprocal schemes.[91] There is a sense, perhaps, that in the 1920s the quest for reciprocity was unrealistic as the American film industry thrived in a *laissez-faire* market and was consistent in its view that if pictures were good they would be shown and be popular. It is ironic that some American companies only became interested in reciprocal schemes as protectionist measures were enacted in Europe, adding an edge of insincerity to cooperative pronouncements which concealed an implicit but fundamental concern to protect Hollywood's lucrative export markets. This instability created a tense atmosphere which had been absent in the earlier, more optimistic schemes to distribute foreign films in the United States. Reciprocity therefore became less of an expression of goodwill between nations and more of a bargaining counter in an increasingly volatile market. As the political battle against *laissez-faire* intensified, advocates of protection for the film industry became more vociferous in their patriotic fervour. The pronouncements of a producer such as Oswald Stoll, who had experienced some success with his films in the American market in the early 1920s, reverberated as hide-bound and anti-American.

In a small but not undistinguished or insignificant way British films contributed to Europe's challenge to Hollywood in the 1920s. Despite the overriding view that American films were superior, British films which did well were not seen as a threat but welcomed as interesting and worthy of exhibition. Once the protection issue became the focus of Anglo-American film relations, opinion was inevitably tempered by fear that Hollywood's films might experience a reduction in screentime all over Europe. This defensive reaction no doubt influenced the opinions of *Variety* reviewers whose generosity towards British films was diminishing by the time films such as *Shooting Stars* and *The Case of Jonathan Drew/The Lodger* were released in 1928. By the end of the silent period the market for foreign films in the United States was mainly identified with the art cinema movement, and the majority of critical adulation was lavished on films from the Soviet Union (Guzman, 1993: 791). British producers continued to aspire to the mainstream market, and with the coming of sound experienced a reduction in direct competition in the United States from other European producers. At the same time they collaborated with French and German companies in multilanguage productions (Higson and Maltby, 1999: 288–92). The Cinematograph Films Act 1927 was of fundamental importance in increasing British production and accelerating the growth of large vertically integrated companies such as Gaumont-British which developed export policies in the 1930s (Sedgwick, 1996). The Act's existence signalled a new *modus operandi* for British cinema, a fact of life with which American distributors had to live. How this impacted British exports will be discussed in the next chapter, but the experience of British films in America in the 1920s left an ambivalent but determined legacy that the advancement of British films depended to a great extent on overseas exhibition for commercial, aesthetic and political reasons.

Notes

1. Figures derived from Guzman's survey (1993). I have checked these figures where possible, but there are a few discrepancies. *Film Daily Year Book* (New York: *Film Daily*) started to separate imports from their lists of films released in the United States each year in 1928, and the figures for 1927 (8) and 1928 (35) for British films are higher than those given by Guzman (5 and 11 respectively). Figures supplied by such lists are variable and, as the *Film Daily Year Book* points out, compilations often included pictures exhibited in the previous year or which had had their original showings several years previously but which had since been revived (1928: 511).
2. See Table III in Dickinson and Street (1985: 13). Figures for films that were on American distributors' books but were never exhibited are unavailable.
3. *Film Daily Year Book* (1928: 953). A study of European films in the United States during the pre-war period would be very interesting as a basis for comparison.
4. See summary of Cohen's views in *Film Daily Year Book* (1925: 43).
5. For debates on the renewal of the Films Act and trade practices see *Minutes of Evidence to the Committee on Cinematograph Films* (1936) London: HMSO.
6. *Exhibitors' Herald*, 15 Nov 1924: 78. A report on European films in the United States published in *Variety* recommended that imports had improved but still needed re-titling 'to get by in the American market and make some money in low price houses', *Variety*, 21 May 1920: 35.
7. *Picture-Play Magazine*, Mar 1921: 103.
8. *Picture-Play Magazine*, Dec 1922: 65.
9. *Variety*, 31 Mar 1922.
10. *Variety*, 3 Feb 1922.
11. Stoll's role in publicizing the 'British slump' of the mid-1920s was intertwined with his desire to persuade the UK Government to impose import duties on American films. See Burrows, 2002.
12. *Exhibitors' Herald*, 15 Nov 1924: 78.
13. *Variety*, 5 Oct 1927: 3.
14. *The Times*, 4 June 1925: 19.
15. The American trade press was also preoccupied with reciprocity. See 'Reciprocity!' in *Moving Picture World*, 7 Mar 1925: 26–7.

16. *Kinematograph Weekly,* 17 June 1926: 51.
17. See *Exhibitors' Herald,* 30 Oct 1926: 39 and 6 Nov 1926: 31 for reports of these events.
18. *Variety,* 31 Dec 1924.
19. *Photoplay,* Mar 1925: 104.
20. *Variety,* 14 Feb 1923: 17.
21. *Picture-Play Magazine,* Oct 1922: 1.
22. *Variety,* 2 Apr 1924.
23. *Variety,* 5 Mar 1923: 7.
24. *Exhibitors' Herald,* 2 Feb 1924: 46.
25. *Photo-Play Magazine,* Mar 1924: 60.
26. *New York Times,* 1 Apr 1924: 19. Compson starred in another version of *Woman to Woman* in 1929 which was made in Hollywood and directed by Victor Saville. Mordant Hall gave it a poor review, based mainly on the narrative which he considered to be 'ridiculous', *New York Times,* 12 Nov 1929: 34.
27. Michael Balcon in draft of article on the career of Sam Eckman, 1952, in Michael Balcon Special Collection, H/23, British Film Institute.
28. *Variety,* 23 Sept 1925 and 3 Nov 1926.
29. *Variety,* 11 Oct 1923.
30. *Exhibitors' Herald,* 18 Sept 1926: 25.
31. Report on the film from *Proctor's News Weekly* (East 58th St. Theatre), vol. 1, no. 10, 16 Aug 1926: 1.
32. *Exhibitors' Herald,* 30 Jan 1926: 46.
33. Although there is a distinction to be made here between a picture being given the resources and attention of roadshowing as compared to a general strategy, such as that adopted by United Artists in the 1930s, of selling 'quality' films on an individual basis. See Chapter 2.
34. *Exhibitors' Herald,* 13 Mar 1924: 32–5 and 5 Apr 1924: 23.
35. *Variety,* 27 Jan 1926.
36. *Picture-Play Magazine,* Nov 1926: 62.
37. *New York Times,* 19 July 1926: 13. This comment is similar to the 'aristocratic-proletarian' appeal of *The Private Life of Henry VIII.* See Chapter 2.
38. *Exhibitors' Herald,* 9 July 1927: 17.
39. *Moving Picture World,* 6 Feb 1926: 573.
40. 'Two Keys to the American market' by J. D. Williams in *Kinematograph Weekly,* 7 Jan 1926. Williams' article is also reprinted in Higson and Maltby, 1999: 389.
41. *Exhibitors' Herald,* 30 Jan 1926: 46.
42. *Moving Picture World,* 6 Feb 1926: 573.
43. *Exhibitors' Herald,* 28 Aug 1926: 27.
44. See *Exhibitors' Herald,* 15 Jan 1927: 59, 24 Dec 1927: 39 and 11 Sept 1926: 67.
45. See, for example, *Exhibitors' Herald* report 21 May 1927: 55.
46. *Exhibitors' Herald,* 12 Mar 1927: 58, 21 May 1927: 68 and 26 Feb 1927: 59–60.
47. *Film Daily Year Book,* 1927, summary of *Variety's* box-office figures.
48. *Film Daily Year Book,* 1927: 17, 23.
49. This correspondence is from the National Archives, Washington DC, US Department of Commerce records: North to Butler, 19 Feb 1926 (RG 151-281).
50. Butler to North, 16 Mar 1926, National Archives, Washington DC, US Department of Commerce records (RG 151-281).
51. *Moving Picture World,* 14 Aug 1920: 35.
52. Arthur Kelly in *Film Daily Year Book* (1927: 919).
53. *Exhibitors' Herald,* 8 May 1926: 21.
54. *Exhibitors' Herald,* 4 June 1927: 61, 19 Feb 1927: 60 and 12 Feb 1927: 68.

55. Dupont was variously described as supervisor, co-director, co-scriptwriter and editor. At that time he was Director General of Production at British National.

56. As remarked earlier, it would appear to be the case that 'costume' pictures were more acceptable in metropolitan areas than in small towns. See comments in *Exhibitors' Herald*, 9 July 1927: 17.

57. *Variety*, 3 Aug 1927 and the *New York Times*, 1 Aug 1927.

58. The Schüfftan process involved using mirrors to combine into a single shot portions of a full-scale studio set with artwork or a miniature component. See Low, 1971: 246.

59. According to Wilcox, Williams was involved in further disputes and went back to New York where he died, leaving his wife penniless. See Wilcox, 1967: 69–70.

60. *Film Daily Year Book*, 1929: 289–93.

61. *Exhibitors' Herald*, 16 Oct 1920: 37.

62. *Variety*, 12 May 1922.

63. *Variety*, 2 June 1922.

64. *Variety*, 30 June 1922.

65. *Variety*, 22 Dec 1922.

66. *Variety*, 21 Dec 1927.

67. *Boston Transcript*, 7 Sept 1926.

68. *Variety*, 13 June 1928.

69. *Variety*, 13 June 1928.

70. *New York Times*, 4 Mar 1928: 7 and 11 June 1928: 27.

71. For an excellent case study of the reception of *Sunrise* see Allen and Gomery, 1985: 91–105.

72. *Variety*, 13 June 1928.

73. It was exhibited in silent cinema retrospectives and distributed on the art circuit. See program notes, New York Public Library.

74. For an account of Negri's career and her place in Hollywood history see Koszarski, 1990: 296–299. On the American success of *The Passion* see Low, 1971: 78 and Gomery, 1992: 173.

75. For a summary of Novello's career with filmography see *The Silent Film Monthly*, vol. VI, no. 6, June 1998: 1–4.

76. A feature on male stars in *Picturegoer*, a British fan magazine, declared that 'Ivor looked more like a Greek God in *Carnival* than anyone I have ever seen' (May 1922: 17).

77. *Picture-Play Magazine*, Sept 1921: 59, 93.

78. *Variety*, 5 Aug 1921.

79. *Variety*, 8 Feb 1923.

80. *New York Times* quoted in Pope, 1954: 53.

81. See 'Ivor Discovers America' report in *Picturegoer*, May 1923: 10–11 and *Picture-Play Magazine*, May 1923: 43. Novello was Welsh and his Italian-sounding name came from his mother, Clara Novello-Davies who was named after an opera singer. See also Noble, 1951: 19.

82. *Variety*, 24 May 1923.

83. *New York Telegraph*, quoted in Williams, 1975: 63.

84. *Washington Times*, quoted in Williams, 1975: 63.

85. Schickel, 1984: 482.

86. Novello in *News of the World*, Dec 1924, quoted in Macnab, 2000: 41.

87. *Moving Picture World*, 3 Jan 1920: 78.

88. *Moving Picture World*, 6 Feb 1926: 573.

89. W. Walter Crotch, Vice-President of the Alliance Film Corporation and author of several books on Charles Dickens, went to New York in 1920 and declared this as a policy for his company. See *Moving Picture World*, 1 May 1920: 659.

90. See, for example, article by Colonel H. A. Browne in *Moving Picture World,* 28 Feb 1920: 1385.

91. *Variety,* 21 May 1920: 35, declared that none of the British films imported in the last year compared with the average American production.

2

The 1930s: Exportable Texts and Stars – Alexander Korda and United Artists

The years 1928–39 were of momentous importance for the British film industry. Adjusting to protection, the coming of sound and the formation of two large vertically integrated companies, Gaumont-British and Associated British, had key implications for the export market. The Cinematograph Films Act 1927 gave the industry confidence to expand even though many of the companies formed in its wake were insufficiently capitalized and soon collapsed. The Act facilitated the emergence of Gaumont-British and Associated British as 'majors', the former pursuing a strident internationalist policy for much of the decade. Gaumont-British was an amalgam of several key companies, including Ideal, the W. & F. Film Service and Gainsborough Pictures. Associated British absorbed British International Pictures, Pathé Pictures and the Scottish Cinema and Variety Theatre chains. Companies such as Gaumont-British which owned cinema circuits were able to command bargaining power as the fate of British films in America became intertwined with Hollywood's anxiety to maintain access to British screens. The existence of protectionist legislation in Britain created tension as Anglo-American film relations embarked on a volatile phase characterized by contradictory impulses that veered between collaboration, goodwill, optimism and suspicion, antipathy and jingoism. While the latter intensified as the Films Act was debated and revised in 1937–8, the decade was nevertheless marked by highly publicized transatlantic crossings with many film company executives, stars and technicians visiting New York and Hollywood to explore joint ventures, star exchanges, promote British films and gain technical experience. From 1928 to 1939 the United States imported a total of 2,393 foreign feature films, 428 of which were British.[1] In terms of notable exports the decade was dominated by the box-office and critical success of Alexander Korda's *The Private Life of Henry VIII* (1933), a film to which reference was made in most subsequent pronouncements on the economic and aesthetic viability of British films abroad. It was not however the only Korda film to make a mark. As well as offering a detailed analysis of the distribution and reception of *The Private Life of Henry VIII,* this chapter will discuss subsequent films that made distinctive contributions to the appreciation of British films in America.

The Impact of the 'Talkies'

In its anxiety to be the first European country to 'wire' its cinemas for sound, Britain was vulnerable to American marketing of sound-film apparatus. By the middle of 1929 Western Electric and RCA, the major American suppliers, accounted for over half the British cinema and studio installations (Dickinson and Street, 1985: 45). The trend for multilingual production attracted many producers such as J. D. Williams, the enterprising Canadian who had already demonstrated an interest in pan-European collaboration and who had distributed British films, most notably *Piccadilly,* in the United States with some success, and had a role in securing effective distribution for *Nell Gwyn* (see Chapter 1). However, this trend was short-lived because of a variety of factors, one of which was the considerably cheaper costs of dubbing (Higson and Maltby, 1999: 292). On the face of it, British producers did not, *vis-à-vis* America, have a language 'problem', so there was not the same incentive to participate in schemes which intended to isolate the European market from the United States. The Paris Agreement of 1930 carved up the world's markets among the dominant suppliers of talking-picture equipment, the major beneficiaries being the United States and Germany. For German films the combination of the talkies with a strong, protected film industry facilitated the establishment of a 'niche' market serviced by specialized theatres in New York which had been growing since the 1920s (Crafton, 1997: 435 and Balio, 1993: 34). Nevertheless, as Crafton has observed: 'Sound enabled the American film industry to solidify its power as the leading exporter of entertainment' (1997: 418). Victor Saville went to New York to study RCA's recording processes and Gaumont-British installed Western Electric equipment in its cinemas while it continued to develop its own system, British Acoustic. Britain's first talkie, *Blackmail* (1929), was distributed by Sono Art/World Wide and played well in theatres in New York, New Jersey and Los Angeles. The actors' diction was praised as 'superior to our home-made' as well as the film's overall quality as 'not just a talker, but a motion picture that talks'.[2] But it had cost £24,000, more than twice the average for a British film (Dickinson and Street, 1985: 42). As film production costs rose in this highly competitive environment, exports were becoming crucial for the survival and growth of the British film industry.[3]

While some British films were criticized for clumsy recording and inaudible diction, others were well reviewed, including Hitchcock's *Murder* (1930) and

Table 2.1 British Films Reviewed in *Variety*, 1930–31

Rating and Description	Number of Films
0 = very poor	3
1 = poor	60
2 = fair – not very suitable for United States	23
3 = good – reasonable chance in United States	18
4 = good – predicted to do well in United States	11
5 = excellent – play very well in United States	4

Victor Saville's *The Office Girl/Sunshine Susie* (1931).[4] A survey of reviews of British films in *Variety*, 1930–32 (Table 2.1) gives a sense of how British films were faring in the early sound period before the release of *The Private Life of Henry VIII*. As noted earlier, such comment is revealing since *Variety* reflected the interests of the majors, and its reviewers had an astute eye for box-office values which were assessed according to Hollywood's standards. Some of the films were reviewed in London and undoubtedly played a role in imparting advice to American distributors as to whether or not they were likely to appeal to American audiences. During the period January 1930 to December 1931, *Variety* reviewed a total of 119 British films. On the basis of a one-to-five point rating the films scored 224 out of a potential 595. A breakdown of the scores is given in Table 2.1.

Admittedly crude, this does give a sense of the relative progress, according to the *Variety* reviewers, which had been achieved by British films in the early 1930s. While *The Private Life of Henry VIII* has been interpreted as an isolated example of British success in America, it is clear that in the years prior to its release some British films were receiving positive comment as evidence of improving standards.[5]

Of the better films scoring four or five points, aspects which were singled out as improvements included non-theatrical direction, snappy dialogue and humour, particularly *Rookery Nook* and *On Approval*, adaptations of the Aldwych Theatre stage farces directed by Tom Walls. *Rookery Nook* was predicted 'to play satisfactorily anywhere in America', especially with 'sophisticated' audiences and reported as 'one of the few British talkers to get a showing break in the United States'.[6] Hitchcock's *Murder* was admired for its technical virtuosity, snappy dialogue and uncluttered sets while British International Pictures's *Atlantic*, a lavish 'international' production directed by E. A. Dupont, about an ocean liner which collides with an iceberg, was deemed 'excellent' and full of suspense.[7] *The Dreyfus Case/Dreyfus*, a BIP production released by Columbia which had also been made in French and German, did very well at the New York box-office, largely because of the Jewish audience.[8] In January–February 1931, British International Pictures (BIP) took several films to the Cohan Theatre in New York for test screenings. These were scrutinized by *Variety*'s reviewers and while the majority did not rate highly, reviews of two which did – *The Middle Watch* and *The Love Habit* – indicate elements which were considered suitable for the American market. As in the 1920s, the addition of American talent was a key factor. *The Middle Watch*, a comedy directed by Norman Walker, starred Hollywood actress Jacqueline Logan whose inclusion ensured that American slang featured in the dialogue would be more comprehensible to American audiences than some previous British attempts. The review also pointed out that American appeal was highly likely because 'Miss Logan does a Bow with the British navy, outwitting all of the officers and the admiral himself', implying that satisfaction was to be gained from Americans gaining the upper hand over British characters.[9] *The Love Habit* was another comedy, an adaptation from a French play by Louis Verneuil and directed by American Harry Lachman. Lachman was praised for his ability to move the camera very little but nevertheless suggest mobility by astute cutting in a 'slick light comedy' which was considered to be a 'novelty' proposition for the US market.[10] Better than any of the BIP offerings, however, was Gainsborough's *Sunshine Susie,* a musical comedy which had been adapted from a successful German film. *Variety* was so enthusiastic that it described the film as 'much better than the average American talker'.[11] Following its box-office success in Britain and positive reviews in America, *Sunshine Susie* was sold to distributors Ameranglo and W. D. Shapiro for six years for an outright fee of $35,000.[12] Also receiving good notices were *Hindle Wakes* and *The Speckled Band,* the second part of a Herbert Wilcox *Sherlock Holmes* series which was described as having a popular audience in New York, repeating Stoll's earlier success with Holmes in the 1920s.[13]

Of the films which scored the lowest ratings of nought to two points, the criticisms included humour being 'distinctly British', so unlikely to appeal to American audiences (*Splinters*); poor transference of stage material to the screen (*Elstree Calling, The Chinese Bungalow*); slowness (*Loves of Robert Burns, Man From Chicago*); too long (*One Embarrassing Night*); technical backwardness (*Almost a Honeymoon*); poor cutting (*Cape Forlorn*); 'muddled foggy dialog' (*The Perfect Alibi*) or poor casting (*Should a Doctor Tell*). Silent films were still being shown in 1930, some of which received merciless criticism, for example, Hitchcock's *The Farmer's Wife*. This film was released in the United States by Super Pictures and played in New York in January 1930. The *Variety* reviewer was not impressed: 'Meritless picture incapable of playing anywhere over here other than the smallest grinds. . . . Both the direction and acting are amateurish'.[14] Reviews of sound films commented on the quality of recording which fast became a criterion of judgement, along with audibility and comprehension of accents. Regional accents were preferable to 'Oxford' accents. It was commented that *Juno and the Paycock,* another Hitchcock film produced by British International Pictures, was assisted by its 'Irish English' whereas *Lord Richard in the Pantry* (Twickenham Film Studios) directed by Walter Forde, was hampered by 'Oxford' accents and use of long vowels.[15] 'Oxford' accents were generally interpreted as potentially alienating for audiences. *Young Woodley,* with a public school setting, was thought to have a chance in the United States only if 'audiences would like a slice from a life about which they know nothing'.[16]

What emerges from this survey is that, in the opinion of *Variety* reviewers, to have a chance in America British films needed to communicate clear and well-recorded dialogue not necessarily in an 'Oxford' accent; include some 'known' element such as an American actor or director; ensure that comedies contained transatlantic comprehension and appeal; subscribe to the technical principles of sharp, continuity editing; keep sets uncluttered and include appealing female stars who would not be 'smothered' by male actors.[17] The impression that these deficiencies were being addressed is confirmed by information in film company records. In a report of a preview screening of *Yes, Mr Brown* (1932) in Flushing, for example, a United Artists salesman reported to the home office in New York that although the acting was 'different – more gesture' and diction was 'a trifle hard to understand', British films had nevertheless improved.[18] The first years after the coming of sound were volatile as British films struggled to find their way in a highly competitive market. With the onset of sound cinema, the art market contracted and did not experience a period of sustained expansion until the late 1940s and 1950s (Wilinsky, 2001: 54–5). While at the end of the silent period the films of Hitchcock and Asquith were candidates (albeit doubtful for some – see Chapter 1) for art cinemas of New York, early British sound films, with their reliance on proven successes on the stage, found themselves in constant comparison with mainstream Hollywood product. In 1932–33 however the situation improved and Korda's success with *The Private Life of Henry VIII* was preceded by several films which were well received by American critics and to some extent at the box-office.[19]

The Private Life of Henry VIII in the United States

It's costume and history of another country, but it has laughs, spice and its presentation is of the best. The business this film will do should convince England's flicker producers that their contention of prejudice on this side has always been a fallacy. (*Variety*'s review of *The Private Life of Henry VIII*).[20]

The Private Life of Henry VIII is something of a *cause célèbre*: it broke box-office records on 12 October 1933, its first day's showing at the Radio City Music Hall, New York, and encouraged other producers to aim at world markets.[21] Alexander Korda was a Hungarian producer and director who had made films in Hungary and Hollywood before coming to Britain in 1932. He went on to become one of the most significant figures in the British film industry, building Denham Studios in 1936. Soon after his arrival in Britain, he formed London Film Productions and experienced his first real success with *The Private Life of Henry VIII,* with a cast including Charles Laughton, Elsa Lanchester, Robert Donat and Merle Oberon. By April 1937 London Film Productions had earned a net profit of £116,290 on the film, a figure that more than recovered its relatively high production cost.[22] Many, however, blamed the example set by Korda for promoting profligacy and overextension, contributing to the famous 'crash' of many British film companies in 1937. Encouraged by confidence in film production as an investment, banks and insurance companies had financed film companies to an unprecedented extent in 1935–7. When returns on their investments proved to be disappointing, the City financiers withdrew their support and many film companies were declared bankrupt.[23] This version of events is oversimplified, however: in many respects *The Private Life of Henry VIII* became a convenient scapegoat for the film industry's domestic problems in the 1930s.[24]

There is a degree of controversy about the impact and significance of the film's American experience. Ian Jarvie has speculated that 'close analysis of the career of the film in the US would, I believe, show that it had in fact a limited release, confined to major cities, and that it gained, by Hollywood's standards, a modest return' (Jarvie, 1992: 144). In fact, what 'close analysis' of the film's career (in *Variety* and *Motion Picture Herald*) shows is that it did do well outside New York, extremely well in some places, holding its own against American films such as *I'm No Angel* (1933). Far from being an insignificant example, I would argue that this was a major step forward for British films and was certainly perceived as such by contemporaries. A report from Pittsburgh, for example, commented that

> leading town comparatively by a wide margin is *Henry VIII* at Fulton, which shows signs of hitting $9,000 and indicating possibility of h.o. [hold over]. Picture has been in the air for some time now, with intelligentsia eating it up and giving house carriage trade it hasn't seen since

Cavalcade [Frank Lloyd, 1932]. Also marks first time in history of house that Friday's business, usually a cropper due to preponderance of other openings, has topped inaugural day's trade. All the more amazing since Charles Laughton is cast's only name and he has meant just a bit more than nothing here in the past.[25]

Reports of comparative good business also came from Boston, Buffalo, Chicago, Cleveland, Denver, Detroit, Los Angeles, Providence, San Francisco, St. Louis and Washington.[26] The film occupied seventh place in United Artists' top grossing rental figures for 1933. In the United States, it grossed $469,646 (probably higher because figures for the last nine months of 1934 are missing from the United Artists ledgers).[27] It was used by its distributor, United Artists, as an example of the money-earning potential of British films. In a circular memo from Harry Gold to all United Artists branch managers, salesmen and bookers in 1936, comparative figures were given to illustrate the film's success as a reissue:

> The Publix Organization in New England were extremely sceptical about playing re-issue *Henry VIII,* and had steadfastly refused to play the picture. We finally prevailed upon them to try the picture out in a couple of situations where they have a policy of a daily change and where, if the picture did not meet with our expectations their losses would be reduced to a minimum.

The results showed that in Fort Fairfield *Henry VIII* grossed $135.00 on one day, higher than popular American films *Call of the Wild* ($107.55) and *Barnum* ($128.30). Similarly, in Houlton a day's gross for *Henry VIII* was $153.45, a figure which was just behind that for *Barnum* ($156.10) and more than *Dark Angel* ($146.90).[28] To put these grosses into perspective, $.25 to $.35 would get most filmgoers into the majority of first-run cinemas in most locations, with the more prestigious theatres, such as Radio City Music Hall in New York or the Fox in Philadelphia, charging a low price of about $.40.[29]

Korda's film was the product of many advantageous circumstances which help to explain its success. The first was the backing from an American company, United Artists (UA), which part-financed the film at the instigation of Richard Norton, a friend of George Grossmith, the Chairman of Korda's production company, London Film Productions. Herbert Wilcox's company, British and Dominion, held exclusive rights to produce quota pictures for UA but agreed to waive the exclusivity contract so that Korda's film would be distributed in America. UA was also anxious to obtain more British films in the hope that its world operations might claw back the $270,000 loss shown in 1932 (Balio, 1976: 95, 133). Since the company was solely a distributor, the British films were not competing with its own product in the same way that might have occurred if it had been a major (Balio, 1993: 35). To encourage exhibitors to book the film, the UA sales team also sanctioned a degree of flexibility on the terms.[30] UA marketed *The Private Life of Henry VIII* in an astute manner in New York and beyond, pitching it to 'highbrow' audiences but at the same time remaining aware of its box-office potential as a comedy with broader appeal. *Motion Picture Herald* reported on the campaign, introducing several key themes which highlight aspects of the American context of reception:

> Every British and Canadian club and organisation in NY was informed of the date, and bulletins were posted at all headquarters and clubrooms. High and elementary school history and English department heads were asked to inform their classes of the historical interest of the picture, and the various NY colleges also cooperated in bringing this information to the attention of students. Special screenings were held for representatives of over 600 local women's clubs, National Council of History Teachers, the Daughters of the American Revolution, and other prominent organisations, whose secretaries signed endorsements of the picture on postcards sent by UA to all individual members. Other screenings were held for magazine and newspaper picture editors and critics with excellent advance publicity results. The local Liggett drug stores carried special 40 by 60 window cards done in the Ripley manner showing the highlights of Henry's matrimonial career, and book stores also plugged the Hackett edition of the king's biography. A clever and humorous angle was carried out in the newspaper ads, wherein the entertainment values of Henry's roaring romances was stressed, and managers who do not choose to sell the historical angle too strongly, should utilize this slant which is carried out in the press books ads.[31]

The film's progress was assisted by the recession in Hollywood, creating a 'space' for new or unusual films. The majors were experiencing a period of crisis as they had overextended themselves 'first in the ferocious battle . . . for control of the country's theatres in the 1920s and then in the tremendous capital investment in studios and theatre equipment for the conversion to sound' (Balio, 1985: 215). In February 1932, *Motion Picture Herald* reported that US distributors were looking to foreign films to meet the product shortage and advised that these would need careful exploitation in order to earn a profit.[32] In 1933 Britain's film exports increased by approximately 50 per cent.[33] Attendances and box-office takings were down in 1933, and America was just beginning to recover from the worst effects of the Depression, assisted by

Roosevelt's "New Deal" programme (Cormack, 1994: 45). *Gold Diggers of 1933* (1933) had been released in June, a film which along with *42nd Street* (1933) articulated the New Deal's philosophy of a united community and their President fighting against the Depression. This ideology is also evident in *The Private Life of Henry VIII*, with its representation of a benevolent king whose subjects understand and support him. The concept of 'aristocratic substitution' in connection with class will be discussed further on, but it is also interesting to consider the film in a New Deal context and note the similarity of its address to notions of 'community' and 'benevolent leadership' in an American context. At one point in *Henry VIII*, for example, 'the people's will' is declared to constitute 'the king's law'.

As David Reynolds has shown, in the 1930s many Americans were both fascinated by and critical of British traditions and institutions, especially the class system (Reynolds, 1981: 23–5). As Sue Harper has hypothesized, *Henry VIII* is a film which demonstrates the idea of an 'aristocratic-proletarian alliance' in the sense that the audience is encouraged to sympathize with Henry – to put themselves in his place – thus forging a cross-class bond which paradoxically confers on the lower echelons in the film a 'superior' status which is characterized by an apparent insight into the king's personal shortcomings and human frailties, particularly as far as women are concerned (Harper, 1994: 20–3 and Street, 1997: 40). From this perspective, *Henry VIII*'s comedic 'key-hole' approach to British history and its potential for readings based on 'aristocratic substitution' can be seen as exercising persuasive influence in America at a time when the historical sense of a common liberal tradition between the United Kingdom and the United States was being interrogated. One review picked up on the film's ability to address American audiences: 'This narrative about the notorious British ruler . . . has been adapted with a good eye to angles of appeal that will register with current audiences'.[34] *Henry VIII* is an example of a British film that uses comedy to critique British institutions, and the film was considered irreverent and unpatriotic by some British reviewers.[35] In the film, Henry's royal status is a burden – he cannot live up to the onerous demands of monarchy, especially repeated pressures from advisers and the populace to prove his masculinity by re-marrying and siring heirs to the throne. Far from being represented as a 'divine being', Henry is weak and pathetic, longing for the personal freedoms enjoyed by his subjects. The demands of the state are depicted as crushing his spirit, with advisers and wives alike exploiting his physical weaknesses.

The film is therefore far from an 'official' history and is much more a comedic character study which nevertheless involves an address to contemporary concerns.[36] As we have seen, in the 1920s, Wilcox's *Nell Gwyn* had adopted this approach with successful results. *Motion Picture Herald* observed in January 1932 that this type of historical film would continue to do well at the box-office, encouraging British producers to follow the example of *Disraeli* (1929), a Warner Brothers film starring George Arliss, which privileged 'entertainment' above historical accuracy. The trade paper also urged British producers to be less 'conscious of their responsibilities to British custom and "culture"' and more willing to jettison their 'reverential awe for British traditions'.[37] *Henry VIII* clearly demonstrated these qualities. Richard Watts Jnr, reviewing the film for the *New York Herald Tribune,* suggested that Laughton's portrayal elicited an effect which detracted from Henry's stately activities, emphasizing the man, not the monarch:

> If there is any fault to be found with Mr Laughton's portrayal by the most captious critics is that he makes the monstrous monarch too likeable a figure to check with the facts of history. . . . Mr Laughton's Henry is a lecherous scoundrel, selfish, unfeeling and gross, but there is about him the petulant air of a spoiled child which makes amazingly for compassion. The manner, also, in which Henry is shown as an amorous old fool, completely at the mercy of the most obvious feminine trickery, tends to make him if far from a heroic, then at least a slyly likeable character.[38]

Nevertheless, it is also important to point out that the 'humanizing' process encouraged by the film does not necessarily imply that the monarchy should be abolished. Instead it proposes that the king faced ordinary dilemmas with which members of the audience could identify: instead of being the focus of attention, the institution of the monarchy is therefore sidelined, or at least we are encouraged to think that Henry would be a happier man if he were not a king. The press book for *The Private Life of Henry VIII* includes a production feature which articulates this position:

> The story . . . is concerned with the romantic rather than the historic phase of Henry's reign. This does not mean that London Films in producing it, or Alexander Korda in directing it, have taken any liberties with the life of England's 'Bluff King Hal' as recorded, but rather that the king is shown as a man with human, loveable qualities and with as many domestic difficulties as any husband who married six times.[39]

The press book material also stresses that the film was based on extensive research into the Tudor period, undertaken by Charles Laughton in particular, to ensure that an 'accurate' representation of the King was conveyed. This in-

Plate 1. Dorothy Gish in *Nell Gwyn* (Herbert Wilcox, 1925)

Plate 2. Charles Laughton and Wendy Barrie in the shot that was banned from the advertising campaign for the 1935 re-release of *The Private Life of Henry VIII* (Alexander Korda, 1933)

Plate 3. Robert Donat and Jean Parker accompanying the castle on its journey across the Atlantic in *The Ghost Goes West* (René Clair, 1935)

Plate 4. Robert Donat and Jean Parker tune into the radio in armour in *The Ghost Goes West* (René Clair, 1935)

Plate 5. The *Daily Express* reacts to the censorship of *Nell Gwyn* (Herbert Wilcox, 1935)

Plate 6.
Jessie Matthews in
It's Love Again
(Victor Saville, 1936)

Plate 7. Jessie Matthews and Robert Young in *It's Love Again* (Victor Saville, 1936)

Plate 8. J. Arthur Rank inspects a poster for *Great Expectations* (David Lean, 1946)

Plate 9. Laurence Olivier in *Henry V* (US release, 1946)

Plate 10. J. Arthur Rank and B. B. Kahane, Vice-President of the Association of Motion Picture Producers

Plate 11. Eastern longings: Deborah Kerr in *Black Narcissus* (Michael Powell and Emeric Pressburger, 1947)

Plate 12. Sister Clodagh (Deborah Kerr) gazes out of the chapel window 'her mind intent – not on prayer – but … going over a love-scene of her own youth' (Virginia S. Tomlinson in *The Tidings* – see Chapter 5) in *Black Narcissus* (Michael Powell and Emeric Pressburger, 1947)

Plate 13. Louis Mazzini (Dennis Price) is released from prison at the end of *Kind Hearts and Coronets* (Robert Hamer, 1949), but realizes that he has forgotten his memoirs.

Plate 14. Alec Guinness and the captain's two lovers, Nita (Yvonne de Carlo) and Maud (Celia Johnson) in *The Captain's Paradise* (Anthony Kimmins, 1953)

Plate 16. The Beatles in
A Hard Day's Night
(Richard Lester, 1964)

Plate 15. Christopher Lee
in *The Horror of Dracula*
(Terence Fisher, 1958)

te 17. Susannah York and
bert Finney in *Tom Jones*
(Tony Richardson, 1963)

Plate 18. Hugh Grant and Andie MacDowell in *Four Weddings and a Funeral* (Mike Newell, 1994)

Plate 19. Robert Carlyle and Ewan McGregor in *Trainspotting* (Danny Boyle, 1996)

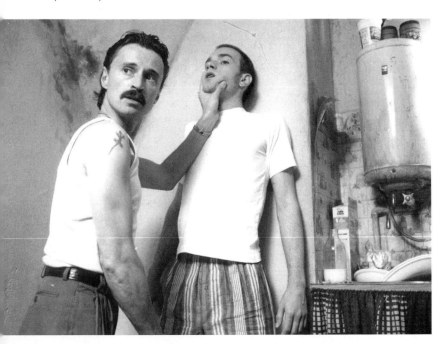

cluded his 'athletic' prowess, which Laughton replicated in the wrestling scene
for which he took training lessons with a professional wrestler. The merging of
Laughton's persona with that of the King was a successful strategy, as re-
counted later by Elsa Lanchester. After a visit to Warwick Castle, a friend reported to Elsa Lanchester that on seeing the painting of Henry VIII by Hol-
bein, an American tourist exclaimed, 'Oh, I know who that is – it's Charles
Laughton!'[40] Laughton's physical likeness to Henry is highlighted in the press
book: 'When he dons the beret of the Merry Monarch, he immediately becomes the King!'[41] Similarly, Merle Oberon, who plays Anne Boleyn, is described as bearing a facial resemblance to the Queen as demonstrated in por-
traits, a resemblance which is enhanced by her costume and jewellery.
Authentic settings are also promoted as a key element of the film, particularly
the filming of the exterior scenes in Hatfield House. The promotional activities
recommended to exhibitors tend to stress the film's comedic elements, including the suggestion of eating and wrestling contests, and lobby displays which
play on the fate of Henry's unfortunate wives: 'Blondes . . . Brunettes and Redheads. . . . They all fell for him . . . under the axe!' In a rather desperate effort
to foster tie-ins with clothing stores the press book rather weakly suggested
that 'the clothes of today are inspired by the fashions of Henry VIII's time', an
observation which rather undercuts claims to literal authenticity.

In its attention to such details, the press book was trying to promote the
film as appealing to a large and varied audience. Key constituents were educa-
tionalists, and it was recommended that *The Private Life of Henry VIII* was
suitable for special screenings for teachers and civic groups. When pitched to
'class' audiences, the film was promoted as history, conferring on it a 'highbrow' status which appealed to those seeking to acquire 'cultural capital'. English history had been widely taught in America until the mid-1920s, but by the
1930s had more or less disappeared as a separate high school subject
(Reynolds, 1981: 23). English authors still dominated literature classes, but it
seems that *Henry VIII*'s own ambivalent engagement with the institution of
monarchy fed into prevailing American attitudes towards the United Kingdom. It seems likely, therefore, that combined with the 'history' theme it was
the film's irreverence and comedy which assured it of longer life at the box-office. *Motion Picture Herald* commented: 'A preview of the picture will enable
the exhibitor to catch innumerable flashes, situations which will make for
powerful advertising copy. He may well place selling emphasis on the comedy,
the flashing performance of Laughton'.[42] Other reviews highlighted these elements, as well as acting, settings, comedy and sex. Charles Laughton's star
persona was a significant factor in ensuring the film's success in America. He
was far from unknown to American audiences: by the time he appeared in

Henry VIII, he had completed six major films in Hollywood, including *The Old Dark House* (1932), *Payment Deferred* (1932), *The Sign of the Cross* (1932) and *If I had a Million* (1932). His performance in *Henry VIII* was awarded with an Oscar, and the film was voted one of the ten best films of 1933 by the *New York Times*' critics.

Henry VIII also appeared at an interesting moment in terms of stricter censorship in the United States. In 1933 the Payne Studies on the impact of films on children were published, and from November onwards Joseph Breen initiated tougher rules for the industry's Production Code. By 1934 films needed approval from the Motion Picture Producers and Distributors of America (MPPDA) before they could be distributed or exhibited. During the years 1932–3, most films were influenced by debates about overt representations of sexuality on screen and many producers avoided taking risks. From this perspective, *Henry VIII*'s risqué subject matter and verbal sexual banter perhaps anticipated the dialogue-based innuendo upon which producers were forced to rely once the Code was in operation. While the film was not censored in 1933, the poster showed Henry in a lustful pose, behind Jane Seymour, pulling her back to kiss her neck (see Plate 2). Such postures by no means typified the film which perhaps reveals tension between advertising concerns and pressures towards conforming to the Production Code. When the film was re-released in 1935, this poster was withdrawn at the insistence of the Advertising Advisory Council and some of the suggestive dialogue was removed from the film.[43]

Henry VIII acquired a celebrated status in American film culture as a case of a British film which deserved to do well: features praised in reviews were commonly used as standards of judgement for subsequent British films, suggesting continuities and contrasts.[44] UA was pleased to deal with good-quality British product, and in 1934 Joseph Schenck visited Britain and wrote back to the company: 'We have a wonderful business here. . . . You cannot conceive what these British pictures are doing'.[45] Ian Jarvie has argued that *Henry VIII* was an isolated, freak example of British success in the United States, citing the comparatively poor reception of London Film Production's (LFP) later imperial films directed by Zoltan Korda, *Sanders of the River* (1935) and *The Four Feathers* (1939) as evidence for this assertion (Jarvie, 1992: 143). In fact, some of these later films did very well at the box-office, particularly *Drums/The Drum*, UA's eighth-highest grossing film of 1938, and *The Four Feathers*, UA's sixth-highest grossing film of 1939.[46]

It is also productive to link *Henry VIII* with comedy, Gainsborough melodramas and similarly irreverent or lavish costume epics. A successor in this tradition is *Caesar and Cleopatra*, which after a vigorous and astute marketing campaign earned $2,000,000 on its first run and was reported as 'doing strong business throughout the country and . . . going over particularly big in Loew houses outside New York'.[47] The film made more money in the United States than in the United Kingdom, and it also fared better with American critics. *Henry VIII* also displays similarities with Hollywood's late 1930s cycle of history/costume films, including *The Prince and the Pauper* (1937), *The Adventures of Robin Hood* (1938) and *The Private Lives of Elizabeth and Essex* (1939).[48] The continued popularity of *The Private Life of Henry VIII* was indicated when the Audience Research Institute conducted a series of reports for RKO in 1940–41. A representative sample of cinema-goers was given a list of 100 films released before 1936 and asked which they liked best and would like to see again: *Henry VIII* came fifteenth on the list, while the American-produced *Cavalcade* came eighteenth.[49]

United Artists and Korda after *Henry VIII*

In 1933–34 the success of *Henry VIII* resulted in an ever-closer relationship between Korda and UA. He signed a contract for sixteen films and became a partner in the company in September 1935 (Balio, 1976: 135). Korda continued to inspire confidence in UA executives. After a pre-screening of some reels of *Rembrandt,* Vice-President Arthur Kelly cabled UA's New York offices: 'I predict that it will be as great as Henry Eight if not better and it is a tremendous production'.[50] UA made great efforts to promote British product with varying results, the most successful post-*Henry VIII* films being *Catherine the Great* (rentals $282,083; 1934), *The Scarlet Pimpernel* ($376,866; 1935), *The Ghost Goes West* ($156,722; 1936, third-highest grosser), *Drums* (1938, eighth-highest grosser) and *The Four Feathers* (1939, sixth-highest grosser). Even so, the figures they earned were hardly spectacular (see below for an explanation of the low figure recorded for *The Ghost Goes West*). Korda's financial problems with LFP's major backer, the Prudential Assurance Company, also caused concern, a situation which tried the patience of his partners in UA (Street, 1986: 161–79). When several LFP films did not earn as much as Korda expected, he accused UA of not marketing them properly, an opinion shared by some UA executives who in turn blamed their regional sales teams who were reprimanded for low bookings (Balio, 1976: 144).

While it was clearly an advantage for Korda to have LFP's films distributed by UA, with the exception of the highest-grossing pictures listed above, they did not earn as much as they might have done had UA been a major vertically integrated company. It is important to note, however, that if UA had been vertically integrated its interest in distributing British films might well have been

Table 2.2 Exhibition of British Films, 1935–36

Company	Year	1st Features Trade Shown + Origin	2nd Features Trade Shown + Origin
MGM	1935	37 (36 US; 1 UK)	17 (7 US; 10 UK)
MGM	1936	34 (34 US)	23 (11 US; 12 UK)
Fox Film Corp	1935	28 (28 US)	30 (19 US; 11 UK)
Fox Film Corp	1936	22 (20 US; 2 UK)	27 (20 US; 7 UK)
United Artists	1936	22 (8 US; 14 UK)	1 (1 Fr)

less pronounced. UA's consistent product shortage made the films an attractive proposition. Maintaining a good supply of British films was crucial since the company depended on profits from the British market. These could not be relied upon from its US operations since the priority was to deliver profits to producers. This had the effect of reducing domestic distribution fees and placing greater emphasis on recovering profits from Britain.[51] Consequently, according to a British exhibitor (see Table 2.2), in comparison with MGM and Fox, companies which produced 'British' films in the United Kingdom, UA had the best record of showing British films as first features to the trade. This confirmed UA's high opinion of the quality of British films but it also reveals their importance to the company's overall finances.[52]

Indeed, UA's policy was to obtain 'quality' films which were offered to exhibitors on an individual basis. The US sales team was urged to develop sophisticated 'showmanship' skills by making every attempt to persuade exhibitors that they could not afford to ignore above-average films such as those produced by LFP.[53] Without the incentive of block-booking, however, the sales teams had to work extra hard to convince exhibitors that every single film was worth a booking. Salesmen reported to the home office that British films were difficult to sell, while UA's reputation for handling quality product exposed them all the more to adverse criticism, especially when UA executives implied that low bookings were caused by inefficient sales teams rather than by competition from major studios who sold their films – good and bad – in all-inclusive blocks. When Paul Lazarus, a UA domestic sales executive, wrote to A. M. Goodman of the Cleveland exchange about pictures which had not been sold during 1934–5, he received a lengthy reply which detailed some of the difficulties of selling British films. The point was made that 'we have very few contracts on [British films] from any of our circuit accounts . . . and with the exception of a booking here and there we received practically no representation on these pictures from these circuit accounts. Invariably, when a picture does not play a first run house it prevents us from selling such pictures to the subsequent accounts'.[54] Another problem was that the films could not be sold as second features, a situation that was likely to change with the reintro-duction of double bills. Goodman assured Lazarus that these difficulties were being addressed by UA salesmen:

> I wish to assure you that no possibility is left unsolicited and is con-stantly being watched, particularly on the pictures on which we have the least contracts. Everyone here is working diligently, the writer is constantly exerting personal effort even with the smallest account to se-cure contracts where it is possible to obtain same, and I am certain our number of contracts will swell as we go along.

Other salesmen complained that the rentals charged for British films were too high, as Fred Anderson of Morris, Illinois, put it:

> I believe that the producer is entitled to all money his pictures will rea-sonably earn. On the other hand the exhibitor must base the price he pays for pictures on the results he has obtained on prior occasions to-gether with what he might reasonably expect the business to be under present conditions.[55]

Even so Lazarus was often unsympathetic, stressing Korda's status as a partner of the company to salesmen who reported that LFP's films did not rate highly with 'cowboys'. In October 1935 Lazarus wrote to Doak Roberts in Dallas:

> It is your job down in Dallas to make a proper market for the English pictures. For a number of years we have had a lot of talk about the cow-boys not being able to understand the English dialogue and a lot of other funny talk like that. After a while, Doak, that kind of line loses its punch. I don't know why we should continue to baby you along on great productions such as Mr Korda has for sale.[56]

Exchanges of opinion such as this between the home office and the sales of-fices illuminate the advantages and disadvantages of distributing through a company such as UA. While Korda's position as a partner gave him bargaining power within the central organization, it had the unforeseen consequence of encouraging high expectations of films the sales teams were required to pro-mote as above-average quality. It was somewhat ironic therefore that in 1941 Korda persuaded UA to finally abandon its policy of booking films singly (Kulik, 1975: 270).

UA's strategy to promote Korda's films as distinctive was also reflected in its press material and correspondence with LFP regarding publicity. While *Rem-*

brandt (1936) was greeted with enthusiasm, Monroe Greenthal, UA's advertising and publicity executive, was frustrated at the lack of communication with LFP about how to market the film in the United States. In July 1936 he devised a special convention brochure and display for Korda's films which he sent to John Myers, LFP's publicity director. Greenthal also sent news of deals he had arranged with major library associations and women's clubs for the promotion of *Rembrandt* as an example 'of a picture which the millions of women and library goers should support'. He requested further information from LFP about the painter and the film together with illustrative stills.[57] Greenthal wrote in frustration to George Schaefer, general manager of domestic distribution at UA: 'I have written to John Myers in London to get me these stills and if we get same, it will mean a lot to our picture. I would appreciate it, if you would stress the importance to Mr Korda to get this material, as in the past, it has been like pulling teeth to get even the ordinary stills on time'.[58] It would appear that LFP was not always as efficient as it might be in supplying UA with publicity material, but despite this problem UA made valiant efforts to make LFP's films stand out as distinctive. The publicity files for *The Four Feathers*, for example, worked towards forging tie-ins with Jaeger for merchandising hats, costumes and jewellery.[59] The exploitation of *The Thief of Bagdad* (1940), the first film to be produced by Alexander Korda Film Productions, involved an elaborate campaign in New York including a costume ball held at Manhattan Beach; window displays on Fifth Avenue; a float of the Djinni from *The Thief of Bagdad* in Macy's Thanksgiving Parade; a skating exhibition at the Rockefeller Centre rink; a 'tumbling act' of three men dressed in Arabian costume carrying a carpet with the film's name written on it; a special Technicolor trailer screened at the Radio City Music Hall and a targeted mail campaign.[60] As proof of the efficacy of these labours, *The Thief of Bagdad* was UA's top-grossing film out of twenty released in 1940, earning just over a million dollars in domestic rentals.

The Ghost Goes West (1935) was a relatively successful post-*Henry VIII* film.[61] Tracing its progress in *Variety*'s box-office reports, it did excellent business at some theatres and was held over by many for several weeks, inviting comments from exhibitors such as: 'Donat acquiring quite a following here' (Kansas City); 'best seven-day opener house ever had' (Los Angeles); 'bucking some strong competition' (St. Louis).[62] UA's head office also received reports of good business from Los Angeles, Ohio and New York.[63] It was in the top ten best films of 1936 nominated by critics from the *New York Times*. A circular to all domestic exchanges urged salesmen to promote the film as suitable for 'mixed class right down to low-brow . . . we have in *The Ghost Goes West* a picture that definitely appeals to everybody. It is not a costume picture; it is not a so-called British picture. It is made strictly to appeal to an American audience'.[64] The film had a French director, René Clair, and was publicized as an 'international' production, featuring several American actors including Jean Parker, who was signed by MGM after appearing as a swimwear model on posters for the Olympic Games, and Ralph Bunker, who was known to millions of Americans as a radio personality. Its major star, the half-Polish Robert Donat, was already known to US audiences in *The Count of Monte Cristo* (1934) and *The 39 Steps* (1935). *The 39 Steps* grossed $43,000 in its first week at the Roxy, New York, and $34,400 in its second, high figures for that theatre which assisted in establishing Donat as a 'known' star.[65] A 'Thirty-Nine Steps' club was started in New York in honour of the film. While the film generally did less well outside New York when it was booked into smaller cinemas, such as in Minneapolis, where it was booked for a four week run, it grossed well and acquired a good reputation for its stars. Also, *The 39 Steps* received more enthusiastic reviews in America than it did in Britain.[66]

As an indication of his international reputation Korda had to increase Donat's salary in order to secure his services which were being courted by Hollywood.[67] The extent of his star potential is demonstrated by a writ served in May 1935 by Warner Brothers against Donat, claiming that he had a contract with the company to make three films. Warners' agent in Britain, Mr Asher, was so desperate to sign Donat that he misrepresented the details of a deal. Crucially, Asher erroneously conveyed the contents of a cable sent by Warners outlining the conditions of any agreement with Donat. Faking urgency, and in order to make Donat sign an agreement in December 1934, Asher implied that Donat would have far more control over the realization of the three projects than was customary for actors in Hollywood. It later transpired that this was not what the studio had in mind. Justice Goddard decided in favour of Donat that the agreement he signed with Warners was a preliminary document, in anticipation of a much more detailed contract that would resolve all the areas of difficulty. The incident shows how representatives of American companies in Britain were under pressure to sign up top British stars who commanded bargaining power. On the other hand, at a time when Hollywood was seeking to limit the influence of actors on film productions, Donat was not able to strike a preferential deal.[68]

A Scottish-American theme also gave the film transatlantic appeal, resulting in a gentle comedy based on a story by Eric Keown published in *Punch*. Donat plays Donald, a descendant of the Glourie clan whose castle is haunted by the ghost of Murdoch Glourie (also played by Donat) who was killed in the eighteenth century as a result of rivalry with the McLaggan clan. In the film's first sequence, we learn that the ghost of Murdoch was hitherto consigned to haunt the castle on the instructions of his dead father, who insisted that his son could not pass to heaven until he had avenged the family honour by forcing a member of the McLaggan clan to kneel before him and apologize. The rest of the film takes place in the twentieth century when the castle is in a state of disrepair and Donald needs to sell it in order to fend off his creditors. When Peggy Martin (Jean Parker), a young American woman, passes by, she is enchanted by the castle and persuades her father, a rich American food magnate, to buy it. Although her American accent is not very pronounced, when Peggy first appears, Donald's housekeeper comments that her accent is 'queer', making perhaps a veiled reference to the debate about the comprehensibility of American and British diction. Fearing that Murdoch's ghost would put them off, Donald conceals its existence and invites the family to dinner to show them around and to consolidate his friendly relationship with Peggy. Peggy returns after her parents have left and encounters the ghost, believing that it is Donald masquerading as Murdoch for a joke. Donald is shocked when Peggy's father, Joe Martin (Eugene Pallette), tells him that he intends to dismantle the castle and rebuild it in Florida. He finally agrees because of his increasing affection for Peggy and because he will supervise the castle's reconstruction in America (Plate 3).

When Donald, the Martins and the remnants of the dismantled castle are on board ship for America, Murdoch's ghost appears and Peggy's father is persuaded by his wife that he should not have purchased a haunted castle. He changes his mind however when Ed Bigelow (Ralph Bunker), a rival 'collector' who has purchased a chateau, sees novelty value in the ghost as a source of advertisement revenue for his own food chain and bids a high sum for the castle. The castle's value is enhanced by this new commercial angle, and Martin wins out but only by increasing the sum of his original offer. The film makes several satirical references such as this to American importation and commercial exploitation of European culture. The ghost is treated similarly as news of its existence reaches the newspapers and a series of sensational reports of sightings of the ghost are published. The arrival of the castle in America is greeted with enthusiasm, illustrated by actuality footage of exuberant crowds, taken out of its original context and inserted in this fictional story for comic effect. There is a key scene when we see images of the American Senate and the House of Lords overlaid with juxtaposed aural extracts from debates in both arenas, including a British discussion of the 'heritage' issue about the export of British culture to America. While the American senators complain about the importation of a ghost 'into our progressive country . . . a relic of medieval superstition . . . which might be acceptable in the effete atmosphere of the British House of Lords', members of the House of Lords are concerned about the uprooting of 'the flowers of Scottish architecture . . . to please the fancy of a millionaire who apparently has no ancestors of his own'. In this way seemingly insignificant incidents become the focus of 'high' politics. Such moments have a satirical but whimsical appeal which anticipate similar use of such techniques in the Ealing comedies, which were also popular in America.

When the ghost arrives in New York, he objects to being shot at by mobsters, and his father agrees that he can stay invisible until the quest to find a repentant member of the McLaggan clan has been concluded. Once in Florida, Donald is upset by the 'Americanization' of the castle, complete with the addition of modern technology and gimmicks such as suits of armour with in-built radios (Plate 4). Again, we have an example of an American appropriation of Scottish culture being satirized as jarring jazz music is heard; the castle is brightly illuminated and set amongst palm trees, a fake moat and gondolas. These images invite a direct comparison with earlier scenes of the castle in Scotland, minimally decorated and located amidst a spectacular Scottish landscape. Since Murdoch has not made an appearance, the Martins, desperate to show off their 'genuine Scottish ghost', persuade Donald to pretend to be the ghost before he returns to Scotland. During the much-awaited event to which many guests have been invited to meet the ghost, it transpires that Ed Bigelow, Joe Martin's food-chain rival, is the last descendant of the McLaggan clan. Donald calls to Murdoch's ghost with the news, and when he appears Bigelow is so scared that he makes the desired apology to the Glourie clan that will set Murdoch free to join his ancestors in heaven. The film ends rather abruptly with the implication that Donald will marry Peggy but without an indication about the fate of the uprooted castle.

The film is therefore 'transatlantic' in its themes and the satire of the American characters is always gentle and sophisticated. As Peggy Martin is being shown around the castle, for example, she says 'You don't know what it means to us to see something that's not new', implying a self-knowingness about caricatured images of Americans as crass and uncultured. Similarly, Donald's love for Peggy outweighs his disturbance about the castle's 'Americanisation', investing the film with an over-arching discourse about love breaking down prejudice. The film's ambiguous ending, however, makes this less convincing, as we are unsure as to what might have followed: will Donald insist that the castle is returned to Scotland or will he begin a new life in America? The film can be seen to make unconscious reference to the many transatlantic crossings which were taking place in the 1930s as producers encouraged British film stars such as Robert Donat to visit and work in America so that they would be more familiar to American audiences. The film's view of Americans suggests a 'special relationship', a fond familiarity rather than a suspicious antagonism. It is these elements in particular which influenced the lavish and light-hearted marketing of *The Ghost Goes West* as a film that would appeal to American audiences.

A comparison of the British and American press books for *The Ghost Goes West* shows that it was marketed in a very specific way in the United States.[69] The British press book highlights Donat as a 'matinée idol of the world'; René Clair's directorial credentials and publicity stunts involving shop window displays of Scottish costumes.[70] While the American material features these elements, it places far more emphasis on Donat as a romantic hero/dare-devil lover, implying that the film contains risqué subject matter. Posters contained captions such as: 'A dashing ghost who made love to every pretty girl he met!'; 'No passion greater than the violence of thwarted love!'; 'A girl with two identical lovers . . . one human . . . the other a ghost!' and 'Shocking, sensational, stirring!' (Plate 20). Korda's involvement is signalled when he is described as 'The man who gave you *Henry VIII*', seeking to establish a link between that successful film and the comedic liveliness of *The Ghost Goes West*. Fashion tie-ins were encouraged, particularly with Jean Parker's costumes that the press book declared were typical of fashions worn by 'the average young girl'. Theatres were advised to stage ingenious publicity stunts including placing luminous cut-outs of the ghost outside cinemas. These instructions were followed by exhibitors. For example, the Keith Memorial theatre in Boston reported that their 'excellent' business for the film was assisted by elaborate stunts, described as 'an inanimate "ghost" answering questions via a p.a. set drew plenty of attention; a truck tie-up, and a play for Scotch population, in addition to an impressive lay out of newspaper publicity'.[71]

The American press book also contained examples of reviews, highlighting one from *New York American* which made the point that everyone in the film is satirized: the Scots, the British, the Americans and ancient institutions. In other publications the film was praised very highly. The *New York Times* heralded it as 'the first important film of the new year, and a joyous one'.[72] Although appreciative of the film, *Variety* was concerned that its humour might be too sophisticated and ironic for the mass audience. The satiric tone and elements of what might be construed as anti-Americanism were not taken seriously and even used to suggest that the American sense of humour was tolerant of self-parody. The *Variety* reviewer declared, for example, that 'the American people as a whole are amazingly good natured about themselves. Had Americans made this film for instance, about the British, or the Scotch, or the French, or any other nation, the screams would have risen to the skies'.[73] It would appear therefore that *The Ghost Goes West* attracted attention for its relaxed attitude towards Anglo-American differences, its irreverent, comic sensibilities and quality of the cast. Many of these elements had been present in *The Private Life of Henry VIII* and with a brief appearance by Elsa Lanchester in *The Ghost Goes West*, Korda's desire to distinguish his productions with the mark of transatlantic success was demonstrated once again.

By far the most successful of LFP's films released by UA in the 1930s had imperial themes, *Drums/The Drum* (1938) and *The Four Feathers* (1939), both of which exceeded the celebrated rentals earned by *The Private Life of Henry VIII*. These 'films of empire' found a US audience and were indicative of a fascination with imperial subject matter that was also demonstrated in Hollywood's own cycle, including *Clive of India* (1935), *Lives of a Bengal Lancer* (1935) and *Gunga Din* (1939). As part of this generic tradition, Korda's biggest box-office winners can be linked with an American fascination with 'patterns of chivalry'. As Fraser has argued, although a rejection of European codes of chivalry, aristocratic values and medieval structures was an integral part of America's democratic and libertarian heritage, in the twentieth century 'the chivalry business had prospered in America with a vengeance' (Fraser, 1982: 14).[74] Cultural reminders of chivalric values persisted in cinema, as represented by the cowboy hero; the romantic private detective; gentlemanly English actors such as Ronald Colman and George Sanders and the 'civilizing' officers and gentlemen of the British empire. Korda's films epitomized these notions of chivalry and heroism, thus tapping into an American preoccupation with chivalry which was complex and at times contradictory. As well as explaining the popularity of Korda's films in relation to ideas about chivalry, I shall also argue that the release of *Drums* and *The Four Feathers* in 1938–39 provided an international context which was particularly receptive to imperial themes. As the Second World War approached, questions of British military strength against Fascism were of key importance to American commentators, isolationist and pro-interventionist alike.

Fraser's insightful analysis of the persistent patterns of chivalry in American culture points the way to understanding how US audiences appreciated films such as *The Private Life of Henry VIII* and *The Four Feathers*. America developed its own versions of chivalry which involved unlikely pairings (Fraser, 1982: 150–55). As I have argued in relation to *Nell Gwyn* and *Henry VIII,* the 'proletarian-aristocratic' alliance involved an attraction of opposites that could easily be related to contemporary American New Deal politics. Charles II and Henry VIII are shown to be 'soul mates' with the populace, downtrodden by their demanding, selfish and scheming courtiers who are the real holders of power. Similarly, both *Drums* and *The Four Feathers* propose that there is little conflict between officers and soldiers or between the empire and the majority of its subjects. Both films therefore endow their imperialist heroes with classic chivalric attributes of good manners, thoughtfulness, bravery and modesty in such a way that the basis of their power – domination and conquest – is underplayed. Any opposition to British rule is cast as dangerous and destructive. In *Drums* Carruthers (Roger Livesey), son-in-law of the British Governor, is therefore gentle, kind and admired by Azim (Sabu), the son of a pro-British Indian prince who is threatened by Prince Guhl (Raymond Massey) who gains Moslem support for his plans to re-conquer territories held by the British. Azim joins the British in defeating Guhl, who alone voices criticism of the British empire, at one point remarking that 'the empire is ready to be carved to pieces'. Guhl's opinions are negated by the film's depiction of the personal and political alliance between Azim and Carruthers as natural and non-exploitative. In recognition of these crucial delineations the *New York Times'* reviewer pointed out that Prince Ghul was evil because his schemes of empire were conceived not out of sympathy for Indian nationalism but out of sheer selfishness. Audiences who might otherwise prefer to favour the cause of Ghul and the Moslems were therefore being directed against their natural sympathies by a film which mobilized complex chivalric structures. Cast as the aggressor, the tyrant Ghul and his territorial ambitions could also be related to the contemporary international situation and the film thus read as an 'effective instrument for cementing the democratic axis' against Fascism and as a 'gloriously High Anglican sermon for peace'.[75]

In *The Four Feathers* Harry Faversham (John Clements) is labelled a coward by his friends and fiancée after he refuses to accompany his regiment to the Sudan to fight with Lord Kitchener. Faversham redeems himself later when, racked with guilt, he goes to the Sudan and impersonates a mute tribesman. Following his old regiment, he performs acts of self-sacrifice and bravery, saving the lives of three men who had presented him with white feathers as a symbol of cowardice when he left his regiment. Although the film is about Faversham's conversion to heroism, it is important that the means whereby he achieves the title of the 'bravest Faversham' are unconventional. At the beginning of the film, the expectations placed on him to demonstrate his bravery in the military are depicted as rigid and unyielding. At the dinner table, General Burroughs (C. Aubrey Smith), his fiancée's father, repeats the same story of his bravery in the Crimean War time and time again.[76] We later learn that Burroughs' supposed heroic act was in fact an accident: he led an important charge at a key moment because his horse was startled, not because of his own ingenious timing. Faversham's bravery is anonymous. Masquerading as the mute tribesman, his true identity is only discovered later when a white feather is found on each of the men he has saved. So, rather than prove his bravery in the conventional way he chooses to flout military structures, reject the pomp and pageantry of military ambition and instead pursue his personal quest to return the white feathers to the individuals who despised him for failing to perform his imperial duty. The film foregrounds an individual's bravery rather than the wider context of British imperialism. The ridiculousness of General Burroughs and his militaristic comrades was, indeed, singled out by the *New York Times* as alien to American values:

> The strangely tortured British ruling-class ethics which motivate the plot are decently buried (thank goodness) in the picaresque confusion incident to the storming of Omdurman, or scenes like the mad Mahdi's savage extermination of Capt. Ralph Richardson's reconnoitring force in the desert. The entire cast, notably including Mr Smith (C. Aubrey Smith) has that air of well-bred just rightness which only a carefully selected native English cast can have in pictures dealing with that curiously foreign race.[77]

For this reviewer, the antics of the British military establishment were viewed with disdain, recognising that the chivalric code expressed by Faversham's actions was of a different nature, perhaps closer to an American understanding of the concept. The film was also appreciated for its spectacle and action-adventure elements, both of which were highlighted in UA's press book for *The Four Feathers*. With reference to the eve of the Second World War, the film proposes that true heroism is not to be equated with aggressive, self-aggrandizing militarism.

By the end of the 1930s, Korda had therefore made a significant contribution towards opening up the American market for British films. Despite the difficulties of gaining access to America's cinemas, the success of *The Private Life of Henry VIII*, *The Ghost Goes West*, *Drums* and *The Four Feathers* showed that British cinema was developing a profile abroad. While financial problems had overtaken LFP, Korda continued to produce films with his company, Alexander Korda Film Productions, but he became more reliant on American finance. With the onset of the Second World War, Korda was forced to move to Hollywood where he completed *The Thief of Bagdad* (1940) and shot *That Hamilton Woman/Lady Hamilton* (registered US, 1941), two pictures which did exceptionally well at the box-office (Balio, 1976: 172). In 1940 *The Thief of Bagdad* was UA's highest grosser, earning just over $1 million in the United States and Canada (total domestic rentals). The following year *That Hamilton Woman* was the third-highest grossing film, earning total domestic rentals of $1,149,499.[78] In 1938 Korda wrote that 'there could be no more serious setback to the British film industry than a retrenching from our world ambitions. To take this retrograde step would be a disaster to the industry economically' (in Davy, 1938: 171). *The Private Life of Henry VIII* had placed 'world ambitions' within the grasp of the larger British producers who, as we shall see in the following chapter, began to view exports as a risky but essential element of a successful national film industry.

Notes

1. *Film Daily Year Book* figures, 1928–39. Germany was responsible for the highest number of imports, although in 1930 British imports totalled 30 and German 26. In the wake of *Henry VIII*, imports from Britain increased in 1934 and stayed at more or less the same level to 1939. See Appendix A.
2. *Variety* reviews of *Blackmail*: 9 Oct 1929; 10 July 1929.
3. As Vincent Porter (1998: 26) has observed, 'The hard commercial reality was that, to cover their costs, most British films, other than those with a very low budget, also had to appeal to overseas audiences, especially those in the United States'.
4. *Film Daily*, 26 Oct 1930: 10; *Variety*, 13 Aug 1930 and 29 Oct 1930 (cutting was advised); Crafton, 1997: 435. *Motion Picture Herald*'s review of *Sunshine Susie*, 9 Jan 1932: 40, was full of praise: 'a sparkle in every foot' while the *New York Times* (27 June 1932: 20), considered the German version to be superior.
5. See Jarvie, 1992: 144, and for a revisionist view Street, 2000: 51–62.
6. *Variety*, 26 Feb 1930 and 17 Sept 1930. The *New York Times* also admired Hitchcock's film, Oct 25 1930: 20.
7. *Variety*, 13 Aug 1930 and 8 Oct 1930.
8. *Variety*, 1 Sept 1931. *Motion Picture Herald*, 6 Feb 1932: 11, reported that *The Dreyfus Case* grossed over $200,000 by early 1932. The *New York Times* (31 Aug 1931: 30) gave it a very positive review.
9. *Variety*, 24 Dec 1930. The *New York Times* was not so enthusiastic, finding the acting good but the direction 'unimaginative' (20 Dec 1930: 20).
10. *Variety*, 4 Feb 1931.
11. *Variety*, 29 Dec 1931.
12. For its box-office success in the United Kingdom see Low, 1985: 35 and details of the American distribution deal are in the Michael Balcon Special Collection, MEB 3/17, British Film Institute. *Sunshine Susie* starred Jack Hulbert, whom Balcon later considered unpopular in America: telegram from Balcon to Boxall, 17 Oct 1934: 'Hulbert fairly difficult', C/9 (New York trip, 1934), British Film Institute.
13. *Variety*, 13 Oct 1931 and 10 Nov 1931.
14. *Variety*, 29 Jan 1930.
15. *Variety*, 29 Jan 1930 and 6 Aug 1930.
16. *Variety*, 16 July 1930.
17. *Variety*, 4 Feb 1931 – report on BIP's test screenings in New York.
18. Hal Horne to Lichtman, Kelly, Buckley, Moskowitz, Gold, Lazarus and Burger, 11 Apr 1933. United Artists archive, 99AN 1E, Box 3.
19. *Rome Express* and *The Good Companions* are particularly notable in this respect. Fox's *Cavalcade* (1932) established a taste for 'English' films; see Glancy, 1999: 72–3. 1933 was a very good year at the box-office for British films in the United States: between them *Be Mine Tonight*, *Rome Express* and *Henry VIII* made more money than the total number of British imports in 1932, *Daily Telegraph*, 13 Jan 1934.
20. *Variety*, 17 Oct 1933: 19. Some of this material on *Henry VIII* has been published in Street, 2000.
21. According to figures published in *Motion Picture Herald*, the Radio City Music Hall took $103,000 during the week ending 21 October, a very high figure when compared

with other grosses of the year; see *Motion Picture Herald*, 28 Oct 1933: 76. According to Karol Kulik, the film made £500,000 on its first world run and twenty years later still earned £10,000 a year; see Kulik, 1975, 89.

22. This figure represents the amount LFP received after 30 per cent had been paid to United Artists, balanced against the film's production cost of £93,710. Bank of England Archive, Securities Management Trust files, 2/34, Lever to Bunbury, 10 May 1937.

23. For an analysis of this situation see Klingender and Legg, 1937 and Dickinson and Street, 1985: 76–88.

24. Although Korda was implicated in the 1937 'crash' in the sense that the financial fortunes of London Film Productions were scrutinized by the Bank of England and instrumental in the decision not to support a Film Bank; see Street, 1986.

25. *Variety*, 14 Nov 1933: 10.

26. See reports in *Variety*, 7 Nov 1933: 25; 14 Nov 1933: 8; 21 Nov 1933: 11; 28 Nov 1933: 8; and 5 Dec 1933: 9. Reports in *Motion Picture Herald* confirm this view: see 28 Oct 1933: 76; 4 Nov 1933: 50; 25 Nov 1933: 51; 9 Dec 1933: 48; 16 Dec 1933: 35; 23 Dec 1933: 52.

27. United Artists rental grosses. I am grateful to Mike Walsh for sending me details of UA grosses, compiled from the UA archive, Madison, Wisconsin.

28. Circular letter 3547, 24 July 1936. Gold to branch managers. UA archive, 99 AN 1H, B1, F1.

29. I am grateful to John Sedgwick for providing me with this estimate.

30. See memo from A.L. Lichtman (UA, New York) 17 Oct 1933 to exchanges giving advice on the need for 'fast work in small situations . . . some discretion can be used for *Henry VIII* in accepting slightly lower than very top prices'. UA archive, Paul Lazarus sales correspondence, 99AN 1E, box 3, University of Wisconsin, Madison.

31. *Motion Picture Herald*, 21 Oct 1933: 6.

32. *Motion Picture Herald*, 'Foreign made films to reopen houses dark for lack of films', 6 Feb 1932: 11.

33. *Kinematograph Weekly*, 15 Feb 1934: 5.

34. *Film Daily*, 21 Sept 1933.

35. See survey of British reviews in Harper, 1994: 22–3. In the House of Commons, pressure was put on the Secretary of State for India (Sir Samuel Hoare) by Sir Frank Saunderson to urge the Indian Government to ban *The Private Life of Henry VIII* on the grounds that it was likely to have a 'detrimental effect on the audience'. The film, however, passed the censors. See *Kinematograph Weekly*, 30 Nov 1933: 1 and 4 Jan 1934: 12; *Parliamentary Debates (Commons), Official Report*, 5th Series, 1933–4, vol. 283, 27 Nov 1933, cols., 484–5, HMSO 1934 .

36. There was even a claim that Korda had plagiarized an American author, Francis Hackett, in his depiction of Henry and interpretation of his 'personal habits'. A law suit was filed in the US District Court in December 1935 claiming that the film had failed to acknowledge its debt to Hackett's biography of Henry VIII, copyrighted in 1929. *New York Times*, 20 Dec 1935: 31.

37. *Motion Picture Herald*, 16 Jan 1932: 12.

38. *New York Herald Tribune*, 13 Oct 1933.

39. See press book for *The Private Life of Henry VIII*, New York Public Library.

40. Letter from Violet Gordon (n.d.) to Elsa Lanchester. Elsa Lanchester collection, Margaret Herrick Library, Los Angeles.

41. The concern to stress accuracy, the likeness of the actor to the king and efforts made to reproduce period detail are consistent with the genre of the historical film; see Quinn, 2000, unpublished PhD thesis, Sheffield Hallam University.

42. *Motion Picture Herald*, 23 Sept 1933: 40.

43. Production Code Administration files, Margaret Herrick Library, Los Angeles and press books file, Billy Rose Theatre Collection, New York. In 1933 the film received a certificate without any problems, but the deletions insisted on in 1935 were enforced and had to be upheld when the film was reissued in 1947. The lines deleted included Henry's 'Am I a King or a breeding bull?'

44. *Variety* reviewed fifty-nine British films in 1933. Those which received the best reviews were *The Private Life of Henry VIII, Rome Express* (Walter Forde), *The Good Companions* (Victor Saville), *Sleeping Car* (Anatole Litvak), *It's A Boy* (Tim Whelan) and *Orders Is Orders* (Walter Forde).

45. Schenck to O'Brien, 11 Jan 1934, quoted in Balio, 1976: 134.

46. See UA figures, UA archive. *Drums* earned $660,771.05 in the United States and Canada and *The Four Feathers* earned $801,564.24.

47. *Variety*, 11 Sept 1946: 27.

48. For a discussion of Warners' 'Merrie England'/historical cycle see Roddick, 1983: 235–48. The review by *Variety* of *The Private Life of Henry VIII* predicted this trend: 'With Hollywood on the verge of a biographical cycle *Henry VIII* will likely provide the slight shove needed to send the coast into an era of historical and costume pictures', 17 Oct 1933: 19.

49. Report LXVII: American Research Institute reports, 1940–41 published on microfilm as *Gallup Looks at the Movies: Audience Research Reports, 1940–50*, Princeton, New Jersey: American Institute of Public Opinion; Eilmington, Delaware: Scholarly Resources, 1979.

50. Kelly to George Schaefer, 16 Sept 1936. UA archive, 99AN 1E, B3, F6.

51. I am grateful to Michael Walsh for pointing out the role of the British market in UA's overall financial strategy.

52. Figures supplied by F. G. W. Chamberlain of Gaiety Cinema, Bristol, 5 Feb 1937 to the Moyne Committee. Public Record Office (PRO), Board of Trade files, BT 64 89/6551/37.

53. See series of papers by Joseph Schenck, UA President, on selling films to exhibitors. UA archive, 99AN 1E, B2, F1.

54. Goodman to Lazarus, 18 Sept 1935. UA archive, 99AN 1E, B3, F5.

55. Fred Anderson to Harry Gold, 1 Aug 1935, UA archive, 99AN 1E, B3, F5.

56. Lazarus to Doak Roberts, 20 Oct 1935, UA archive, 99AN 1E, B3, F5.

57. Greenthal to Myers, 7 Aug 1936, UA archive, 99AN 1D, 3, 9.

58. Greenthal to Schaefer, 7 Aug 1936, UA archive, 99AN 1D, 3, 9.

59. UA archive, 99AN 1D, 3, 9.

60. Monrie Greenthal circular, 4 Dec 1940, UA archive, 99AN 1H, 3, 1.

61. It grossed $156,722 in the USA, UA's third-highest grossing film out of sixteen in 1936. The recorded gross compiled from UA's records is missing 1937 figures which accounts for the disparity between UA's accounts and box-office reports in the trade press.

62. *Variety*, 5 Feb 1936: 10; 12 Feb 1936: 3; 19 Feb 1936: 10. *The Ghost Goes West* featured regularly in *Variety* box-office reports throughout its first run.

63. See Telegram from Harry Gold to LA exchange, 5 Feb 1936; Gold to Libson, 11 Feb 1936; Telegram from Arthur Kelly, 1 Nov 1936. UA archive, 99AN 1E, B3, F6. Karol Kulik (1975: 140) contends that the film was 'immensely successful at home and overseas'; Rachael Low (1985: 171) describes it as 'tailored for the American market' and Tino Balio (1976: 144) refers to it as a 'success'.

64. Circular letter no. 3410, 14 Jan 1936. UA archive 99AN 1E, B3, F6.

65. *Variety*, 16 Oct 1935: 10.

66. I am grateful to Mark Glancy for sharing his researches into the reception of *The 39 Steps*. See H. M Glancy, *The 39 Steps* (forthcoming, I. B. Tauris, 2002).

67. At the tenth meeting of the Moyne Committee, Korda claimed that LFP had to increase Donat's salary from £6,000 to £25,000 to appear in *The Ghost Goes West* in response to an American offer of $35,000. Public Record Office (PRO), Board of Trade files, BT 64/92/6757/38.

68. Warner Brothers writ and judgement, RD1/9/1/1-2; Robert Donat Collection, John Rylands Library, Manchester.

69. See press books for *The Ghost Goes West* at the British Film Institute Library.

70. Donat did not approve of this kind of merchandising. In a letter to Alexander Korda he wrote: 'Did you know that the Ghost's costume was exhibited in the window of an Edinburgh store(s) [sic]? This seems to me to be not only poor publicity, but damn silly! Why stress the material properties of the Ghost, anyway?' RD1, file 1/239: Donat to Korda, 21 Feb 1936 in Robert Donat Collection, John Rylands Library, Manchester.

71. *Variety,* 5 Feb 1936: 10.

72. *New York Times,* 11 Jan 1936: 9.

73. *Variety,* 15 Jan 1936.

74. I am grateful to Jeffrey Richards for alerting me to Fraser's work on chivalry.

75. *New York Times,* 30 Sept 1938: 24.

76. This scene is later parodied in *Kind Hearts and Coronets.*

77. *New York Times,* 4 Aug 1939: 11.

78. UA grosses.

3

The 1930s: Exportable Texts and Stars – Herbert Wilcox, Michael Balcon and Reciprocity

During the 1930s Michael Balcon and Herbert Wilcox made significant attempts to win American screentime for 'exportable' films and stars. Inspired by the success of *Nell Gwyn* (1925) and *The Private Life of Henry VIII*, Herbert Wilcox pursued an 'internationalist' policy with historical films which demonstrated that British films did not have to stifle national themes in order to be successful in America. Michael Balcon became the British film industry's unofficial ambassador whose relations with American stars, producers and distributors did much to enhance the reputation of British films in America. Balcon promoted British star Jessie Matthews with an international audience in mind. As exemplary texts, the films of Jessie Matthews provide an opportunity to analyse questions of transatlantic appeal, cross-cultural address and the nature of British stardom. These efforts took place within a context of official and unofficial enthusiasm about Anglo-American cooperation.

Debates about the viability of British films overseas dominated discussions in 1936–7 before the renewal of the Films Act. The desire for 'reciprocity', or the recognition that bargains might be struck with the Hollywood majors who were anxious to protect the lucrative flow of dollars earned by their films in Britain, was exploited by producers such as Basil Dean and commentators on the financial state of the British film industry including Simon Rowson. The basic belief in *quid pro quo* arrangements, or the forging of a 'special' economic relationship between Britain and the USA, extended from schemes designed to increase the overseas earning power of British films to Michael Balcon's highly publicized transatlantic crossings and meetings with Hollywood movie moguls. A reciprocity clause was incorporated into the 1938 Films Act, legislation that was, as I have argued elsewhere, intimately bound up with the Government's aim to encourage American production in Britain and to enlist American support against Fascism (Street, 1985). Instead of concentrating on Anglo-American relations and official policy, this chapter is therefore concerned with the 'unofficial' diplomacy of producers' own schemes, hopes and ambitions for the US market.

Herbert Wilcox and the American Market

Like Korda, Herbert Wilcox was another significant British producer to be linked with United Artists (UA). As in the 1920s Wilcox concentrated his efforts on producing films throughout the following decade which were intended for American distribution. In 1927 he formed a new company, British and Dominions, which survived the transition to sound, purchased studios at Elstree and acquired star attractions, including Jack Buchanan and Anna Neagle, from stage comedy revues. From April 1933 to the end of 1935, UA distributed British and Dominions' films, the most successful in the United States being *Bitter Sweet* (1933), *Sorrell and Son* (1934) and *Escape Me Never* (1935).[1] *Bitter Sweet* took $20,000 in one week at the Rivoli, New York, and Anna Neagle received high praise for her role, described by the *New York Daily Mirror* critic as 'a dazzling English beauty'.[2] While Wilcox was optimistic about forging links with American companies and establishing international reputations for his stars, in the opinion of Richard Norton, a director of British and Dominions, the UA sales team did not devote their best efforts to selling British films.[3] As we have seen in relation to Korda, this charge was arguably without foundation since UA's central distribution strategy and position as a minor American company made it difficult to sell films which were designated as 'quality' product, to be sold on an individual basis in a market dominated by the major circuits.

Indeed, there were many complex reasons why films which were expected to do well earned very little in America. Wilcox's sound version of *Nell Gwyn* (1934) is an interesting case in point.[4] As we have seen, the 1925 version did good business at the American box-office and established the formula which Korda exploited to such good effect with *The Private Life of Henry VIII*. Wilcox's generally good box-office sense and discovery of Anna Neagle suggested that the irreverent, comedic approach to history would once more earn dollars and continue to enhance the reputation of British films. Like the silent version, *Nell Gwyn* provided audiences with a lively, popular heroine. Much of its humour depended on gentle sexual banter between Nell and King Charles (Cecil Hardwicke) who despite their liaison occupy the moral highground above the machinations of the corrupt court. The film also forged the aristocratic-proletarian alliance which I have argued was conducive to American audiences' enthusiastic reception of *Henry VIII* in the context of the New Deal. The press book touched on these elements when it described Nell as 'the idol of the crowd . . . a nation's greatest girl friend!' It also quoted a review in the *Hollywood Reporter* which compared Cecil Hardwicke to Charles Laughton and reminded showmen of the success of the silent version, 'one of the biggest box-office successes in motion picture history, grossing well in the millions'.[5]

A major problem for *Nell Gwyn*, however, was the delay of its release by nine months because of problems with the US censors.[6] Unlike *Henry VIII*, whose sexual innuendo was sanctioned because it was released just before the Production Code Administration (PCA) devised a strict regime of script vetting, *Nell Gwyn* could not escape the rigours of the new system. PCA officials saw the film in July 1934 and recommended that it should be refused a certificate because it was unacceptable to show the King's mistress living in luxury and profiting from their relationship (Plate 5). The censors did not, however, dismiss it out of hand and suggested that a way forward might be to claim that the film was historically accurate. As Joseph Breen, director of the PCA wrote:

> It may be perfectly necessary, and perfectly acceptable, to allow the showing of a 'kept woman'. That fact of itself does not condemn the picture. Generally, it should be avoided; but, when necessary for legitimate plot motivation, it may be acceptable. Much depends on the manner in which the 'kept woman' is treated. If she is a sympathetic character, or if she is made to appear that in allowing herself to be a 'kept woman', that reprehensible action is made to appear justified or acceptable, then the 'kept woman' theme is wrong. On the other hand, if the 'kept woman' theme is introduced as drama to point a moral, or to teach a lesson, and if it is definitely shown to be wrong; if it is established clearly in the minds of the audience that such a life is a life of sin, then the theme or the incident may be acceptable.[7]

When Breen saw the film he agreed that adultery was 'glorified' and insisted that the picture could only obtain a release in the United States if objectionable scenes were replaced with those which reinforced the view that Nell's behaviour was immoral.[8] The PCA office contacted UA and Wilcox suggested the insertion of a prologue showing Nell destitute with a moral articulated by distraint officers whose comments occasion the story told in flashback.[9] Breen's office considered this to be a good solution, especially when accompanied by an epilogue which hammered the point home even more forcefully. Both the censors and UA were aware of the sensitivities of British producers who saw the rigorous censorship system as another barrier for British films in the United States. Joseph Schenck of UA wrote to Breen that care must be taken with regard to *Nell Gwyn* since 'it is an English picture and we do not want to be too hard on them as they may think we are doing it to stop the progress of their pictures in America'.[10] Breen replied that he was keen to see the film released and was doing all he could to make it acceptable within the confines of the Code: 'I have not the slightest desire to be anything but helpful to the British producers. Indeed, I am disposed to go out of my way to be constructively helpful'.[11] In March 1935, a compromise was struck whereby a prologue and epilogue were added, and the line 'let not poor Nellie starve' was allowed to stay because it was of 'great historical significance'.[12]

The critics' verdict on the delayed release of *Nell Gwyn* and the intervention of the censors was mixed. Most referred to the moralistic additions of a prologue and epilogue, for example *Variety* commented that the prologue 'sets it off on the wrong foot'.[13] In a letter to the *New York Times*, Edith Jardine from Brooklyn complained that 'this tag at the head and tail of the main picture is historically false in every detail. And it seemed to me intrinsic and clumsily out of key with the film as a whole'.[14] Other reviews found that the film nevertheless had merits, for example Andre Sennwald of the *New York Times* considered it to be 'witty, audacious. . . . The one distinguished talent of the British film studios is the historical photoplay, and they exercise it handsomely'.[15] While the *New York Herald Tribune* admired its bravado and acting, particularly the performance of Cecil Hardwicke, Wilcox's direction was found to be lacking in tempo in parts.[16] Other reviews praised the settings and Anna Neagle's acting.[17] But the film was certainly not the success it had been in Britain, and it is tempting to conclude that the heavy-handed prologue and epilogue did indeed upset the film's balance between comedy, history, subtlety and didacticism which was thus reflected at the box-office.

It is also possible that UA's publicity campaign created expectations which were not met by the film, especially in its emasculated form. The posters suggested sexual allure and thrilling incidents: 'Her glamorous lips. . . . Her daring, her bewitching charm lured a king from his throne! The adventurous private life of a devil-may-care wench who rose from a lowly music hall to become the uncrowned queen of a monarch!' As with *The Private Life of Henry VIII*, the press book also gave the film a 'highbrow' gloss when it stressed that considerable research had been undertaken into the historical period in which the film was set. It pointed out that the stage at Drury Lane had been reproduced exactly and that the make-up and headdress worn by Neagle was copied from a portrait in the National Gallery. Cecil Hardwicke's 'exhaustive' research into the King's life was described as culminating in his own conclusion that 'the man was no more the immoral libertine than were other fashionable folk of his day'. Anna Neagle was reported to have suffered during the scene in which she wears an enormous hat on stage: 'This cumbersome chapeau caused indentations on the fair Neagle brow which forty-eight hours of cold applications barely eradicated'.[18] Yet these claims were contradicted by the press material's overall advice: 'Be sure not to sell *Nell Gwyn* as history but sell it as a live wire, flesh and blood entertainment – which will excite your audience and start the word-of-mouth comment that means so much to your box-office'. Caught between historical pretension and salacious comedy, the press book assumes that the film can be appreciated on both levels. After the intervention of the censors, however, the benefits from an ambiguous address could hardly be reaped on a film which punished its charismatic, popular heroine in so heavy-handed a manner.

From 1935 Wilcox pursued a two-pronged policy of making films directed primarily at the domestic market and those which were intended to appeal to American audiences. An example is *This'll Make You Whistle* (1936), an adaptation of a stage musical which involved American collaborators for the songwriting, and dance numbers staged by American choreographer Buddy Bradley (Low, 1985: 247–8). Wilcox continued to promote the career of his wife, Anna Neagle, and secured an important contract with RKO-Radio for the distribution of *Victoria the Great* (1937), their most successful film in Britain and America in the 1930s. The RKO contract was the result of frantic negotiations after Wilcox's usual distributor, C. M. Woolf, refused to contribute production finance because he disagreed with Wilcox's casting of Anna Neagle in the lead role. Although RKO provided finance and a distribution contract, Wilcox still had to contribute his own money and obtained studio credit from Korda to shoot it at Denham. The film had its world première in Ottawa, and it was awarded the Gold Cup of All Nations at the Venice Film Festival. In New York it played to 'packed houses' and Wilcox was made an honorary member of the American Institute of Cinematography (Wilcox, 1967: 116). *Variety* attributed its American success to audiences' fascination with the British monarchy since the recent Broadway run of *Victoria Regina,* a play by Laurence Housman. Also significant was its release soon after the British Abdication Crisis of December 1936, as well as its resemblance to American films such as *Cavalcade* which 'glorified England, her traditions and checkered history'.[19]

While *Victoria the Great*'s reverent, obsequious depiction of the monarchy was very different from the approach taken by Korda in *The Private Life of Henry VIII,* a similar bond between the monarchy and the population is suggested. The film's focus on the 'private' aspects of Victoria's marriage to Albert, for example, gave the film a similar sense of intimacy with the Queen's personal trials and tribulations. Victoria and Albert are presented as peacekeepers whose timely intervention prevents the sending of a potentially war-mongering telegram to the United States. They also support the people when they advocate the repeal of the Corn Laws to reduce the price of bread. Although the film lacks the salacious elements that had proved to be so popular in Korda's film, *Victoria the Great* nevertheless delivered a comforting portrait of a caring, benevolent monarchy. In the context of the escalating international crisis at the end of the 1930s, the film's concern to stress that the monarchy was peace-loving, sensible and deserving of respect carried symbolic reassurance about contemporary politics.

On the strength of such enthusiasm for the film and after an American tour in 1938 with Anna Neagle, Wilcox secured a ten-year contract with RKO-Radio. The contract was for Imperator, a company he had formed to make *Victoria the Great,* to produce three to four films a year, for Neagle to make one film each year in Hollywood and for guaranteed bookings for the films in the United States. Surveys by the Audience Research Institute demonstrated that Anna Neagle's star rating was increased by the RKO connection.[20] The deal was extremely important in representing the confidence American distributors had placed in British films by the end of the decade. As Low comments: 'The importance of this contract should not be underestimated. Had the war not intervened Wilcox, like Korda, might have achieved what all the big British producers had been aiming at, a real market in America' (Low, 1985: 250).

Michael Balcon, Gaumont-British and Internationalism

The growth of the film industry in this country during the past few years, and the welcome extended to British pictures, not only in our own Dominions but in the vast American market, have proved beyond doubt that in order to progress still further we must pursue a production policy ever less and less parochial and more and more international in appeal. 'Internationalism' sums up Gaumont-British policy.[21]

In June 1936 Michael Balcon described his company's policy in the above terms. While Balcon was not a major participant in the official reciprocity debates, his efforts to forge links with American companies and institute a transatlantic exchange of stars were just as important in enhancing the reputation of British films as players in the world market. The strategy of internationalism was concentrated in the years 1934–6 when Gaumont-British sent Arthur Lee to New York to oversee American distribution. Balcon visited America several times in search of Hollywood stars who might be exchanged with British, and he was greeted enthusiastically by the American press. Don Mersereau, general manager of *Film Daily,* wrote to him in October 1934: 'Your presence, personality and spirit has been a tremendous factor in establishing in the minds of Americans that your organization is one to be looked up to and respected'.[22] Balcon attended the US première of *Chu Chin Chow* (1934) at the Roxy Theatre, New York, a film which was reported to have run for two weeks and broken the house record.[23] The managing director of the Roxy praised other Gaumont-British films and confirmed that they had been profitable for two years. As Sedgwick has observed 'the diffusion of G-B's films in the US from late 1934 represents a dramatic change from the earlier situation where Fox had distributed the occasional G-B film' (Sedgwick, 1996: 338). Balcon's visits were not only in search of stars, but his keen observations on US studios and the nature of the American market led him to conclude that the British films which were likely to do best were 'dramatic subjects and musicals'.[24] At the end of 1935 Gaumont-British announced a cluster of star signings including director Raoul Walsh, actor Robert Young, who was to star with Jessie Matthews in *It's Love Again* (Plates 6 and 7), and Sylvia Sidney, who was hired by special arrangement with Walter Wagner for a film to be written and directed by Hitchcock.[25]

Yet for all these valiant efforts Balcon's internationalist strategy failed to reap the profits required to sustain a major high-budget production drive. Gaumont-British executives placed the blame squarely on the entrenched interests of the American film industry rather than on the public's reaction to the films (Higson, 1995: 124). Gaumont's distribution agency could not compete with the economic advantages enjoyed by the vertically integrated Hollywood majors. As Sedgwick's (1996: 333–48 and 2000: 211–29) statistical analysis of the box-office careers of Gaumont-British films in the United States 1934–6 reveals, their overall performance was disappointing. Part of the problem was that most of the films were shown in independent cinemas which held a weak position in the overall market, struggling against the majors' block-booking practices. The film that did best was *Transatlantic Tunnel* (1935), a futuristic adventure film based on a German novel published in 1913 by Bernhard Kellermann and directed by Maurice Elvey. *Variety* predicted that the boldness of its ideas, the Anglo-American cast, combination of realism, romance and adventure would ensure it 'big box-office'.[26] The cast included Richard Dix and Helen Vinson, both from Hollywood; C. Aubrey Smith and George Arliss, both British-Hollywood; and the British actor Leslie Banks.[27] Set in the 1950s, the film is about the development of a transatlantic tunnel and the tragedy it brings to its American director, engineer McAllan, 'Mac', (Richard Dix) when his British wife Ruth (Madge Evans) suspects that he is having an affair with Varlia, the daughter of a British millionaire who has helped to finance the scheme. Further personal sacrifices are at the heart of the drama as McAllan's wife and son suffer when working on the tunnel: she loses her sight and their son is killed. Mac and Ruth become further estranged as work on the tunnel consumes Mac. The couple are, however, united at the end of the film as the tunnel is finally completed. While German and French language adaptations of Kellerman's novel had been made simultaneously in 1933, the British version was distinguished by a greater emphasis on the marital problems experienced by the film's central couple (Richards, 1999: 25–7). As such, the Anglo-American couple is symbolic of the tortuous collaborative relationship between the two countries as the tunnel scheme is beset with problems before finally reaching successful completion.

The construction of the tunnel and the various setbacks suffered by the project suggest that genuine Anglo-American cooperation must be worked at very hard. The film evidently alludes to contemporary hopes about the likelihood of an Anglo-American alliance against Fascism. George Arliss and Walter Huston make a brief, three-minute appearance as the British Prime Minister and US President announcing the successful completion of the project on television, broadcast all over the world. Arliss declares that for the promotion of peace 'the Atlantic tunnel will be greater than any treaty'. Similarly, Huston proclaims that the tunnel will divert money 'hitherto wasted on wages of soldiers and munitions of war' into 'useful and peaceful channels'. The tunnel is therefore symbolic of Anglo-American cooperation both in terms of contemporary discussions about reciprocity between the film industries and in relation to the developing European crisis. As Telotte (1999: 149) has commented: 'The final images of mutual celebrations in New York and London upon the tunnel's completion, presided over by those same leaders, reaffirm this dream of a new era of peace and understanding among peoples, and emphasize the tunnel's status as a kind of monument of this new age'.

Other films that did comparatively well were *The 39 Steps* (1935), *It's Love Again* (1936), *Chu Chin Chow, Iron Duke* (1934), *Rhodes of Africa* (1936), *Secret Agent* (1936), *First a Girl* (1935) and *Evergreen* (1934). The films which were held over for two-week runs, indicating a favourable initial performance, were *Evergreen* (Uptown Theatre, Kansas City) and *It's Love Again* (Music Box, Seattle). However, as Sedgwick's survey also reveals, 'the performance of these films in terms of box-office receipts is generally poor when compared with rival films playing simultaneously or films immediately preceding/following' (Sedgwick, 1996: 345). It would appear, therefore, that while Balcon's internationalist policy was laudible for its aspiration, it failed to deliver what it set out to achieve: equitable market prospects for British films and sustained box-office profits. With more consolidated economic power, such as that held by the Rank Organization in the 1940s, Balcon would undoubtedly have reaped greater benefits from the production drive (Higson, 1995: 125). Largely due to internal dissention and financial instability Balcon left Gaumont-British at the end of 1936 and became head of MGM's production unit in Britain, a position which, ironically, had been earned on the basis of his good reputation in Hollywood.

Marketing an International Star: Jessie Matthews

Miss Matthews, on stage musicals on the other side, looks to be a find.
– *Variety* on *The Good Companions*
Her individual dancing is delightful.
– *Motion Picture Herald* on *Evergreen*
The feminine counterpart of Fred Astaire.
– *New York Times* on *Evergreen*
Jessie Matthews at her best, and where her name can carry it's due for nice business.
– *New York Review* on *It's Love Again*

Despite Balcon's problems with Gaumont-British, he did achieve transatlantic exposure in terms of positive reviews, publicity and comparative box-office success with musicals starring Jessie Matthews (See Higson, 1995: 126–31).[28] Matthews had started her career as a member of the chorus in London stage revues. Balcon signed her to a two-year contract on the strength of her performance in her first film, *Out of the Blue* (1931). Her reputation was the most international of all British stars in the 1930s, and her most well-known films in America, *Evergreen* (1934) and *It's Love Again* (1936), established her as the 'dancing divinity' in a decade when Hollywood musicals, particularly those choreographed by Busby Berkeley at Warner and the Fred Astaire and Ginger Rogers musicals at RKO, dominated American and European screens. Several Hollywood companies tried to lure her to Hollywood, and RKO is reported to have bid $50,000 for her to co-star with Fred Astaire, an offer that never materialized (Thornton, 1975: 139). Further offers were received from studios including MGM, each time being rejected by Matthews because of personal problems and ill health (Richards, 1985: 223). In 1935 Michael Balcon wanted to exchange her services for those of Hollywood star Myrna Loy.[29] Balcon had to tread very carefully with Matthews, agreeing with reluctance to allow Sonnie Hale, Matthews's husband, to star in *First a Girl* even though he considered Hale to be 'definitely bad' in the American market.[30] A combination of difficult and conflicting circumstances prevented her from making a film in America until 1943 when her career had started to decline. But in the 1930s she was definitely one of Balcon's most important stars and a lynchpin of his internationalist strategy. She appeared with American stars including Robert Young and Jack Whiting, and many of her dance routines were choreographed by American jazz expert Buddy Bradley. Higson has analysed *Evergreen* as a classical narrative film that was deliberately tailored 'to make a mark in the international arena' (1995: 132). As such, *Evergreen* and other Matthews' films were constantly compared to an 'ideal' Hollywood standard of musical performance. Comparatively speaking, they measured up quite well, although it was generally acknowledged that American musicals were faster paced. As we have seen, American reviewers often recommended that British films should be cut, indicating a certain rigidity about film style and testament to the assumption that to be successful, Hollywood's 'universal' cinematic strategies should be adopted by other nations. As well as showing how Matthews was publicized in the United States, the following analysis will focus on her films' connection with modernity, particularly their art deco/*moderne* style which I shall argue was an integral aspect of their transatlantic address and appeal.[31]

Matthews' first major film role was in *The Good Companions* (1933), a musical adaptation of J. B. Priestley's popular novel about a group of unlikely companions who take to the road as a theatrical troupe. The difference between the reception of this film and Matthews' later work demonstrates how quickly she was groomed for international stardom and how from *Evergreen* onwards the 'look' of her films became more and more influenced by Hollywood. Even though the stage version of *The Good Companions* had failed on Broadway, the film version was distributed in the United States by Fox and greeted with mixed reviews. Mordaunt Hall of the *New York Times* was the most enthusiastic, describing Jessie Matthews as 'charming', and most other reviewers praised her performance in what they considered to be an otherwise disappointing adaptation.[32] Despite praise for its use of English locations, criticism of the film focussed on its poor sound quality, difficult accents and technical faults. The film's slow pace was singled out as its most serious deficiency:

> One continuously wishes that the production had been smoother, that the continuity and plot lines had pursued a steadier course. What it needs, furthermore is 'visual flow' – begging your pardon for bringing up that old descriptive phrase which Hollywood proficiency has almost made possible to throw into the discard. In other words, it doesn't steadily create an illusion from just these faults.[33]

At that time British musicals were not considered to be on a par with Hollywood's, as expressed by another New York reviewer who commented: 'The dancing and singing aren't good enough to make one forget such things as *42nd Street* and even that gala-gala *The Golddiggers of 1933*'.[34]

Compared with Matthews' later films *The Good Companions* was inadequately marketed. Fox's rather poor quality and low-key publicity displays a striking contrast with the astute and imaginative campaign undertaken by United Artists for *The Private Life of Henry VIII* in the same year. Somewhat predictably, Fox's press book for the film emphasized Priestley's novel as the source text and recommended tie-ins with book shops and libraries, hardly appropriate venues for promoting a musical. Newspaper advertisements had drawings of Matthews rather than glossy, attractive photographs. Priestley's name was billed above Matthews', and she was rather oddly described as 'nature's most beautifully formed girl'.[35] Fox was clearly uncertain about the best way to promote a British film, perhaps because the company had little confidence in its real prospects outside New York. The *Variety* reviewer also expressed concerns about the film's suitability for American audiences:

> A long and rather draggy story with a musical background that will probably be restricted on this side because of its foreign nature, notably its very English accent, characteristics, etc. As entertainment it rates less than fair. Miss Matthews, on stage musicals on the other side, looks to be a find who would develop with better material.[36]

As we shall see, in later musicals Matthews managed to overcome these reservations with a complete change in musical performance, set design and star presentation that was more acceptable in the American market. While in 1933 she was received reasonably well but hardly enthusiastically by American critics, in just a few years their praise for her was unequivocal. In subsequent years the Museum of Modern Art, New York, held several retrospectives of her films, indicating the longevity of her image as a British star who gained a following in the United States.[37]

When *Variety* reviewed *Evergreen* in January 1934, it was perceived as 'important in that it is the first musical from across the sea that comes this close to competing successfully with the best efforts of Hollywood'.[38] An analysis of the American press book shows how Gaumont-British pitched it to American exhibitors far more successfully than Fox's campaign for *The Good Companions*.[39] The Gaumont-British office in New York arranged for special stills to be shot which were used as tie-ins with merchandisers selling furs, jewellery, telephones, glasses and records. Matthews' name was billed above the film title, and she was described as 'a new personality' and 'the new wonder star'.

Although she had appeared on Broadway in musical-comedy stage revues in the late 1920s and was known as the lead in *The Good Companions,* Matthews was promoted for *Evergreen* as a star on the brink of recognition. Her qualification as a star was highlighted by 'advance specials' that described her hard-working, professional attitude and how she assisted other members of the cast and crew: 'Long hours and tedious rehearsals to find proper camera angles had no terrors for her. With the application of a serious collegiate Miss Matthews made a careful study of every detail of her new calling'. Her rise to fame from the chorus in revues directed by Charlot and C. B. Cochran, noted theatrical impresarios of the London stage, was also charted. Other aspects intended to demonstrate American appeal included items on the contribution of Rogers and Hart to the music and lyrics; the Edwardian and modern costumes and studio recreation of the Tivoli music hall.

Evergreen was also distinctive in its use of art deco/*moderne* sets, in particular in the 'Dancing of the Ceiling' sequence, and represented the beginning of a trend that was to distinguish her subsequent films. Later dismissed by American critic William K. Everson as 'trivial and superficial', Matthews' films and their display of art deco designs related very much to the 1930s in terms of consumption and consumerism. They also bore close resemblance to other films that utilized the style including the Astaire-Rogers musicals and MGM's *Topper* films.[40] Designed by celebrated German production designer Alfred Junge, the sets create a fascinating European-American dynamic that reflected America's adoption and commercialization of a style that originated in Europe.

In both Britain and America, art deco related to the diegetic world of Matthews' films as well as to the external environment in which they were viewed. Cinemas represented the most extensive use of art deco in public architecture, a classic example being New York's Radio City Music Hall where several British films were premièred. As a style, art deco became prominent from 1925, after the Exposition Internationale in Paris which provided a showcase for the decorative arts. When American designers adopted the style, it evolved into a combination of streamlined forms, geometric shapes and utilized designs and materials which could be adapted for mass consumption. Sometimes referred to as *moderne,* the style featured prominently in Hollywood's films, creating a sense of luxury and modernity from MGM musicals to the creations of Van Nest Polgese at RKO for films such as *Top Hat* (1935).[41] As with the Astaire-Rogers musicals Jessie Matthews' films displayed a crucial interrelationship between the dance numbers, their sets and narrative intent. This sense of transatlantic exchange – between classic European art deco and American consumer culture – was absorbed by Gaumont-British for Matthews' star vehicles.

Unlike earlier, more elitist art forms, art deco was democratic in its ethos, its emphasis on modernity and mass production in turn celebrating the use of cheap, new materials such as chrome and plastics. While the interiors in Jessie Matthews' films were opulent and the epitome of luxurious art deco design, the availability of mass-produced furniture, fittings and clothes inspired by the movies meant that even in the Depression people could adapt what was available for their own consumption (Massey, 2000: 79–91). Matthews' films showcased new designs which were an integral aspect of her musical performances (Street in Conrich and Tincknell, 2002). Her costumes also advertised the latest fashions, particularly glamorous evening gowns which emphasised the feminine body or skirts which by the late 1930s were becoming fuller. Hats were dramatic and exaggerated, often inspired by Surrealism, and several of Matthews' films required her to wear elaborate headpieces which emphasised her large eyes. Gaumont-British's press books for her films exploited these novelties and encouraged tie-ins with local American stores.

Examples of striking art deco sets appear in *Evergreen* (the 'Dancing on the Ceiling' number and the diegetic show 'Springtime in Your Heart'); *First a Girl* (1935; the 'Casino des Folies' sequence); *It's Love Again* (Matthews' performances as 'Mrs Smythe-Smythe'); *Sailing Along* (1938; her impromptu performance of 'My Souvenir of Love' in an art deco apartment) and *Gangway* (1938; the ocean liner). With their affinity to modernity, sophistication and elegance, the art deco sets contributed to an overall impression that Matthews' films represented a major advance for British cinema without losing a sense of distinctiveness. As one review of *It's Love Again* remarked:

> Picture rates as the outstander . . . to come from the other side for production values, imaginativeness, lighting and staging. It can hold its own with the average Hollywood musical without resorting to the standard Hollywood plot and without using a half-mile stage for dancing numbers supposed to be done within a theatre. London is catching up rapidly.[42]

Indeed, even though Matthews' films bore stylistic resemblance to Hollywood cinema, they featured plots which dealt with British or European themes and locales such as 'middle England' (*The Good Companions*); the London music hall (*Evergreen*); Paris and Vienna (*First a Girl*) and Paris (*Head over Heels*, 1936). Also, as Bergfelder has observed, there is a resemblance between the brand of modern femininity represented by Matthews and that of female stars in German cinema of the early 1930s (Bergfelder, 1997: 42). This somewhat complicates the idea that the films were 'internationalist' and therefore devoid of national identity. Rather, as with Korda's films, they projected a sophisticated address which cut across and extended national boundaries. Jessie Matthews' accent could not have been more 'English' and, as I have argued, the use of art deco sets represents not only an homage to set design at MGM and RKO but also to the style's European heritage. The ocean liner in *Gangway* perhaps represents the ultimate symbol of transatlantic fluidity, locating British cinema as a 'travelling' enterprise. With their different approaches Alexander Korda, Herbert Wilcox and Michael Balcon were all heading in the same direction but, as we have seen, the path was not always clear. Assistance came from the Government in 1938 in recognition of the difficulties they had experienced in America, arguably too late to alter the fundamental economic inequalities that prevented unexceptional films from gaining effective American distribution.

The Economics of Exportability: Basil Dean, Simon Rowson and Reciprocity

When the Cinematograph Films Act 1927 was reviewed in the mid-1930s, producers put forward ideas about how to improve the chances of British films in the home market and overseas. Whereas in the 1920s the desire for reciprocity did not find expression in legislation, a decade later producers' attempts were successful. In his evidence to the Moyne Committee which reviewed the Films Act and produced a report in 1936, Simon Rowson was concerned about the American majors' block-booking policies which made it difficult for British films to find screentime both at home and abroad. He was nevertheless optimistic about striking bargains with American distributors: 'The conditions precedent to the negotiation of a treaty do exist. In the important value of this market we have something to give or withhold which is regarded as essential to the continued production of American pictures on their present scale'.[43] Rowson was referring to the recognition that Hollywood's profitability depended on maintaining an aggressive export strategy and, as its most lucrative overseas market, Britain was therefore in a position to use this fact strategically. Over the next eighteen months several schemes were examined by the film trade, elements of which were incorporated into the Cinematograph Films Act 1938.

The first plans were devised by the Film Group of the Federation of British Industries, an organization which included major British producers and was chaired by Basil Dean of Associated Talking Pictures (ATP). Dean was a stage producer who had founded ATP in 1929 as a means of utilizing stage talent for the screen. Dean's attitude towards reciprocity was influenced by his involvement with two American companies, Paramount Famous-Players Lasky and RKO in the late 1920s and early 1930s. His co-production plans with Paramount involved two films, *Escape* and *The Return of Sherlock Holmes*. The production of the former film was delayed by problems securing the agreement of John Galsworthy, author of the original story, who insisted that 'not a single sentence of dialogue other than that which he has written himself or approved himself is to be spoken'.[44] Dean planned to work with Paramount on the picture, shooting on location in Britain and then finishing the picture in Hollywood. A disagreement arose between Dean and Paramount when the American company wanted to postpone the production of *Escape,* preferring instead to concentrate all energies on a more commercial prospect, *The Return of Sherlock Holmes,* a film that was duly produced and released in America.

Dean eventually made *Escape* as part of a co-production deal he made with RKO. In 1929 Dean had forged links with RKO in the hope that ATP's films would obtain fair distribution in America, and in 1931 he became RKO's general European representative. But relations were no better than they had been with Paramount. Dean's contract stipulated that he present RKO with story ideas and British stars. He did this, but in the course of their correspondence, it appears that Dean's ideas were not considered to be good box-office potential by RKO. One proposal, a 'Sapper' story as a star vehicle for Jack Buchanan, was dismissed as 'wishy-washy material from which it is hopeless to expect you could make a good picture'. As an indication of the divergence between British and American conceptions of good picture material, Lee Marcus of RKO commented in notes he sent to Dean that the story was 'manufactured – nothing real or alive about people or events; no real conflict. This is hack work. Get more action, unexpected twists – imagination'.[45] These disagreements continued as RKO dismissed proposal after proposal in similar terms, including an idea for a film based on the Schneider Cup aviation race that was rejected because 'the story lacks naturalness, and there is a considerable lack of real emotional appeal'.[46] By the time ATP released *Looking on the Bright Side* (1931), starring Gracie Fields, the company had made nine films but had not received any returns from their distributors. Relations between ATP and RKO deteriorated when it became apparent that RKO was more interested in buying up exhibition interests in Britain than in offering British films as first features to American exhibitors.[47] They were particularly keen for ATP to make cheap quota pictures, frankly admitting that 'these pictures will never see the light of day in the US'.[48] Discouraged and disappointed, Dean withdrew from all dealings with RKO when his contract as European manager was terminated in 1932, 'in view of retrenchment policy and general conditions'.[49] As well as differences of opinion over suitable story material, then, it must not be forgotten that like the other Hollywood companies, RKO was hit badly by the Depression at the beginning of the 1930s and that this influenced their commitment to British producers. In January 1933 RKO went bankrupt, so Dean's dismissal was as much as anything else a consequence of economics (Balio, 1993: 15).

These bitter experiences undoubtedly influenced Dean's attitude towards securing statutory incentives for reciprocity. In February 1937 a subcommittee was formed to examine the question of reciprocity which submitted a scheme in March. The proposal offered renters the option of satisfying their quota requirements in the normal way or by contributing towards the cost of a British film in exchange for its foreign distribution rights. While this basic principle was accepted, producers were divided over the stipulated minimum cost of the British films: whereas producers like Dean wanted this to be relatively high so that quality would be ensured, others were concerned that the supply of films might be reduced, a view that was supported by the Cinematograph Exhibitors' Association. Eventually a proposal was put forward to the Board of Trade in June 1937 whereby renters choosing to opt for reciprocity as a means of satisfying quota requirements were either to contribute £10,000 to the cost of production in return for foreign distribution rights, or to acquire for at least £10,000 the foreign rights for a British film already made.[50] The Board of Trade received these suggestions favourably and endorsed the related principle that a reciprocity clause in the new Act might induce Hollywood to contribute production finance for British films.

The linking of the question of American distribution with the cost of British films reflected the opinion of Simon Rowson, who made a strong case in his evidence to the Moyne Committee that the profitability of Hollywood's films related to their costs. Quoting examples of 'specials' such as *Ben Hur* (1925, reported to have cost £500,000), *Mutiny on the Bounty* (1935, £400,000) and *David Copperfield* (1935, £300,000), he estimated that 'even the normal expenditure on the great majority of the ordinary pictures ranges between £60,000 and £125,000'.[51] (Other production costs of LFP films are given in Table 3.1.) While many British films did not have budgets this high, the production costs of Korda's films were commensurate with those of Hollywood pictures.[52]

John Sedgwick has similarly concluded that in the mid-1930s, the film budgets of Gaumont-British 'were at least comparable to those of the bulk of films emanating from the major Hollywood studios, although the number of films produced by G-B was less than half their typical output' (Sedgwick, 1996: 336). It would appear therefore that as far as the largest companies were concerned, British films were being made with budgets which would, on the face of it, place them in a good enough position to aspire to foreign distri-

Table 3.1 Costs of Films Produced by London Film Productions
(by date of first trade show, London)

Film	£ Cost of Production
The Private Life of Henry VIII	93, 710
Catherine the Great	127,868
Don Juan	114,239
The Scarlet Pimpernel	143,521
Sanders of the River	149,789
Moscow Nights	52,326
The Ghost Goes West	156,062
Things to Come	241,028
The Man Who Could Work Miracles	133,104
Rembrandt	138,945
Men Are Not Gods	93,765

bution. While Rowson's argument about British film budgets being shadows of their Hollywood counterparts is therefore incorrect, his location of key problems within the marketplace explained that, while several British films had done very well in America, the reluctance of the majors to distribute them on a large scale continued to restrict their impact. As we have seen with Korda and United Artists, the method of distribution was crucial and the reciprocity proposals should be interpreted in the light of Rowson's concern that quota legislation could be used as an incentive for the majors to open up their booking systems to welcome British films. The good progress of British films in the United States towards the end of the decade, particularly the success of Wilcox's *Victoria the Great* and Korda's films, indicates that the 'problem' of market conditions abroad was beginning to be addressed.

To this end, the Cinematograph Films Act 1938 stipulated that a British film costing at least £22,500 in labour costs and acquired for overseas distribution for more than £20,000 exempted its renter from registering it for quota; if the rights cost above £30,000, double quota exemption was achieved. While many producers feared that this would encourage American production in Britain, a trend that the Board of Trade encouraged, it did imply a commitment to overseas distribution as an essential component of bigger budget filmmaking. As far as the history of British films in America is concerned, the Act therefore validated the aspirations of Korda and Balcon. On the part of the Hollywood majors who had lobbied for multiple quota credits and a reciprocity clause, the willingness to put more money into quota films and to release them abroad validates Rowson's argument that 'we have something to give or withhold'. These elements, however, contained a somewhat double-edged nature which put pressure on British films to live up to their status as products worthy of protection and export. It also encouraged companies such as MGM to establish studios in Britain to produce 'British' pictures.[53] This generated fears about British production being subject to 'foreign control' (Dickinson and Street, 1985: 100). As far as the Americans were concerned, however, the familiar argument continued to be made that if films made by British companies proved to be as successful as those made by American companies in Britain, they too would receive the foreign distribution contracts which made bigger budget production viable. The reciprocity provisions therefore placed the responsibility of overseas distribution on the Hollywood majors whose negotiating skills had won them concessions which protected their interests. At the same time they were potentially of great benefit to British films which needed to be given a chance in the most competitive market of all.

British Film Exports at the End of the 1930s

While the decade was dominated by the overseas success of Korda's *The Private Life of Henry VIII,* there were other significant interventions in the American market. In the early 1930s British films were considered to be improving and in subsequent years Korda's contract with United Artists ensured that British films were given a high profile in the trade press. *Henry VIII* had profited from a combination of favourable circumstances which showed that given conducive conditions, British films could receive widespread distribution and hold their own against American films. Korda produced several other films which were also well reviewed and profitable, films that were far from amorphous 'international' spectacles, but displaying sophisticated engagements with Anglo-American themes (*The Ghost Goes West*) or tapping into American fascination about British history and 'patterns' of chivalry (*Drums* and *The Four Feathers*). Despite these examples, there is no doubt that British films were unable to compete on equal terms with Hollywood. UA found it difficult to persuade exhibitors to book British films since they were in competition with groups of films offered in blocks by the majors. Michael Balcon tried to confront this problem by establishing his own distribution network, but the films could only be sold to independents. Consequently, despite excellent reviews and considerable comment in the American trade press, British films found it difficult to sustain *Henry VIII*'s remarkable record. When Basil Dean obtained a contract with RKO, the company did not book ATP's films in first-run cinemas and appeared to be concerned only about controlling British cinemas. However, even though UA did not own cinemas and did not possess the economic advantages of the majors, the company's insistence that British films were 'quality product' had advantages. The status of British cinema was enhanced and UA's extensive marketing campaigns and press books indicate a genuine belief in the product.

Reviews were also important in establishing a mode of discourse about British cinema, its features, whether it was improving, and so forth. Both *Variety* and the *New York Times* reviewed British films regularly and provide an excellent register of opinion as to the viability of British films in the American market. Recurrent issues emerge such as what constituted a 'quality' film, confirming the view that production values were related to the increasing costs of film production. Diction and accents were perceived as problematic in the early sound years. Many exhibitors complained that British accents were difficult for their patrons to understand, and some films were even dubbed with American accents, for example *White Face* (1933). The 'Oxford' accent in particular was disliked and actors such as Robert Donat were given diction training to make their voices clearer. Standards tended to be related to the conventions of Hollywood cinema, but the importance of varied and authentic locations continued to be promoted as positive attributes of British films. What emerges is not a desire for British films to be indistinguishable from American but the advocacy of distinctive films which conformed to classical conventions, particularly in terms of pace and editing. Films with transatlantic subjects, such as *Transatlantic Tunnel* and *The Ghost Goes West,* were indicative of the attempt, generally received positively by critics, to exploit Anglo-American themes. In these instances 'reciprocity' can therefore be seen to transcend economic policies, contracts and star exchanges into narrative concerns.

On the eve of the Second World War, British cinema was, arguably, in a strong position to take advantage of the Films Act which endorsed and encouraged bigger budget film-making. British film exports to the United States did not dramatically fall in the late 1930s: in 1938 forty-four films were exported and in 1939 the figure was thirty-seven.[54] In 1938 three British films were listed by the *New York Times* in the top ten best films: *The Citadel* (MGM-British); *Pygmalion* and *The Lady Vanishes.* Korda had recovered from losing LFP and Denham Studios and was successful with his new company, Alexander Korda Film Productions. The industry had weathered two major crises – the coming of sound and the financial crash of 1937 – although its structural problems undoubtedly persisted (see Sedgwick, 2000: 230–53). Despite problems earlier in the decade, Wilcox made profits from *Victoria the Great* and *Sixty Glorious Years* (1938). A new British major, the Rank Organization, absorbed Gaumont-British, and after the Second World War, made a

concerted attempt to take up where Balcon had left off in his quest for overseas distribution. Into the next decade 'internationalism' therefore continued
to sum up the aims of many British producers.

Notes

1. *Bitter Sweet* earned $90,553; *Sorrell and Son,* $183,003; and *Escape Me Never,*
   $195,830: UA rental grosses.
2. Reported in *Kinematograph Weekly,* 14 Sept 1933: xii (overseas supplement).
3. Norton considered that 'the man out in the field did not want to sell them', quoted in
   Low, 1985: 149.
4. *Nell Gwyn* earned only $36,526 in the United States in 1935: UA grosses. It was how-
   ever a box-office success in Britain, Low: 1985: 148 and found favour with the critics,
   Harper, 1994: 51–2.
5. Press book for *Nell Gwyn,* New York Public Library.
6. The operation of the Code and its impact on British films will discussed at greater length
   in Chapter 5.
7. Joseph Breen to Vincent Hart, 28 July 1934. PCA file on *Nell Gwyn,* Margaret Herrick
   Library, Los Angeles.
8. Telegram from Breen to Hart, 1 Aug 1934. PCA file on *Nell Gwyn.*
9. Telegram from Richard Norton to Breen, 28 Feb 1935. PCA file on *Nell Gwyn.*
10. Schenck to Breen, 26 Feb 1935. PCA file on *Nell Gwyn.*
11. Breen to Schenck, 5 Mar 1935. PCA file on *Nell Gwyn.*
12. Memo by Breen, 14 Mar 1935. PCA file on *Nell Gwyn.*
13. *Variety,* 26 June 1935.
14. *New York Times,* 7 July 1935.
15. *New York Times,* 20 June 1935.
16. *New York Herald Tribune,* 20 June 1935.
17. *New York Sun,* 20 June 1935; *New York Daily Mirror,* 16 June 1935.
18. Press book for *Nell Gwyn,* New York Public Library.
19. *Variety,* 25 Aug 1937.
20. See Audit of Marquee Values, April 1940 and report no. XX for RKO, published on mi-
    crofilm by the American Institute of Public Opinion, 1979.
21. Michael Balcon, *World Film News,* vol. 1, no. 3, June 1936: 6.
22. Don M. Mersereau to Balcon, 18 Oct 1934. Michael Balcon Special Collection, C/83,
    British Film Institute.
23. Chairman's speech to Gainsborough Pictures, Dec 1934: Michael Balcon Special Collec-
    tion, C/50.
24. Telegram, Balcon to Boxall, 17 Oct 1934: Michael Balcon Special Collection, C/9 (New
    York trip, 1934).
25. *Gaumont-British News,* 13 Dec 1935: Michael Balcon Special Collection, C/71.
26. *Variety,* 30 Oct 1935.
27. See reports of New York showings in *Variety,* 30 Oct 1935: 28–9.
28. The box-office reports on Matthews' films in American trade papers do not indicate that
    they made major advances on previous British films but they suggest that her most
    popular film was *It's Love Again.* See reports in *Variety,* 10 June 1936: 7, 19; 19 Aug
    1936: 10, which confirm that it was shown outside New York. Unfortunately, the Mi-
    chael Balcon Special Collection does not contain computed overseas grosses for Gau-
    mont-British films.
29. *Hollywood Reporter,* 9 Mar 1935: 15.

30. Telegram, Balcon to Maurice Ostrer, 25 Mar 1935, Michael Balcon Special Collection, C/696.
31. Some of this work also appears in my chapter on Jessie Matthews in Conrich and Tincknell, 2002.
32. *New York Times,* 10 Oct 1933.
33. *New York Sun,* review by John S. Cohen Jnr, 11 Oct 1933. On the other hand, William Boehnel, writing in *Town and Country,* 1 Nov 1933, observed that after seeing *The Good Companions* and *The Private Life of Henry VIII,* he concluded that 'British films have suddenly become pretty alive and vital'.
34. *New York Evening Post,* 10 Oct 1933.
35. American press book for *The Good Companions,* New York Public Library.
36. *Variety,* 17 Oct 1933.
37. *Evergreen* was shown as part of a season on European musicals in May 1995. The *New York Times,* 24 Nov 1995 reported on a six-film retrospective held at the Walter Reade Theatre, Lincoln Center and described Matthews as epitomizing 'a glamorous Depression era flapper with a streak of innocent mischief'.
38. *Variety,* 15 Jan 1934.
39. Press books, New York Public Library.
40. Everson, 1975, and *Movieline,* vol. 11, no. 7, April 2000: 36–38.
41. Anne Massey explains that the *moderne* adopted many of the traits of art deco but made them more industrial and consumerist: 'America had emulated European style since the colonial era and art deco was adopted in the same tradition of emulating European fashion. This came at a time when America was asserting herself as a world power and when the industries upon which her wealth was created – films, electronic goods, cars – were maturing. However, art deco carried qualities of the risqué. This was addressed through the adoption of the *moderne* after 1929 to represent a more futuristic and American image' (2000: 91).
42. *New York Review,* 27 May 1936.
43. Simon Rowson, evidence to the Moyne Committee, 30 June 1936, paragraph 22: 112.
44. Basil Dean to Walter Wanger (Paramount Famous-Players Lasky), 12 Oct 1928. Basil Dean Collection, 4/1/18, John Rylands Library, Manchester.
45. Lee Marcus to Basil Dean, 8 June 1931. Basil Dean Collection, 4/2/20.
46. Marcus to Dean, 18 Aug 1931. Basil Dean Collection, 4/2/24.
47. The Basil Dean Collection contains material on the conflict between Dean and RKO over the management of the Leicester Square Theatre. See 4/2/39–42.
48. Marcus to Dean, 10 Mar 1931. Basil Dean Collection, 4/2/11.
49. Cable to Dean from RKO, 7 May 1932. Basil Dean Collection, 4/2/85. For an account of these events see also Dean, 1973: 101–75.
50. Details of the Film Group of the FBI's reciprocity schemes are in the Basil Dean Special Collection, British Film Institute.
51. Simon Rowson, evidence to the Moyne Committee, 30 June 1936, paragraph 17: 111.
52. Figures from the Prudential Assurance Company archive.
53. Glancy points out that while the films were shot at Denham in Britain 'they were controlled entirely by MGM in Hollywood' (1999: 2).
54. *Film Daily Year Book,* 1939 and 1940, figures.

4

The 1940s: Prestige, History and Shakespeare

During the 1940s, British films experienced the highs and lows of overseas distribution. After a number of British films had been reviewed favourably and earned commercial success during the Second World War, the Rank Organization, the largest vertically integrated combine controlling approximately 600 of Britain's 4,000 cinemas and nearly half of British sound stages, was well placed to launch a further offensive.

Methodist entrepreneur J. Arthur Rank entered the film business in 1934 when he established British National (Plate 8). By 1941 his company was evolving into a major combine, absorbing Gaumont-British. In 1936 Rank bought into Universal and, together with American financiers, had a seat on the Universal trustee board. This link provided concrete grounds for optimism about gaining a secure distribution outlet for British films in the United States. By dint of its control of the most important 'key' cinemas in Britain, the Rank Organization was also in a position to strike deals of unprecedented magnitude with the Hollywood majors. As in the previous decade, Hollywood's financial dependence on Britain for overseas profits was a major factor in bargaining for reciprocal arrangements for the distribution of British films in America.

In recognition of the advances made by British films, Eric Johnston, President of the Motion Picture Producers of America (MPAA), announced that in 1946 British films grossed $3.7 million in the United States, a figure he estimated would exceed $10 million in 1947.[1] The trade press featured many articles on deals between Britain and Hollywood, particularly Rank's celebrated links with United Artists and Universal.[2] In June 1947, executive John Davis announced deals with American majors that would give Rank's films playing time in 3,000 US theatres.[3] Yet, although the Rank Organization gained the greatest possible access to American screens, the company suffered considerably when it fell from grace in the aftermath of the Dalton Duty crisis of 1947–48.[4] The crisis resulted from the British government's decision to impose a 75 per cent *ad valorem* duty on American films from August 1947 until June 1948. In 1949, due to a combination of adverse circumstances, the Rank group announced in its annual report a net loss of £746,747.[5] As studies of Rank's overseas policy have concluded, the imposition of the duty had serious consequences for the goodwill which had been created between Britain and Hollywood (Murphy, 1984: 164–78 and Macnab 1993: 162–87). Recovery was slow and difficult, drawing attention once again to the British film industry's structural weaknesses and vulnerable position in world markets. At the end of the decade, the Plant report (1949) on the *Distribution and Exhibition of Cinematograph Films* concluded that while the best British films had done well in America, the recovery of the industry could not be expected to result solely from overseas funds.[6]

The economic and political context was intimately related to the reception of British films. As in the 1930s, Anglo-American film relations were intertwined with international policy, and at times it seemed as if cooperation was a test case for the endurance of the 'special relationship'. The hard commercial reality of American dependence on the British market reared its head on several occasions, making many British producers suspicious of welcoming, positive American comments about British films. Still haunted by his experiences as head of MGM-British, Michael Balcon was a firm believer that the British film industry should conquer its own market before pursuing an aggressive export policy.[7] On the other hand, there was considerable debate about the costs of British films and whether exportation implied high budgets and special distribution tactics.

Whether the British government had a role to play in supporting the domestic industry beyond quota protectionism was also at the heart of many official discussions. The 1938 Cinematograph Films Act established the Cinematograph Films Council (CFC), a body charged with reporting to the Board of Trade on the progress of the British film industry. In 1940 a CFC subcommittee report published figures relating to the costs and revenues of sixty-one British films produced between 1 January 1937 and 30 June 1938. The report showed that the most expensive films, costing over £75,000 (which was not that high in relation to the cost of the average Hollywood film), derived 41 per cent of their net receipts from overseas. The subcommittee remarked that 'it is obvious that the manufacture of products which are capable of furnishing foreign exchange upon this scale should be fostered'.[8] Such opinion was taken seriously and film exports were a notable feature of subsequent official dealings with Hollywood. The 1948 Anglo-American Film Agreement, for example, which settled the Dalton Duty dispute, permitted American companies to take no more than $17 million out of the United Kingdom in respect of the earnings of their films in the United Kingdom, plus dollars equivalent to the earnings of British films in America.[9] The ideals of reciprocity therefore persisted into the 1940s in the face of Hollywood's intense resentment of quota protectionism.

Although the fortunes of British films abroad during this turbulent decade have received some academic attention, most notably from Murphy (1983), Macnab (1993), Swann (2000) and Ryall (2001), it is the intention of this chapter to provide detail on aspects which deserve closer analysis. Rank's attempt to gain access to the American market gave film exports a high profile, resulting in some celebrated examples, including *In Which We Serve* (1942), *The Seventh Veil* (1945), *Brief Encounter* (1945), *Henry V* (US release, 1946), *Caesar and Cleopatra* (1946), *Hamlet* (1948) and *The Red Shoes* (1948). Their relative success in a highly competitive market was supported by critical commentary, as evidenced by a nationwide survey conducted by *Film Daily* and sent out to press reviewers and radio film commentators. The survey revealed that 53 per cent of respondents considered that their local audiences would welcome foreign films, particularly British films. One critic from Mobile, Alabama, for example, commented: 'I don't believe many Mobilians enjoy foreign pictures. However, the last few British films that have played here have received favourable comment. I think their stories far better than those Hollywood uses, the acting more sincere, and the background music is generally beautiful'.[10] The two films most frequently mentioned, *The Seventh Veil* and *Henry V,* reflect a split between popular melodrama and 'highbrow' taste. While it is commonly assumed that most British films were marketed as 'highbrow' product for small, elitist, city-based audiences (see Swann, 2000: 29–30), it is clear that the patterns of distribution and reception were more complex. This suggests that American audiences were exposed to a variety of British films and reacted to them in interesting ways. These trends and perhaps surprise successes will be examined in the following case studies.

The Second World War

During the early years of the war, there was considerable disruption to British studios and cinemas. Despite this the industry produced an average of sixty feature films a year, a third of the annual average output of the 1930s (Political and Economic Planning, 1952: 83). The wartime films were popular and highly regarded. Just after the war, Samuel Goldwyn commented that at last British films had found a distinctive style of their own, 'broader and more international' than Hollywood's films and expressive of 'the intimate universality of everyday living'.[11] The British film industry and Hollywood benefited from a rise in cinema attendance in both countries, a 'boom' period for the major studios that reached a peak in 1945–46 (Schatz, 1997: 290). A number of British films were well received by American critics and, on occasion, held their own against Hollywood's in the US market (Schatz, 1997: 156). In particular these included films with wartime themes such as *The Invaders/49th Parallel* (1941), *One of Our Aircraft is Missing* (1941), *In Which We Serve, The Immortal Batallion/The Way Ahead* (1944) and *Johnny in the Clouds/The Way to the Stars* (1945).[12] Three British films – *Brief Encounter, Stairway to Heaven/A Matter of Life and Death* (1946) and *Henry V* – were in the *New York Times* list of top ten features of 1946. *Henry V* was the runner-up to *The Best Years of Our Lives* (1946) as best film. The National Board of Review voted *In Which We Serve* as best English language film of 1942 and featured other British films in its lists, even those such as *Colonel Blimp/The Life and Death of Colonel Blimp* (US release, 1945), which were not commercial successes (Schatz, 1997: 244). This points to a critical appreciation of British films which translated into healthy box-office revenue in several cases, most notably *In Which We Serve* (US gross, $1,516,069), *Henry V* (US gross, $1,254,788) and *Caesar and Cleopatra* (1946: US gross, $1,363,371).[13] In September 1946, *Variety* reported that while *The Seventh Veil* had originally been cast as a 'sleeper', it went on to do very well at the box-office. Similarly, while *Brief Encounter* had originally been intended for art-house exhibition, the film did good general business after an astute exploitation campaign by the Prestige unit at Universal.[14] It would be erroneous to claim that Hollywood's domination was seriously threatened, but British films had made headway in America in terms of critical acclaim and relative box-office profits. At the end of the war, political goodwill, represented by Anglo-American military cooperation and America's commitment to post-war economic assistance for European recovery, was reflected in an enhanced appreciation of British films.

Of all the wartime successes, *In Which We Serve* accords closely with Goldwyn's description of British films that conveyed 'the intimate universality of everyday living'. An elaborate instance of wartime propaganda, the film did excellent business in both countries as well as receiving high critical praise. George Freedley of the *New York Morning Telegraph* emphasized its political context:

> It is my earnest desire to persuade as many people as possible to see this film, not only because it is a magnificent venture in motion picture making, but because it will do as much as anything to cement the solidarity which exists in the United Nations and so quicken the progress of the war.[15]

In Which We Serve was marketed and distributed by United Artists, the company that paid £100,000 in advance of its American release.[16] The press book material stresses its 'universal appeal' to 'every class and age in society', and draws on the idea of the Anglo-American 'special relationship' as allies against fascism.[17] Of particular appeal to Americans who objected to the British class system was the film's suggestion that class conflict had been subsumed by the war effort, projecting an image of a united, more democratic, community at war. The film's 'realism' is also singled out in the press book as a positive quality, even to the extent of remarking that Celia Johnson (Mrs Kinross, wife of Captain Kinross, played by Noël Coward) 'is a wife and mother in real life' and that John Mills, who plays a sailor, had experience of life in the services (the army). Another realistic detail that features prominently in the advertising material is the rigours of filming the 'story' of the ship, HMS Torrin. As the ship sinks after being bombed in a battle off Crete, the water in which the survivors swim is covered with patches of oil and floating wreckage. The press book recounts how the actors had to endure this experience, made realistic by the use of castor oil and other ingredients, their bodies protected by a layer of Vaseline. As actors they are therefore invested with a sense of courage and fearlessness which equates them with the fictional characters they play in the film. UA's press book included ideas for radio campaigns including interviews with British or American officers to talk about 'the splendid morale in both British and American navies'. Another recommendation was for showmen all over America to suggest a public holiday, a 'United Nations Naval Day', to their city councils for the purpose of 'giving a lift to war-time morale based on the memorable example of the British fighting men and their families shown in *In Which We Serve*'. Special screenings with British consuls in attendance were also suggested as good publicity. The poster exploited the film's romantic angles, illustrated with the caption: 'Throbbing emotion of a million wartime romances!' The timing of its release was also important, just over a year after America entered the war and when allied cooperation against fascism was accelerating. On 21 December 1942, *Life* magazine declared it movie of the week together with a lavish picture spread and reports of Noël Coward entertaining American servicemen in London.

Despite the intensity of the 'special relationship', the not always congruent dynamics of Anglo-American film relations were nevertheless in the background. At the beginning of the war, the British government was concerned about conserving dollar reserves, and one of the biggest drains was the large amount – reported as equivalent to £6 to 10 million – remitted by American companies in respect of their films screened in British cinemas (Street, 1997: 11). From 1940–42, restrictions were placed on the amount of dollars that companies could transfer to the United States, forcing them to retain 'blocked funds' in Britain while at the same time export the customary number of films to Britain. As an incentive to overseas distribution, it was stipulated that American companies' quota requirements could be honoured by purchasing the foreign rights to British films. A much-publicized instance of this strategy was David Selznick and Samuel Goldwyn's purchase of the American rights for UA to British National's feature film *Contraband* (1940) for £45,000.[18] Sidney Bernstein was also able to strike a deal with the American majors whereby each undertook to distribute at least one British feature film and two shorts per year.[19] A tough stance could not, however, be maintained after America entered the war in December 1941, and from October 1942 the majors were permitted to remit all their earnings in dollars back to the United States. This relaxation of restrictions occurred at the time *In Which We Serve* was being heralded as the cinematic embodiment of Anglo-American naval cooperation.

The quota was severely criticized by American film producers who feared that after the war its restrictions would be intensified. Nathan Golden, Chief of the Motion Picture Division of the US Department of Commerce, was opposed to quotas and currency restrictions that necessitated American companies producing 'British' films.[20] Charges made by British producers that their films were discriminated against in America were rebuffed by the MPAA and reported to the US State Department. The department's Office of International Trade insisted that 'the United States market is completely free of any restrictions in respect of the entry and exhibition of foreign films'. Success stories were listed, including *In Which We Serve, Henry V* and *Caesar and Cleopatra*, leading to the conclusion that British films had made 'impressive progress' in the American market, 1942–46.[21] As in the 1930s, the desire to protect American interests in Britain influenced the extent of goodwill that was extended to British films. This is not to argue that American opinion was insincere, but to recognize the degree of self-interest that inevitably crept into the debate.

Rank, United Artists and *Henry V*

UA continued to demonstrate an interest in distributing British films, and after Korda's stock was sold in 1944, transferred its allegiance to Rank. Rank was the most powerful British film company and during the war made plans to pursue assertive export policies in peacetime. Rank did not take Korda's place as a partner in UA but secured the expertise of Arthur Kelly and Theodor Carr, two former UA employees, in the establishment of Eagle-Lion Films, a worldwide distribution venture that was in operation until 1951 (Balio, 1976: 200

and Balio, 1987: 17–39). Rank was also keen to make deals with experienced distributors, and to this end UA obtained the domestic distribution rights in 1944 for six of Rank's top films: *Mr Emmanuel* (1944), *Colonel Blimp, Johnny in the Clouds, Blithe Spirit* (1945), *Caesar and Cleopatra* and *Henry V*.[22] UA had a good reputation for distributing and publicizing British films. *Caesar and Cleopatra* and *Henry V* made the greatest impact, but it appears that the company seriously miscalculated in the case of *Colonel Blimp,* causing Rank to complain to the US Federal Trade Commission about UA's handling of the film.

Colonel Blimp was first reviewed by the American press on its British release in 1943. Reaction was generally favourable with reservations about its longer than average feature length. Perhaps as a reaction to these perceptions, UA did not release the film in the United States until March 1945, arguably too late to capitalize on its wartime message (Chapman, 1995: 46). It is important to note, however, that the distribution deal with UA took place in September 1944, making the release delay only six months. The film was cut from 163 to 148 minutes and, instead of being aimed at 'class audiences', was inappropriately marketed for a mass clientele. As Jay E. Gordon remarked in a study of motion picture advertising in 1951, *Colonel Blimp* was pitched erroneously with serious box-office consequences (it grossed $275,472 in rentals for UA in the United States):

> Instead of leaning heavily on the art of David Low, the cartoonist who created Colonel Blimp and made him Britain's favourite, those responsible for advertising this picture in America chose to high-light all the posters and materials with a bosomy girl in a suggestive pose. The people who paid to see what was advertised were disappointed, for many were not of a temperament to enjoy the good colonel; but, more's the pity, the people who could have enjoyed *Colonel Blimp* were repelled by the advertising, and did not venture into the theatre.[23]

Indeed, the poster showed Colonel Blimp in a lecherous pose, creating an expectation of titillating farce that the film did not deliver. While it was common for Hollywood to highlight any film's romantic angles, in this case the decision to invest the film with a bawdy sentiment was clearly misguided. It is likely that this experience alienated Rank from UA and was instrumental in ending their association towards the end of 1945, with the exception of films already committed to UA including *Caesar and Cleopatra* and *Henry V.* Rank had no reason however to complain about UA's handling of these two films. The decision to distribute via Universal was also likely to have been determined by Rank's part ownership of the company and the need to concentrate product in the hands of a distributor that was free from the internal squabbles that dogged UA. Although it did not own cinema circuits, Universal appeared to be a promising partner at the end of the war, announcing a profit of $3 million for the year ending July 1945. Rank announced an American distribution contract with Universal in the summer of 1945, and news of their collaborative venture, United World Pictures, followed on its heels in December, after the problematic release of *Colonel Blimp* but prior to the contrasting success of *Henry V* and *Caesar and Cleopatra*.[24]

While the release of *Henry V* has been criticized by Swann (2000: 34) as being elitist and aimed only at academics, an examination of UA's 'roadshow' campaign reveals the astute and detailed planning that went into the film's American distribution, resulting in considerable profits and enhancing the reputation of British films.[25] It also created an instructive precedent for Universal's later successful marketing campaign for *Hamlet* (1948). *Henry V* was first released in America on 3 April 1946 at the Esquire Theatre, Boston, and then in Los Angeles, Baltimore and Chicago. The New York première followed in June at the New York City Centre where it played for forty-six weeks, the longest Broadway run of any British film. It was distributed throughout the United States for three years, won numerous awards and was one of UA's most successful films as the fourth highest grosser out of twenty films first released in 1946.[26]

Henry V had been released in London in November 1944, but the first evidence of planning for UA's American distribution was nearly a year later in an October 1945 memorandum from Jock Lawrence of the Lawrence Organization, Rank's publicity representative in New York, to Harold Auten of UA's Home Office in New York.[27] The details of the roadshow release were not yet in evidence, but there was a sense that the film would need careful treatment: 'playing down Shakespeare' but highlighting the film's colourful spectacle, the Battle of Agincourt, Laurence Olivier and the romance angle (Plate 9). Olivier was known to American audiences since he starred in several successful Hollywood films including *Wuthering Heights* (1939), *Rebecca* (1939), *Pride and Prejudice* (1940) and Korda's *That Hamilton Woman* (1941). At that point Lawrence considered that *Henry V*'s British nationality should be a major selling point: 'It is not a Hollywood film and should not be viewed in comparison to Hollywood films, in my opinion. The cast is perhaps the greatest ever assembled in the history of British films. In America, it means little so its importance comes from use of the British angle'. Interestingly, Auten annotated this comment in the margin with a caution: 'Play down. Art is international', implying some concern about identifying a film too closely with a particular nationality. How to persuade those who were ignorant of Shakespeare to see the film was a major point of discussion, indicating that general release was on the cards at this early point. A follow-up memorandum listed the 'pros' and 'cons', this time including Shakespeare as a positive element but continuing with the perceived problems over the film's nationality:

Pros

1. It is Shakespeare.
2. It has sex interest.
3. It is new and 'different'.
4. It has a musical score.
5. It is entirely non-controversial and can be shown anywhere, at any time, to any audience.
6. It cost a great deal of money.

Cons

1. It is British.
   It is historical – and British History!
3. Its theme is 'Good Old England'.
4. Its difficult dialogue.
5. Its 'highbrow' connotation.[28]

The latter points were explained in terms of anti-British feeling outside metropolitan centres, suggesting that a foreword might be added to emphasize the Anglo-American 'special relationship': 'This picture belongs to America as much as to Great Britain, for it is the story of a common ancestor and a common heritage'. In addition, it was feared that Midwestern towns might object to an overt expression of British patriotism and history: 'Don't overlook the fact that it was in Chicago, Illinois, that Mayor Thompson took it upon himself to fight King George V', demanding that 'all history books which had any reference to England in them be withdrawn from all schools'. To offset the difficult dialogue, UA was considering making it 'intelligible to the average American', presumably by dubbing. Likewise, to prevent audiences being alienated by the film's 'highbrow' connotations, the memorandum recommended that publicity should feature comic strips of Shakespeare's plays and promote the adoption of *Henry V* as a high-school set text. The publicity executives were clearly perplexed about how to market the film, and it was some months before the eventual strategy was devised, a strategy that depended less on general release and more on selective roadshow programming aimed primarily at schools and the educated audience. Ironically, despite this slant, the film managed to do well in unexpected locations, occasionally 'crossing over' from its anticipated audience to non-metropolitan centres.

The roadshow devised by Paul Lazarus, UA's advertising and publicity chief, in collaboration with Harold Auten, proceeded according to the following content and pattern.[29] A roadshow, normally associated with 'prestige' films, involved the distributor renting or leasing theatres in selected locations, undertaking the entire mechanics of exhibition, including advertising and projection. Theatres were rented on a 'four wall' basis, which involved UA paying the owner a flat fee for taking over the theatre and its staff, paying for advertising and tickets in exchange for retaining the entire box-office revenue. UA's branch managers arranged first-run bookings for *Henry V* in theatres in or near the centre of a town or city, preferably with a relatively small seating capacity and on the 'worst' days of the week. Weekends were avoided, and the film played for only a few days at a time, targeted primarily at colleges and high schools. The aim was to make a short, sharp impact, as explained in the instruction notes provided by UA's head office to branch managers: 'Always remember it is far better to have a short successful engagement – go out in a blaze of glory – and return again to the theatre at a later date "By Popular Demand" – rather than to "die" through overestimating the playing time'.[30] As far as possible, tickets were sold in advance with a sliding scale of prices; discounts were available for students and school groups. Once a booking had been made, local schools were contacted, group bookings encouraged, and local newspapers and radio stations were provided with advertising copy and features. As well as schools, UA agents were advised to target other potentially receptive groups including church and service clubs and Roman Catholics. Advertising material was to be placed with radio and record dealers (RCA Victor released a record of the original musical score with William Walton conducting the London Symphony Orchestra), bookshops, libraries and museums.[31] The Theatre Guild's decision to sponsor *Henry V* by allowing UA access to its subscription lists in twenty cities for the dissemination of advertising material was an unprecedented and prestigious association.

As the roadshow progressed, the 'four wall' policy was replaced with percentage contracts, splitting the costs and revenues with the theatre owner, typically at a 60:40 per cent ratio. An agent from UA would accompany the film to each venue and supervise its publicity and exhibition, moving on to the next city when the run had finished. As many as twenty-five agents were thus employed in the early stages of the roadshow, 'college men who are thoroughly conversant with the technique of the picture as well as the methods of getting the greatest number of potential *Henry* patrons into the theatre'.[32] All advertising materials were generated from UA's head office including posters, window displays and pamphlets. Atypically, there was no press book for *Henry V*, emphasizing its 'special' status. Fearing that individual theatre managers could not be trusted to promote *Henry V* in a consistent or appropriate manner, UA was determined to keep total control of the process. As Auten explained to C. K. Olson, a US branch manager in Denver, Colorado:

> It is absolutely suicidal for us to allow any local manager of any theatre to handle *Henry V* however good and excellent that man may be for the good reason that our *Henry* is a peculiar bird and requires an expert to handle same.[33]

The final phase of the roadshow started in October 1948 and was less elaborate. Agents no longer accompanied the film to each particular engagement but were responsible for overseeing the progress of several venues simultaneously. Prices were reduced, and UA split the expenses and profits with the theatre on a 50:50 basis.

When the film was released, it was accompanied by a plethora of enthusiastic reviews. *Variety*'s reviewer praised UA's discriminating release strategy, an opinion endorsed by the exhibitor-biased *Motion Picture Herald*.[34] While its status as 'filmed Shakespeare' was acknowledged, as well as the fact that this might make *Henry V* difficult for some audiences to understand, the film's cinematic qualities featured in many reviews including use of Technicolor; the Battle of Agincourt sequence (compared to Eisenstein's work by the *LA Times*); use of costume and scenery; 'sensuous composition' (*New York Times*) and 'action' scenes.[35] Several reviews declared that it was superior to a Hollywood production, as the *New Yorker* wryly observed, 'Even the horses are more tastefully dressed than most of the girls in a Hollywood spectacle'.[36] Unsurprisingly, Anglophile Bosley Crowther wrote a very positive review in the *New York Times,* declaring Olivier's film to be 'a stunningly brilliant and intriguing screen spectacle'.[37] Reported in many newspapers, the New York première was a celebrity event attended by Laurence Olivier, Vivien Leigh and guests from the Old Vic Company, as well as political figures including Sir Alexander Cadogan and representatives from the United Nations. The feature was accompanied by a seventeen-minute Technicolor newsreel of the Victory parade in London, an exciting event in itself since it was only the second newsreel to have been made in Technicolor.[38] To accompany the film, UA sent out a simple four-page programme that stressed the play's cinematic potential ('it almost insists on motion picture treatment') and reproduced quotations from British reviews. While UA's advertising campaign for the film was not costly, in this way similarly effusive American press reports did much to encourage the impression that *Henry V* was essential viewing.

In the field, the efforts of UA's agents to promote the film all over the United States provides a fascinating and well-documented case study of the marketing of a British film.[39] Agents were required to report every forty-eight hours to Harold Auten on conditions and business, providing an insight into regional responses to *Henry V* as well as accounts of the problems encountered during the roadshow. Auten calculated that less than 5 per cent of the population in any one given situation would be interested in seeing *Henry V* and that UA could rely on 50 per cent of the enrolment of colleges and universities for sales.[40] Care was to be taken in choosing small theatres, but on several occasions the agents complained that the film had been booked by district managers at inappropriate venues. Milton Hale, an agent reporting to Auten from Klamath Falls, Oregon, for example, was amazed that a booking had been arranged at the Rainbow Theatre, 'a house that caters to nothing but Mexicans and Indians and plays westerns and third run'. He was so incensed that he transferred the booking to another theatre without official approval from UA's head office.[41] Similar complaints were made about 'lousy' theatres in San Bernando and Vallejo, California.[42] Having to negotiate favourable terms with circuits was necessary but led to disputes over pricing and advertising. Several of the Californian agents' reports describe conflicts with Fox-West Coast, a circuit that was permitted a 50:50 deal with UA (as opposed to the usual 60:40 arrangement). Fox-West Coast theatre managers assumed that UA's agents would do all the work to promote the film and were often unwilling to receive instructions from 'outsiders'. When they did lend a hand, they ignored the careful pre-publicity instructions and materials provided by UA, leading to incidents such as the erection of an inappropriately 'gaudy' banner that had to be removed by the UA agent.[43] Towards the end of 1947, Auten commented that such conflicts let down the campaign: 'During a period of twenty months we have played approximately three hundred engagements, and the only situations in which we have encountered any rebuff have been from the exhibitor himself and not the public'.[44]

Box-office reports showed that UA had been correct to target the film at a specific, educated audience. When the film opened in Boston, it played to full houses for several weeks and similarly good business was reported from Berkeley and Sacramento, California; New Canaan, Greenwich and Westport, Connecticut; and Westchester, New York. College towns were a sure bet, but occasionally the film did well in surprising locations. Alec Nyary, the agent in Dallas, reported to Auten, for example, that some Texans had supported the film in the unlikely venue of San Angelo:

> One day receipts in San Angelo are considered of record proportions for that little Chicago counterpart of Texas, noted for its juvenile delinquency and such. We will never know why the cowboys attended en

masse, though probably it had something to do with my stressing the horse opry (sic) aspects of our masterpiece in my press releases here.[45]

'Hundreds' of Chinese patrons were reported in Stockton, California, a town where many Chinese students lived who attended university at Berkeley or Stanford. On this occasion, the agent was able to question these audiences about their liking for the film. Many had seen it previously and were prepared to travel a considerable distance for a repeat viewing.[46] Encouraged by the full support of the local university, the patronage of students in Iowa netted profits for *Henry V* in the Midwest. Nevertheless, some areas were beyond the pale, particularly industrial towns such as Birmingham, Alabama, or parts of Florida, Colorado and Wyoming. Weather conditions – either a heatwave or snow and ice – could have an adverse affect on screenings, as did economic hardship that made the comparatively high admission price prohibitive for some areas. Some agents reported that schools and colleges in their areas were too poor to hire the film or that they did not own a movie projector.[47] By contrast, high profits were received from established art theatres such as the Tower in Oakland, California, that had a reputation for screening foreign films including *Rome, Open City, Brief Encounter* and *Blithe Spirit*.[48]

UA's success with *Henry V* was heralded as a breakthrough for British films, as significant a step forward as Korda's *The Private Life of Henry VIII* had been in the 1930s. When *Variety* surveyed exhibitors' attitudes towards foreign films in 1947, *Henry V* featured prominently as a significant booking all over the country. While this survey drew attention to the problems some exhibitors experienced with British films (mainly to do with difficult dialogue and accents), it confirmed that several films were gaining ground and that in some places British films were the only foreign product shown. New York was definitely the best outlet for foreign films. Of ninety-nine top theatres in greater New York over 50 per cent exhibited foreign films and ten of the thirty-two venues in midtown Manhattan, encompassing the important first-run theatres on Broadway, screened foreign films regularly. Some places welcomed British films with open arms, particularly Chicago, where *Henry V* ran for twenty-one weeks 'outlasting all other films for 1946 including the national top grosser, *The Belles of St Mary*'. Table 4.1 summarizes *Variety*'s results and comments, comprising a useful snapshot of opinion on British films in 1947.[49]

What is striking is that all of these films were produced under the auspices of the Rank Organization, that they were being shown and, in some cases, doing well. British films were able to take advantage of the fact that they could be exhibited at cinemas associated with foreign films yet at the same time not suffer from being stigmatized as 'other' (apart from the common complaint

Table 4.1 *Variety* Survey of British Films, 1947

Town/City	British Film	Comment
Boston	*Seventh Veil; Henry V; Stairway to Heaven*	Doing better all the time; 10 downtown stands out of 20 showing 1st run foreign films.
Buffalo	*Henry V*	Henry did well; British films more or less only foreign films shown; moderately favourable reaction.
Chicago	*Henry V*	British prestige films doing well high-calibre entertainment features.
Cincinnati	*Seventh Veil; Brief Encounter*	*Seventh Veil* played four weeks; *Brief Encounter* fared poorly; so-so returns for several British films.
Cleveland	*Henry V*	*Henry* the only foreign film to do well.
Denver		Exhibitors divided over British films.
Detroit	*Caesar and Cleopatra; Henry V; Brief Encounter*	All three films did top business; most foreign films difficult for audiences to understand.
Indianapolis	*The Man in Grey; Brief Encounter; Henry V*	James Mason popular; core audience for British films that could grow; *Brief Encounter* shown at first-run venue.
Kansas City	*Brief Encounter*	Foreign language films do better than British.
Los Angeles	*Seventh Veil*	Doing well; no competition for US films.

about diction and accents). While that set them up for comparison with Hollywood's films, it is clear from this survey that 'core' audiences existed, and that the best exhibition prospects lay in first-run 'downtown' venues rather than in local neighbourhoods. It also pointed to the sense in identifying an audience for British films and concentrating advertising and marketing campaigns accordingly.

UA's elaborate strategy for *Henry V* could not be taken as representative of how most British films were handled, but many believed that this was the key to a more sustained advancement for British films including Richard Griffith, assistant curator at the Museum of Modern Art, New York, who wrote a series of articles on British films in the American market for *Sight and Sound*, 1949–50.[50] Griffith believed that the success of UA's roadshow strategy proved that the key to profits lay in small, unambitious openings. As well as *Henry V*,

Table 4.1 *Continued*

Town/City	British Film	Comment
Milwaukee	*Caesar and Cleopatra*	Foreign language films do better; *Caesar* going splendidly until storm cut business
Minneapolis	*Brief Encounter; Wicked Lady; Bedelia*	Good box-office; no shying away from foreign films.
Omaha		British films more or less only foreign films shown; friendly press attitude.
Philadelphia	*Stairway to Heaven*	James Mason popular; British films more or less only foreign films shown; better as first-run shows than in neighourhoods.
Pittsburgh	*Stairway to Heaven; Seventh Veil; Caesar and Cleopatra; Henry V*	Indifferent results; not much prospect in neighbourhoods; tough for foreign films.
Seattle	*Wicked Lady; Brief Encounter*	*Wicked Lady* a "slow take"
San Francisco	*Henry V*	Good market for foreign films.
St Louis		Problems with diction; difficult for foreign films; conservative area.
Washington, DC	*Caesar and Cleopatra*	Did well midtown

he cited *Brief Encounter, I Know Where I'm Going* (1945), *Hamlet* and *The Red Shoes* as examples of films that had been released selectively and then attracted a wider audience. While there is sense in this argument, his antipathy to big-budget spectaculars appears to have influenced his judgement about *Caesar and Cleopatra*, a film released on a general basis whose returns, Griffith claimed, 'dropped like a falling barometer' after the big opening, and when word of mouth advertising gave it a reputation as a poor imitation of a Cecil B. DeMille picture.[51] Actually, *Caesar and Cleopatra* earned more than *Henry V*, garnering $1,363,371 in US rentals for UA, the third-highest grosser of 1946. Ironically, then, UA's greatest successes with British films were the result of completely different release strategies.

Caesar and Cleopatra was somewhat controversial because of its cost (£1,250,000), ambition and spectacle (Drazin, 1998: 230). While in their different ways *Henry V* and *Brief Encounter* demonstrated generic elements of 'Britishness', *Caesar and Cleopatra* bore closer resemblance to Hollywood's epics. The cast was headed by Claude Rains and Vivien Leigh, stars who were not American but best known for their performances in Hollywood films. *Variety*'s reviewer considered that high production values swamped a vague story and that the 'spearhead' of Rank's American campaign was a disappointment.[52] On the other hand, Bosley Crowther of the *New York Times* appreciated the productive combination of director Gabriel Pascal and writer George Bernard Shaw in 'making a conventional drama both intellectual and spectacular'.[53] UA's strategy was 'to hit 116 spots simultaneously' and reports of its progress throughout the United States demonstrate that Griffith's 'falling barometer' analogy was not an accurate reflection of its career.[54] In September 1946, *Variety* reported that 'British Pix Finally Click in the US', recording how *Caesar and Cleopatra* played approximately three hundred engagements in twenty-three days and broke many house records, out-performing successful Hollywood films such as *The Kid from Brooklyn* (1946) at the Astor Theatre, New York. *Variety* concluded, 'the film is doing strong business throughout the country and is going over particularly big in Loew houses outside New York'.[55] Although the film was more successful in the United States than in Britain, the problem for Rank was that UA retained 47 per cent of the rentals and, combined with the film's high cost, did not benefit much from its overseas earnings. *Variety* later commented on its high record of bookings but poor rate of return to Rank: '*Caesar and Cleopatra* . . . was good for $2 million in rentals but proved of minor help to dollar-starved Britain. It's estimated that only $500,000 from *Caesar* reached England after Technicolor print costs, distribution fees and a whacking $500,000 and more for advertising expenses were deducted. *Caesar* has copped top bookings to date, a total of 10,000 throughout the country'.[56] On balance, therefore, *Henry V* was more financially rewarding. Above all, it could play the card of British culture and its roadshow set a precedent that was followed by Rank's other American link, Universal-International.

Rank, Universal and *Hamlet*

Not only is it an attraction which will draw non-filmgoers from their caves, but it is a superior movie by even 'box-office' terms. Loaded with smouldering melodrama of a rich Shakespearean sort and pregnant with deep and burning passion, it is a film which will fascinate the modern version of the 'groundlings' as well as the heavy intellects. (Bosley Crowther, *New York Times*, Oct 1948)

Henry V provided a blueprint for the successful distribution of *Hamlet*. Universal-International (U-I) gave it the roadshow treatment and then a general release, proving Crowther's theory that it had the potential to transcend 'high-brow' appeal. *Hamlet* appeared in *Variety*'s anniversary list of top-grossing films with a record sum of $3,250,000 to date for a British film.[57] It grossed $738,572 alone at the Park Avenue Theatre, New York, where it played for sixty-six weeks until January 1950.[58] It was the first British film to win an Academy Award for Best Picture (of 1948), as well as a host of other awards and nominations.[59] Rank had been involved with Universal since 1936 and, as previously noted, formed United World Pictures with Universal. The company was established to offer British and American films to exhibitors in a package, an aim that was prevented by the outlawing of block-booking by the US Department of Justice in June 1946 (Murphy, 1984: 169). Such an arrangement might well have benefited British films which, as observed in the 1930s, often suffered from being isolated from the main cache of releases. In response, U-I was formed in 1946 as an amalgamation of Universal and International Pictures to accelerate 'prestige' production and effect reciprocal distribution terms. From that date, the US distribution of Rank's films was divided between Eagle-Lion and U-I, and the latter's acquisition of the rights for *Hamlet* represented U-I's more dominant status (Balio, 1987: 21).

Hamlet was accompanied on its roadshow by a special field staff supervised by Jefferson Livingston, a U-I publicist who had been employed by UA for the *Henry V* roadshow. Theatres were rented on a 'four wall' basis, and the field officer would generally supervise the film's first engagements, employ local staff to assist with publicity and advertising and then move on to the next venue. A special publicity unit was established at head office and a pre-publicity campaign was devised.[60] *Hamlet* opened in Boston in August 1948 and in New York the following month, playing to packed houses and greeted with rave reviews. It then proceeded on its roadshow to other key cities. Universal put a major effort into pre-publicity, organizing press screenings, radio interviews and preparing advertising material.[61] After the film was clearly a success in its first venues a special manual was written, 'Five easy steps to a successful *Hamlet* engagement', impressing on the field team the importance of extensive promotion: 'play up romance, adventure, spectacle . . . forget highbrow dignity'.[62] The 'highbrow' elements were not, however, neglected in the roadshow. Links with schools were fostered when letters were sent to educators, urging them to facilitate attendance at *Hamlet* for the good of their communities. High schools were also presented with library stills and clippings of reviews. Schools and colleges were given special rates and study guides were given out free. In some locations – for example, Los Angeles – people who had worked on the *Henry V* roadshow were employed as local experts.[63] While some field staff complained about the non-cooperation of Fox-West coast managers, a familiar cry from the experience of handling *Henry V,* on the whole the roadshow ran smoothly and resulted in extensive bookings.[64] Milton Hale, an ex-UA employee and *Henry V* roadshow expert, was interviewed on the radio about the popularity of *Hamlet.* He explained U-I's tactics, likening the pre-publicity and work of the field staff to the preparation for a legitimate stage production. According to Hale, the film's main patrons were 'discriminating' theatre-goers; school and college students; a large female following and, to some extent, the regular cinema-goer who appreciated it as 'entertainment'.[65]

After *Hamlet* won the Academy Award, Universal decided to offer it on general release at the end of 1949 and re-releases occurred on a regular basis into the 1950s. U-I capitalized on the Oscar success by launching a further advertising campaign for which it had prepared, prior to the announcement, in the hope that the film would win an award (Plate 27). Jock Lawrence, Rank's representative in New York, insisted that U-I paid for the heightened pre-Oscar campaign on the grounds that 'The British have not been conditioned to the Hollywood system of taking ads to praise one's own creative efforts. We have had express instructions from London that we may not participate in such Academy trade advertising'.[66] In keeping with this modest attitude, or perhaps not wishing to tempt fate, Laurence Olivier would not agree to be interviewed by Louella Parsons until the Oscar ceremony was over.[67] In a survey of post-Oscar takings, U-I's returns proved that the film experienced an extended lease of life after the announcement of the award.[68]

Unusually, in 1950 *Hamlet* was re-booked in New York's first-run circuit theatres at the same prices as the original run, which had lasted over a year.[69] Elsewhere, prices were reduced to normal rates and unusually profitable screenings were reported in neighbourhood theatres in New York.[70] For the general release, the promoters downplayed high cultural elements, emphasizing the film's appeal as 'The greatest ghost story of them all', advertised with an accompanying caption: 'Shrouded in mist, clad in rusty armor, a horrifying spectre stalks the great stone battlements of the ancient castle. Its one command is . . . kill . . . kill . . . KILL!'[71] Discussions of ghost/horror posters reveal that the general release was indeed aimed at a much wider audience than the art-house. The artwork of the ghost was debated at length, particularly the extent to which the ghost should be 'cadaverous' or 'spectral'. This detail was certainly not a trivial one for, as a member of the advertising team pointed out, the logic of the 'cadaverous' approach was that 'we wanted to hit as low as possible with this type of selling and not make the picture appear too imaginative and arty'.[72] Indeed, U-I was having to scale down its operations and forget specialized distribution. Despite the success of *Hamlet,* like the other Hollywood studios U-I's overall profits had turned to losses in the recession at the end of the 1940s (Schatz, 1997: 340). It is ironic that in this way *Hamlet* accompanied Universal in its journey towards the distribution of Hammer horror films in the 1950s, concentrating on low-budget productions and leaving prestige behind.

Rank, Eagle-Lion and *The Red Shoes*

In 1954 *The Red Shoes* was listed forty-third as an all-time top-grossing picture with record earnings for a British film of $5 million.[73] It is perhaps curious that of all Rank's productions this unusual film took flight. Powell and Pressburger's Technicolor melodrama about the conflict between love and ambition in the world of the ballet included a fifteen-minute ballet sequence and was longer than average feature length. There were few 'big names' in the cast. Moira Shearer, the female lead, was a ballerina from the Sadler's Wells Company who had never starred in a film before. Yet *The Red Shoes* was well reviewed, apart from some reservations about its length, melodramatic narrative and the ballet-within-the-film. Bosley Crowther hailed it as 'a visual and emotional comprehension of all the grace and rhythm and power of the ballet', whereas *Variety* doubted its appeal beyond a limited audience.[74] Some reviewers were perplexed by the 'Red Shoes' ballet, a sequence that eschewed conventional stage representation, utilizing many cinematic techniques to create an impressionistic link between the Hans Christian Anderson fairy tale on which it was based, and the personal dilemmas facing the film's central characters.[75] Others were inspired by the film to write ecstatic comments, for example, Cecelia Ager in the *New York Star,* described it as 'a bewitching production . . . utterly enchanting'.[76] Whatever the verdict, a survey of the many reviews it attracted shows that above all a climate of expectation was created to see something different and, possibly, exceptional.[77] The film's British nationality was not a major feature (although Rank was mentioned in many reviews) and with its international cast and continental locations could not be easily associated with any particular genre of British films. Powell and Pressburger were however known in the United States. Apart from the problems of *Colonel Blimp,* Powell and Pressburger's films were relatively popular, particularly *Stairway to Heaven* and *I Know Where I'm Going* (1945) which acquired a following in New York and other cities.[78]

The Red Shoes' narrative about the tempestuous world of a ballet company appeared to transcend national boundaries by tapping into a fast-growing culture and 'craze' among young American women for classical dance. This might seem puzzling, in view of the film's portrayal of the bitter conflicts within the company and its devastating verdict on the high personal price to be paid for the pursuit of art and ambition. Nevertheless, this core group of enthusiasts was targeted in the film's exploitation campaign. As the distributor of *The Red Shoes*, Eagle-Lion's press book recommended tie-ins with a range of merchandisers of shoes; records (Sir Thomas Beecham's recordings and Brian Easdale's score for 'The Red Shoes' ballet); jewellery; books; art materials (Degas reproductions) and flowers.

While *The Red Shoes* was not a historical comedy, a war film or Shakespeare, it gathered its reputation as 'unusual quality product' by being released selectively by Eagle-Lion on a roadshow basis (Balio, 1987: 34). Since Eagle-Lion distributed the lower end of Rank's films, it must be concluded that the company had no idea that the film would be so successful. While U-I was lavishing attention on *Hamlet*, Eagle-Lion decided that the only chance for *The Red Shoes* was to build up its reputation in key cities, appealing to an audience of ballet enthusiasts, schools and the art market which was expanding by the late 1940s.[79] As with *Hamlet*, Academy Awards success in 1948 (Best Color, Art Direction and Best Score) prompted the advertising department to design new posters that claimed, 'There has never been a motion picture like *The Red Shoes* – already seen by 10 million people!'[80] (Plate 26). This strategy paid off: by March 1949 *Variety* reported that it was 'showing remarkable building power', doing excellent business for Eagle-Lion, which as distributor retained 60 per cent of the rentals.[81] By the time distributing fees and advertising costs had been paid, Rank received less than half of the grosses, although the deal with Universal permitted Rank to hold up to $2 million in earnings from Universal's films in Britain as a recoupment of profits on *Hamlet* in the United States. A similar stipulation in the deal with Eagle-Lion gave Rank a further $1.2 million.[82]

Unfortunately, these examples of extraordinary success were not sufficient to carry Rank's entire production programme into profit. Information submitted by Rank to the Board of Trade on the earnings of films released during the period January 1947 to December 1949 confirm that *The Red Shoes* and *Hamlet* carried the company through a difficult period, saving Rank from showing substantial losses. Although both films had higher than average budgets (*The Red Shoes* cost £505,581 and *Hamlet* cost £572,530, while the average cost of the other thirty films for which Rank supplied information was £233,000), they resulted in high takings at home and abroad. The films that Rank recorded as yielding the highest amounts to the producer from American sales, after the deduction of commission and expenses, were *Great Expectations, The Man Within, The Red Shoes* and *Hamlet*.83

British Film Exports at the End of the 1940s

The 1940s was a difficult but significant decade for British film exports. As the case studies have shown, several key films managed to gain an unprecedented extent of American screentime. Yet adverse circumstances prevented a sustained advancement, circumstances that made the achievements of *Henry V, Hamlet* and *The Red Shoes* all the more remarkable. Two boycotts proved to be of key importance, although their impact should not be exaggerated. The spirit of Anglo-American collaboration that pervaded the war years receded during the 'Dalton Duty' dollar crisis and the American boycott of 1947–48. It became extremely difficult for Rank to sustain an export campaign that was predicated on 'prestige' films and at the same time accelerate general production in order to keep Britain's cinemas open. Eric Johnston, President of the MPAA, admitted that the bitterness of feeling caused by the duty had a negative impact on the reception of British films in America.[84] Soon after the dispute was settled, the Sons of Liberty, a radical Jewish organization, advocated a boycott of British films in protest against British policy in Palestine. While this did not have the same impact as the dollar crisis, there is some evidence that it exacerbated anti-British attitudes.[85] At the same time, it is striking how quickly ill-feeling was dissolved. Anglo-American film relations could see-saw at an incredible rate, at one moment hostile while the next, cordial and accommodating.

What is most important is that neither United Artists nor Universal were prejudiced by political conflicts. From an analysis of their records, both companies made great efforts to promote British films. Their distribution organizations involved hundreds of employees who tried to sell British films all over the United States. Coordinators' reports, submitted to Universal, confirm that at the grass roots 'field men' promoted British films and reported on the expansion of the art market into which many of them were absorbed. Some reports produced surprising results, for example, an account of the excellent box-office receipts for *Hungry Hill* (1946), a melodrama starring Margaret Lockwood, at the River Oaks Theatre, Houston, Texas.[86] They also provide evidence for the link between art cinema and the increasingly popular drive-in theatres that proliferated in the 1940s. A report written in May 1949 recorded that art films, including British, were being shown in areas that were previously resistant. Birmingham, Alabama, was such a territory, and the successful exhibition of British films in drive-in theatres persuaded theatre managers that an art market was worth cultivating. While this new attitude had to overcome 'bitterness toward anything English, which has been going on here in the South for generations', it was done out of commercial necessity, for 'the pictures get a respectable gross, and in a good many instances they exceed top American made pictures'.[87] As with the distribution of *Henry V* and *Hamlet,* a picture emerges of careful and astute handling of British films, their advertising campaigns and placement in relevant theatres.

The expansion of the art market was well underway by the end of the 1940s. Paradoxically, this could cause problems for British films. The success of *Hamlet* and *The Red Shoes* meant that many art cinemas were committed to playing those films for long runs, leaving little space for other British films.[88] But it also had the effect of causing Universal's sales team to consider how to promote British films for general release. A general release strategy was judged to be the most appropriate for the Ealing comedy *Tight Little Island/ Whiskey Galore!* (1948), a film that was distributed for 'classes' and 'masses'[89] (Plate 28). As a result good business was reported in Chicago, Houston, Minneapolis and New Haven, as well as in drive-in theatres.[90] When a branch manager in New Haven was unable to book *Tight Little Island* into a first-run venue in Hartford, he booked it into a subsequent-run house where it grossed more than the average Universal release at a first-run house.[91] In this way British films were able to attract audiences that became familiar with their differences, paving the way for the wider success of Ealing films in the 1950s.

The roadshow strategies and selective releasing policies used for *Brief Encounter, Henry V, Hamlet* and *The Red Shoes* were of key importance in building up enthusiasm for British films. They also increased the popularity of British stars. British names (Anna Neagle, James Mason, Margaret Lockwood, Phyllis Calvert, Stewart Granger, Laurence Olivier and Robert Donat) appeared in surveys of the 'top 120 stars' conducted throughout the 1940s by the Institute of Audience Research.[92] 'Core' audiences were targeted and many non-cinema-goers were attracted. On the other hand, although they were more of a gamble, films on general release, including *Caesar and Cleopatra,* could also make profits. Publicity and advertising departments were attuned to marketing British films for both specialized and general audiences. As the campaign for *Hamlet* demonstrated, the same film could be presented either as 'highbrow' culture or as an exciting ghost story: same film, different audience. This reveals that film companies were becoming attuned to the fracturing of the cinema audience, recognizing the existence of different 'taste publics' and marketing a film accordingly.

Film reviews often set the tone of a campaign, recommending how and to whom it should be pitched. *Variety* noted a direct correlation between the box-office success of foreign films and their reviews: 'American critics . . . now have the actual life-or-death say on British and foreign imports. . . . In key cities, it's the crix, first and last, who call the tune'.[93] The opinion of the New

York and film trade press was influential since reviews were quoted in press books, included in publicity material and often used as templates for local reviewers who had been unable to see the film. This was certainly the case with *Henry V* and *Hamlet*. While both *Caesar and Cleopatra* and *The Red Shoes* were subject to a degree of criticism, on the whole their good critical reception created a climate of anticipation. Their different novelty values – expense and spectacle for *Caesar and Cleopatra* and the ballet sequence in *The Red Shoes* – gave them a particular, if not controversial, cachet. While *Brief Encounter* was well reviewed by the New York press, it was also praised by *Variety* and *Motion Picture Herald*, trade papers that were most attuned to box-office potential. *Variety* did not consider its British theme and actors a barrier to American reception, stating that it was 'a notable addition to the growing list of British-made features qualified to appeal to world markets'.[94] Noël Coward's name featured prominently on the posters that were annotated with the caption: 'A story of the most precious moments in a woman's life. It could happen to you!'[95] (Plate 25). This aspect – realism – was also foregrounded in reviews that commented on the film's sensitive depiction of extramarital temptation. In this way a consensus emerged about the film's merits that linked it with Coward's previous work, particularly the realism of *In Which We Serve*, giving melodrama a respectable reputation.

British melodramas of a more 'lowbrow' nature had a more difficult time with critics and at the box-office. As we shall see in Chapter 5, *The Wicked Lady* (1945) caused considerable controversy with the censors. Despite its risqué reputation the majority of critics were not impressed. *Variety* accused it of distorting British history in a way more often associated with Hollywood's films, while Jack D. Grant of the *Reporter* lambasted it as 'an over-stuffed bore. J. Arthur Rank cannot hope to win and influence friendly American audiences with British product so dull and limping'.[96] On the other hand, the reviewer in *Film Daily* considered that the settings and costumes bore 'the authenticity of scholarly research. . . . It is ribald, clever and has unusual wallops. Mason has superb moments on the scaffold and how the femmes will go for his interpretation of the brazen highwayman'.[97] This perhaps confused critical reception was reflected in its mediocre box-office. This is also the case with *Bedelia* (1946), a British attempt at the *film noir* genre that was criticized in *Variety*: 'Its appeal is for femmes, but aside from select situations its fate will be the duals. Margaret Lockwood's marquee magnetism isn't sufficient to carry it, and the picture won't evoke press peans [sic] nor glowing word-of-mouth'.[98] Once again, for every bad review a much better one can be found, for example *Film Daily* described *Bedelia* as 'a cleverly built up crime and punishment drama with a fresh twist. Ably played, it stacks up as a good bet'.[99] Similarly, *Box-Office* considered it to be 'entirely deserving of favourable comparison with its Hollywood counterparts'.[100]

The most successful melodrama, however, was *The Seventh Veil*, not produced by Gainsborough but by Sydney Box with the Theatrecraft/Ortus company. More than any other film, it made James Mason a recognized star in the United States and did better box-office business than any other British melodrama.[101] Although the film cost £92,000 to produce, by February 1948 worldwide sales grossed £750,000 and box-office receipts exceeded £2 million.[102] Indeed, Marcia Landy recalls an enthusiastic reception for Mason from critics and audiences in Cleveland, Ohio (Landy, 2000: 67). Mason featured regularly in research reports on the top 120 film stars produced by the Audience Research Institute. His 'Marquee Value', as calculated by surveys of principal audience groups throughout the 1940s, showed a consistent improvement. According to the same registers, in 1948 Stewart Granger's star rating increased.[103] This shows that as well as the 'high' cultural values of films such as *Henry V,* films operating outside that milieu could also do well. They were, however, harder to place and market than films with an obvious appeal to arthouse audiences. Since most British films were destined for exhibition in art theatres it was easier, for example, for a film such as *Brief Encounter* to fit into that niche than the bawdier approach to melodrama as represented by films such as *The Man in Grey* (1943; Plate 22) or *The Wicked Lady.* Against the expectation of 'high class' presentation they were often interpreted by reviewers as poor relations to the 'prestige' films such as *Hamlet.*

I have argued that the film reviewing process was an integral aspect of the perception and reception of British films. On the whole, the positive reception given to many British films increased their chances as 'bookable' options as well as their status as marketable and appealing texts. This was particularly crucial in the 1940s because of the American film industry's own difficulties from 1947 onwards, during the recession when there was a product shortage. British films looked to obtain more effective US distribution during a period when a market – the growth of art cinemas – was opening up for them and when the Hollywood majors' monopoly over exhibition was challenged by the Paramount antitrust case of 1948 that forced the studios to 'divorce' their theatre circuits (Schatz, 1997: 4). With block-booking also outlawed, in theory this created greater opportunities for British films. Despite the volatile nature of Anglo-American film relations, major deals were still being announced. In 1948 Alexander Korda, for example, obtained an advance of $1.5 million in respect of future American earnings of *Anna Karenina* (1947), *Mine Own Executioner* (1947) and *An Ideal Husband* (1947).[104] The 'blocking' of dollars in Britain, an integral feature of the Anglo-American Film Agreements 1948–

50, assumed that as well as producing in Britain, the Hollywood studios would also purchase the US distribution rights of British films. Therefore, despite the turbulent crises and conflicts that beset Anglo-American film relations, and the varied performance of British films at the American box-office, by the end of the decade there were grounds for optimism about the future of British film exports.

Notes

1. *Kinematograph Weekly,* 6 Mar 1947. In fact they earned $5.8 million in 1947, $1.4 million of which was remitted to British producers after distribution and advertising costs had been deducted. See Public Record Office, BT 64/2370, notes of a meeting between Eric Johnston and Harold Wilson, 3 Mar 1948.
2. *Kinematograph Weekly,* 14 Sept 1944 and 6 Dec 1945.
3. *Kinematograph Weekly,* 19 June 1947.
4. American companies boycotted the British market when the British government imposed a 75 per cent *ad valorem* duty on American films from August 1947. The duty was intended to offset Britain's acute dollar shortage. Rank attempted to fill the resulting product shortage, and the dispute was settled by the March 1948 Anglo-American Film Agreement which devised a 'blocked earnings' solution. See Street, 1997: 14–15.
5. *Kinematograph Weekly,* 10 Nov 1949.
6. *Kinematograph Weekly,* 8 Dec 1949 for full details of Plant report and trade commentary.
7. *Kinematograph Weekly,* 25 Nov 1943.
8. Public Record Office, Kew Gardens, London: BT 64/61/17793.
9. Although, since these amounts had to be divided up among the majors, there was little incentive to push British films in the United States as a source of additional dollar remittance. Universal therefore opted out of the 'B' pool agreement which was an adjunct to the main agreement. It stipulated that in addition to the $17 million, companies could remit additional monies equal to the amount of dollars earned by British films in the United States (*Kinematograph Weekly,* 1 Sept 1949). In the 1950 Anglo-American Film Agreement the 'B' Pool was abolished, but provision was made for the purchase of overseas distribution rights of British films on a different basis.
10. *Film Daily* survey reported in *Sight and Sound,* vol. 15, no. 60, Winter 1946–47.
11. Samuel Goldwyn, quoted in H. H. Wollenberg, 'British films overseas' in *Sight and Sound,* vol. 15, no. 60, Winter 1946–47.
12. Caution should be taken over the box-office performances of these films. UA grosses, for example, report poor rentals for *Johnny in the Clouds* even though it was highly regarded by the critics and had an Anglo-American theme.
13. UA grosses. *Variety* reported the first-run grosses of *Caesar and Cleopatra* to be higher at $2 million (figures reported in *Film Industry,* vol. 1, no. 5, Nov 1946: 11). Similarly, a document in the UA collection claims that *Henry V* grossed over $3 million. See Harold Auten, UA head office to all salesmen, 2 Sept 1948, UA Archive, State Historical Society, Madison, 99 AN/90-1-2.
14. *Variety,* 11 Sept 1946: 27 and 19 Feb 1947: 19.
15. *New York Morning Telegraph,* 18 Jan 1943.
16. This figure is given by Filippo Del Giudice in correspondence with the Board of Trade, April 1948 in BT 64/2366 (Public Record Office).
17. *In Which We Serve* press book, New York Public Library.
18. *Kinematograph Weekly,* 23 May 1940 and 30 May 1940.

19. *Sight and Sound,* Dec 1949: 34.
20. *Kinematograph Weekly,* 6 Jan 1944.
21. Gerald Mayer, International Division of MPAA to Clair Wilcox, Office of International Trade, US State Department, 28 Mar 1947. National Archives, Washington D.C., 841.4061.MP/3-2847.
22. *Kinematograph Weekly,* 14 Sept 1944.
23. Jay E. Gordon, 'There's really no business like show business' in *Quarterly of Film, Radio and Television* (formerly *Hollywood Quarterly*), vol. 6, no. 2, Winter 1951: 180.
24. *Variety,* 11 July 1945: 3; *Kinematograph Weekly,* 1 Nov 1945 and 6 Dec 1945. Further details of Rank and Universal will follow in the discussion of the US release of *Hamlet.*
25. The following analysis is based on the *Henry V* Road Show File, 1946–49, US Mss 99AN, 9D, four boxes of material held at the UA archive, State Historical Society, Madison, Wisconsin, hereafter referred to as HVRSF.
26. The film was declared best film of 1946 by the National Board of Review; Olivier won the top acting award of 1946 from the New York Film Critics' Circle. In the Academy Awards, *Henry V* was nominated as Best Picture and nominations were also received by William Walton, Olivier and for art direction. At the Oscar ceremony *Henry V* received a special award.
27. Lawrence to Auten, 26 Oct 1945; HVRSF, 99 AN/9D-1-3.
28. HVRSF, 99 AN/9D-1-3; General Policies, October 1946–Feb 1949.
29. *Variety,* 10 May 1948: 3 and see description of HVRSF in UA archive catalogue.
30. HVRSF, 'Instructions as to booking and handling of *Henry V',* 99 AN/9D, box 1.
31. HVRSF, 'Selling angles and exploitations suggestions', 99 AN/9D-1-3, box 1.
32. 'Instructions as to booking and handling of *Henry V',* 99 AN/9D, box 1.
33. Auten to Olson, 9 July 1947, HVRSF, 99 AN/9D-1-16; Colorado and Wyoming, Nov 1946–Nov 1947.
34. *Variety,* 24 Apr 1946 and *Motion Picture Herald,* 26 Oct 1946: 24.
35. *LA Times,* 15 June 1946; *New York Times,* 17 June 1946.
36. *New Yorker,* 22 June 1946. The *New York Journal American* made a similar comment about the film's superior taste, 17 June 1946.
37. *New York Times,* 18 June 1946.
38. *New York Times,* 18 June 1946.
39. HVRSF, see correspondence filed by State, 99 AN/9D-1-13 (Northern California); 9D-1-16 (Colorado and Wyoming); 9D-3-11 (Texas); 9D-2-3 (Florida); 9D-2-14 (Massachusetts).
40. Auten to B. B. Gamer, Talgar Theatre, Lakeland, Florida, 24 Nov 1947; Florida records, 9D-2-3.
41. Hale to Auten, 12 Aug 1947; 9D-1-13.
42. Kolmar to Auten, 9 Aug 1947; 9D-1-13.
43. Kolmar to Auten, 11 July 1947; 9D-1-13.
44. Auten to B. B. Garner, 24 Nov 1947; 9D-2-3.
45. Nyary to Auten, 6 Dec 1947; 9D-3-11.
46. Nathanson to Auten, 22 July 1947: 9D-1-13.
47. Beacon to Auten, 16 May 1947; 9D-1-16.
48. Kolmer to Auten, 20 June 1947; 9D-1-13.
49. *Variety,* 18 June 1947: 16, 18. This survey has been cited as evidence that British films were not making any progress (see, for example Balio, 1987: 34) without presenting the details which, as Table 4.1 shows, indicates that some films were doing well.
50. Richard Griffith, 'Where are the Dollars?', *Sight and Sound,* Dec 1949, Jan and Mar 1950.
51. Griffith, *Sight and Sound,* Dec 1949: 34.
52. *Variety,* 2 Jan 1946.

53. *New York Times,* 8 Sept 1946.
54. *Variety,* 28 Aug 1946: 3.
55. *Variety,* 11 Sept 1946: 3.
56. *Variety,* 17 Mar 1948: 4.
57. *Variety* anniversary box-office listings, 5 Jan 1949.
58. Universal archive, USC, box 600/23/19057, Coordinator's report 22, 10 Jan 1950.
59. As well as the film being awarded Best Picture, Laurence Olivier won Best Actor. It also won awards for black and white art direction and costume design, and nominations were received by Olivier for Best Director; by Jean Simmons for Best Supporting Actress; and for Best Scoring of a Dramatic Picture.
60. Details of Universal's handling of *Hamlet* are taken from the Universal archive, University of Southern California, USC, box 445/21/14059.
61. Universal archive, USC, box 453/21/12743; minutes of *Hamlet* meeting, 14 June 1948.
62. Universal archive, USC, box 453/21/12743: 'Five easy steps'.
63. Universal archive, USC, box 445/21/14059, Livingston to Lipton, 5 Aug 1948.
64. Universal archive, USC, box 453/21/12743, Herzoff to Livingston, wire, n.d. complaining about Fox-West Coast not contributing enough to advertising expenses for *Hamlet.*
65. Universal archive, USC, box 700/7/21644, interview with Milton Hale, n.d.
66. Universal archive, USC, box 453/21/12743, Lawrence to Lipton, 7 Mar 1949.
67. Universal archive, USC, box 453/21/12743, Lawrence to McFadden, 3 Mar 1949.
68. Universal archive, USC, box 453/21/12743, Livingston to Lipton, 31 Mar 1949 and subsequent correspondence.
69. Universal archive, USC, box 445/21/14059.
70. Universal archive, USC, box 769/36/23857, Coordinator's report 22, 15 Feb 1950.
71. Universal archive, USC, box 558/22/16931.
72. Universal archive, USC, box 700/7/21644, Ramsay to Lipton, 31 Oct 1950.
73. *Variety,* 13 Jan 1954.
74. *New York Times,* 23 Oct 1948: 9; *Variety,* 4 Aug 1948.
75. See, for example, *The Boston Christian Science Monitor,* 18 Sept 1948.
76. *New York Star,* 22 Oct 1948.
77. See reviews file on *The Red Shoes,* New York Public Library.
78. *Sight and Sound,* Jan 1950: 40. Michael Powell wrote to Reginald Allen at Universal that 'we have had more fan letters on it than any other', 9 Feb 1948, Universal archive, USC, box 417/25/12473.
79. See reports on expansion of art cinemas in *Variety,* 19 Feb 1947: 19; 18 June 1947: 16.
80. Press book for *The Red Shoes,* New York Public Library.
81. *Variety,* 9 Mar 1949: 4.
82. Balio, 1987: 34 and *Variety,* 22 Mar 1950.
83. See figures supplied by Rank to the Board of Trade contained in BT 64/4490 (Public Record Office).
84. Notes of a meeting between Eric Johnston, Fay Allport, the British Ambassador and Sir John Macgowan, 6 Feb 1948; Public Record Office, BT 64/2370.
85. *New York Times,* 18 Oct 1948: 28; 20 Oct 1948: 28; Oct 28, 1948. L. J. McGinley reported in a Coordinator's report to Universal on 31 Dec 1948 that the Sons of Liberty boycott had a negative impact on bookings for *I Know Where I'm Going, The Mikado* and *The Brothers Quartet.* Universal archive, USC, box 600/23/19057.
86. Universal archive, USC, Coordinator's report 12, 3 Feb 1949, box 600/23/19057.
87. Universal archive, USC, Coordinator's report 17, 6 May 1949, box 600/23/19057.
88. Universal archive, USC, Coordinator's report 18, 3 Mar 1949, box 600/23/19057.
89. Universal archive, USC, Coordinator's report 20, 25 Oct 1949, box 600/23/19057.
90. Universal archive, USC, Coordinator's report 26, 21 Apr 1950, box 769/36/23857.
91. Universal archive, USC, Coordinator's report 28, 20 June 1950, box 769/36/23857.

92. American Institute of Public Opinion: 'Continuing Audit of Marquee Values', published on microfilm by Scholarly Resources, 1979.

93. *Variety,* 26 Nov 1947: 4.

94. See reviews of *Brief Encounter* in the *New York Times,* 26 Aug 1946; *New York Herald Tribune,* 26 Aug 1946; *Variety,* 28 Nov 1945 and *Motion Picture Herald,* 15 Dec 1945.

95. *Brief Encounter* press book, New York Public Library.

96. *Variety,* 20 Nov 1945; *Reporter,* 9 Dec 1946.

97. *Film Daily,* 12 Dec 1946.

98. *Variety,* 29 Jan 1947.

99. *Film Daily,* 30 Jan 1947.

100. *Box-Office,* 1 Feb 1947.

101. Universal archive, USC, John Joseph (Universal) to Rank, 5 Apr 1946, box 708/6/23174.

102. Figures quoted by Dennis Holman in 'Sydney Box', *Film Illustrated Monthly,* vol. 3, Feb 1948: 12.

103. See 'Continuing Audit of Marquee Values', published on microfilm by Scholarly Resources (The American Institute of Public Opinion), 1979.

104. *Financial Times,* 3 Mar 1948.

5

Questions of Censorship and Ideology

Censorship played a key role in the planning and production of films in America. As in Britain, the system was self-regulatory, designed to offset the threat of state censorship. The Production Code Administration (PCA) was established in 1934 by the Motion Picture Producers and Distributors of America (MPPDA), in response to 'moral panic' about Hollywood scandals and motion picture representation. State and municipal authorities already had the right to censor films, and these local boards continued after the PCA was established. But the guiding authority was the PCA, directed by Joseph Breen who devised the 'Code' with fellow-Catholic Martin Quigley, proprietor of the *Motion Picture Herald*. The majority of cinemas owned by the majors agreed not to show films without a PCA seal. Statutory provision was not therefore necessary to ensure that its decisions were complied with, a situation that held sway until the mid-1950s (Maltby, 1996: 235–48 and Slide, 1998: 1–9). Far from being imposed from without, the Code was an integral element of Hollywood's economic and political procedures. The PCA represented 'the establishment of an institutionalised process of negotiation over the content and ideology of every movie' (Vasey, 1997: 9). The industry's economic prerogatives – to dominate the home market and pursue an aggressive export policy – also acted as a determining influence on the content of Hollywood's films. As a result they steered clear of controversy, avoided offence to other nations and produced a 'permissible field of representation'. This consisted of a world that operated 'according to Hollywood', an 'exotic, sensual cousin of the realm outside the cinema, simultaneously familiar and strange to its worldwide audiences, who are as certain about what is morally right and wrong in this utopia as they are about whether the star or his best friend will get the girl in the final scene' (Vasey, 1997: 3).

Negotiating the US censorship system was a requirement for British producers who wanted to have their films shown in American cinemas. In the 1930s films were submitted to the PCA by American distributors in their British versions, while by the 1940s producers sent scripts direct to Breen's office for advice about the changes needed to obtain the all-important PCA seal (Slide, 1998: 24). This resulted in a complex negotiating process during which many scripts were altered. In their anxiety to obtain a seal and distribution for their films, British producers were often grateful for Breen's advice and in many cases accepted his recommendations uncritically, even enthusiastically. When Powell and Pressburger submitted a draft script of *Black Narcissus* to Breen in 1946, they welcomed his suggestions: 'We appreciate your insistence on dealing firmly and constructively with all these points, as it has certainly resulted in improving our story as well as making it more acceptable to all audiences'.[1] As experts on making motion pictures acceptable to a wide variety of audiences, Breen's staff at the PCA were well qualified to work with British producers who occasionally presented them with problem cases, some of which will be analysed in this chapter. Like film reviewers, the censors acted as a gauge for American reception. In their correspondence with British producers, Breen and his staff were particularly keen not to cause offence, especially in view of the studios' dependence on Britain as a key overseas market. On occasion, however, the pressures to conform to the Code by the letter conflicted with a desire to demonstrate goodwill and not appear to be obstructive. While the case of *Nell Gwyn* was discussed in Chapter 3 as an example of a film whose box-office chances may well have been adversely affected by changes insisted on by the censors, this chapter will consider the extent to which other films were affected by the work of the PCA. Crucially, the PCA's files provide an insight into the censorship process and the pressures of dealing with British films against a background of wider Anglo-American film and political relations.

Mr Breen Regrets

If it were left to me I would not touch the thing at all. (Joseph Breen on *The Wicked Lady*, September 1946).

For the most part relations between the PCA and British producers were cordial. As Slide has commented, 'With remarkable equanimity and good feeling, Breen and his staff would work with British producers, taking on the unenviable task of making a script or even a finished film acceptable under the requirements of the Production Code' (Slide, 1998: x). It was as if Breen thought many of the Code's strictures were ridiculous, yet he felt compelled to insist that they were observed. Many of the case histories read as unbelievably rigid in their adherence to a system that from many perspectives was riddled with

inconsistencies. As with American films, the way the Code was operated in relation to British films – applied in a crude and mechanistic manner – resulted
in curious anomalies that often subverted its conservative intentions. The file
on *The Wicked Lady* exposes some of these issues and tensions.

In February 1946, William Burnside of Eagle-Lion sent a script of *The
Wicked Lady* to the PCA. Based on a melodramatic historical novel by Mag-
dalen King-Hall, the story concerned the daring activities of Barbara (Margaret Lockwood), an unscrupulous woman who marries a nobleman and out
of boredom masquerades as a highwayman, has a passionate, adulterous affair
and commits murder. When the film was released in Britain, it was an enormous box-office success. Producer R. J. Minney went ahead with shooting the
film despite Breen's following comments on the script:

> This basic story is unacceptable because of its extremely low moral
> tone. This story contains several incidents of adultery, illicit sex, mur-
> der, rape, unacceptably intimate details of a bridal night, many offen-
> sive lines referring to mistresses, etc., and an unacceptable dance
> sequence. Further, except for one or two characters, nearly all of the
> principal characters in the script are involved with illicit sex of some
> sort.[2]

A year later, Breen saw the finished film and his reaction was unchanged with
the added objection to 'fifty scenes showing the breasts of several of the
women partially and "substantially" uncovered'.[3] Yet his office tried to be accommodating over the film, not least because of the delicate nature of Anglo-
American film relations after the Second World War. Universal, the studio now
handling *The Wicked Lady*, was especially concerned not to alienate Rank or
provoke an anti-American press campaign in Britain, claiming that the film
and, by implication, the British film industry, had been discriminated against.[4]
On the other hand, Breen was caught in a difficult situation since leniency towards *The Wicked Lady* would be resented by American producers who had
only just been reprimanded for revealing 'breast shots' in *The Outlaw* (1943).
Universal adjusted the offensive shots and Breen viewed the film in July 1946.
He advised the excision of several lines including sexually suggestive dialogue
such as 'I've heard you say that in other circumstances' and 'We must be together – just once – tonight'. Breen recommended that re-shooting might be
the best option since he considered that 'if it can be made reasonably acceptable for the American market, you have a great money-maker. You really have
something in *The Wicked Lady* and it justifies every effort to make it acceptable'.[5] Apart from the 'breast shots' there were a number of problems concerning *double entendres*, language and scenes on beds. Re-shooting did take place

of scenes written by Jock Lawrence, Rank's representative in America, using the 'framing' technique with Patricia Roc telling her story through a diary. To allay criticism or a British backlash, the *New York Times* was primed with text for a 'Thank you Mr Breen' story.[6] Indeed, according to Lawrence, the retakes were a success, and the film was granted a PCA certificate in November 1946.

Despite this toning down of the sexual content, the film was advertised as 'The most talked about picture of the year!' concerning 'the lusty adventures of a daring highwayman and his partner in danger'. Ironically, the controversy over the 'breast shots' diverted attention away from major cuts and in the end the film was reduced by only five minutes (from 103 to 98 minutes).[7] It is not entirely clear which scenes were re-shot, but from the amiable British reaction it would appear that the film was not regarded as ruined. In fact, Lawrence reported that Sydney Box thought it was better than before.[8] The case showed that adhering to the strictures of the Code placed Breen in a difficult position but that in certain circumstances – in this case delicate Anglo-American film relations – a compromise could be reached. On the British side, an American release was important to Rank's overseas campaign, even if the film had not originally been intended for international audiences. In this way a modified film reached American screens. Unusually, very little was changed in response to Breen's initial advice on the script, and his next encounter with the film was as a finished product. By that time the basic elements of the narrative were set and 'pruning' therefore occurred rather than complete revision. Universal was also involved with the case, proving that negotiations with distributors persisted into the 1940s. In the event, Universal's willingness to sponsor costly re-shooting was probably a better option than the more crude excisions forced on other films.

The case shows that producers were not disturbed by the thought that two versions of the same film might be in circulation. If satisfying the Code was a step towards American distribution, cuts and re-shooting were considered to be a small price to pay. This indicates a factory-conception of film-making that was in keeping with Gainsborough's reputation for balancing the books and efficient studio management. In this context the modification of a product for a different market was not a travesty but a strategic decision to maximize profits wherever possible. As the advertising material reveals, the spirit of the film was nevertheless retained, an element that was essential for the marketing of James Mason as an attractive villain. One suggestion for lobby advertising, for example, featured close-ups of Mason and Lockwood described as 'Fearless Highwayman! Shameless Beauty!', and hinted at the risqué elements that had been so popular with British audiences: 'With reckless guns and ruthless lips . . . that tempted the Devil in each other!'[9] The poster included the caption:

'Hers is the story of violent love and love of violence!' and was illustrated by a close-up of the pair in an embrace, Lockwood reclining backwards, bare-shouldered with the details of cast and title placed over, and covering up, her controversial chest (Plate 23). In this way the advertising material alluded to the well-publicized struggles over the 'breast shots' with Breen's office. *The Wicked Lady* therefore benefited from its reputation as a salacious film, a strategy often used by distributors in order to create a climate of anticipation as well as seeking some recompense for problems with Breen's office. The trailer scripts also show how even though the film had to be toned down for American audiences, its reckless and thrilling spirit was retained with Mason described as 'that mean magnificent Mason man', and Lockwood as 'the most exciting woman who ever made light of her marriage vows and traded love for danger'.[10] In this way the illicit pleasures to be derived from the film were made explicit, a situation that, ironically, had been created by the censorship system that sought to have them repressed.[11] Direct reference was also made to Mason as 'mean' on a poster, indicating that audiences would recognize him as such from *The Man in Grey* (1943). It is however probable that after all the build-up, audiences were disappointed with the film. When an exhibitor in Maryland ran a British Film Festival in 1947, he reported that while *The Wicked Lady* was an obvious choice for the programme, together with *Notorious Gentleman/The Rake's Progress* (1945) and *The Ghost Goes West,* it was evident that *The Wicked Lady* 'suffered too much from the censors to be entirely satisfactory'. On the other hand, he cited James Mason as a popular star.[12] This was confirmed by surveys conducted by the Audience Research Institute throughout the 1940s.[13]

Bedelia, another controversial film starring Margaret Lockwood, had to be adjusted even more drastically in response to the Code (Plate 24). The producer, Isadore Goldsmith, arranged for an alternative ending to be shot when Breen pointed out that a suicide (of a sane person to evade the law) was in contravention of the Code.[14] In the British version (based on a novel by American writer Vera Caspary who collaborated on the screenplay), Lockwood plays a *femme fatale* who commits suicide at the end of the film to escape justice; in the American version, she gives herself up.[15] Again, we see the same grateful reaction to a major change. Goldsmith was advised of the position by Breen and shot two endings. As a trial he screened both versions of *Bedelia* in Hollywood and afterwards he wrote to Breen that:

> The result was amazing. Almost unanimously, and especially by women, I was told that the American ending, which is the alternative ending suggested by your office, is by all means better for American audiences and will prove much more satisfactory commercially than the

British one. . . . I now feel that had it not been for the influence of your office I would never have thought of producing an ending different than the one with the suicide. In other words, the influence of your office made me shoot the surrender ending which now proves, in the United States, a hundred times better commercially than the ending used in Britain. Please understand that I am grateful for the advice given by your office and as soon as the film is released here I shall do my best to bring this fact to the knowledge of my British fellow producers.[16]

In this way the reactions of trial audiences converged with the censor's advice, a rare test that most British producers could not afford to organize.

On other occasions, as the following case of *Black Narcissus* reveals, Breen's office did not act in isolation from dominant pressure groups which were sometimes too powerful to control. The censorship of this film was one of the most controversial cases in the 1940s and will be used as an opportunity to explore the textual consequences of American censorship. As we shall see, the version of *Black Narcissus* released in America excised some key sequences that provide a basis for a wider discussion of the film in relation to its immediate historical context.

'Condemned!': The Forbidden Spectacle of *Black Narcissus*

All we Catholics should gang up on this picture – and with Mr Breen's help see that the stinky thing is stopped. I can't see how it got past your office – if it has. Anyway, we ought to let Rank keep his 'rank' pictures and take them back to England. (Eleanor Lewis to Joseph Breen's secretary, 1947)

Black Narcissus, based on Rumer Godden's novel (1939), is Powell and Pressburger's 1947 film about a community of British nuns who set up a school and hospital in the Himalayas (Plate 11). They are led by Sister Clodagh, a young nun who is given the responsibility of overseeing the operation. As they settle, they discover that their assumptions and beliefs are challenged by their new environment. They find themselves diverted from their duties when they begin to experience feelings of sensual longing which are linked to their present predicament and to their past lives. In particular, Sister Clodagh is haunted by memories of a love affair in Ireland, an emotional attachment that preceded her life as a nun. The film culminates with a series of dramatic events, largely revolving around the disturbed Sister Ruth, who plunges to her death after a struggle at the bell tower with Sister Clodagh. In the end the nuns fail to make their mark in the East and they leave the old palace. The film obtained a certificate from the British Board of Film Censors (BBFC) without any trouble, but in America its history was completely different.

The release of *Black Narcissus* in the United States was beset with controversy, providing an example of how in the short term, a British film could be adversely affected when its release was held up by the process of censorship. Several key sequences, including flashbacks of Sister Clodagh's past life in Ireland, were excised from the American release print. The cuts were the result of the work of the Catholic Legion of Decency (LOD) rather than the PCA.

As we have seen, American censorship was very strict, and Joseph Breen's office wielded a considerable degree of authority over which films, and in what form, were released. Many had to be cut in order to receive a PCA certificate, which was necessary to obtain a screening for a film. The Breen office was not, however, the only organization with control over film content. The LOD, formed in 1934, also censored films and worked in close collaboration with the PCA (Black, 1997). Its collusion with and influence over the PCA reflects the power of Catholicism in many metropolitan centres all over the United States. A film's release could be boycotted and even prevented if the LOD disagreed with a PCA decision to issue it with a seal.

Operating alongside the PCA Code, the Legion devised its own categorization system in 1936 (A1 = unobjectionable for general patronage; A2 = unobjectionable for adults; B = objectionable in part and C, the rating given to *Black Narcissus*, = Condemned). In many cases, such as that of *Black Narcissus*, this rating system was utilized as an authoritative register of disapproval. The purview of the Legion extended beyond judgement over particular films to extensive comment on the affairs of the film industry. One of the key figures who colluded with the Catholic-dominated PCA and with the LOD was Martin Quigley, co-author of the original PCA code and a prominent Catholic film industry press baron. Producers who tried to challenge the Legion, for example David Selznick over *Duel in the Sun* in 1946–47, found no support from fellow producers and ended up having to comply with the Legion's insistence on cuts. The case of *Black Narcissus* came at a time when the LOD was therefore at the height of its power – so powerful that in this case it was able to challenge the judgement of the PCA itself. *Black Narcissus* was the first major film to cause controversy with the LOD since their protracted opposition during 1941–43 against another 'Condemned' film, *The Outlaw*.

The debate over the censorship of *Black Narcissus* can therefore be related to the LOD's influence over cinema and, in view of the film's setting and thematic preoccupations, to a wider context of East-West relations. On a broader level, the case provides an example of how censorship is representative of a convergence of systems of power and authority rather than the activity of a single organization. In this way the interaction between different institutions can be seen to exert an overall context of constraint, revealing the many complex ideological preoccupations at stake in the process. It is clear that the existence of a framework of negotiation between the PCA, LOD and the film industry contributed to the tenacity and longevity of the censorship system in the United States.

As early as April 1945 a 'very rough draft' of *Black Narcissus* was sent to Joseph Breen's office, and a warning was given that it might cause offence in religious quarters.[17] The story was considered to be risqué from the start. Breen wrote:

> We are apprehensive that any motion picture in which there would be even the slightest implication of sex sin or sexual longings or desires on the part of the women consecrated to religion, would give great offence to religious-minded folk in this country and might well call forth very vigorous and, possibly, violent protest from them.[18]

Powell and Pressburger gave assurances that this would be avoided, and further scripts were sent and revised, including some lines spoken by Mr Dean, the English agent who helps the Sisters settle in. Breen instructed: 'Please change the underlined word in Mr Dean's line, "I've come to mend a loose joint in *your* pipe". The plumbing must not refer to water closets or toilets. We question the further line "I swear to you, Sister, it's only the pipe I'm interested in" in order to avoid the sex inference which embarrasses the Sister'.[19] The PCA passed *Black Narcissus* in June 1947, with the proviso that a foreword should be added, making it clear that the nuns were Anglo, as opposed to Roman, Catholic. The foreword was written by Breen: 'Throughout the world a group of faithful nuns of the order (fill in name) carry on the charitable work of the Church of England. Outside of the British Empire not much is known of their activities. Each year they are given the choice of renewing their vows as nuns. To them and to their work we dedicate this film'.[20] In Breen's opinion, the film was 'superb', assuring Father John McLafferty of the LOD, New York, that 'we need have no serious worry about this picture on any score'.[21]

In the meantime, however, the LOD was not happy and had begun its protest in April 1946 when news of the film was picked up by the Archbishop of Calcutta from an item in the *Times of India*.[22] The LOD, with its powerful organization all over the United States and with contacts in the United Kingdom, began an elaborate and effective campaign against the film's release. The LOD was highly influential in the Catholic press, and in July 1947 a damning review by Virginia S. Tomlinson was published in *The Tidings*, the Catholic weekly of the Los Angeles diocese.[23] Tomlinson described the film's portrayal of the nuns as 'hysterical, frustrated, neurotic, lovestarved and worldly'. She also wrote: 'It is a long time since the American public has been handed such a perverted specimen of bad taste, vicious inaccuracies and ludicrous improbabilities'. She also noted that in the version she had seen, the foreword was printed only on the programmes. The scene which caused most offence was Sister Clodagh's flashback of her past life in Ireland and her love for Con, a man she wishes to marry but who in the end rejects her. We assume that this rejection is connected with her decision to join the Sisterhood. Tomlinson wrote of this: ' Sister Clodagh . . . kneeling at the altar, her mind intent – not on prayer – but . . . going over a love-scene of her own youth' (Plate 12). This proved to be a most controversial sequence, the excision of which had profound consequences for the film. Predictably, the scenes of Sister Ruth putting on red lipstick were severely criticized by the Catholics as a representation of a nun who demonstrated the twin evils of a rebellious attitude coupled with sexual desire.

Tomlinson's review had serious consequences. Father Patrick J. Masterson, a powerful figure in the LOD, sent it to Universal-International (the film's US distributors) and informed *The Tidings* that 'You may be sure that the boys at Universal saw it and paused. We're trying to add some more fuel to the flame, in the hope of getting Mr Rank to bring his picture back to England and perhaps dump it on the way over'.[24] The review also persuaded Martin Quigley to join in the crusade against the film in the United States. He disseminated the review widely, which encouraged the writing of the 'Notre Dame letter', a key communication in the controversy. This was written by a committee appointed by the Sisters' Vocation Institute which met at Notre Dame University to discuss how to increase dwindling recruitment to the various Sisterhoods. The letter, written in July 1947, protested against the film, declaring that the foreword was inadequate and that the film 'ridiculed all religion'.[25] It was felt that the average cinema-goer would not distinguish between Anglican and Roman Catholic nuns. The 'modern world' was blamed for the shortage of Sisters, a situation that would not be helped by a film like *Black Narcussus,* which depicted the nuns as unhappy, or at least not entirely content, with their choice. The strident letter was sent to J. Arthur Rank, Nate Blumberg (President of Universal-International), Eric Johnston (President of the MPAA) and to Joseph Breen's office. Breen's secretary was sent a copy by a Catholic friend who sent an accompanying note: 'All we Catholics should gang up on this picture – and with Mr Breen's help see that the stinky thing is stopped. I can't see how it got past your office – if it has. Anyway, we ought to let Rank keep his "rank" pictures and take them back to England'.[26] As a result of this protest, the foreword to the film was changed, this time emphasizing that the *Anglican* nuns were from 'Protestant Orders', renewing their vows annually.[27] As the Episcopal Church of the United States did not join in the Roman Catholic protest, we can assume they had no objection to the film.

Prominent members of the LOD were invited to a special screening of the film in August 1947, after which they nevertheless proclaimed it to be a 'Condemned' picture, some fathers objecting to its 'Freudian' implications.[28] The term 'Freudian' was used in a pejorative sense, referring to the film's portrayal of women who are in danger of failing to control their emotions and of rebelling against authority, particularly their 'problem' with their vocation which is explained in terms of their being frustrated in love. Others objected to its images of the 'pagan' East as seductive, offering a more attractive environment than the West. Hedda Hopper publicized the controversy and news spread fast of the Legion's ban.[29] Universal-International arranged some high-profile preview screenings in New York and Los Angeles, but wider distribution was prevented by protests and lobbying by the LOD. Rank attended the glittering Anglo-American première at the Cathay Circle Theatre, Los Angeles, on 7 July 1947, a significant event in his campaign to publicize Anglo-American cooperation. When, however, the film opened in Los Angeles and the LOD intensified its campaign, bookings elsewhere were cancelled.[30] This furore was extremely bad timing for Rank, who was in the midst of the Dalton Duty and American boycott crisis. The Legion's campaign continued and by September Powell, Pressburger and Universal were forced to consider cutting the film. The cuts, ten in all, were suggested by Martin Quigley and reduced the film by 900 feet in total. These cuts included Sister Clodagh's flashbacks of Ireland; close-ups of sister Ruth putting on lipstick and stockings, and parts of Sister Ruth's scenes with Mr Dean, the man with whom she is infatuated. The explanatory foreword was further developed: 'A group of Protestant nuns in mysterious India find adventure, sacrifice and tragedy'. The 'C' ban was thus removed and *Black Narcissus* was finally released.

News of the cuts reached the press. The *New York Times* published a letter by a man who had seen the film in the summer of 1947 at a preview screening in New York and was dismayed to see the cut version later, claiming that the film was deprived 'of much of its impact and logic'.[31] By contrast, John O'Connor of Universal claimed that the editing had been done under the supervision of Emeric Pressburger who considered the changes to be 'fair, reasonable and just'.[32] The ridiculousness of aspects of the LOD's criticisms and their frustration in practice was made clear by William K. Everson in his notes for a Museum of Modern Art retrospective. Everson pointed out that one of the cuts had exactly the opposite effect of what was intended. Mr Dean's reprimand of Sister Ruth when she attempts to seduce him was removed from the sequence. This resulted in the insinuation that the seduction had taken place and triggered off Sister Ruth's subsequent madness.[33]

Reviews varied between *Variety*'s quip that it was '*Brief Encounter* in the Himalayas . . . a story of sex-starved nuns and a man', and *American Cinematographer*'s praise for the film's art direction, costume design and Technicolor cinematography by Jack Cardiff.[34] The *New York Times* described it as a 'curiously fascinating psychological study', while the reviewer for *Time* magazine was concerned about the East not being portrayed as strange enough: 'lovely as some of the Technicolour [sic] photographs are, they bring little of the strangeness to the audience's eyes', implying that portrayal of the East demanded an even more extreme realization.[35] The most recurring adjectives used in reviews were 'different', 'strange', 'unusual', 'daring', 'exotic', 'provocative', 'controversial', 'curious' and 'challenging'. Whatever the aesthetic and ideological consequences of the cuts, the film nevertheless made profits in America (Macdonald, 1994: 292). Ironically, it was American director Martin Scorsese, a Catholic, who resuscitated Powell and Pressburger's reputation in the 1980s.

The case of *Black Narcissus* generated a vast bulk of documents that raise interesting questions about the consequences of American censorship. The religious issue predominated, but it also had wider implications. Participants in the controversy were not only concerned about the portrayal of the nuns, they were also uncomfortable with the film's vision of the East as seductive and enchanting. It is clear from the documents that the East-West dichotomy was one of the themes which commentators drew out. In many ways *Black Narcissus* can be read as a film that implicitly references the decline of the British Empire. Just as the Sisters are forced to withdraw from their 'civilizing mission', the British had been forced to withdraw from India (India Independence Act, July 1947). As bearers of Western influence, the women in *Black Narcissus* fail to offer the East a sustained alternative to sensibilities which the film privileges as seductive. In the aftermath of the Second World War, the world was rapidly becoming a de-colonized one, with the United States assuming an ever-increasing economic and political role, displaying many of the imperialist assumptions formerly held by the British Empire.

The excision of Sister Clodagh's flashbacks in particular draws attention to their function in the film itself. Even if it was convenient to remove them (in terms of ease of editing), it is clear that they play an important role in the film's narrative. Their excision has many fascinating consequences, but first it is necessary to consider the function of the flashbacks in the British version. The first flashback occurs when Sister Clodagh is in the chapel, after she has been talking to Sister Philippa in a field and has commented on 'this place, with its strange atmosphere and new people', gazing at the stunning landscape. In the chapel, we see Clodagh with the shadow of a cross on her face in monochrome, a symbol of Christianity used here to indicate stasis and repression. In stark contrast, she looks up at the window whose frame reveals the outside which is full of colour and movement, introducing Sister Clodagh's flashback via overlapping dialogue and a dissolve. The flashback opens with a wide, open space: a pastoral Irish scene as Clodagh and her boyfriend Con are fishing. Their conversation is about him being restless and her contentment at staying in Ireland; she seems peaceful, happy. The dissolve from her face in the flashback to the present suggests a contrast between someone who was full of life and hope and the nun who must forever cast her eyes downward in a spirit of sacrifice and humility. Another flashback is occasioned by the sound of a dog barking outside the chapel. In the flashback we hear hounds barking and see horses. The horses are galloping very fast, jumping over hedges and when we return to Sister Clodagh we see her thrilled, animated expression. Back in the present, she hears the dog bark again and we see the Young General arriving on a Tibetan pony, creating a direct link between her memory and present environment.

The flashback is important in awakening a haunting memory, thus establishing a connection between the East and the West. The formal devices of a dissolve combined with overlapping sound indicates a smooth and related connection between the past and the present.[36] Furthermore, the flashback has been prepared for by the shots which emphasize 'looking'; 'spaces' which are characterized by looking and longing. Without Sister Clodagh's flashbacks, we get no literal sense of her past, or the idea that the West might be capable of offering similar sensual experiences to the East, thus threatening the Orientalist dichotomy of East vs. West (Said, 1985; 1995 ed). As Maureen Turim (1989) has shown, the flashback is an intriguing device which introduces narrational complexity. While the main narrative thrust of the film suggests in Orientalist terms that East and West are opposed, the flashbacks indicate a sense of shared sensuality and natural beauty which works to reduce this dichotomy. Sister Clodagh's flashbacks are usually occasioned by an element of the present, constituting an 'associative memory' which then unfolds. Flashbacks also assist in reinforcing the audience's identification with a particular character. As the nun in charge of the Order, Sister Clodagh's role is important as a sensible woman who represents stability. Knowledge of her past threatens to shatter this position of authority and responsibility, indicating that in many respects she is as vulnerable as Sister Ruth, whose function in the film is to represent 'hysterical' and rebellious femininity. From this perspective, Ruth represents what Clodagh might easily become: hysterical and uncontrollable, a figure of threatening madness. Again, boundaries are blurred rather than reinforced. Priya Jaikumar (2001: 66) has also noticed how 'Sister Ruth is arguably a distended reflection of all the weaknesses and deviances that the nuns, and particularly Sister Clodagh, experience in their encounter with (and responses to) Mopu'.

It seems that the controversy over *Black Narcissus* was not therefore simply confined to the objections of the Catholic Church. The film was certainly considered to be an attack on the Church, the issue that exercised most critics. However, as we have seen, it was also viewed as an attack on Western civilization. Virginia S. Tomlinson's review explicitly says that '[Rank] is attacking the known sanctity of a group of women whose lives are (as he says) dedicated to sacrifice and work and who stand for all that is holy and above reproach in a rocking world'. Religion thus stands in for stability, Western civilization, stasis, 'tamed' and sacrificial femininity. What we know and trust must not be seen to be under threat. Its defeat in *Black Narcissus* by powerful 'rocking' forces of sexuality, desire, nature, beauty and freedom appeared at a significant juncture in East-West relations when political divisions were being established and (re-established) after the Second World War. With hindsight, it is therefore significant and intriguing to observe that the American print cuts out the scenes which blur a rigid East-West divide at a time when, as Said acknowledges, the United States was adopting the Orientalist mantle in the East (1995: 4). Sisters Ruth, Clodagh and Philippa were looking outwards, beyond their immediate responsibilities, their memories perhaps contributed to the film's suggestion of the existence of a utopian space, a convergence between a remembered past and a more challenging future where strict divisions between East and West are no longer operable. By excising the flashbacks, the Legion of Decency therefore unwittingly punished the nuns and, by implication, optimists in the West, for daring to 'see too far'.

'Fair Representation': *Oliver Twist* and the Censors

The history, institutions, prominent people and citizenry of all nations shall be represented fairly. (Production Code, section on 'National Feelings')

The other major conflict with the PCA in the 1940s was over *Oliver Twist* (1948). Somewhat ironically (Rank was a deeply religious man) it also involved religious groups, but this time Jewish concern over the issue of the 'stereotypical' representation of Fagin. The case is an example of how when it was drawn to his attention, Rank was persuaded of the problems and did not press for a US release. Instead, the pressure to reach a compromise with the PCA came from the distributor, Eagle-Lion. In May 1947 Breen commented on a draft script which had been sent to him by A. R. Allen, the Pacific Coast representative of Rank, based at Universal City. As well as advising against the usual details concerning language; young boys drinking liquor; sexually revealing costumes and brutality, Breen added the caution:

> Assume you will bear in mind the advisability of omitting from the portrayal of Fagin, any elements or inferences that would be offensive to any specific racial group or religion. Otherwise, of course, your picture might meet with very definite audience resistance in this country.[37]

The film was made, without apparent heed of this warning. When *Oliver Twist* was viewed at a private screening by the Anti-Defamation League of B'nai B'rith, the portrayal of Fagin by Alec Guinness was condemned as 'a grotesque Jewish caricature stereotype'.[38] Aware of this reaction, Breen assured Francis S. Harmon of the PCA office in New York that Rank had no intention of releasing the film in America.[39] For a while Rank did nothing, but after Eagle-Lion had purchased the distribution rights, *Oliver Twist* was again scrutinized by Breen's office in 1950. Breen wrote to Jock Lawrence that the film was still unacceptable on the grounds that Fagin was an 'unfair representation' of Jewry.[40] The press got wind of the controversy and was avid for further details. Against Rank's wishes Eagle-Lion appealed against the PCA's decision to refuse the film a seal. The case was the first time a distributor had pressed for an appeal without the producer's consent. Rank even offered to reimburse Eagle-Lion their expenses in connection with preparing the film for distribution.[41] Despite this gesture the distributors were adamant and determined to release the film.

Some change in the situation occurred in January 1951 when *Oliver Twist* was viewed by four representatives of the National Conference of Christians and Jews. Their verdict was that the film would not arouse anti-Semitism since

> the make-up of Guinness presents a Fagin so far removed from twentieth-century American Jews in appearance and in occupation that we see no likelihood of a widespread transfer in the minds of American audiences to their Jewish neighbors.[42]

Breen informed the President of Eagle-Lion films that he had re-examined the film to see if there was a way forward. He suggested substantial cuts (69 cuts – 749 feet) to 'eliminate wherever possible the photography of the character of Fagin' and in so doing take care not to damage the film, clarity of plot or dramatic continuity.[43] Eagle-Lion agreed to the cuts, the revised version satisfied

Breen and the film was finally granted a certificate in February 1951. Later, in April, without seeing the final cut version but just before the film was released in America, Bob Benjamin, a representative of the Rank Organization in the United States, passed a cable from David Lean, the film's director, to Breen. Lean's cable made detailed suggestions for cuts. He claimed to be 'distressed that my film should have been interpreted by some in such a way' and advised against extreme or obvious cutting:

> If audiences are aware of cuts they will imagine that what has been deleted is unspeakable anti-Semitic propaganda and the thought of such unfounded assumption gravely disturbs me. Above all I have idea of short scene wherein respectable Jewish leader offers services of his community to police when hunt for Fagin is on. Object would be to demonstrate indignation of Jewish community that one disreputable member endangers reputation of the many.[44]

Nevertheless, Breen refused to reconsider the matter.[45] Even with the sixty-nine cuts, reviewers still found Guinness' Fagin disturbing. *Motion Picture Herald*, for example, wondered why a 'less unfortunate' visualization was not possible and that an otherwise excellent film suffered from caricature.[46] Indeed, Breen had warned Rank against the use of such stereotypes and in the early correspondence cited the example of advice given to MGM in 1935 about taking care not to cause offence in any screen portrayal of Fagin.[47] On the other hand, the *Motion Picture Daily* reviewer shared Lean's opinion that Fagin had been based on the original Cruikshank illustrations for the novel and that 'by any standards of fairness . . . one must say that the sordidness depicted in him [Fagin] are human qualities and not racial'.[48]

It is remarkable that David Lean and Rank did not take heed of Breen's advice. In view of Rank's attitude towards the controversy, seeking to distance himself from the aims of Eagle-Lion, it would appear that a gross error had been made. The film certainly bears out the charges of caricature and stereotype, and it is interesting that these were considered to be reasonable for the British market but not for America. After all, there were many Jews in Britain who were equally likely to take offence at this particular representation of Fagin. With its financial difficulties, Eagle-Lion was keen to push whatever 'prestige' films came its way, and the case reveals the lengths to which a company would go in order to obtain a release for what it considered to be a good film. For a company concerned to penetrate the American market, it is interesting that Rank did not consider that *Oliver Twist* ought to be made with international distribution in mind. On the other hand, it is tempting to interpret this case as an example of gross insensitivity, if not commercial folly. In the event, the film was one of more than 200 that were acquired by United Artists when the company bought Eagle-Lion in 1951, the crop earning reasonable box-office returns that kept UA afloat (Balio, 1987: 45). Eagle-Lion had anticipated rental grosses to the tune of $3 million for *Oliver Twist,* but reports of its first screenings recorded 'fair' business in the Southwest, New England and Detroit, leading executives to expect something more in the region of $1 million. When the film was shown at the Capitol Theatre, Boston, the house was picketed by a Jewish labour organization. However, when it opened in New York in August 1951 at the Park Avenue Theatre, it did 'remarkable' business that continued for six weeks, despite the hot summer weather.[49]

Britain and the Decline of the Code:
Kind Hearts and Coronets and *The Captain's Paradise*

The previous examples were particularly dramatic instances of clashes between British producers and Breen's office. Many other British films were subject to revision, including highly regarded British 'classics'. *In Which We Serve,* for example, was censored even though it was considered to be an essential element of war propaganda. Swear words were deleted, as well as derogatory references to Italians in the First World War. Carl Milliken of the PCA explained to Robert Hilton at United Artists that 'the function of the Code is not to be patriotic, it is to be moral. The function of the Code is not to create authenticity nor realism'.[50] In this case the argument had been used that a realistic representation of life on board ship would undoubtedly involve sailors swearing. In his defence of the Code, Milliken is clearly aware of its role in forging a distinction between realism and the fiction of 'the world according to Hollywood'.

Another interesting case of a celebrated film being revised for American audiences is *Kind Hearts and Coronets* (1949), the Ealing black comedy in which the leading character, Louis Mazzini (Dennis Price) murders members of his family (all played by Alec Guinness) in order to inherit what he considers to be his lawful birthright. This film in particular had a difficult experience with the censors, although, as the contrasting case of *The Captain's Paradise* shows, in just three years it was possible to exploit the Code's increasing vulnerability to contravention. Arguably, if *Kind Hearts and Coronets* had been released a few years later, the American version would have been much closer to the British.

After examining several treatments for the film, submitted in the spring of 1948, Breen's office warned against any attempt 'to justify the leading character's career of murder', elements of 'illicit sex and adultery' or the use of religious characters for ridicule.[51] Problems with the film continued after it had been shot, particularly the ending that was unclear as to whether Louis would be hanged, and the film's alleged 'improper treatment of adultery'.[52] Lawrence responded with the news that Michael Balcon had devised an alternative ending, an additional scene with the prison governor receiving Louis's memoirs in which he had confessed to the murders but inadvertently left in his cell (in the British version it is not clear whether the memoirs will be discovered and read)[53] (Plate 13).

Breen viewed a revised version in February 1950 and granted approval if further deletions were made concerning 'brutality' in the scene in which Louis kills the Duke (Ethelred) and afterwards comments, 'so be quiet'; Edith's statement in the witness box in support of her husband, Louis; reference to the clergyman as a 'boring old ass' and scenes with sexual suggestiveness.[54] In all, these deletions reduced the length of the film by six minutes and Balcon's 'alternative ending' was added so that there could be no doubt that Louis was punished. The reception of Ealing comedies in America will be considered in the next chapter, but suffice it to say here that despite the intervention of the censors to remove its risqué elements, moral ambiguity and *double entendres, Kind Hearts and Coronets* was well reviewed and did good business in arthouse cinemas.

In the early 1950s, major changes in the film industry, particularly the Paramount divorcement decree, began to break down the censorship system. The PCA's authority 'depended on vertical integration and the majors' oligopoly' (Maltby, 1996: 248). When independent distributors and exhibitors began to challenge its decisions, or exhibitors screened films that had not been granted a seal, the PCA was not empowered to insist that they be reprimanded. United Artists refused to cut *The Moon Is Blue* in 1953, and when it was screened without a seal, it broke box-office records. This precedent encouraged other distributors to follow suit. The Production Code was duly revised in 1954 and 1956, and in 1968 the Code was abandoned in favour of a voluntary rating system (Slide, 1998: 7). Interestingly, debate over a British film, *The Captain's Paradise* (1953), was causing controversy at this important juncture in the history of American censorship.

The Captain's Paradise involved the issue of adultery. Alec Guinness plays a sea captain whose idea of paradise is to have simultaneous relationships with a domestic, home-loving wife in Gibraltar and a lover in North Africa (Plate 14). Breen's first reaction to the draft shooting script was that 'this basic story is thoroughly and completely unacceptable. . . . It is a story of gross adultery which is justified and made to seem right and acceptable'.[55] Nevertheless, the film was shown without a certificate in New York and when Breen saw it he still considered it to be unacceptable.[56] United Artists, the distributor, had even given it a tentative code number that had to be removed when Breen refused to grant it a seal. The Legion of Decency agreed with the PCA that until suitable changes or cuts were made *The Captain's Paradise* ought to be denied a seal. It seems that the LOD still wielded considerable power since UA eventually agreed to alter the film in accordance with its suggestions. A prologue and epilogue were added, claiming that the story bore no resemblance to real life. The epilogue stated:

> We have to conclude that this is a fairy tale. It never happened. It couldn't happen. If it has ever occurred to you as a possibility, forget it. There are all kinds of laws, divine and human, against it. To say nothing of the scandal. Our considered advice is to go home now and have a good cup of hot cocoa and bring a cup to your spouse – the only one you have.[57]

This warning assured Breen that the film could be awarded a seal. But the incident of the 'dummy' certificate showed that it was difficult to police the so-called 'voluntary' system, and that in the wake of the controversy over *The Moon Is Blue* companies were feeling their way towards independence. While in this case the LOD proved to be the decisive force, it is likely that the more vulnerable position of British films in the American market determined the extent to which distributors were prepared to challenge the PCA. While *The Moon Is Blue* was able to obtain screenings without a certificate, *The Captain's Paradise* had to be treated more circumspectly. Nevertheless, it is an important case and the fact that a prologue and epilogue were added, rather than substantial changes to the main body of the film, shows that by the early 1950s the censorship system itself was breaking down under the weight of its own rigidity. While the letter of the Code appeared to have been honoured, the narrative of *The Capatin's Paradise* and the comedic performance by Alec Guinness ensured that the logic of its irreverent spirit was retained.

Censorship was clearly an important hurdle for British films. The PCA's files show that they received full attention from Breen's office and that in many cases extreme effort would go into modifying films. While this could be a difficult and problematic task, throughout his years at the PCA Breen established a good relationship with the majority of British producers. As we have seen, this inadvertently created a history of collaboration rather than conflict. In the 1940s in particular, there is evidence of an acute awareness that decisions over censorship might alienate large British companies such as Rank that held the key to Britain's cinemas, cinemas that were so necessary for Hollywood's overseas profits. On the other hand, British producers found it difficult to challenge Breen's suggestions, since in the 1930s and 1940s exhibition was more or less impossible without a PCA seal. Occasionally, British films were released by independent distributors without a seal, but this was rare. One striking example was UA's release of *Brewster's Millions* (1935). After Breen had seen the film in 1935 he advised on some cuts to remove 'vulgarity', otherwise, he warned, the film would not be awarded a seal. After apparently accepting this, UA appealed direct to the MPPDA in protest against Breen's decision. Special screenings were arranged by UA in March 1935, but senior studio executives backed up Breen's decision and Will Hays informed UA that the appeal had been rejected. UA released the film without a seal (Slide, 1998: 41–2). Similarly, an independent distributor, Pax Films, refused to cut a major sequence that referred to illegitimacy in Michael Powell's *Edge of the World* (1938). The film was screened without a seal in New York (Slide, 1998: 58–9). The problem was that such actions were taken by independents, and to access the majority of America's screens, British films had to comply with the Code that had been endorsed by the majors. A gauge of a British picture's value to the distributor was the extent to which compromises were made with Breen's staff. The case of *Oliver Twist* shows that even when a producer was prepared to sacrifice an American release, a distributor determined to press ahead could not be stopped.

The power of the Legion of Decency could, as the case of *Black Narcissus* reveals, be immense. When Barbara Hall interviewed Albert E. Van Schmus who worked for RKO and then at the PCA from 1949, he was of the opinion that Breen refused to be pressured by the extreme views of the LOD.[58] While this might have been the case by the mid-1950s, a decade earlier the LOD's power was considerable. However, even in 1953, as *The Captain's Paradise* illustrates, the LOD was still able to collaborate with the Breen office in a decisive way. As a Catholic, Joseph Breen was their natural ally for the enforcement of a Code that had been devised with the assistance of yet another Catholic, Martin Quigley. British films also had to negotiate with the BBFC, an organization that maintained a good relationship with the PCA. As with Hollywood's films, a process of double censorship occurred, having to satisfy both domestic and foreign censors. Complex negotiations would take place, often in the planning stages and in drafts of scripts. So British films were undoubtedly influenced by 'the world according to Hollywood' in that they were subject to the same strictures as American films, deleting the swear words, references to adultery, controversial issues of religion and cruelty to animals. For Hollywood's producers the Code was such an important constraint it is likely that many of its restrictions were anticipated and so never challenged. This form of internalized, 'unofficial' censorship also occurred in Britain, but more with the BBFC in mind than the PCA, which is why British films often presented Breen with unexpected subject matter and portrayals. The extent of reportage of censorship conflicts is striking, creating an aura around particular films, such as *Black Narcissus,* that had suffered at the hands of the LOD. In the case of a film like *The Wicked Lady,* reviews advertised the deletions so that, in combination with suggestive publicity material, the film was nevertheless appreciated as forbidden viewing. Unwittingly, therefore, censorship became part of the wider experience of British films in America.

Notes

1. Powell and Pressburger to Breen, 28 Mar 1946. Production Code Administration (PCA) file on *Black Narcissus,* Margaret Herrick Library, Center for Motion Picture Study, Los Angeles.
2. Breen to Burnside, 9 Feb 1945: PCA file, *The Wicked Lady.*
3. Breen to Johnston, 13 Feb 1946: PCA file, *The Wicked Lady.*
4. Breen's reported discussion with Blumberg in Breen to Johnston, 13 Feb 1946: PCA file, *The Wicked Lady.*
5. Summary of viewing of *The Wicked Lady* by Breen, R. J. Minney (producer) and Jock Lawrence (Rank Organization, New York Vice-President), 16 July 1946: PCA file.
6. Lawrence to Breen, 26 Aug 1946: PCA file, *The Wicked Lady.*
7. *Variety,* 11 Dec 1946.
8. Lawrence to Breen, 18 Sept 1946: PCA file, *The Wicked Lady.*
9. Press book for *The Wicked Lady,* New York Public Library.
10. Trailer scripts for *The Wicked Lady,* Margaret Herrick Library, Los Angeles.
11. For the press reaction to *The Wicked Lady* and *Bedelia,* see Chapter 4.
12. W. Ray Gingell of the Hiser-Bethesda Cinema, Maryland, reporting on his British Film Festival in *Film Industry,* vol. 3, no. 16, October 1947: 7.
13. 'Gallup Looks at the Movies: Audience Research reports, 1940–50', published by Scholarly Resources, 1979 (microfilm).
14. Although, a few years later, Vicky's suicide, possibily because of its unorthodox representation in *The Red Shoes* was not an issue for the PCA.
15. It is interesting that Caspary, best-selling author of *Laura,* on which director Otto Preminger's thriller of 1944 was based, was employed to work on the British film, co-authoring the screenplay with Herbert Victor, Isadore Goldsmith, Moie Charles and Roy Ridley. She appears to have played no direct part in the censorship controversy which was handled by Goldsmith. Caspary sold Eagle-Lion the film rights to *Bedelia* on condition that Caspary could work on the screenplay in England. Information contained in *Bedelia* press book.
16. Goldsmith to Breen, 31 Oct 1946: PCA file, *Bedelia.*
17. 20 Apr 1945, PCA file on *Black Narcissus,* Margaret Herrick Library.
18. 26 Apr 1945, PCA.
19. Breen to Allen (Rank Organization), 17 Apr 1946, PCA.
20. 5 June 1947, PCA.
21. Breen to Pressburger, 1 Oct 1946, report of advice given to McLafferty, PCA.
22. 10 Apr 1946, LOD file on *Black Narcissus,* Margaret Herrick Library.
23. 11 July 1947, LOD file on *Black Narcissus,* Margaret Herrick Library.
24. 23 July 1947, LOD file on *Black Narcissus,* Margaret Herrick Library.
25. 20 July 1947, LOD and PCA files on *Black Narcissus,* Margaret Herrick Library.
26. Eleanor Lewis to Miss Taylore (Breen's secretary), n.d. PCA.

27. See memos dated 20 June and 19 July 1947, Universal archive, USC, box, 411/17/12704.
28. 5 Aug 1947, LOD file on *Black Narcissus*, Margaret Herrick Library. Press release to this effect was issued 14 Aug 1947.
29. *LA Times*, 12 Aug 1947.
30. 26 Sept 1947, LOD file on *Black Narcissus*, Margaret Herrick Library.
31. Herbert Morris in the *New York Times*, 21 Mar 1948: 5.
32. Editor's comment on Morris' letter, the *New York Times*, 21 Mar 1948: 5.
33. William K. Everson, programme notes for *Black Narcissus*, 1980, Museum of Modern Art, New York.
34. *Variety*, 9 Aug 1947 and *American Cinematographer*, Dec 1947.
35. *New York Times*, 14 Aug 1947 and *Time*, 25 Aug 1947.
36. This connection is also in Rumer Godden's novel in which present events trigger past memories.
37. Breen to Allen, 13 May 1947, PCA file on *Oliver Twist*.
38. Cable from Harmon to Johnston, 7 Sept 1948, PCA file.
39. Breen to Harmon, 14 Sept 1948, PCA file.
40. Breen to Lawrence, 22 Nov 1950, PCA file.
41. Breen to Schreiber, 8 Dec 1950, PCA file.
42. Everett Clinchy, National Conference of Christians and Jews to Nate Spingold, Columbia Pictures, 5 Jan 1950, PCA file.
43. Breen to Macmillen, President of Eagle-Lion Films, 18 Jan 1951, PCA file.
44. Lean to Bob Benjamin, 2 April 1951, PCA file.
45. Breen to Benjamin, 13 Apr 1951, PCA file.
46. *Motion Picture Herald*, 5 May 1951.
47. Correspondence on earlier versions of *Oliver Twist* in PCA file.
48. *Motion Picture Daily*, 10 Apr 1951.
49. *Variety*, 6 June 1951: 6; 15 Aug 1951: 9; 22 Aug 1951: 3; 19 Sept 1951: 5; 10 Oct 1951: 8.
50. Milliken to Hilton, 12 Oct 1942, PCA file, *In Which We Serve*.
51. Stephen S. Jackson (PCA) to Reginald Allen (Rank), 20 Apr 1948, PCA file, *Kind Hearts and Coronets*.
52. Breen to Lawrence, 18 Nov 1949, PCA file.
53. Lawrence to Breen, 29 Nov 1949, PCA file.
54. Breen to Lawrence, 1 Feb 1950, PCA file. See also account of this case in Slide, 1998: 89–91.
55. Breen to Morris Helprin (London Film Productions, New York), 23 Oct 1952, PCA file, *The Captain's Paradise*.
56. Breen to Robert Blumofe (United Artists), 16 Nov 1953, PCA file.
57. Robert Benjamin (United Artists, New York) to Breen, 10 Dec 1953, PCA file.
58. Barbara Hall, transcripts of interviews with Van Schmus, 1990–92, Oral History 100; Margaret Herrick Library, Los Angeles.

6

The 1950s: British Films as Art and Entertainment

During the 1950s British films were able to take advantage of the growth of the art-cinema movement. As a percentage of foreign films imported into the United States, British films regularly represented at least 20 to 30 per cent of the total, reaching a peak in 1954 when they occupied 34 per cent of the import market.[1] At the beginning of the decade, it was estimated that British producers earned £3 to £3.5 million annually from abroad, virtually the same as they did from their home market (Political and Economic Planning, 1952: 250). In 1959 *Variety* published film-rental figures acquired from thirty-three independent and five major companies, placing British films at the top, having earned a high figure of $27,167,250 for seventy-six films, a sum that exceeded the combined US earnings of French, Mexican, Italian and Japanese films.[2] While these figures would appear to represent a major step forward for British films, it was still rare for them to break into the mass market, as the Rank Organization discovered with its subsidiary Rank Film Distributors of America, formed in 1957 but dissolved only two years later due to 'difficulties existing in the industry'.[3] By this time, however, the increase in the number of American independent exhibitors and distributors gave British films a greater chance than ever before to gain screentime in the increasingly important art and foreign film market.

British and foreign-language films benefited from changes in the Hollywood studio system that enabled them to occupy a 'niche' market in major cities and college towns. Whereas in 1950 there were eighty-three art cinemas in the United States, this figure increased to 200 in 1956, and ten years later had risen to 664 (Balio, 1987: 224 and Gomery, 1992: 181).[4] The rise of the 'drive-in theatre', another venue for British films, was striking in this period, having expanded from twenty-four in 1945 to over four thousand by 1956 (Thompson and Bordwell, 1994: 384).[5] Ironically, this growth in the independent exhibition sector coincided with the American film industry's most sustained period of retrenchment when production declined (Sklar, 1999: 81).

Divested of their cinema chains in the wake of the Paramount case, the majors had to develop new strategies to control the market.[6] European currency restrictions and protectionist legislation continued to force the American majors to produce films abroad and distribute them in America. As *Variety* pointed out, 'It is becoming increasingly difficult to distinguish between the "pure" British films and those which, while British quota pictures, were financed by American money'.[7] Foreign films were in a good position to fill the product shortage, giving a new lease of life to former newsreel and second-run theatres that were converted into art cinemas. A plethora of small distribution companies were established specifically to cater for the influx of British and foreign-language films, and, despite the difficulties of the late 1940s, Universal continued to handle British films. In 1958 United Artists consolidated its interest in foreign films by acquiring Lopert Films, an independent art-film distributor that had absorbed Rank Film Distributors of America (Balio, 1987: 226). As competition from television also threatened Hollywood's hegemony over screen entertainment, the 1950s was a decade of decline and readjustment.

There were social as well as economic reasons for the increase in film imports and their appreciation by art-house audiences. The 1950s was a paradoxical decade when the pursuit of success and illusions of class harmony coexisted uneasily with doubt and fragmentation (May, 1989: 2). Cold War politics formed the background to wider social anxieties. The quest for distinction and social status was marked, exposing the myth of American society as united, middle class and equal. *The Lonely Crowd,* an influential sociological study 'of the changing American character' by Riesman, Glazer and Denney, first published in 1950, argued that Americans had lost their sense of 'inner-directed' individualism and become 'other-directed', or overly concerned with the example and approval of their peers and contemporaries. The typical 'other-directed' person was young, affluent, educated, upper middle class and living in the larger American cities. The book's central thesis argued that:

What is common to all the other-directed people is that their contemporaries are the source of direction for the individual – either those known to him or those with whom he is indirectly acquainted, through friends and through the mass media. This source is of course 'internalized' in the sense that dependence on it for guidance in life is implanted early. The goals toward which the other-directed person strives shift with that guidance: it is only the process of striving itself and the process of paying close attention to the signals from others that remain unaltered throughout life. This mode of keeping in touch with others permits a close behavioral conformity, not through drill in behavior itself . . . but rather through an exceptional sensitivity to the actions and wishes of others (Riesman et al., 1953: 37–8).

This description of a quest for conformity and acute awareness of peer distinction anticipates the later work of French sociologist of culture, Pierre Bourdieu. Bourdieu's ideas about 'cultural capital' have been extremely influential in understanding how taste is a form of social distinction (Bourdieu, 1984). It is useful to consider the expansion of the art market in the United States within this context, as an indicator of social status and method of analysing how 'niche' audiences developed and changed over time. As Wilinsky (2001: 82) has noted, in this way familiarity with the latest foreign imports invested an individual with 'cultural capital' that was premised on a rejection of mass culture. As we shall see, British films occupied ambiguous territory as 'foreign' but not 'foreign-language' product. While able to take advantage of the expansion of the art market, they were often considered to be lacking in the exoticism or formal adventurousness of French or Italian films. In this process the role of the film critic became extremely important as a gauge of shifting opinion, particularly in the case of foreign films that were analysed, deciphered and judged by critics. The reputation of a foreign film often stood or fell on a reviewer's verdict, and British films were no exception to this rule. As Haberski (2001: 104) has observed, during this period the increased importation of foreign films made a decisive impact on American film criticism, broadening reviewers' horizons and suggesting new directions for cinema, and, by implication, Hollywood cinema.

As we have seen in previous chapters, many British films were frequently marketed as 'highbrow' product, catering for an educated clientele that expanded in the 1950s. The GI bill made a college education accessible for former servicemen, many of whom had served overseas and developed an interest in European culture (Wilinsky, 2001: 83). In 1948 Rank's publicity chief, Sydney Wynne, went to New York to research the reception of British films in America. He reported that British films should target the 'untapped' potential audience of non-cinema-goers aged over thirty years.[8] While this was an astute observation that recognized the importance of 'niche' audiences, American surveys conducted in the 1950s observed the changing composition of movie audiences, in particular the increased attendance by young, higher-income and educated groups (Sklar, 1999: 82-3). This audience bears close resemblance to Riesman, Glazer and Denney's 'other-directed' population. Indeed, the typical art-house patron had above average education and attended lectures, opera, ballet, appreciated fine art, and preferred the experience of seeing a film in a cinema rather than on television.[9] It is therefore not surprising that Alexander Korda's decision to release the television rights of some of his older films for

one year to WPIX, an unaffiliated New York television station, and their les-
sees in 1948, was unpopular with the critics and art-house fans who did not
own televisions.[10] The art theatres themselves reflected this pretension to high
cultural status, with their lavish decoration and facilities, including the display
of experimental art. The practice of booking films as single features and exhib-
iting them for weeks at a time was more akin to the presentation of stage plays
and their promotion as high cultural experiences (Gomery, 1992: 187).

Hollywood's adjustment to the consequences of divorcement, the decline in
cinema attendance and reduction in production provoked a number of surveys
about the cinema audience. Foreign films featured in a study of art-theatre
audiences (Smythe, Lusk and Lewis, 1953: 28–50). The survey was conducted
in 1951–2 at the Illini Theatre, Champagne-Urbana in eastern Illinois, during
six weeks when six different films were playing, including two British, *The
Tales of Hoffmann* (Powell and Pressburger, 1951) and *Last Holiday* (1950,
starring Alec Guinness). These two films did particularly well in the United
States: *The Tales of Hoffmann* had earned $1,150,000 for United Artists in
rentals by the end of 1952.[11] Apart from these two, the only other foreign film
mentioned in the survey was *Rashomon* (Japanese, 1950). Interviews were
conducted with 728 patrons, consisting in large part of young, casual cinema-
goers from the local university. The survey showed that critics' opinions highly
influenced this group and that of foreign films, British were rated the most
highly. Four British films (*The Red Shoes, Tales of Hoffmann, Hamlet* and
Oliver Twist) appeared in the 'top ten' best pictures named as the most enjoy-
able by those who attended the art cinema regularly and only one, *The Red
Shoes*, was named by the casuals. The longer list of 'best films' included two
Ealing comedies, *The Lavender Hill Mob* and *Kind Hearts and Coronets*.
These citations show a definite familiarity with, and popularity of, British
films. Interviewees were also asked about their attitudes towards foreign films:
this revealed a marked difference between regular customers who appreciated
them and casuals who disliked them except for British films. Both regulars and
casuals liked British films and on the whole foreign films were admired for
their realism, high quality and good acting. Influenced by Riesman's character
typology, the study concluded that the 'typical' art-cinema enthusiast was an
'other-directed' person:

The . . . larger group of casual patrons show in their movie behavior
and attitudes the characteristics of the other-directed character type in
its more sophisticated aspects. Their movie tastes and habits are what
would be expected from peer-group oriented marginal competitors in
consumption, whether the field of play be the unusual cocktail, the ex-

otic anecdote, the salad dressing mixed at the table, or the choice of magazines, books and movies. (Smythe et al., 1953: 50).

The high standing of British films in this study is striking, even if it does appear that this particular cinema did not show many foreign-language films. As far as this theatre was concerned, 'art' cinema included Hollywood, for example, A Streetcar Named Desire (1951), All About Eve (1950) and Cyrano de Bergerac (1950). These films are hardly what we would categorize as art cinema today, but their mention is significant in an analysis of 'a small but integral part of the nation's motion-picture business' (Smythe et al., 1950: 28). It shows that in the early 1950s the art-cinema audience was not necessarily identified solely with foreign-language films and that British films occupied a large part of it, alongside Hollywood's 'serious' dramas. A study of the critical and cultural reception of European art films screened at the Brattle Theatre in Cambridge, Massachusetts, reveals, however, that as the 1950s progressed British films increasingly occupied a 'non-foreign' category of their own, as art films became more and more identified with foreign-language product (Lane, 1994).

The Accent Issue

Respondents to the Illini Theatre survey did not mention that British accents were a problem, whereas foreign language and dubbing could be negative factors (Smythe et al., 1953: 43). This is a major change from previous commentary that raised the issue consistently. In the early sound period, critics commented on the difficulties they had understanding British accents, occasionally resulting in the extreme action of dubbing films with American accents, as for example in Whiteface (1932), an adaptation of an Edgar Wallace play produced by Michael Balcon. The fixation on difficult accents as a major reason for the failure of British films in the mass market raises interesting questions about cross-cultural address and toleration of regional expression within conceptions of a 'standard' English language. By the early 1950s British producers were more attuned to the necessity for clear diction and sound reproduction. Contemporary commentary indicates that it was becoming less of a problem, particularly since many British films were not destined for exhibition outside art theatres. As many audiences became aficionados of British films, the British accent did not grate so much, particularly when care was taken in response to twenty years of criticism.

Michael Truman, Ealing's chief editor, was sent to America to edit Ealing's films for the American market. His reports home shed light on the work needed to make British films acceptable and, indeed, ensure their success. A good example was his work with *Passport to Pimlico* (1948; US release, 1949; Plate 29), a comedy that broke records in the Trans-Lux Theatre, New York and was described by *The Washington Daily Post* as 'a kind of British humour that survives export'.[12] Truman studied preview reactions to the film and concluded that audiences were 'restless' during the slow opening:

> The Americans are impatient by nature. They are used to having their characters introduced quickly and without any delineation – a couple of key lines, one or two tricks and a gag, then finding out more as the story develops. In Britain, however, we draw the characters more carefully and establish them before the story itself develops.[13]

Truman therefore cut the opening sequences, although ironically Bosley Crowther, the Anglophile film critic at the *New York Times,* considered this 'injudicious' since 'some of the picture's charm was lost'.[14] In the late 1940s, therefore, Ealing was prepared to 'adapt' films for America, whereas Crowther's opinion indicates that 'niche' films did not necessarily have to conform to rules of 'classical' film narration. Truman did not find that there was prejudice against British films – on the contrary, he was 'surprised at the number of people who had nothing but praise for our pictures and the interest they were taking in them'. As far as accents were concerned, his researches led him to conclude that it was not so much the accent that was the problem, but the way words were 'drawled out', indistinct and difficult to follow: 'Although they probably speak more rapidly than we do, they enunciate each syllable separately, keep air between the words and balance their weight in the sentences to form colour and emphasis'. Interestingly however, at the preview of *Tight Little Island/Whiskey Galore!* (1948; US release, 1949), American audiences did not strain so much to understand the speech because of the Scottish enunciation that was more akin to the American way of speaking. Consequently, only a few sentences were cut at the beginning of the film. In 1946 *Picturegoer* made a similar case which linked the increase in regional British accents to a growing acceptability and comprehensibility of British films in America:

> Fortunately, without sacrificing character and ideas, many of our producers and directors are now obtaining an English that is acceptable to American ears. There is no more of the so-called Oxford accent. Lines are not being 'thrown away' in the Mayfair manner. One of the main objections to British pictures is being swept away.[15]

While this would help to explain the success of films such as *Tight Little Island,* it does not, however, account for successful films which continued to use

'Oxford' accents, for example, *Hamlet* or *Kind Hearts and Coronets*. It is possible that what *Picturegoer* is alluding to is the context in which the accents are used: in the case of the latter, it would have flown in the face of verisimilitude to have Louis Mazzini as the impoverished aristocrat speaking in anything other than an 'Oxford' accent. The more significant observation concerns the lines not being 'thrown away', which chimes with Truman's theory about the importance of precision and pacing rather than the accent itself.

Other investigations confirmed this need for closer attention to diction and the quality of sound-recording equipment. When an American exhibitor visited Britain in 1946, he recommended that attention to technical precision in sound reproduction would enhance the appreciation of British films. Similarly, British cinematographer Ronald Neame visited Hollywood and reported on voice training given to all new actors. Documentarist Ken Cameron advised that the Hollywood practice of extensive post-synchronizing gave quick and clear results.[16] Such commentary provides evidence that the need to 'adapt' films for particular audiences was becoming an accepted element of exportation. British films benefited from this at the same time as their appreciation by 'niche' audiences rendered their difference more acceptable as a positive attribute.

This thesis was developed by Richard Roud in a survey (Table 6.1) of British films in America published by *Sight and Sound* in 1956–7. Roud observed that 'American audiences like their British films British. They do not, generally speaking, take to British films deliberately designed to suit the American market'. As a survey, it is deficient in many respects, acknowledging that 'it is impossible to get any exact figures about how well or how badly British films have done in America', but its observations and findings, based on information about British films popular in the United States supplied by contacts in three companies, the Rank Organization, Associated-British Pathé and British Lion, are nevertheless interesting.[17]

Roud concluded from his survey that British comedies, particularly those starring Alec Guinness, were more likely to succeed in America than 'social-problem' films. This view was confirmed by reviewers in the *New York Times*, although by the late 1950s their enthusiasm for British 'new wave' films showed that opinion was shifting. Jympson Harman of the Rank Organization informed Roud that two films, *Scott of the Antarctic* (1948) and *The Blue Lamp* (1949) had been unexpected failures in America. Roud explained these cases in terms of the former film's 'stiff upper-lip' patriotism and the latter's shortcomings in comparison with American police thrillers. Immersed in the art-cinema world of New York, Roud however reported long runs for Ealing comedies, John and Roy Boulting's *Private's Progress* and *The Captain's Para-*

Table 6.1 The Roud Survey, 1956–57

The Rank Organization	Associated-British Pathé
The Purple Plain (UA, 1955)*	*Top Secret* /US title: *Mr Potts Goes to Moscow* (Stratford, 1954)
The Million Pound Note/US title: *Man with a Million* (UA, 1954)*	*Last Holiday* (Stratford, 1950)
Where No Vultures Fly/US title: *Ivory Hunter* (Universal, 1952)*	*South of Algiers*/US title: *The Golden Mask* (UA, 1954)
Doctor in the House (Republic, 1955)*	*Happy Ever After*/US title: *O'Leary Night*/*Tonight's the Night* (Allied Artists, 1954)
The Cruel Sea (U-I, 1953)*	*Happy Go Lovely* (RKO, 1951)
Genevieve (U-I, 1954)	*Duel in the Jungle* (Warner Bros, 1954)
To Paris with Love (Continental, 1955)	*The Dam Busters* (Warner Bros, 1955)
The Ladykillers (Continental, 1956)	
The Lavender Hill Mob (Universal, 1951)	
The Man in the White Suit (Universal, 1952)	
The Planter's Wife/US title: *Outpost in Malaya* (UA, 1952)*	**British Lion**
West of Zanzibar (Universal, 1955)*	*Private's Progress* (Distributors Corp of America, 1956)
The Card/US title: *The Promoter* (Universal, 1952)	*Geordie*/US title: *Wee Geordie* (Times, 1956)
Christopher Columbus (Universal, 1949)*	*I am a Camera* (Distributors Corp of America, 1955)

*Films that obtained limited circuit runs

dise, the film that had been scrutinized by the Production Code Administration. By the end of 1954 *The Captain's Paradise* had grossed just over $1 million for United Artists.[18] While Roud's survey was clearly biased towards New York, it is significant that in his desire to advance his thesis about the importance of British films as being identified unquestionably as 'British', he sidelined the existence of films that could be described as 'Anglo-American' in casting, setting and genre. Indeed, their place in Roud's survey illustrates the impact of 'internationalism' in film production in the 1950s. Several of the films mentioned by Roud had American stars, including *The Purple Plain* and *The Million Pound Note* which both featured Gregory Peck. Non-British settings were also a feature, and several were shot in lavish Technicolor. *The*

Planter's Wife starred Claudette Colbert and was set in a Malayan rubber plantation. *The Purple Plain* was set in the Burmese jungle, and *Where No Vultures Fly*, *West of Zanzibar* and *Duel in the Jungle* were all set in Africa. Roud noted that these films were more likely to be distributed beyond art houses, but that the costs involved did not necessarily result in higher profits than those gained from bookings such as the lucrative seventeen-week run of *Genevieve* at the Sutton Theatre in New York. This is a fair point, although in the case of Universal, the company that distributed comedies as well as 'international' pictures, the dual approach was a strategic response to the opportunities presented by divorcement.

Promoting British Films: Universal and Rank in the Early 1950s

Universal's profits rose in the 1950s: the company made a recovery from declaring a loss of $1.1 million in 1949 to registering profits of $4 million in 1955 and 1956 (Finler, 1988: 288). The distribution of foreign films played a part in this recovery, but more so in the first half of the decade than the second, resulting in Rank's decision to establish Rank Film Distributors of America in 1957.[19] During the years 1948–55, Universal distributed sixty-three British films, a total that decreased to fifteen in 1955–58.[20] After 1952 Rank was no longer a stockholder in Universal, which explains Rank's weaker position in terms of insisting its films were marketed as aggressively as, say, *Hamlet* had been in the late 1940s. In general, the Rank Organization increased its overseas earnings in the 1950s, but more so outside the United States (Porter, 1997: 129). Towards the end of the decade, Universal did not sustain its profits, reporting a loss of $2 million in 1958. The number of foreign films distributed by the company decreased. The following year, however, Universal had made a remarkable recovery, declaring profits of $4.7 million. This quick turnaround of fortunes was possible because unlike the traditionally more dominant majors, Universal adjusted particularly well to the television age with its demand for product in subsequent-run theatres and on television (Gomery, 1986: 160).

An insight into the changing market for British films can be ascertained from reports compiled by Harry Fellerman, head of Universal-International's Special Films Division, 1952–3. Fellerman's reports included information on bookings, rentals and notes on the performance of particular films. It is possible to glean from them an impression of the types of British films that did the best business, as well as the problems of trying to succeed in both the commercial and art markets. An indication of the comparative popularity of thirteen British films can be ascertained from the Table 6.2, compiled by Fellerman in

Table 6.2 British Films Distributed by Universal, 1953

Film Title and US Release Date	Contracts	$ Received
A Queen is Crowned (June 1953)	3,249	562,930
The Promoter (Oct 1952)	819	369,325
Ivory Hunter (June 1952)	11,865	754,105
The Lavender Hill Mob (Oct 1951)	2,136	510,339
The Man in the White Suit (Apr 1952)	1,264	426,740
Pool of London (Nov 1951)	280	35,708
The Browning Version (Oct 1951)	460	98,627
The Importance of Being Earnest (Dec 1953)	332	143,481
Crash of Silence/Mandy (Feb 1953)	177	34,214
Penny Princess (Mar 1953)	182	20,597
I Believe in You (Apr 1953)	78	18,120
Island Rescue (June 1952)	558	80,667
The Stranger in Between (Aug 1952)	361	63,979

December 1953. American release dates have been added to provide a greater sense of the films' comparative performance.

Table 6.2 confirms some of Roud's observations, especially the popularity of Ealing comedies (*The Lavender Hill Mob* and *The Man in the White Suit*) and box-office strength of *Where No Vultures Fly/Ivory Hunter*, a film that was also very successful in the United Kingdom. Additional information in the report recorded that *Ivory Hunter* had sold well in New Orleans, Jacksonville and in Florida.[21] In *The Promoter/The Card*, Alec Guinness proved to be such a draw that it attracted bookings in Atlanta, Georgia, in a circuit that had previously been resistant to British films. The high number of contracts and earnings in a relatively short period of time for *A Queen is Crowned*, a colour film of the Coronation of Elizabeth II, narrated by Laurence Olivier, illustrates a continuing fascination with the British monarchy, although in the longer term the film was more successful outside the United States.[22] Social-realist films – Ealing's *Pool of London, Crash of Silence/Mandy* and Basil Dearden's *I Believe in You* – did not attract many bookings, again confirming Roud's views about the poor American box-office potential of such films. On the other hand, an adaptation of a classic stage drama, Oscar Wilde's *The Importance of Being Earnest,* resulted in a relatively high number of bookings prior to the film's release and good opening takings. The figures represent Universal's share of the takings, so in real terms these films earned more. Information on the division of takings between the theatre and distributor are provided in the reports so that, for example, after playing for a long run of eighteen weeks *The Promoter/The Card* grossed $146,090, yielding a rental figure of $61,923, or just under half the gross. *The Importance of Being Earnest* grossed $61,923 in the Baronet Theatre, New York, leaving Universal with $31,036.[23] The poor performances of *Crash of Silence/Mandy, Penny Princess* and *I Believe in You* in art-houses resulted in the decision to bill them alongside Universal films on general commercial release.

The *Cruel Sea* (US release, 1953) was reported as doing well by a number of branch managers. The Eastern Division manager, for example, considered that the film compared favourably with top U-I product in several spots in his territory. A series of meetings were held in Hollywood in December 1953 to discuss the marketing of Rank films in the United States. These were attended by staff from the New York office; foreign and advertising sales executives; divisional, district and branch managers; field publicity men and Hollywood production executives. The meetings show that in 1953 at least, Rank's films were being taken very seriously and that 'without Rank revenue our domestic figures would not look so good. . . . The Rank product must be treated absolutely no different from the pictures from our own studio'.[24] On the other hand, John Davis of Rank complained about the returns received by the company from the showings of British films in the United States. The Universal sales executives blamed their branch managers for not promoting them as specialized product: 'we have definitely not shown a strong enough effort in the handling of the Rank product'. These comments indicate the volatile nature of the American market in the early 1950s. Companies such as Universal were looking to British films and films produced by independents to fill their product shortage. Apart from the Ealing comedies – although *The Titfield Thunderbolt* (US release, 1953) was an interesting instance of one that did not do well – and some of the 'Commonwealth' spectacular adventure dramas such as *The Ivory Hunter,* clearly several of Rank's films did not prove to be as lucrative as both companies had hoped.

Correspondence between the Rank Organization's offices in New York and Universal's advertising department in the early 1950s sheds light on the promotion of British films. A recurring problem was the fact that many British stars were unknown to American audiences; the studio was keen to develop publicity that emphasized their distinctiveness. Occasionally, it therefore proved difficult to market British films which used American stars in a deliberate attempt to gain greater acceptability. An 'at home' layout devised for Yolande Donlan, star of *Penny Princess,* for example, was rejected by several leading magazines because the feature had 'no special British flavour' or foreign identity.[25] Donlan was an American actress living in the United Kingdom.

Although she had appeared in small roles in American films, she was best known as a stage actress. On the other hand, a careful handling of Joan Collins' introduction to America resulted in a more positive response. *Parade* magazine rejected an idea for a feature entitled, 'Two girls from Britain named Joan', referring to Joan Greenwood (in *The Importance of Being Earnest*) and Joan Collins. But Collins attracted interest, and *Parade* arranged for their photographer in Britain to visit her, resulting in a front-page colour cover and inside features. After this introduction other magazines requested information about her. Petula Clark proved to be more of a problem for Universal's advertising team, again because she was not connected with a major success. Popularity was not the only significant factor, however, and Universal stressed to Rank that in order to publicize British actors the features on their films had to incorporate items of 'novelty' or 'special interest'. Jeff Livingston of Universal-International's Special Films Division summarized the position in 1953, confirming the view that advertising based on the distinctiveness of British films was most likely to succeed:

> While no layout can be sure of placement in advance, our opportunities for placement are best when we turn a negative aspect into a positive one by utilizing the foreign locale or 'local color' to give the layouts we get from Britain a different flavour from those the publications are bombarded with from Hollywood. . . . Here in the US we can sell to the magazines the different customs and unique locales of different countries more easily than we can sell stars, not too well known, in conventional activity.

A year later a series of meetings was held to discuss problems in connection with publicity, advertising and promotions for Rank films.[26] A bone of contention between Rank and Universal's publicity team was the low number of British stars who went to America to publicize their films. On the occasions when they did visit, for example when Michael Redgrave and Valerie Hobson were present for the US premières of their respective star vehicles, *The Importance of Being Earnest* and *The Promoter*, effective publicity was much easier to arrange. Universal recommended that as a long-term policy British stars should be sent to the various key exchanges, including Boston, Chicago, Washington DC and Philadelphia, where art-theatre income was healthy. The greatest problem in the mid-1950s was obtaining features in fan magazines for British stars. Universal was caught in a difficult situation in this regard since the magazines refused to allocate column space to personalities whose popularity had not been demonstrated by the receipt of fan letters. Again, Universal recommended an expensive but potentially effective solution – for the Rank Organization to invite the key editors of fan magazines to Pinewood to meet the British stars: 'As guests of Rank, they will be obliged to devote a certain amount of space to British films. This will be helpful in instilling in the readers a desire to know more about the British personalities and a curiosity to see them in their films'. This proposal is interesting in terms of its intended address. As previously noted, British films were considered most suitable for the art market, but comments such as this, about the need for their stars to be more visible in America, indicates that publicity was still being sought according to the conventional norms of Hollywood exposure. On the other hand, the desire to make British films distinctive reveals that this strategy was not necessarily incompatible with the pursuit of 'niche' audiences or that stardom was not a factor in the marketing of art films.

Advertising credits were also an important factor in marketing foreign films. Universal was sent posters and other material by Rank that was often considered to be inappropriate for America. Credit lists on British posters, for example, were too long in comparison with American posters that singled out star names and key associations for a particular picture, such as an adaptation of a novel by a popular writer. Furthermore, Universal complained that Rank sent material on forthcoming films all at once, preventing a continuous flow of daily production news similar to the material a Hollywood unit man would normally send to the home office. The result of this poor management of publicity information from the Rank end of the operation was that reviews and reports of British films would appear in influential publications such as the *New York Times* before Universal received news of them or advertising material that could be used in conjunction with reviews.[27] Although Universal possessed an adequate supply of biographical information, they were hampered by a 'paucity of location stories' and the snippets of news reporters were used to obtaining from stars and technicians during the course of shooting a much-hyped film. Another recurrent problem was that Rank sent Universal publicity stills too late after a film had been completed. As Sheldon Gunsberg of Universal's Advertising Department complained:

We received some exciting photos in connection with *West of Zanzibar* and immediately submitted them to *The New York Times* for a Sunday break. Their objection, as has happened before, was that while the stills were very good, they were no longer timely because news about completion of *West of Zanzibar* had already appeared in Stephen Watts' column. If we had received these photos one month earlier, we might have gotten an important Sunday break similar to the one we had in connection with the first days of shooting on *The Cruel Sea*.

This correspondence reveals the tensions between Rank and Universal that contributed to the establishment of Rank Films Distributors of America. Universal felt frustrated and let down by Rank's lack of cooperation with publicizing films in the United States, while the Rank Organization felt that Universal should be doing more to obtain general releases for British films. Again, publicity was a key factor, and it appears to be the case that Rank was not responding to justifiable criticisms of their publicity work. The stills sent to accompany films intended for general release, such as *West of Zanzibar* and *Ivory Hunter*, were not considered to be up to the standard required in terms of conveying a sense of the pictures' key dramatic moments.[28] This observation is interesting in terms of Hollywood's convention of connecting pre-release publicity with a film's genre and narrative trajectory. By contrast, the British posters sent to Universal were far more static in their composition, veering towards a more literal impression of a film. As with publicity stills, Hollywood's posters would frequently depict actors in exaggerated poses, capturing the essence of a film's drama, rather than simply reproduce an image of a star. In the case of British films, whose stars were often not well known in America, more animated representations were therefore considered to be more alluring and effective.

Rank responded to Universal's criticisms by agreeing to open studios and facilities in Britain to visiting American fan magazine editors. Nevertheless, Universal's publicity department continued to feel torn between devoting the time, money and energy necessary to ensure more effective advertising for British films and concentration on their own films. Philip Gerard of Universal-International's publicity department in New York expressed this dilemma in a letter to David Lipton, head of Advertising and Publicity in Hollywood:

There is much we can do with the Rank product, both pre-production and during shooting, but this is a responsibility and a chore that can take considerable time and effort and cannot be done on the run. I have always felt that the primary responsibility for myself and the staff was to Universal-International, and I am aware of the fact that Rank is very much part of the U-I operation, but, it is difficult to try to do justice to both. If we were to do what can be done for the J. Arthur Rank pictures, in the production planning stage and the follow through stage, we would have to devote lots more time to this operation – I would have to devote more time and certainly the staff would. Such pictures as *Magnificant Obsession, Sign of the Pagan* and others in work, have a much greater potential for publicity than our past product, and if we are diverted to the advance handling and extras on the Rank product, some of our own pictures will have to suffer.[29]

From the mid-1950s Universal distributed fewer British films, no doubt influenced by the above conflicts over presentation. While the art market provided a lucrative base for films such as Ealing comedies that had established stars, it was not so easy with the bulk of Rank's releases. As a studio whose fortunes were, on the whole, rising in the 1950s, Universal was not prepared to divert attention from films that were proving more successful at the box-office. As we shall see, this was a factor that influenced the company's decision to distribute Hammer's horror films in the late 1950s.

Ealing and Alec Guinness in America

Surefire for the art house trade in the US.
—*Variety* on *Kind Hearts and Coronets*
At kidding the British, no one equals the British themselves.
—*Time* on *Passport to Pimlico*
The production of Michael Balcon and direction of Alexander Mackendrick play up national foibles and do a good job of caricaturing the English.
—*Reporter* on *Tight Little Island*
An artistic gem at the art houses and perhaps even at the neighborhoods.
—*Hollywood Reporter* on *The Ladykillers*
There is every good reason why Alec Guinness should be the darling of the British Treasury and the toast of the London City. . . . For certainly the pictures in which he appears are the most amusing, if not the most profitable exports from Britain.
—*The New York Times* on *The Man in the White Suit*

Of all the British films that were distributed in the United States in the 1950s, most sources point to Ealing comedies as the most successful. Although the comedies were only one element of Ealing's total generic output, it is clear that these films in particular made an impact. While the majority were distributed by Universal (*Tight Little Island/Whisky Galore!, The Lavender Hill Mob, The Man in the White Suit,* and *The Titfield Thunderbolt*), two of the most popular, *Kind Hearts and Coronets* and *Passport to Pimlico* were handled by Eagle-Lion, and *The Ladykillers* by United Artists. Universal also distributed one of Alec Guinness' most popular non-Ealing films, *The Promoter/The Card,* while *The Captain's Paradise* and *Last Holiday* were distributed by Stratford and Continental, respectively. They were sought after by distributors, particularly Continental, an independent company that was anxious to make a deal with Michael Balcon as late as 1957, when Ealing was in decline and the phase of Guinness comedies was more or less over. When Balcon tried to impress Continental with *The Shiralee* (1957), a film directed by Leslie Norman set in Australia, it was rejected. On the other hand, Continental was envious of MGM's agreement with Balcon to distribute *All At Sea/Barnacle Bill* (1957; US release, 1958), a film starring Guinness that is regarded as being inferior to the 'classic' comedies, representing 'an unmistakeable end of the line for Ealing comedy' (Barr, 1977: 165).[30] The incident nevertheless shows that Guinness' image as a British money-maker persisted until the end of the 1950s.

To a great extent Ealing's American success was inextricably bound up with the popularity of Alec Guinness, investing the films with theatrical kudos. A report in 1952 noted:

> Art house trade has developed a marquee name in the person of Alec Guinness, British thespian currently starring in America in J. Arthur Rank's *Lavender Hill Mob* and *The Man in the White Suit*. Although Guinness has appeared in many British pictures seen in this country, it wasn't until *Mob* that he developed into the solid box-office personality that he is. *Suit* is doing record business in New York, with Guinness getting sock newspaper and magazine breaks.[31]

Even in films that were not a great success in the United Kingdom, such as *Last Holiday*, a poignant drama scripted by J. B. Priestley about a man who is told he has a month to live, Guinness was received in enthusiastic terms by American critics and art-cinema patrons. Praise for his acting abilities featured in many reviews, for example, Bosley Crowther described an ability to suggest 'intense emotional moods through his perfect command of stoicism' in *Last Holiday*.[32] On other occasions, such as his performance as 'The Professor' in *The Ladykillers*, what was admired was the way Guinness 'sinks his personality almost to the level of anonymity'.[33] One of Ealing's more complex comedies, *The Man in the White Suit*, received an excellent critical reception in America, in large part attributed to the satirical sophistication communicated by Guinness with his 'dead-pan manner'.[34]

The majority of the Ealing comedies were exhibited in art theatres, occasionally 'crossing over' into a wider market, as with *Tight Little Island*, a film that grossed well outside 'the sophisticated centres' in places such as Houston, Burlington (Vermont), Minneapolis, Charlottesville, Milwaukee, Maynard, New Bedford (Massachusetts) and Stamford (Connecticut).[35] In an astute piece of marketing, Universal devised a supplementary advertisement that made much of the film's opposition to Hollywood values. The following text was in the advertisement as well as the trailer for *Tight Little Island*: 'Here's news! Our next attraction. Did not cost $2 million! Did not take two years to make! Did not have a star-studded cast! Is not a great spectacle!' The advertisement however went on to quote reviews that stressed its unusual qualities: 'Like Scotch whiskey, it is a peculiarly British product with strong transatlantic appeal'.[36] Another review made a connection between the film's subject matter – a liquor shortage – and American experience: 'Its story will particularly delight and amuse Americans who remember the national thirst inspired by the eighteenth amendment'.[37] As a result, 'word-of-mouth' publicity had a direct impact on the box-office when takings went up after its first week's exhibition in Boston and Chicago.[38] Marcia Landy recalls that as well as being exhibited in New York, Boston and Chicago, Ealing films 'also made their way to college campuses and to a dwindling but still viable cinema-going public' (Landy, 2000: 68). As the work of editor Michael Truman reveals, the studio acknowledged that changes might be necessary for the films to 'cross over' into a wider market. In certain cases, however, this was not deemed necessary. No attempt was made to show *The Man in the White Suit* outside of the art market, so it was possible to prepare it for specialized exhibition by showing the longer than average UK trailer.[39]

As reviews attest and in support of Roud's thesis, the films were praised for their 'Englishness', their distinctive satire of national identity and the performances of Alec Guinness. Reviewers appreciated their distinctive 'take' on postwar British society, and it is interesting to consider why this held such an appeal for American art audiences. A recurrent theme is self-parody, a quality that had been so admired in films going back to *The Private Life of Henry VIII*, indicating a link with a tradition of satiric comedy. While it is common to interpret the Ealing comedies as a reaction to post-war restrictions and expressive of nostalgia for the wartime sense of community, it was their unsettling, probing facets that were picked up by American reviewers. 'Satire' is a recurrent word, as well as reference to some of the films' almost anarchic tendencies. One review of *The Man in the White Suit*, for example, identified the 'sly and trenchant undercurrents that run beneath its surface of stuffy conventionality and pomposity'.[40] Reviewers expressed amazement at the depths of satire evident in *Passport to Pimlico*, agreeing that elements of 'Britishness' did, indeed, deserve to be caricatured, particularly 'the obstinate pride and pompous sense of superiority of Britons generally'.[41] Indeed, remembering seeing these films in America on first release, Marcia Landy endorses the opinion that the films were 'able to communicate vulnerable aspects of British national culture, presenting an image of crisis rather than legitimation' (2000: 68).

Landy argues that while ostensibly very 'British' in theme, the Ealing comedies 'travelled well' because of their appropriateness to 1950s American society: 'What we recognized, if perhaps inchoately, was that the films were an antidote to the rhetoric and actions of Cold War America' (2000: 69). The stance of many of the Ealing films against government restrictions and authority figures can, indeed, be considered in the context of Cold War politics and the rise of Riesman's 'other-directed' characters. There is an irony in the fact that the people who sought to distinguish themselves from the mass by cultivating minority tastes and ideas were more than likely members of the art-house audiences that appreciated Ealing comedies. While, as Landy remembers, a liking for these apparently nonconformist films invested a person with a certain 'hipness', in an intriguing way their content critiqued post-war social values that threatened to destroy notions of community and unity. Just as the Cold War encouraged suspicion, division and prejudice, Ealing films advocated a perpetuation of the apparent social cohesiveness of wartime society. As in *Passport to Pimlico* and *Tight Little Island/Whiskey Galore!*, they celebrated people who did not conform to the new *status quo*, 'little men' who refused to be subject to bureaucratic authority. In Riesman's terms, the heroes of Ealing comedies were more 'inner-directed' individualists than 'outer-directed' characters desperate to fit in with their peers in an increasingly fragmentary society. Care must however be taken in applying a broad generic gloss to Ealing's films. As Barr has shown, they were diverse, complex and sometimes reactionary in their engagement with contemporary issues (Barr, 1977: 106).

Hammer Horror in America

Universal was attracted to British horror films after the success of *The Curse of Frankenstein* (1957), Hammer's first horror film that was distributed by Warner Brothers. Produced on a low budget of £65,000, the film grossed £1 million in the United States (Murphy, 1992: 162). The film was part-funded by a bank loan from the Chemical Commercial Exchange Bank of $168,000 at a rate of 6 per cent interest, to be paid out of the proceeds. In the distribution contract, Warners took a fee of 30 per cent and launched an appropriate pre-release exploitation campaign that created a climate of anticipation for *The Curse of Frankenstein*. This campaign clearly contributed to the film's box-office success, as noted by *Variety*.[42] The première in San Diego, California, was heralded by a 'horrorthon', and on its opening day the film took almost as much as the theatre's usual weekly takings. The première was an example of an 'event' opening, lasting twenty-four hours during which the film was shown eight times. A similar opening was held in New York where a variety of gimmicks were used to attract an aura of excitement about the picture. Exploitation 'stunts' included free admission to those wearing Dracula, Frankenstein or other monster costumes; the provision of a nurse's aide and first aid assistance for those who found the film too terrifying; the distribution of masks to young patrons; the attendance of actors dressed up as Dracula, Wolf Man and Mr Hyde and a letter-writing contest for patrons to write about their 'most terrifying moment'.[43] Radio features also prepared audiences to be scared out of their wits by *The Curse of Frankenstein,* urging them not to faint. Showings in drive-in theatres were accompanied by similar 'horrorthon' and 'screamière' stunts. In the Stanley Theatre, Baltimore, a young woman was invited to see *The Curse of Frankenstein* alone in a 3,000 seat house, afterwards appearing on radio stations to give her reaction.[44]

These arrangements were clearly successful as far as audiences were concerned. Warner Brothers' files list the various box-office records achieved by the film, as well as the noticeably young audience it attracted. 'Exceptional' business was noted at the Paramount and Fenway Theatres in Boston, for example, as well as in other locations.[45] As such, *The Curse of Frankenstein* was the first British film to take advantage of the changing nature of the cinema audience, exploiting its appeal to the young people who frequented drive-in theatres. Some contemporary commentators identified *The Curse of Frankenstein* as a sure bet for horror fans and, unusually for a British film, recognized that 'it should sell well in all but the sophisticated situations'.[46] This astute observation clearly testifies to the film's popular, as opposed to critical success, revealing that young audiences were more influenced by Warners' pre-publicity than by the press. Hammer horrors were clearly the exception to the 'arthouse only' rule, although in subsequent decades the films were shown in British retrospectives at the Museum of Modern Art, New York.

Not all critics were impressed with *The Curse of Frankenstein,* some of them rather disapproving of the exploitation stunts that had drawn in so many people. This film is clearly an example of how word-of-mouth and extravagant publicity could, on rare occasions, be more important than critical opinion. In particular, resentment was expressed at Hammer's apparent 'borrowing' of Universal's horror themes and characters from their 1930s cycle of horror classics. Bosley Crowther thought that nothing new had been added: 'Everything that happens in their picture has happened the same way in previous films'.[47] This inevitable comparison tended to obscure the distinctiveness that was the beginning of Hammer's style, as the following reviews reveal: 'A frail facsimilie of the original haunting classic. The British concept of the monster just doesn't have it'; 'This monster, to come right out with it, is too darn vulnerable to be much of a threat. . . . For those who remember the old thrillers, it will be prettier but less melodramatically gripping'.[48] Other reviewers argued that with all the build-up, the film should have been scarier, as it failed to satisfy the horrific expectations that had been suggested by Warners' campaign.[49] On the other hand, a perceptive reviewer for *New York Journal American* was able to see that Hammer's film had something different to offer that departed from the Universal formula:

> Despite its melodramatic title *The Curse of Frankenstein* is a superbly acted picture. I'm not going to compare Boris Karloff and Bela Lugosi, previous monsters, with Christopher Lee . . . because I think top laurels should go to Peter Cushing. . . . You could almost hear the nerves snapping in the audience at the Paramount last night.[50]

This review is important because it indicates a recognition that Hammer horrors did not have to repeat past formulas in order to be successful. Indeed, *The Curse of Frankenstein* is 'characterised by a mordant realism and dark humour rather than macabre symbolism and expressionist excess'. This style was a feature of the horror films directed by Terence Fisher, less exotic than the Universal horror cycle, but distinguished instead by 'urbanity and restraint only occasionally disrupted by shocking images' (Murphy, 1992: 164, 163). The use of colour was also a departure from previous Frankenstein films, a feature that prompted an interesting discussion about the extent to which colour enhanced the realism of the horror genre. While some reviewers considered that this did indeed increase realism others, such as the *LA Times* critic, held on to a generic association between horror and black and white: 'Subverting everything, of course, is Technicolor; its creamy tones fatally dissipate all the grimness vital to the genre'.[51] The distinctive use of colour in Hammer horrors was further developed in subsequent films, particularly *Dracula/Horror of Dracula* (1958), a film that capitalized on the success of *The Curse of Frankenstein*.

Recognizing that Hammer had revived the horror film in a profitable manner, Universal distributed the company's next film, *Horror of Dracula,* and sold the remake rights of their Gothic horror films to Hammer (Murphy, 1992: 168). Although Warners had launched an impressive publicity and exploitation campaign for *The Curse of Frankenstein,* Universal was more experienced with 'showmanship' strategies. As Philip Gerard of Universal wrote to Dennison Thornton at Hammer: 'We at Universal have a reputation for being the "showmanship" company in the industry and it [*Horror of Dracula*] is a "natural" for our selling and merchandising organization'.[52] Universal was impressed with James Carreras, co-founder with Anthony Hinds of Hammer, a production company that had been formed in 1947. Carreras had faith in Universal's exploitation plans and contacted Archie Herzoff in Universal's California office with an enthusiastic report on the film's progress: 'The picture looks sensational, and if really well handled by your boys should take a fortune. In my opinion it is twice as horrific and twice as big as *The Curse of Franken-stein*.[53] The deal with Universal stipulated that the film would be played in 'top theatres', released at the same time as *The Thing that Couldn't Die,* an American film that took second billing to Hammer's film.

When he visited New York, Carreras gave interviews to the trade press, and several members of the cast, including Peter Cushing and Christopher Lee, joined Carreras and Hinds for the New York première at the Mayfair theatre. Unlike Universal's previous experience with the Rank Organization and its non-cooperative attitude towards the norms of American movie publicity, the Hammer team assisted Universal by going to America and giving many press and radio interviews. The studio also sent Universal information about the stars and other publicity material.[54] When the film opened it was accompanied by similar stunts to those Warners had used for *The Curse of Frankenstein,* encouraging the opinion that the picture was a 'shocker'. A few days before *Horror of Dracula* was shown at a cinema in Flint, Michigan, its overenthusiastic manager dressed up as Dracula and paraded through the town only to be charged with committing a breach of the peace.[55] More successful stunts included contests for the 'bride' of Dracula; the handing out of wills before the film was shown and award of prizes, including a 'courage' cocktail and pocket-book edition of *Dracula,* for the first 200 patrons. Instead of including a still of Christopher Lee, Universal's poster featured a drawing of a long-fanged creature with large, white piercing eyes, illustrated with the caption: 'The terrifying creature who died . . . yet LIVED!'

Despite the spirit of collaboration between Hammer and Universal, this campaign conflicted with Hammer's desire for their film to be treated as a 'high-class' horror production. This point was made by James Carreras in response to some of Universal's 'gory' posters for the film:

> I don't like the advertising I have seen put out by your New York office which is on the lines of old Dracula pictures – a hideous face and bats flying about all over the place. Our Dracula is handsome and sexy and not the old Bella Lugosi type. His victims are young attractive women. The campaign in London is on the horror sex lines and I would be grateful if you would re-examine.

Again, the reluctance to distinguish Hammer films from their Universal predecessors prevented their difference from being foregrounded at the publicity stage. When shooting the film Fisher was highly aware of the Dracula audiences were expecting:

In my film, when Dracula made his first appearance, he took a long time to come down the stairs but it seems a short time because you're waiting to see what he's going to look like. Because, the first time, everybody was ready to laugh their bloody heads off – I've seen it in cinemas again and again – they thought they were going to see fangs and everything. They didn't of course. Instead they saw a charming and extremely good-looking man with a touch, an undercurrent, of evil or menace. (Fisher quoted in Hutchings, 1993: 115)

It seems that Fisher's observation applied equally to critics.

The showmanship stunts nevertheless paid off, as attendances were high, particularly among teenagers and young couples. A telegram reporting on the film's opening at the Warner Theatre, Milwaukee, conveys Universal's excitement at having backed such a profitable film:

Terrific opening day gross $1562 Warner Milwaukee. Indicates solid week with anticipated smash weekend. One of the top figures within year excepting *Kwai*. . . . Audiences primarily teenagers including many young couples. Evening attendance males and females about equal. Reaction great with screen thrills audibly permeating audiences. Voluntary comments excellent.[56]

Regional takings were reported as 'excellent', especially in areas that did not normally welcome British films. The opening at the Michigan Theatre, Detroit, for example, was 'good' for a theatre whose patronage was 50 per cent black; 10 per cent teenagers and 5 per cent children.[57] Many trade and critical reviews predicted its good box-office takings, largely because of the precedent set by *The Curse of Frankenstein*.

Reviewers were more impressed with *Horror of Dracula* than they had been with *The Curse of Frankenstein*. Critics were beginning to appreciate Hammer's style, as well as the use of Technicolor, a more expensive process than the Eastman colour used for *The Curse of Frankenstein*. The *Harrison's Report* verdict was particularly positive: 'Of all the *Dracula* horror pictures thus far produced, this one, made in Britain and photographed in Technicolor, tops them all. Its shock impact is, in fact, so great that it may well be considered as one of the best horror films ever made'.[58] This time colour was considered to be an aid to realism. Indeed, in *Horror of Dracula*, the Technicolor was not garish and used to good effect in conjunction with the work of cinematographer Jack Asher and the disciplined directorial style of Terence Fisher that was characterized by a 'mordant realism and dark humour' (Murphy, 1992: 164).

The success of these films persuaded Universal to continue to distribute Hammer's films. Carreras was astute enough not to be tied to a single distributor, and over the years Hammer product was handled by other large companies, including Columbia (*The Revenge of Frankenstein*, US release, 1958 and *Curse of the Mummy's Tomb*, US release, 1965); United Artists (*The Hound of the Baskervilles*, US release, 1959) and Fox (*Dracula – Prince of Darkness*, US release, 1966). The international success of Hammer's films was acknowledged in 1968 when Carreras received a Queen's Award for Industry.

While Hutchings (1993) has examined Hammer and other British horror films in relation to trends in contemporary British society, as with Ealing's films it is interesting to consider why they were so successful in the United States. Their emphasis on sexuality was an obvious attraction, particularly Dracula as a dangerous but compelling carnal lover. The use of colour, costumes and settings also received high praise. Landy (2000: 69) has argued that Hammer horror 'capitalized on the anxieties of the time. Such films worked over issues of authority gone awry and of beleaguered masculinity and femininity'. While this argument is not explicit in contemporary discourse on the films, it is nevertheless useful to relate Hammer to American experience. Since the studio was working with the models established by Universal in the 1930s, the early Hammer films were bound, to a certain extent, to acknowledge the generic expectations associated with the earlier films. As Hutchings has shown, Hammer worked with and revised these models in significant ways so that elements of continuity – for example, the monster or particular iconographic traditions – remained but new elements and emphases were added. Whereas many critics responded in a somewhat confused manner to *The Curse of Frankenstein*, their reception of *Horror of Dracula* shows that in a relatively short period of time they had adjusted to Hammer's revision of previous characteristics of the horror genre.

Just as Hammer's early Frankenstein and Dracula films can be seen to relate to issues of an increasingly threatened male authority in relation to the social changes that were taking place in Britain at the end of the 1950s, the cycle's international popularity implies that these gender issues were equally relevant to other societies. Hutchings (1993: 101–6) has argued that in Universal's Frankenstein films the monster represented the underclass, to be feared and pitied. By contrast, in Hammer's version it is Frankenstein (Peter Cushing) who is the central character, representing an urbane authority figure who is 'monstrous' but at the same time 'heroic'. He does not represent the underclass but is an aristocrat who is forced to engage with bourgeois society because of his profession as a scientist. The pathetic monster (Christopher Lee) is merely an extension of Frankenstein's unsentimental, calculating and cruel ambitions.

He is single-minded and ruthless and exploits those, particularly women, who threaten the achievement of his goals. As such, Frankenstein's character and values represent a rejection of contemporary, bourgeois social values: his creation of the monster puts science before humanity and family. In the late 1950s, it is not difficult to relate these preoccupations to contemporary concerns in Britain and America about the consequences of scientific experimentation, the instability of the nuclear family and bourgeois society. The Cold War preoccupation with the possibility of a nuclear holocaust is relevant here, as Frankenstein's experiment results in an abject creature whose 'birth' results in death and destruction. As with the Ealing comedies, it is the inner-directed character that represents individualism and threatens prevailing social norms. Frankenstein is the rebel, but he is not part of a wider community as his actions signal a far more dangerous and sinister future than the safe, non-confrontational past recreated in Ealing's films.

Similarly, in *Horror of Dracula* the vampire is an authority figure, but this time he is attractive to women, making them desirous and sexual, even if their awakenings are, ultimately, subservient to his own ends. The increased emphasis on sexuality was a significant development in the genre. As David Pirie (1973: 87) has observed, Christopher Lee's Dracula was 'the villain . . . he was always meant to be, the charming, intelligent, and irresistible host who is on the point of turning the cozy Victorian world upside down' (Plate 15). The result is a humanized and attractive villain who is associated with desire and danger. While he is a compelling figure, the film works towards destroying the deviant sexuality and threat to bourgeois family life he represents. Again, *Horror of Dracula* can be read as a response to changes in Western societies in the late 1950s. In the American context, the publication of the Kinsey report in 1954 demonstrated that women engaged in, and enjoyed, a far greater degree of sexual activity than had previously been assumed. In this context the 'horror' of Dracula represented the dire consequences of sexual temptation and the disturbing features of carnal lust. As such, the films reference masculinity under threat in a complex and symbolic manner. While Dracula is contained as he turns to dust at the end of *Horror of Dracula,* the Hammer cycle of subsequent Dracula films confirmed that he would never be completely destroyed.

Conclusion: British Films as Art and Entertainment

By the end of the 1950s, British films had made their mark in the ever-expanding art market, as well as the occasional success outside. British films had attracted important distributors and were appreciated for their distinctiveness, particularly Ealing comedies with their satirical elements. British accents were complained about far less than in previous years as studios paid more attention to pacing and enunciation, demonstrating a greater sensitivity to the requirements of overseas markets. In terms of critical appreciation, the 1950s was an important decade when British films began to acquire a 'prestige' category of their own, a subdivision of 'foreign films' that presented exhibitors with fewer problems than foreign-language product, even after the introduction of dubbing and subtitling. Also, as Wilinsky (2001: 31) has noted, there were distinctions between different sorts of British films. These were between the prestige Rank productions which, as we have seen, received top promotional treatment from Universal, and the smaller films that played primarily in small, independent art cinemas. The National Board of Review consistently placed British films at the top of their lists throughout the 1950s.[59]

This enhanced status, based on the English language, also presented problems in that British producers assumed that it gave them a chance to break out from the art market. As we have seen, this was possible, even with a film such as *Tight Little Island* that would appear to have a narrow national address. Wide distribution was more likely to occur, however, with films like *The Purple Plain* and *The Ivory Hunter*, which were more 'international' in terms of their themes, concerns and personnel. Indeed, the 1950s was a key decade in the development of the 'international' film, especially with an increasing number of films being shot in Europe and Africa. *The African Queen* (1951) was registered as a British film, even though its producer and director were American. The outstanding box-office success of *The Bridge on the River Kwai* (1957), produced by an American company but directed by David Lean and starring British actors Alec Guinness and Jack Hawkins, together with American star William Holden, demonstrated that big financial returns could result from productive international collaboration. *The Bridge on the River Kwai* was listed by *Variety* as one of the highest-grossing films of 1958, eventually earning $15 million. Apart from this, the only British registered film to exceed $5 million in the United States before 1960 was still *The Red Shoes*. So while the decade was certainly characterized by an expansion of the art market, by dint of the common language and the increasing trend for American companies to produce films abroad, British films were still potentially active in the wider arena. In Britain, however, the production of 'British' films by American companies was criticized because of the perceived threat to genuinely domestic production.

Against the background of major changes in the structure of the American film industry, competition from television and changing leisure patterns, the film market was volatile for all concerned. This encouraged an intense preoccupation with box-office returns, an anxiety that undoubtedly influenced John

Davis at Rank, who was determined to register international success on an equivalent scale to Hollywood. Since the major American companies were on the defensive throughout the 1950s, it was frequently pointed out that while foreign films had invaded the market, they nevertheless did not earn as much money as Hollywood's. S. H. Fabian, President of the Stanley Warner cinema circuit, was keen to point out that while in 1958 the major studios produced approximately half the films they had produced in 1951, thirteen had grossed over $5 million, and the only 'foreign' films that did well were those produced by American companies on location in Europe.[60] Such comment naturally obscured the advances made by British films in 'niche' markets and the extent to which they kept pace with the changing composition of the cinema audience. It also concealed the fact that British producers were dependent on American distributors for their share of rental grosses, a share that was often frustratingly small since many of the companies were new, dealing primarily in foreign product that did not yield large returns.

Universal's records provide an insight into the practical problems of marketing films during a period when such major changes were taking place. British films presented them with an opportunity to develop campaigns based on product differentiation, such as the pre-publicity for *Tight Little Island*. Stardom continued to be a major factor in motion-picture marketing, even in the art market. The name of Alec Guinness proved to be a box-office draw that was exploited by all the companies that distributed films in which he starred. As yet the cult of the 'auteur' was not sufficiently developed to displace stars as the major incentive for movie attendance. As Hollywood's output was dwindling, and in the context of divorcement, pre-release marketing became all the more important as the studios could no longer rely on securing an automatic release for their films. American film companies had to spend more time and energy on marketing British films, time and energy that often conflicted with their desire to promote their own product. In a major study of motion-picture audiences published in 1950, the opinion of reviewers was found to be the most important factor in communicating knowledge about a film, along with trailers and newspaper advertisements. Posters and billboards were low on the list of influential material (Handel, 1950: 69). As the marketing of early Hammer horror films demonstrates, the end of the decade saw a shift away from the dominance of critical opinion towards exploitation, pre-publicity campaigns and word-of-mouth advertising. Managers of art cinemas consulted critics' opinions before they booked a film, whereas for managers of drive-ins attention to the needs of the youth audience placed more stress on advertising.[61] The success of Hammer represented a key shift in the audience for some British films, a young clientele that can be regarded as the beginnings of the 'cult' audience that was attracted by subsequent British films and genres. In this way British films continued to attract 'niche' audiences and grapple with issues of product differentiation in the context of trends towards 'internationalism', discussed in the next chapter.

Notes

1. Figures from *Film Daily Year Book*, see Appendix A. Another source of film industry data, the *Motion Picture and Television Almanac* (New York: Quigley) put the figures even higher, averaging 150 films a year that were available for distribution, illustrating the generally healthy state of British imports in the 1950s.
2. *Variety*, 15 Apr 1959: 30. French films earned gross rentals of $8,345,825; Mexican, $3,301,000; Italian, $1,508,450 and Japanese, $933,000. The British figure was inflated by the success of *The Bridge on the River Kwai* which earned $14 million in the United States in 1958. Although registered as British, this film had been produced by an American company. The *Variety* report noted that such films inflated the dollar earnings of 'British' films and that 'the "pure" British films, such as the Rank releases, failed to make similar headway in 1958'. An exception was *Pursuit of the Graf Spee*.
3. *Variety*, 19 June 1957; 17 Mar 1959.
4. Although it should be noted, as Wilinsky (2001: 89) stresses, that the exact number of art-houses operating is open to debate, since different sources give different figures. However, what can be said is that they grew considerably during the post-war period.
5. A 'drive-in theatre' was an outdoor theatre. Audiences sat in their cars and viewed a film on a large, elevated screen, and cars were fitted with small speakers to transmit the sound. Their expansion is explained by the growth of the suburban family in the 1950s. See Gomery, 1992: 92–3.
6. The US Supreme Court's decision in 1948 on the Paramount case was the culmination of federal antitrust action against the Hollywood studios. The court ruled that production and exhibition should be divorced and unfair booking practices eliminated. Studios were thus forced to sell their exhibition interests, breaking the vertically integrated structure of the film industry.
7. *Variety*, 15 Apr 1959: 30.
8. *Variety*, 6 Oct 1948: 4.
9. For a description of the art-house audience see Wilinsky, 2001: 93–103.
10. Barbara Wilinsky (1997) argues that the broadcast of Korda's films on television was stymied by bad timing and did not reap the financial rewards expected by WPIX. It could also be argued that British films were not the most appropriate to be the first films broadcast on American television. Since art-house audiences for the most part did not own televisions, the television audience was more than likely not appreciative of Korda's films. Also, the values privileged by the 'art-house experience' could not be replicated on early television transmissions. Several of the Korda pictures, such as *The Thief of Bagdad*, demonstrated spectacular values that did not translate well to television.
11. *Variety*, 7 Jan 1953, anniversary edition, Herrick Library, Los Angeles.
12. *Film Industry*, vol. 7, no. 61, 17 Nov 1949: 15.
13. Michael Truman in *Film Industry*, vol. 7, no. 61, 17 Nov 1949: 8.
14. *New York Times*, 27 Oct 1949. The *New York Herald Tribune* also criticized the re-editing of *Passport to Pimlico*, 27 Oct 1949.
15. *Picturegoer*, 25 May 1946.
16. 'Anglo-American Tourists' article in *Film Industry*, vol. 1, no. 6, Dec 1946: 8–12.

17. In all these cases, the British companies distributed the films in the United Kingdom and provided production finance. Additional information on US titles, US distributors and release dates has been added.
18. *Variety*, 5 Jan 1955, anniversary edition, Herrick Library, Los Angeles.
19. *Motion Picture Herald*, 28 June 1952.
20. Figures compiled from *Motion Picture and Television Almanacs* (New York: Quigley), 1948–58.
21. Coordinators' reports, box 706/6/24614/15; Universal archive, University of Southern California, (USC).
22. Odeon Theatres, Annual Report to 27 June 1953, pp. 4, 6, quoted by Porter, 1997: 129.
23. Report by Fellerman, 10 Mar 1952; 706/6/24614/15, USC.
24. Report by Ben Cohn and Harry Fellerman of sales executives' meetings, Hollywood, Dec 1953; box 706/6/24614/15; Universal archive, University of Southern California (USC).
25. Livingstone to Roberts, 12 Nov 1953, Rank Organization file, box 59/23/19042, USC.
26. The following material is contained in an office memorandum to Jeff Livingston to Sheldon Gunsberg (Universal), 10 May 1954; box 59/23/19042, USC.
27. Information on day-to-day relationship with Rank, as established in Livingston to Davis, 21 Mar 1951 and still in force in 1954; box 59/23/19042, USC.
28. Livingston to Jamieson, 31 Aug 1954; box 59/23/19042, USC.
29. Gerard to Lipton, 21 July 1954; box 59/23/19042, USC.
30. See correspondence between Walter Reade and Michael Balcon, I/1996, June-Dec 1957 in the Michael Balcon Special collection, BFI, London.
31. *Variety*, 23 Apr 1952.
32. *New York Times*, 14 Nov 1951: 39.
33. *Variety*, 28 Dec 1955.
34. *Motion Picture Daily*, 2 Apr 1952.
35. Memorandum to bookers, box 426/25/11999, USC.
36. *Time* review quoted in advertising material for *Tight Little Island*, USC.
37. *Philadelphia News*, 9 Feb 1950.
38. Lipton to O'Keefe, 12 Dec 1949 on trailer and performance record for *Tight Little Island*, box 426/25/11998, USC.
39. File on *The Man in the White Suit*, box 437/21/12956, USC.
40. *Motion Picture Daily*, 2 Apr 1952.
41. *Cue*, 29 Oct 1949.
42. Warner Brothers archive, file 174B on *The Curse of Frankenstein*, USC. *Variety*, 24 July 1957 observed: 'Although Warners in general has been putting its production stress on planned blockbuster high-budget releases there will actually be considerable accentuation of exploitation of which *The Curse of Frankenstein* is a first sample'.
43. Warner Brothers archive, file 649 (A), *The Curse of Frankenstein*, USC.
44. *Box Office*, 10 Aug 1957.
45. *Hollywood Reporter*, 24 July 1957.
46. *Film Daily*, 25 June 1957.
47. *New York Times*, 8 Aug 1957.
48. *New York Mirror*, 8 Aug 1957 and *New York Post*, 7 Aug 1957.
49. *New York Herald Tribune*, 8 Aug 1957.
50. *New York Journal American*, 7 Aug 1957.
51. A reviewer for the *New York Herald Tribune*, 11 Aug 1957 commented, for example, that 'Your blood will run cold when the blood runs red in the film'. The *LA Times* quotation was published on 18 June 1957.
52. Gerard to Thornton, 4 Nov 1957; box 428/25/11880, USC.

53. Carreras to Herzoff, 14 Feb 1959; Universal archive, box 428/25/11880, USC.
54. Thornton to Gerard, 5 Nov 1957; box 428/25/11880, USC.
55. *St Paul's Dispatch,* 18 June 1958: 50.
56. Katz to Lipton, 8 May 1958; box 428/25/11880, USC.
57. Johnson to Lipton, 2 June 1958; box 428/25/11880, USC.
58. *Harrison's Reports,* 10 May 1958.
59. See summaries of awards published annually in the *Motion Picture and Television Almanac.*
60. *Variety,* 15 April 1959: 28.
61. Bart Pirosh, executive of Pacific Drive-Ins, commented: 'I don't think reviews mean anything in our theatres'. On the other hand, Max Laemmle, manager of an art theatre in Los Angeles remarked that he paid close attention to reviews when scouting for new films to book. *Film Quarterly,* Winter 1965–66, feature on exhibitors.

7

The 1960s: New Money, New Identities

The art market continued to be an important outlet for British films in the 1960s when they earned more money at the American box-office than ever before. This increased profitability was largely explained by the influx of American capital for British film-making and the production of 'British' films by American companies. As long as the technicians and casts were predominantly British, films sponsored by American companies qualified as British quota films and were entitled to subsidies from the Eady Levy, a production fund established by the British Government in 1950. The fund was accumulated from a levy on cinema tickets that was distributed to producers of British-registered films on the basis of their box-office takings (Street, 1997: 16). The most successful films were therefore well rewarded, leading to criticism when American companies such as United Artists received $2.1 million, or 15 per cent of the Eady fund, as a result of the success of their British-registered James Bond film *Thunderball* (1965).[1] 'Internationalism' was prevalent, and it became increasingly difficult to identify films that had been produced without American assistance. Table 7.1 shows the total North American rental figures for British registered films, including some very high earners. All of these films were made with American participation. Table 7.1 excludes films that earned less than $3 million.[2]

To provide a sense of comparison, the top-grossing film of the decade was *The Sound of Music* (1965), which took the enormous sum of $79.8 million. Other high earners were *The Graduate* (1968, $44.1 million), *Doctor Zhivago* (1965, $47.2 million) and *Mary Poppins* (1964, $45 million). Occasionally foreign-language films did extraordinarily well, for example *La Dolce Vita* (Italian, 1960, $8 million) and *Un homme et une femme* (French, 1966, $6.3 million). The figures represent accumulated rentals to 1990, allowing for the addition of proceeds from reissues. Although many foreign films did not exceed rentals of over $3 million, the table illustrates the impact of American-financed 'British' films. By the end of the 1960s as much as 90 per cent of films

Table 7.1 Rentals for British Films in the 1960s

Film Title (Date, Company)	$ Rentals (in millions)
Thunderball (1965, UA)	28.6
2001: A Space Odyssey (1968, MGM)	25.5
Goldfinger (1964, UA)	22.9
The Dirty Dozen (1967, MGM)	20.4
Lawrence of Arabia (1962, Columbia)	20.2
You Only Live Twice (1967, UA)	19.3
To Sir With Love (1967, Columbia)	19.1
Romeo and Juliet (1968, Paramount)	17.5
Tom Jones (1963, UA)	17.0
Oliver! (1968, Columbia)	16.8
The Guns of Navarone (1961, Columbia)	13.0
A Man for all Seasons (1966, Columbia)	12.8
Casino Royale (1967, Columbia)	10.2
The Lion in Winter (1968, Embassy)	10.0
From Russia With Love (1964, UA)	9.9
On Her Majesty's Secret Service (1969, UA)	9.1
Dr No (1962, UA)	6.4
Blow-Up (1966, MGM)	6.3
A Hard Day's Night (1964, UA)	6.2
Help! (1965, UA)	5.4
Dr Strangelove (1964, Columbia)	5.0
The VIPs (1963, MGM)	4.7
Yellow Submarine (1969, UA)	3.7
Darling (1965, Embassy)	3.6
Far From the Madding Crowd (1967, MGM)	3.5
A Funny Thing Happened on the Way to the Forum (1966, UA)	3.4

made in Britain had US backing (Dickinson and Street, 1985: 233). While the success of the British 'new wave' attracted American finance, other incentives for production in the United Kingdom were the relatively cheap production facilities and labour. With cinema admissions on the decrease, US companies were prepared to diversify their operations in order to secure a stable supply of films. The decade was therefore marked by a combination of exuberance tempered with anxiety about British cinema. It was gratifying to see Britain as a magnet for overseas investment; on the other hand, there was the danger that over-dependence on external sources of finance would last only as long as that

Table 7.2 British Features Imported by the United States, 1957–68

Year	British Film Imports	% British Film Imports to Total	Total Imports
1957	78	33	233
1958	68	26	266
1959	37	15	246
1960	51	22	233
1961	54	16	331
1962	49	18	280
1963	44	15	297
1964	64	18	360
1965	60	20	300
1966	60	20	295
1967	63	22	284
1968	48	18	274

money was available. This concerned commentators such as Penelope Houston who felt that 'British film impresarios, far from being stimulated by the competition, as one feels someone like Korda would have been, are largely standing down; and British film-makers are choosing to get their money from American sources'.[3] At the end of the 1960s, when American finance was largely withdrawn, British producers were left to their own devices, without a strong infrastructure of commercial or state support for indigenous production.

The United States continued to import a high number of foreign films throughout the 1960s. As Table 7.2 illustrates, British films represented an average of 20 per cent of total film imports.[4] While this figure might appear to be comparatively low, the reputation of British films and American fascination with British youth culture gave them a greater status than, say, the high number of imports from Mexico.

The larger companies, including Embassy Films, Continental, United Artists, MGM, Universal and Fox, threatened to squeeze smaller distributors out of business in the scramble for foreign films.[5] The impact of theatre divorcement continued to affect the majors' control of the market. Since fewer films were being produced in Hollywood, the market was uncharacteristically receptive to foreign product, even though the most spectacular earners continued to be American films. According to a survey based on data published in *Variety* of distributors' shares from box-office receipts of foreign films shown in the United States and Canada, British films earned more than those of any other foreign country between 1956 and 1964, their earnings rising from $6,300,000 in 1957 to $29,098,000 in 1964.[6] The comparative figures for France were $3,176,000 (1957) and $2,951,000 (1964) and for Italy, $1,768,000 (1957) and $9,396,000 (1964). It is important to note that these proceeds benefited the larger American distribution companies who had co-financed many of the films (Guback, 1969: 86–9).

The British 'New Wave' in America

It will be apparent that the majority of the 'Angry Young Man', or British 'new wave' social-realist films produced between 1958 and 1963 did not rate highly at the US box-office. None of them grossed over $3 million. As well as the annual publication of an 'All-Time Rental Champs' table, *Variety* produced an additional list of the highest-grossing films in the previous year which charted the progress of less spectacular, but notable successes. In a survey of these 'anniversary' editions, 1959–66, with the exception of *Tom Jones*, the only non-Beatles or James Bond films to be listed were *Look Back in Anger* (grossed $850,000 in 1959); *The L-Shaped Room* ($700,000 in 1963) and *The Pumpkin Eater* ($740,000 in 1965).[7] The latter two films had been financed by Columbia.

American companies played a small part in the early development of the 'new wave'. *Look Back in Anger* was an exceptional case, co-financed by Warners on the strength of Richard Burton's Hollywood reputation, the international success of the play and Warners' links with Associated-British (Dickinson and Street, 1985: 238). Yet the 'classic' social-realist films, including *Room at the Top* (1959), *Saturday Night and Sunday Morning* (1960), *The Entertainer* (1960), *A Taste of Honey* (1961), *A Kind of Loving* (1962), *The Loneliness of the Long Distance Runner* (1962), *Billy Liar!* (1963) and *This Sporting Life* (1963), gained a high critical reputation and introduced many new actors and directors. Their influence was crucial in attracting American finance for projects such as *Tom Jones*, which sought to utilize the talents of Albert Finney, identified by *Variety* as 'a man to watch', in a non-social-realist film.[8]

With low budgets and no designs on overseas markets, the British 'new wave' was a prime example of the eruption of an indigenous film movement that nevertheless travelled well to American art cinemas. American reviewers were often more enthusiastic about the films than British critics who were disturbed by a film such as *Room at the Top* (1959) with its bold treatment of class and sex (Walker, 1974: 49). Despite reservations about the intelligibility of strong regional accents, American critics did not consider the films to be parochial or irrelevant to American concerns. *Newsweek* declared *Room at the Top* to be 'the first top-drawer British picture in a long time which presents British life as it is lived today rather than during England's finest hour or back in medieval times. . . . England enters the realm of topical films of social significance'.[9] A. H. Weiler of the *New York Times* remarked that although *Room at the Top* took place 3,000 miles away 'it is as close to home as a shattered dream, a broken love affair or a man seeking to make life more rewarding in an uneasy world'.[10] The same reviewer commented that *A Taste of Honey* 'travelled well' as 'a fittingly unadorned, sometimes drab, vehicle freighted with meaning and compassion that is universal despite its seemingly restrictive locale'.[11] *This Sporting Life* was described in similar terms: 'Above all, they have caught in truly dramatic, poignant and vivid style a drab universally recognizable world from which there is no escape'.[12] These comments are not surprising, in view of previous American appreciation of films that exposed and interrogated the inequalities of the class system. Many of the films' leading characters desired to break free from the restrictions of their class backgrounds, producing a variation on the familiar heroes of American populist cinema. Within the art market, the films' engagement with questions of British class and regional identity was clearly a major source of their appeal. Such issues applied, in different ways and emphases, to American society. America's social security system implied the existence of classes; Arthur Marwick has pointed out that 'the official image was of a vast classless majority being taxed in order to provide benefits for the tiny unfortunate "low income group"' (Marwick, 1980: 310). It was clearly the case, however, that social, economic, gender and racial inequalities persisted.

At an even broader level, the wider significance of *The Entertainer* was not lost on Bosley Crowther, who recognized a parallel between the film's depiction of the decline of music-hall performer Archie Rice (Laurence Olivier) and Britain's post-imperial crisis after Suez:

> Possibly he [John Osborne, author of the play and co-author of the screenplay] intended its ruthless and dismal exposé of a fading figure in a fast-declining pastime to be reflective of the position of Britain today, and its trailing of the tattered glories of vaudeville to suggest a greater passing of prestige. . . . *The Entertainer* is a devastating picture of a hollow, hypocritical heel and of the pitiful people around him who are drowned in his grubby vanity.[13]

The critique in cinematic form of the institution of the Borstal reform school in *The Loneliness of the Long Distance Runner* was also appreciated, particularly the grating Midland accents that were aligned in the mind of one American reviewer with the film's vivid expression of class antagonism.[14] *Variety*, the trade paper that had criticized British accents so much in the past, even likened the dialogue in *A Taste of Honey* to poetry.[15] The films' direction, screenplays, acting and cinematography also received high praise. Many reviews refer to other examples of the 'Angry Young Man' film, indicating that they were perceived as a British genre associated with the introduction of new talent and challenging themes. While their opposition to Hollywood's norms has been noted by Landy (2000: 71–2), specific films, particularly *This Sporting Life*, were singled out as distinctive, in this case for eschewing a happy ending.[16] Their stars, particularly Rita Tushingham and Tom Courtenay, were commented on for their lack of glamour, but praised for their acting abilities. Instead of being measured against standards set by Hollywood, these films were appreciated for their difference, particularly their willingness to depict sex in a frank and explicit manner, while at the same time developing serious and 'universal' adult themes.

Despite their reputation for rebelliousness and sexual content, the films were however perceived by some reviewers as moralistic, a relief from the more threatening erotic charge of, say, Italian cinema that had a far more risqué reputation. Apart from the occasional deletion, the 'new wave' films did not provide the PCA with controversial cases for censorship. Some of the films, including *Room at the Top*, were released without a PCA certificate, and as the 1960s progressed this became more and more common.[17] It is ironic that to some extent the films were welcomed because, despite their reputation for being about youth and anger, most of them ultimately upheld contemporary values. In *Room at the Top*, for example, Joe Lampton (Laurence Harvey) pays dearly for his attempt to climb the social ladder. A film such as *Saturday Night and Sunday Morning* is vague in its political agenda, compared with a film such as Lindsay Anderson's *If . . .* (1968), which perplexed reviewers who worried about its overtly political message.[18]

The conservatism of some reviewers was indeed revealed by comments including those made about Albert Finney as Arthur Seaton in *Saturday Night and Sunday Morning*, praised as 'a very exceptional specimen in the run of the working class'. Seaton was admired for his 'uncommon share of humor, courage, pride and dignity', as opposed to 'the devious, self-pitying rogues and weaklings we have seen in a lot of modern-day films'. He was likened to 'everyman', the good worker with spirit who was confined and repressed by the dehumanizing pressures of cities and industrialization.[19] His confidence and bravura were admired, the critic in *Newsweek* even going so far as to declare: 'Arthur emerges as one of the few really distinctive characters of recent movies'.[20] A warning to youth was identified in *A Kind of Loving*, a film that was applauded for dealing with 'the sobering notion that young people must be prepared to accept responsibilities when they start playing seriously with romance'.[21] The sense of social responsibility and ultimate conservatism of the films was therefore a significant element in their applause from American critics, anticipating the readings of scholars such as John Hill which identify the films' non-progressive ideologies (1986). While the films' treatment of women and resolutely masculinist – even misogynist – stance is not foregrounded in contemporary American reviews, the character of Jimmy Porter (Richard Burton) in *Look Back in Anger* was severely criticized, described, for example, by the *Variety* critic as 'selfish, incredibly rude, almost psychopathic'.[22] In this way American criticism is instructive as to the degree to which British cinema was seen to be entering into a new phase as well as indicating contemporary limits of tolerance as far as controversial themes were concerned.[23] Critics, like the middle-class audiences who attended art cinemas, applauded the 'new wave' because it was challenging, but did not go too far.

United Artists and *Tom Jones*

Apart from James Bond films, UA's biggest success with a British film in the 1960s was undoubtedly *Tom Jones,* which grossed $17 million, an enormous sum for a British film (Plate 17). In 1962 UA had presented Tony Richardson of Woodfall Film Productions with an attractive contract for *Tom Jones,* an adaptation of Henry Fielding's novel. Woodfall was an independent company that had produced *Look Back in Anger, Room at the Top, The Entertainer* and *A Taste of Honey.* Richardson had tried to obtain British finance from Bryanston Films and other sources, but not enough could be obtained to cover the relatively high budget of approximately £350,000 (Walker, 1974: 133–6). UA's backing was secured with the assistance of Bud Ornstein, UA's head of European production in London and the persistence of David Picker, an executive in New York. Ornstein sent Richardson's script to New York where Picker ensured that it was read in Los Angeles with its box-office potential in mind. He advised executives at UA's home office that the script was 'ribald, bawdy, Hogarthian; it jumps from bed to bed, from adventure to misadventure – it could be great fun. It does have, of course, its serious overtones, but essentially it is a wild caricature of times in England in the seventeen hundreds. . . . Made by these picturemakers, I see this as a potentially important worldwide grosser'.[24] It was clearly envisaged as a break from social realism, an irreverent comedy that could be linked to a tradition of popular historical costume pictures associated with *The Private Life of Henry VIII* (1933). From Richardson's point of view the deal with UA was an achievement because the company not only provided 100 per cent finance, but also a producer's salary and a cut of the profits for the leading actor, Albert Finney. Profits were divided equally between Woodfall and UA, until UA's share equalled the cost of production; thereafter Woodfall received 75 per cent and UA 25 per cent (Walker, 1974: 137–8 and Balio, 1987: 243).

UA's handling of the film for its American release was extremely important in maximizing its profits (Balio, 1987: 243–4). Since the cast was more or less unknown, it was crucial that 'word-of-mouth' advertising was secured, particularly via good reviews that created a climate of favourable expectation for *Tom Jones*. Previews were held in New York, Los Angeles, San Francisco and Chicago, to which selected critics and exhibitors were invited. One review described *Tom Jones* as 'the most imaginative film since *Citizen Kane*'.[25] After its première and first run in New York in October 1963 at an art cinema on the upper East Side, the film was released selectively in other metropolitan areas. Reviews were crucial in establishing *Tom Jones'* reputation as a 'must-see' film. Bosley Crowther described it as 'one of the wildest, bawdiest and funniest comedies that a refreshingly agile filmmaker has brought to the screen . . . a roaring entertainment that develops its own energy as much from its cinematic gusto as from the racy material it presents'.[26] The enthusiasm of American critics surpassed that of the British who were preoccupied with its innovative and non-moralistic approach to the adaptation of Fielding's novel.

Tom Jones was released all over the United States in the spring of 1964 after winning Academy Awards for best picture, director, screenplay and musical score. Albert Finney was hailed as an impressive new star. Recognizing that the film appealed to 'highbrow' and general audiences, UA used two different poster designs for its advertising campaign. For art-house audiences, the rather subdued British poster was used, whereas for general US audiences, a bawdier one was produced which featured a drawing of Tom, arms in the air with his shirt open to the waist, being pawed by five voluptuous scantily-clad women (Balio, 1987: 234, 244). The tone was set for a risqué viewing experience that boasted rampant sexuality as its major component. While the poster was intended for general audiences, in many ways it had much in common with the advertising for foreign-language films that had a reputation for being shocking in terms of sexual morality. Ironically, then, the bawdy poster had a place in both general and art markets. While its high box-office takings meant that *Tom Jones* managed to 'cross over' from the art market, exhibitors identified the film most clearly with discerning audiences. An executive from a chain of drive-in theatres, for example, found that the film's risqué sexual morality was objected to by drive-in customers who favoured 'good family pictures'. On the other hand, the proprietor of an art cinema in Los Angeles reported that *Tom Jones* had been extremely popular.[27]

Tom Jones was in many ways a landmark film of the decade. Its release in 1963 marked a new phase for British film-making as well as an acceleration of American investment. As Alexander Walker commented, 'Just when the "new realism" was drooping for want of refreshment, its energies were revived by *Tom Jones* and redirected away from a scene that had staled from over-familiarity and repetitiveness. The sense of "having a good time" spilled out of every frame of *Tom Jones*' (1974: 139). Judging from comments in reviews and on the evidence of its box-office success, its appeal for American audiences was related to its technical innovations, narrative concerns and symbolic resonances for the 1960s.

Tony Richardson's approach to the adaptation of Fielding's novel was innovative in his deployment of many techniques associated with the *nouvelle vague*. These included effects that both involved and distanced the audience. The use of a narrator, a device borrowed from the novel, at key points in the film introduced a voice of ironic counterpoint. A literary device was therefore employed to suit the prevailing trend in cinema of the 1960s to foreground a film's sense of self-reflexivity. This occurs, for example, when Tom Jones is introduced as a man 'of whom the opinion of all was that he was born to be hanged' at the same time that he is being established as the film's attractive hero. As he plunges into a cluster of ferns with Molly, the narrator tells us that we shall not see the details of Tom's sexual encounters: 'It shall be our custom to relieve such scenes for taste, decorum and the Censor Dictate. In this way we shall seek to make up for our incorrigible hero'. This comment addresses the audience as people who are aware of the construction of Tom's story and of the need for his exploits to be handled in a particular way in order to maintain sympathy. It also calls on their knowledge of the wider context of censorship, inserting a playful comment by the film-maker on the unintentional consequences of the constraints imposed by censorship. Later in the film, when Tom has been turned out by Squire Allworthy and is on the road to London, he links up cheerfully with some redcoat soldiers. Yet the narrator warns us that they are dangerous, encouraging a protective attitude towards Tom: 'His [Tom's] first adventure was with a party of those men whose profligate ways could be conducted with safety only with the protection of red coats'. Such comments distance Tom from the 'profligate' behaviour of others. While on the face of it many of Tom's adventures would appear to be profligate and amoral, including his persistent unfaithfulness to Sophie Western, he is nevertheless presented as kind, full of life, chivalrous, charismatic and handsome, qualities that place him in a different category from the soldiers. This is confirmed when later we see Tom rescue a woman from being raped by a redcoat. These narrative devices pull us in to root for Tom but also alert us to the need for our own compliance in his construction as a hero. Another typical distancing device occurs at the end of the film. When Tom is at the gallows, the narrator interrupts the 'unhappy' ending of Tom being hung and assures us that indeed, we will see him being rescued so that he can marry Sophie: "T'would be the devil's own nonsense to leave Tom without a rescuer'. Sure enough, the noose is cut for the 'happy ending' we have been expecting.

A similar sense of knowingness about the mechanisms of cinematic narration occurs with Richardson's device of having some of the characters directly address the camera and, by extension, the audience. This happens at key points, for example, in acknowledgement of a scene witnessed by the audience but not by other characters in the film. When Tom discusses Molly's family with Sophie, he defends Molly's father's sheep-stealing by referring to his need to feed his 'hungry' daughters. Tom's look to the camera acknowledges that the audience understands a different interpretation of 'hungry' in connection with the scene of him being pursued by the sexually rapacious Molly. This sense of self-reflexivity is also evident when the film abandons dialogue and reverts to a pastiche of silent films, for example, at the beginning of the film when we learn how Squire Allworthy discovered Tom, an abandoned child, in his bed. When Tom is falling in love with Sophie, the film presents an extremely stylized montage of them spending time together in a boat and in the fields. With persistent use of handheld cameras for many of the location scenes, there is a feel of the home movie, endowing these scenes with a sense of intimacy that militates against their otherwise hyper-romantic representation. Indeed, the film is bathed in sunshine, presenting an idealized image of the English countryside that was well suited to the soft colour effect achieved by cinematographer Walter Lassally. This is in contrast to the harsher tones used for London towards the end of the film, a technique that links the thematic preoccupations of *Tom Jones* with the black and white 'new wave' films that were more typical of Woodfall's output. The country is privileged above the city where Tom is subject to the machinations of society women. *Tom Jones* thus relates to a tradition of pastoral romanticism and the association of the city with corruption and amorality that featured in many British and American films, particularly the *film noir* genre.

Walker has observed how an eighteenth-century setting allowed John Osborne, who adapted Fielding's novel for the screen, and Richardson

> to carry their commitment to social realism with a light conscience. The
> 'two Englands' of the rich and poor, the 'haves' and 'have-nots', had
> been the basis of that conscience: now that they intermingled so row-

dily and colourfully in a picaresque comedy, Woodfall were freed from the patronising sympathy which the screen had begun extending to the poor, trapped, inarticulate people in the depressed areas of the mid twentieth century. (Walker, 1974: 139)

As in the 'new wave' films, class is an issue in Tom Jones. Tom is a 'foundling' who has been brought up by Squire Allworthy as his own son. He lives the life of a gentleman but appears to share an empathy with the poor and harbour no pretensions of superiority, unlike many of the other characters. He is a democratic hero. On closer examination, however, the film, like the novel, accepts the dominant ideology that in order for Tom to be fit to marry Sophie, he must be the son of Squire Allworthy's sister, rather than of the servant Jenny Jones. The film's desire to construct a 'happy ending', with Tom as the legitimate heir to Allworthy's fortune and therefore eligible to marry Sophie, cancels out the possibility of offering a more progressive conclusion. As in Room at the Top, at the end of Tom Jones the fundamental structures of class remain intact.

In terms of gender issues and sexual morality, Tom Jones can be related to the context of increased sexual freedoms of the 1960s in Britain and America. Reviews described the film as 'wild', 'bawdy', 'exhilarating' and 'racy' and subsequent writers such as Alexander Walker have related Tom Jones to the 'Swinging London' films of the mid-1960s. In this spirit Tom is presented as the object of women's desire – they pursue him and sex is represented as joyous and liberating. UA's poster encapsulated this impression of the film as a lusty romp. Yet as in the 'new wave' films, sex is not without consequences in Tom Jones, particularly for women. The existence of a double standard is revealed when Molly becomes pregnant. We feel sorry for her until it is revealed that she has had many lovers and that Tom is not necessarily the father. She is outcast by the village and presumably continues to suffer when the child is born. Her story is not followed through, and we are expected to accept that female promiscuity must be punished. On the other hand, Tom does not have sex with Sophie, the 'pure' heroine who is rewarded for her abstinence by winning Tom in marriage, the film's traditional and validated goal. As Thumim has noted, the only exception to the film's punishment of female sexual desire is with the character Jenny Jones, also known as Mrs Waters, in the famous dining scene with Tom where the mutual engorgement of food is a symbolic enactment of their sexual lust for each other (1992: 105). Unusually, Jenny does not suffer for this bold assertion and subsequent enactment of her desire. Thus for all its reputation as a challenging, comedic exploration of sexual liberation, Tom Jones nevertheless subscribes to the dominant, generally conservative, mores of the period.

As an 'exportable' text, *Tom Jones* delivered pleasures that had attracted American audiences to previous British films. These included the showcasing of the English countryside and country values in a romantic, idealized manner. With its stress on pleasure and sensuality, *Tom Jones* can be compared to *The Private Life of Henry VIII* and Gainsborough's costume melodramas. It offered a star in Albert Finney and also introduced Susannah York as Sophie Western. Both were more conventionally good-looking than many of the leading actors of the 'new wave', such as Tom Courtenay or Rita Tushingham. A key element of Tom's appeal was his courteous behaviour, rescuing maidens in distress and subscribing to basic codes of decency. As we have seen in previous chapters, America's fascination with patterns of chivalry continued with the rapturous applause received by *Tom Jones*. While, as I have argued above, the issues of class and sexuality were not subject to rigorous scrutiny or revisionism, the film did offer the exhibition of sexual freedom with a light, celebratory touch that was appealing without being threatening. With a film that was destined for general as well as art-house audiences, this balance was astute and, as it turned out, lucrative.

A Hard Day's Night

UA's next new venture was with the Beatles, Britain's most successful pop group, who became very popular in the United States after television exposure on the *Ed Sullivan Show* and a sell-out American tour at the beginning of 1964. *A Hard Day's Night* was a low-budget film intended to provide UA's record division with a soundtrack album that would further exploit the group's inroads into the American market (Balio, 1987: 249; Plate 16). A deal for three films was signed with the Beatles, facilitated by independent American producer Walter Shenson. Shenson had key contacts that proved to be significant in establishing a relationship with the Beatles. He had worked with Peter Sellers and knew Richard Lester, who was hired as director of *A Hard Day's Night*. Since the Beatles admired Sellers and fellow comedians the Goons, whose television show had been directed by Lester, the involvement of both Shenson and Lester was a key incentive for them to agree to make a film. For this purpose Shenson formed Proscenium Films, a company whose stock was owned two-thirds by Shenson and one-third by the Beatles. The deal was fairly lucrative from the Beatles' point of view since they received a fixed sum for each film plus 30 per cent of the profits.[28] Shenson also received a producer's fee plus 30 per cent, while UA, as financier and distributor, took 40 per cent (Balio, 1987: 250). The film was shot quickly and efficiently at £20,000 less than the original budget of £200,000 (Neaverson, 1997: 12, 28 n.8).

In America the soundtrack album was released before the film opened in August 1964. The film was therefore a tie-in vehicle for the album, which sold over 1.5 million copies in two weeks. Special 'premières' were held before *A Hard Day's Night* was released, preparation for which simulated the build-up to a pop concert. For these events admission prices were high and seats had to be reserved. A 'teaser trailer' was available for theatres to advertise the coming of the Beatles' first film. In combination with advance radio publicity and advance booking, UA capitalized on Beatlemania in a way that recognized the totality of the fans' devotion, seeking to replicate the aura of their live performances.[29] When *A Hard Day's Night* went on general release, 1,000 prints saturated the market, taking advantage of the Beatles' increasing popularity in the United States (Balio, 1987: 251). UA's marketing was astute and hard-hitting, yielding high grosses on first release. The sale of Beatles merchandise accompanied the film's exploitation. The poster, with its listing of tracks, 'Beatles favorites', reflected the importance of the album, as did instructions to exhibitors to forge tie-ins with record stores and radio stations. Additional material accompanied the film's release, including a free short film for television that had been made on location when *A Hard Day's Night* was being filmed. The press book also included information on each Beatle, seeking to distinguish their individual personalities, much as in the film. This individuation constituted a core element of the film's appeal. Although it was about the Beatles, each member of the group was given a key sequence for the development of his personality. Supplemented by a similar technique in interviews and other publicity, fans became aware of their individual identities, a crucial method of soliciting loyalty while at the same time consolidating the impression that the Beatles were 'ordinary' people.

One poster attempted to forge a wide appeal, claiming that the film appealed to 'hip, sharp, dynamic, forward-looking, new fangled adults' as well as teenagers. Some reviewers rejected this idea, arguing that 'since the film makes no pretense of being other than bait for teenage audiences, it seems senseless to attempt to judge it by adult standards'.[30] The film's social commentary was alluded to in some reviews, but on the whole the critical response was to the film's comedic elements and liveliness.[31] The comedy was not, however, considered to be meaningless and took many reviewers by surprise. Bosley Crowther was impressed, likening Alun Owen's comedic script to the Marx Brothers' humour, and admiring the film's surrealist elements: 'It is much more sophisticated in theme and technique than its seemingly frivolous matter promises'.[32] Indeed the press book singled out John Lennon as a jazz enthusiast 'with an unconventional sense of humor', the author of *John Lennon in His Own Write*, a book of drawings, prose and verse that the *Sunday*

Times reviewer (quoted in UA's press book) compared to the work of Lewis Carroll, the Goons, Ivor Cutler and James Joyce. One reviewer identified Lennon's anti-establishment humour as 'camp': 'One cannot help wondering why so much of the fun had homosexual overtones. Such a quantity of queer has certain implications, a drift which whispers things about the Beatles. Must they be counted among the flaming creatures or was this false fire?'[33] The film did not include elements of heterosexual romance in order to perpetuate the idea that the Beatles were all 'available' bachelors. But the likening of the humour to camp is an interesting observation. While elements of the sensibility are evident, it is important to note that the solid working-class lads are contrasted with a middle-class, stereotypically effete television producer who is coded as homosexual in a way that the Beatles are not.

The essence of the film's appeal to American critics and audiences was located therefore in its unusual humour. The Beatles' quick wit and repartee was also an important factor in their US appeal. This had been demonstrated on their arrival at Kennedy Airport when reporters bombarded them with questions to which they replied with characteristic irreverence, wit and verve (Neaverson, 1997: 22). *A Hard Day's Night* included a sequence in which the Beatles are asked similar questions at a reception in a television studio. When asked 'How do you find America?' John Lennon replied, 'Turn left at Greenland'. Their humour was inflected with surrealism, performed in a deadpan manner and communicated a sense of knowingness about their predicament as pop stars who were answerable to an insatiable media. Crucially, the film grants the Beatles with working-class sagacity and the ability to be self-reflexive about their role as pop stars. These qualities transformed their image from being a group for teenagers to one with mass appeal; hence the admiration of the 'adult' audience, including 'highbrow' critics such as Bosley Crowther. As 'working-class lads made good' they endorsed the notion that talent could overcome class barriers. At the same time *A Hard Day's Night* invested the group with insight into their exploitation by the middle-class media. In this way the film touches on similar issues of class that surfaced in many other 1960s British films.

In stylistic terms, Lester's direction attracted praise, for example *Newsweek* appreciated the film's combination of 'sight gags and documentary realism' and its 'semi-abstract, Antonioni-ish chases'.[34] Indeed, the film was a combination of documentary-style realism and techniques associated with the *nouvelle vague*. Real locations were used to convey a world that was convincing in its replication of 'a day in the life of a Beatle'. Handheld camera and black and white photography gave the film a realist aesthetic while Lester also employed antirealist devices. These included speeded-up images, slow motion and 'surprise' moments which break the illusion of actuality. An example of this would be the number 'Can't Buy Me Love' which we do not see the Beatles perform; instead, it is used as a background effect for a sequence when they escape from the television studio. In this sequence Lester uses many unconventional camera techniques and angles as the Beatles run about outside, celebrating their temporary freedom. Neaverson has attributed this technique to Lester's desire to convey the full emotion of the song rather than simply film the Beatles performing it (1997: 19). This approach was certainly innovative in terms of the pop musical, raising it above the level of those produced to promote Cliff Richard or Elvis Presley. Clearly then, *A Hard Day's Night* was not dismissed as frivolous entertainment for an unsophisticated youth audience. Reviews were much more appreciative of it than for *Help!* (1965), the next Beatles film which was in colour, featured extensive foreign locations and cost twice as much as *A Hard Day's Night* to produce. While *Help!* possessed attributes associated with the 'international' film, its predecessor, with its British settings, themes and low budget proved once again that British films did not have to stifle their sense of national identity in order to appeal to American audiences. As one reviewer put it, 'The first Beatle movie was a lucky one. There was something extra under the chocolate and vanilla. *Help!* is all ice cream, and with no napkin either'.[35]

The Midas Touch: James Bond in America

The James Bond series was an even greater success at the American box-office, yielding rentals that equated with those earned by Hollywood's most popular films. While United Artists provided the capital that made the Bond films possible, in many respects the series was imbued with a spirit of 'Britishness' – albeit selective – that makes them fascinating as examples of texts that crossed cultural boundaries. Operating from a British production base at Pinewood for all but two of the films, and using a large number of British technicians and leading actors, the films were not devoid of national identity. As we shall see, several Bond films were particularly concerned with themes that related to both British and American issues, not least the nature of the Anglo-American 'special' relationship. They can also be seen to relate to popular European adventure films (Bergfelder, 2000: 149). United Artists backed the Bond series because of the persuasive enthusiasm of Harry Saltzman and Albert R. 'Cubby' Broccoli. Both were producers based in Britain; Saltzman was a Canadian and Broccoli an American. In 1961 Saltzman, a co-founder of Woodfall Films, had procured an option from Ian Fleming, British author of the James Bond novels, to produce film adaptations of all the titles except *Casino Roy-*

ale. When Saltzman failed to raise the finance necessary to make the first film in Britain, he went into partnership with Broccoli, who had wanted to film the novels in the 1950s (Chapman, 1999: 54–5). In America, Columbia was not prepared to fund the high budget requested by Saltzman and Broccoli, to produce either *Dr No* or *Thunderball,* but Arthur Krim and other United Artists executives decided to go ahead, as long as the budget did not exceed $1 million. Another condition insisted on by UA was the assurance that the Bond films would be registered for British quota and hence qualify for subsidies provided by the Eady fund. A deal with UA was finalized in 1962. This ensured that a series, rather than a single film, would be produced over the years, with UA entitled to exclusive distribution rights for ten years (Balio, 1987: 257–9).

UA launched *Dr No* in an appropriate fashion, creating a climate of anticipation for Bond followed by a saturation of the market. Since it was the first film in the series and unproven as a box-office success in America, UA's campaign was astute but not nearly as extensive as the marketing of subsequent Bond films. Fleming's James Bond novels had enjoyed some popularity in the United States. UA therefore featured Fleming's name on posters and sent prerelease information about *Dr No* to the press and exhibitors. Recognizing that *Dr No* was likely to penetrate the mass market, the film was not treated as 'niche' material. Critics, particularly in the 'highbrow' papers, were hesitant and even dismissive in their evaluations of the action-based spy thriller. While he grew to appreciate the Bond formula, Bosley Crowther described *Dr No* as a 'lively, amusing picture . . . not to be taken seriously as realistic fiction or even art. . . . It is strictly a tinselled action-thriller, spiked with a mystery of a sort'.[36] Trade papers such as *Motion Picture Herald* and *Variety* recognized the series' box-office potential and high entertainment values. *Variety's* reviewer described *Dr No* as 'an entertaining piece of tongue-in-cheek action hokum'. Its ironic sense of humour and exhilarating opening sequence, key trademarks which featured in subsequent Bond films, were identified as keys to box-office success.[37]

Sean Connery as James Bond was a key factor in establishing the series' identity in the next few years, gaining respect from critics who might otherwise have been dubious. *Dr No's* success in Europe encouraged UA to devote time and energy on establishing Connery as a new star. He toured the United States in March 1963, attending exhibitors' conventions, press receptions and special screenings. American reviewers spotted Connery's box-office potential, describing Bond as 'a screen hero . . . definitely here to stay'.[38] In retrospect, it does appear to be the case that Connery 'should be credited with having established a new style of performance: a British screen hero in the manner of an American leading man' (Chapman, 1999: 81). He exuded the glamour associ-

ated with Hollywood stars and was compared to Cary Grant for his 'easy, un-
bound grace' and 'confident physicality' (Walker, 1974: 190). His accent, with
its soft Scottish inflection, was comprehensible and contrasted with the more
stereotypically 'establishment' British accents of Bond's superiors in London.
In this respect he was differentiated as somewhat special, in a class of his own
as the agent who carried out orders but undertook missions with considerable
individuality. In particular he demonstrated an ironic sense of humour and la-
conic manner that, in conjunction with his physical agility, mental ingenuity
and sexual prowess, invested him with a distinctive screen persona.

Bond's fame in America was not, however, achieved overnight. *Dr No's* career at the US box-office was reasonable, excellent for a British film, but not of
the spectacular proportions of its successors. Its huge box-office in Europe
however demonstrated its ability to appeal overseas and facilitated the production of *From Russia With Love* (1963) and *Goldfinger* (1964). *Goldfinger* was
the film to establish Bond as a major box-office draw in America. The pre-release campaign prepared the way, drawing on a more popular knowledge of
Bond than had been possible with *Dr No*. 'Novelty' aspects of *Goldfinger*
were selected as key features in the trailer and other pre-publicity, including
Honor Blackman's judo bout with Connery and subsequent surrender to his
sexual advances, the plot conundrum of Goldfinger's plan that involved controlling but not stealing the gold in Fort Knox and Bond's near-castration tor-
ture with Goldfinger's laser. These 'teaser' moments were showcased as thrilling experiences that typified the film's numerous other pleasures. UA produced
a promotional film that was shown on television before its release and a pre-
recorded interview with Connery was sent to hundreds of radio stations.
'Sneak' previews were arranged for the press and exhibitors. Shirley Eaton,
who played Jill Masterson, the character who dies early on in the film by being
sprayed with gold paint, toured the United States in advance of the film's release. The famous Aston Martin DB5, showcased in the film with its ingenious
gadgets, was also shipped to America in time for the New York première.[39]

The policy of market saturation was utilized on a major level, opening in
more than forty cities simultaneously so that rental grosses were amassed at an
impressive rate. UA pocketed the lion's share of the first-run proceeds, splitting
the box-office gross with exhibitors at a ratio of 90:10 per cent, the larger figure retained by UA. After the deduction of advertising, publicity and house
overhead expenses, UA retained as much as 80 per cent of the film's first-run
grosses (Balio, 1987: 261). 'Bondmania' ensued, manifesting itself in increased
sales of Fleming's novels and the production and marketing of Bond-related
merchandise, particularly toy models of Bond's Aston Martin. UA's advertising
campaign for *Goldfinger* and lucrative tie-ins with manufacturers represented

a precursor of the now established link between film marketing and consumerism. In particular, the release of the title theme of each film, recorded by popular artists such as Shirley Bassey and Tom Jones, provided an instantly recognizable 'extra' text that recalled the particular film, created anticipation for subsequent films in the series and an interest in reissues.

The Bond films succeeded in the American market by establishing a recognizable 'formula', each film extending and elaborating the basic codes. Balio (1987: 263) has summarized it as follows:

> The formula consists of the famous gun-barrel logo, which begins every picture, followed by the distinctive 'James Bond theme', the precredits sequence, and then the main titles, the latter typically accompanied by a title tune. The plot consisted of a series of what Broccoli called 'bumps' – that is, a series of self-contained action sequences strung together as set pieces. Most of the plots, said Penelope Houston, 'are just variations on Jack the Giant Killer, with appropriately extreme trimmings. Dispatched by M, the Prospero of the Secret Service, Bond stages a one-man assault on a fairytale stronghold furnished out of *House and Garden* and the travel supplements. The ogre (Dr No, Mr Big, Ernst Stavro Blofeld) captures him; there is a great smash-up; and Bond swims, skis or shoots his way out'. For each picture, the producers introduced a new exotic locale, a new James Bond woman, and fantastic gadgets to enliven the formula.[40]

This shorthand description manages to convey some of the key elements but does not engage with the films' deeper thematic and ideological preoccupations that challenge their dismissive categorization as mere 'escapism'. As a subgenre of the spy thriller, the James Bond series created a set of expectations that centred on the display of new technology, gadgets and multifarious exotic locations, combined with plots about world conspiracies that can loosely be aligned to contemporary ideological issues (Bennett and Woollacott, 1987). As well as being inflected with politics, the Bond films tapped into popular cultural traditions that encouraged American appreciation. Chapman suggests some important links, looking back to Paramount's 'Bulldog Drummond' films of the 1930s; the Dick Barton Special Agent series, 1946–51; Hitchcock's *North By Northwest* (1959) and in anticipation of the modern Hollywood action movie. He argues that the films combined the British spy thriller with high production values normally associated with Hollywood's films (Chapman, 1999: 47, 49, 21, 69). In turn the Bond series influenced American television spy series such as *The Man From U.N.C.L.E.*, contributing to a cross-cultural and cross-media dialogue which is also evident from charting the influence on

American television of imported British television series such as *The Avengers* (Miller, 2000).

Several observations can be made about the series' appropriateness for American consumption. At a thematic level, the Bond films clearly draw on certain assumptions about power politics in the context of the Cold War, foregrounding an idealized, even mythical, concept of an Anglo-American 'special relationship'. As we have seen, despite their obsession with the British empire, Fleming's novels were popular. As Chapman has pointed out, the novels convey 'a nationalist fantasy in which Britain's decline as a world power did not really take place. One of the ideological functions of the Bond narrative is to construct an imaginary world in which the *Pax Britannica* still operates' (Chapman, 1999: 39). While this might have been tolerated in the novels, their adaptation for the screen privileged an assumed Western supremacy that was premised on Anglo-American cooperation. This was partly a result of their Anglo-American production history as well as their release in the 1960s. Ironically, if it were not for the Eady Levy and its insistence on the inclusion of key British personnel in order to qualify for subsidy, the Bond films might have been completely different, less Anglophile or even with an American James Bond. This was certainly the case with the very first screen adaptation of a James Bond novel that was broadcast on American television in 1954. In this version of *Casino Royale,* Bond is played by an American actor (Barry Nelson) and, in contrast to the novel, America, rather than Britain, is the dominant power. Despite this switch, the choice of Fleming's novel arguably demonstrates a fascination with the power-political nexus that in the process of adaptation placed America in an identificatory role vis-à-vis Britain. In UA's films Bond was once again British, but this time in defence of a sort of *Pax Britannica-Americana* that departed sufficiently enough from the novels to satisfy both partners. In the post-war period, America possessed the attributes of an imperial power, exercising control and influence in both political and economic spheres while perceiving a threat from the East. In the context of the Cold War, the 'special relationship' implied an empathetic bond between powerful Western nations. These international tensions were referenced in the films: while the Cold War featured in *From Russia With Love,* the threat of Communist China was alluded to in *Goldfinger* and *You Only Live Twice* (1967).

The 'special relationship' was evident in many of the Bond films, not only in their nostalgic representation of Western imperialism, but additionally in their optimistic faith in Anglo-American cooperation. As Miller points out, social, cultural and political ties between Britain and America had been strengthened during the Kennedy presidency. After his assassination in 1963, America was even more receptive to British cultural imports: 'Internal anxiety took precedence over the anxiety of influence, further opening the door for artefacts from other cultures' (Miller, 2000: 33). In this context the Anglo-American special relationship evident in the Bond films was appreciated and even enhanced.

Bond frequently teams up with an American ally in order to thwart the forces of sinister organizations such as SPECTRE. As Chapman has noted, 'In the Bond films, as in the novels, the 'special relationship' was rather more equal than *realpolitik* would allow' (1999: 78). In *Goldfinger*, for example, Bond is answerable to representatives of both British and American secret service organizations. Felix Leiter, the American who charts Bond's progress when he is in America on the trail of Goldfinger, watches over Bond with almost paternal care, admiring his notorious reputation with women. When he sees Bond walking with Pussy Galore, he remarks, 'That's my James'. This American affection for the charming Englishman is a notable aspect of *Goldfinger*, extending to key elements of plot as Goldfinger's plans threaten the gold supplies of both the US Treasury and the Bank of England. 'Operation Grandslam' involves exploding the gold reserves held at Fort Knox with an atomic bomb provided by Communist China. The gold will be therefore contaminated for fifty-eight years so that economic chaos will disable the West while the untouchable gold increases in value. While the plot is typical of James Bond films, this fear was not irrelevant to the contemporary political scene: China exploded its first atomic bomb shortly before the American release of *Goldfinger* (Chapman, 1999: 102). In *Thunderball* the sinister organization SPECTRE hijacks nuclear bombs, demanding a ransom from NATO powers to prevent the destruction of a major British or American city. Once again, it is Bond and Leiter who lead the mission to recover the bombs, working well together although Bond is the more charming and dominant character. Thus the Bond films foster the notion that the British secret service works in close collaboration with America in a 'special relationship' that protects the world against plots hatched in the East.

Chapman has observed, 'The Britishness of the Bond films has been one of their main selling points' (1999: 14). It is important however to note that the 'Britishness' represented was very selective. Tim Bergfelder has commented that in the Bond films 'Britishness constituted itself less as an identity or as a sense of place, but as an accumulation of consumer products, fashion accoutrements and self-mocking stereotypes' (2000: 150). 'Sense of place' was however relevant as a shorthand iconographic presentation of the locale of the British secret service. While some of the locations were in Britain, they were usually presented with an establishing shot of the London skyline dominated

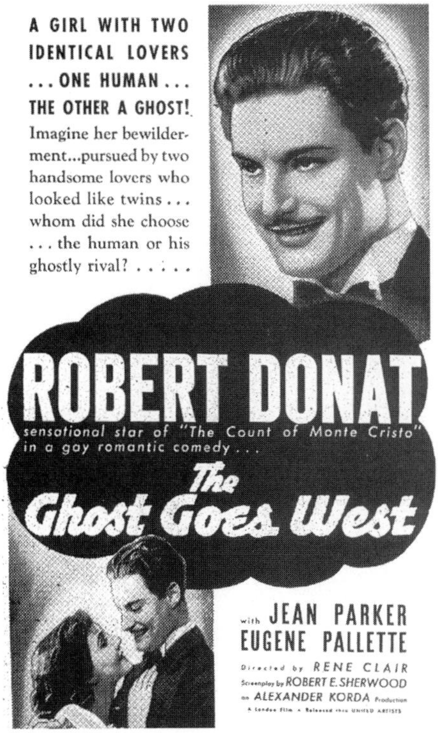

Plate 20. US poster for
The Ghost Goes West (1935)

Plate 21. US poster for
The Thief of Bagdad (1940)

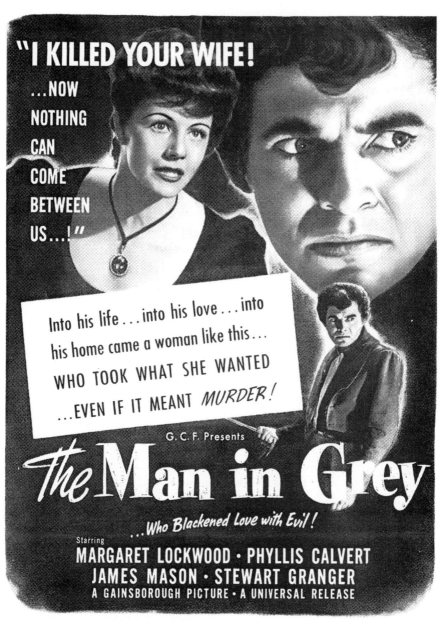

Plate 22. US poster for *The Man in Grey* (1943)

Plate 23. US poster for *The Wicked Lady* (1945)

Plate 24. US poster for *Bedelia* (1946)

Plate 25. US poster for *Brief Encounter* (1945)

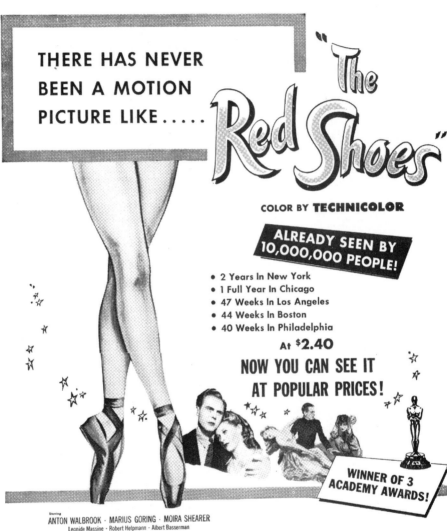

Plate 26. US poster for *The Red Shoes* (1948)

Plate 27. US poster for *Hamlet* (1948)

Plate 28. US poster for *Tight Little Island/Whiskey Galore!* (1948)

Plate 29. US poster for *Passport to Pimlico* (1948)

Plate 30. Article from *Country Life* on British comedy abroad

by Big Ben, as a prelude to revealing the palatial interiors of the intelligence service, including the central meeting room with its combination of classical paintings and the latest technology. This is a mise-en-scène of grandeur and power, harking back to the British empire but at the same time shown to be a hive of technological invention. Bond's superiors are 'establishment' figures with accents to match. By contrast, he is more of an individualist, shown to be charismatic and talented, his personal foibles tolerated because of his talent as an agent. Although the relationship between Bond and his superiors is somewhat patrician, there is no doubt that Bond is an unquestioning executor of Her Majesty's business. Bond is therefore coded as an individualist who nevertheless acts out of loyalty to Britain and NATO: a man who is different from, yet not at odds with the British establishment. As a screen hero Bond therefore represented 'Britishness' but of a meritocratic rather than a class-based nature. As previously noted, Connery's Bond did not possess the same class inflections as his superiors, to some extent placing him in a more 'classless' category. As Miller has observed, the post-Kennedy assassination context of the reception of Bond permitted Americans 'to reconfigure Bond as a noble individualistic warrior fighting for a better world' (2000: 33).

Chivalric codes were also an element of Bond's screen persona. In early trailers, he was described as a 'gentleman agent'. Despite his exploitative treatment of women and lack of moral scruples about killing those who got in his way, Bond demonstrated chivalric attitudes that manifested themselves largely through his charm, wit and irony. Nevertheless, as I have argued elsewhere, although operating in a different generic context, the Bond films were preoccupied with concerns similar to those of the British 'new wave' films, particularly in terms of their presentation of a masculine fantasy of freely available sex without commitment (Street, 1997: 87). These themes were evident in many other films produced in the 1960s and can be seen to provide mythic expression for the so-called 'sexual revolution'. In this sense, the Bond films gave licence to new sexual mores. Their modernity was also signalled by their technology fetishism, fast cutting style and spectacular locations, attributes that came to epitomize the big-budget action movie. Unlike other films sponsored by American finance in the 1960s, the Bond series survived into the following decades, earning the title of the most successful series in film history.

Hollywood and Bust: The Withdrawl of American Finance

Despite the success of many British films in America, at the end of the decade *The Economist* reported on a crisis in Hollywood that had a serious impact on film production in Britain.[41] During the years 1969 to 1971 the majors suffered catastrophic losses and pulled out of 'runaway' production activities in Britain. In 1969 MGM and Warners showed losses of $35.4 million and $42 million respectively, in 1970 United Artists registered losses of $45 million and Fox of $76.4 million and in 1971 Columbia was in the red to the tune of $28.8 million.[42] When American finance was withdrawn from British production, indigenous sources could not make up for the loss, resulting in a crisis in the British film industry (Dickinson and Street, 1985: 238). In a dramatic reversal of earlier trends, the total number of films imported by America fell in the late 1960s and 1970s to the lowest levels since the Second World War.

While the art-film market had been healthy for over twenty years, the films still did not make as much money as major Hollywood releases. The major studios competed with independent distributors for the best foreign films, making it more and more difficult for the smaller companies to survive in the congested New York art market as the decade progressed.[43] In the mainstream arena, the trend for blockbuster pictures inflated the market, raising the stakes and risks of film production to such an extent that a company's financial fortunes could stand or fall on a single film. As Table 7.1 illustrates, it was films such as the Bond series that earned big money, not low-budget art films featuring unknown stars. Stocked up with a plentiful supply of films after a hectic scramble for product, network television was satiated and reduced its purchase of film rights at a time when any extra income would have been ploughed back into production. The majors were forced to retrench and restructure in the wake of the recession. Interest moved away from foreign films to 'a new kind of movie' such as *The Graduate* (1968) or *Bonnie and Clyde* (1967) that reflected indigenous concerns and appealed to youth audiences.[44] Ironically, perhaps, the subsequent phase of 'new American cinema' was profoundly influenced by the European films that had been exhibited in art cinemas (Thompson and Bordwell, 1994: 707–10).

During the decade, British film culture had been appreciated overseas in its multifarious dimensions, including critical enthusiasm for the 'new wave', considerable investment in the 'Swinging London' cycle and the development of James Bond as a lucrative Anglo-American collaboration. Actors who appeared in British films, including Laurence Harvey, Richard Harris, Julie Christie and Albert Finney, became international stars. Directors such as John Schlesinger found subsequent work in Hollywood. Pinewood was firmly established as one of the world's most important studios for technical expertise and facilities. Although after 1967 British films were not doing as well as in previous years, there were still interesting exceptions such as *To Sir, With Love*, set in an East End London school and starring American actor Sidney Poitier as a crusading teacher, which grossed $19.1 million, more than either

Tom Jones or *From Russia With Love*. This proved once again that success in America did not necessarily depend on lavish historical settings or action-adventure thrills.

Murphy has commented that 'the 1960s saw a greater number of significant and exciting films made in Britain than at any time before or since' (1992: 278). Although the *New York Times'* reviewer was concerned about the radicalism of Lindsay Anderson's *If . . .*, the film was noted as a 'beautifully and solidly constructed satire'. Warner-Seven Arts backed *Performance* (1970), even though the studio became concerned about its controversial content and many reviewers found it distasteful. When it opened in Manhattan, it played to capacity audiences, largely because of the casting of Mick Jagger, and has since become a highly regarded 'cult' film. The 1960s had therefore been a crucial decade for British films in the United States. Indeed, on the strength of the enhanced international stature of British film-making, many directors found work and were able to experiment with film form in ways that disproved Truffaut's comment – made in 1962 – that the terms 'cinema' and 'British' were incompatible (1978: 140).

Notes

1. Penelope Houston, 'England, Their England' in *Sight and Sound*, vol. 35, no. 2, 1966: 56.
2. This table has been compiled from *Variety*, 15 Oct 1990: M-140-196, which expanded on previous annual listings and for the first time lowered the minimum dollar rental figure to $3 million (previously it had been $5 million). This allowed for a greater number of British films to show in the table. It is unlikely that the figures were adjusted for inflation, so comparisons between particular years should be made with caution.
3. *Sight and Sound*, vol. 35, no. 2, Spring 1966: 55.
4. Figures compiled from *Film Daily Year Book*. The period 1957–68 has been chosen to cover the main dates incorporated in this chapter and to convey a sense of the importance of British imports from the end of the 1950s to the mid-1960s.
5. See Bosley Crowther, 'Is it really boom or is it bust for foreign films?', *New York Times*, 7 June 1964, II: 1.
6. These figures are lower than the ones quoted in *Variety*'s list of 15 Oct 1990, but it should be remembered that the later figures represent earnings accumulated over thirty years and not just for a single year.
7. Although according to Alexander Walker *Room at the Top* was shown 'widely and profitably in the United States' (1974: 50). *Room at the Top* does not, however, feature in *Variety*'s lists as a large earner. Balio claims that *Saturday Night and Sunday Morning* 'earned over half a million profit'. The figures for *Look Back in Anger* are surprisingly high, contradicting the view that it did not do well internationally (Balio, 1987: 238–9). Compared with the grosses for Ingmar Bergman's films, the figures for *Look Back in Anger*, *The L-Shaped Room* and *The Pumpkin Eater* are high. Bergman's *The Virgin Spring* grossed $700,000 and the average gross for his early films was $350,000 (see Balio, 1987: 231).
8. *Variety*, 9 Nov 1960.
9. *Newsweek*, 6 Apr 1959: 113.

10. *New York Times*, 31 Mar 1959: 26.
11. *New York Times*, 1 May 1962: 33.
12. *New York Times*, 17 July 1963: 19.
13. *New York Times*, 4 Oct 1960: 49.
14. Bosley Crowther, *New York Times*, 9 Oct 1962: 44.
15. *Variety*, 20 Sept 1961.
16. *New York Times*, 17 July 1963: 19.
17. *Blow-Up* (1967), a British-registered film directed by Antonioni, was refused a seal and MGM decided to distribute it anyway, resulting in a box-office hit. This case is generally regarded as instrumental in the development of the MPAA's ratings system (Monaco, 2001: 61).
18. *New York Times*, 10 Mar 1969.
19. *New York Times*, 4 Apr 1961: 44.
20. *Newsweek*, 10 Apr 1961: 103.
21. *New York Times*, 2 Oct 1962: 46.
22. *Variety*, 3 June 1959.
23. Dwight MacDonald, film critic of *Esquire*, was an Anglophile but did not approve of the 'Angry Young Man' cycle. He objected to any implication of a blurring of the high-low cultural divide that the films appeared to represent.
24. David Picker to Arnold Picker, 23 Apr 1962 from United Artists Archive, State Historical Society, Madison, quoted in Balio, 1987: 239.
25. No source is given for this quotation, but it is taken from the UA Archive's clippings file on *Tom Jones* and quoted in Balio, 1987: 243.
26. *New York Times*, 8 Oct 1963: 48.
27. Feature on 'The Exhibitors' in *Film Quarterly*, Winter 1965–66.
28. This figure is considerably higher than the 7.5 per cent quoted by Walker, 1974: 232.
29. United Artists' press book for *A Hard Day's Night*, New York Public Library. All subsequent information on the film's publicity is taken from this source.
30. *Film Daily*, n.d. Review in PCA file in Herrick Library, Los Angeles.
31. See *Variety*, 14 July 1964 and the *New Republic*, 10 Oct 1964.
32. *New York Times*, 12 Aug 1964.
33. *Film Quarterly*, vol. XVIII, no. 1, Fall 1964: 54.
34. *Newsweek*, 24 Aug 1964.
35. *Film Quarterly*, vol. XIX, no. 1, Fall 1965: 58.
36. *New York Times*, 30 May 1963: 20.
37. *Motion Picture Herald*, 3 Apr 1963.
38. *Variety*, 17 Oct 1962.
39. See 'The Making of *Goldfinger*' and 'The *Goldfinger* Phenomenon', special features on *Goldfinger*, DVD (UA/MGM, 2000).
40. The quotation from Houston is from *Sight and Sound*, 34, Winter 1964–65: 15.
41. 'Hollywood and Bust', *The Economist*, 29 Nov 1969: 69–70.
42. See 'Studio revenues and profits' chart in Finler, 1988: 285–6.
43. Bosley Crowther , 'Is it really boom or is it bust for foreign films?', *New York Times*, 7 June 1964, II: 1.
44. *Time*, 8 Dec 1967: 66–76.

8

The 1970s to 2000:
British Films and the 'New' Hollywood

In the 1970s, the Hollywood majors began a slow period of recovery from the recession at the end of the previous decade. Hollywood survived near bankruptcy and since then has demonstrated a striking capacity to adjust to new conditions within the film industry and the increasingly 'globalized' economy. The key to survival has been the expansion of markets for film production at home and abroad, fuelled by demand for product from television networks, cable and satellite services, home video and DVD outlets, and in multiplex cinemas. Hollywood has maintained its dominant position through a series of mergers with large corporations such as Gulf + Western, the conglomerate that took over Paramount in 1966; Rupert Murdoch's News Corporation, the Australian company that absorbed Twentieth Century in 1985; and Sony's acquisition of Columbia in 1989. By diversifying operations, the risks of relying solely on film production were reduced, enabling companies to concentrate on expansion at home and overseas. Another extremely significant development has been the partial return to vertical integration, achieved by the acquisition of cinemas and control of distribution by the reconfigured 'majors'. The strength and resilience of this corporate environment lies in its propensity for 'synergy', or a series of productive relationships with allied companies, creating direct links between screen entertainment and associated merchandise, technical facilities and other media (Neale and Smith, 1998: 57–73).

Bolstered with financial muscle provided by these mergers with large conglomerates, Hollywood has raised the costs of blockbuster film-making to sky-high levels. At the same time, independent producers have often turned to the major companies for secure distribution and exhibition outlets. The 'Americanization' of art cinema has created competition within a market that was formerly dominated by foreign-language and British films. In this way it is still difficult for foreign films to penetrate a system geared to privilege domestic product. On the other hand, much as in previous decades, some foreign films are successful, largely because they have managed to negotiate a space in the market as 'specialized' films. Occasionally, these films have also 'crossed over' to reach wider audiences. Co-production arrangements also facilitate greater access to American screens, repeating a 'classic' strategy in which commercial arrangements are just as important as the quality of the individual film. As this chapter will demonstrate, particular companies, such as the distributor Miramax, have been extremely important in facilitating the entry of British films into the American market, combining a good sense of the product and its potential audience with intelligent marketing strategies.

A comparative analysis of US film imports 1967–69 and 1987–89 demonstrated that the majority originated in Britain and other European countries (Ogan, 1990: 63–5).[1] Not having the disadvantages of foreign-language films that, with the exception of certain celebrated cases, have found it particularly difficult to obtain distribution in America, British films continued to occupy a particular space in the market. Even though the 1970s is generally perceived to have been a difficult decade for British cinema, as Table 8.1 illustrates, the same number of films managed to earn similar proportional rentals as in the 1980s, a decade when British cinema is considered to have experienced a short-lived 'renaissance'. As with Table 7.1, it is important to note that the figures here represent accumulated rentals to 1990 so that films released just before that date would have had less opportunity to benefit from re-releases. The amount earned by the individual distributor also depended on the contract negotiated with the exhibitor, a key division not reflected in the table. Nor do these sums indicate the amount of money returned to the producer. On the other hand, they do provide a sense of the films' comparative popularity as well as the extent to which blockbusters inflated both the costs and potential earnings of films.[2]

The appearance of films which might otherwise be regarded as American is explained by the use of British studios and technicians for the *Superman* films, *Alien* and *Full Metal Jacket*. The continued popularity of James Bond is also evident. Other trends can be discerned which relate to previous and subsequent imports from Britain. The first of these is the success of British comedies, particularly the Monty Python films and *A Fish Called Wanda*. The Python films relate to surrealist comedy that had been popularized in America by Peter Sellers with the *Goon* show, and was evident to some degree in *A Hard Day's Night*. The Pink Panther series also made an impact, again featuring Peter Sellers. *A Fish Called Wanda*, starring ex-Monty Python comedian John Cleese, was directed by Charles Crichton who had worked for Ealing studios. Reviewers compared *A Fish Called Wanda* to the traditions of Ealing comedy which, as we have seen, gained some popularity in the United States. While it does not appear on the table, *Local Hero* (1983, earned $3 million) can also

Table 8.1 Rental Earnings of British Films, 1970s and 1980s

1970s		1980s	
Titles	Rentals	Titles	Rentals
Superman (1978)	$82.8m	*Superman II* (1981)	$65.1m
Alien (1979)	40.3	*Superman III* (1983)	37.2
Moonraker (1979)	33.9	*Octopussy* (1983)	34.0
The Spy Who Loved Me (1977)	24.4	**Chariots of Fire** (1981)	30.6
A Bridge Too Far (1977)	20.4	*A Fish Called Wanda* (1988)	29.7
Return of the Pink Panther (1975)	20.2	*Never Say Never Again* (1983)	28.2
The Pink Panther Strikes Again (1976)	19.8	*For Your Eyes Only* (1981)	26.6
Diamonds Are Forever (1971)	19.7	*A View to a Kill* (1985)	25.3
Murder on the Orient Express (1974)	19.1	**Gandhi** (1982)***	25.0
Tommy (1975)	17.8	*Full Metal Jacket* (1987)	22.7
A Clockwork Orange (1971)	17.0	*Time Bandits* (1981)	20.5
Live and Let Die (1973)	16.0	*Licence to Kill* (1989)	16.7
Dracula (1979)	10.7	**The Killing Fields** (1984)	16.0
Monty Python's Life of Brian (1979)	10.5	*A Passage to India* (1984)	13.9
Barry Lyndon (1975)	9.2	**A Room with a View** (1986)	12.0
Death on the Nile (1978)	8.8	*The French Lieutenant's Woman* (1981)	11.3
The Day of the Jackal (1973)*	8.6	**The Mission** (1986)	8.3
The Odessa File (1974)**	5.7	*Monty Python's Meaning of Life* (1983)	7.3
Monty Python and the Holy Grail (1975)	5.2	*Eye of the Needle* (1981)	6.7
The Eagle Has Landed (1977)	4.2	*The Mirror Crack'd* (1980)	5.5
Straw Dogs (1971)	4.0	*Henry V* (1989)	4.5
Mary, Queen of Scots (1972)	3.6	*Brazil* (1985)	4.5
The Man who Fell to Earth (1976)	3.0	*1984* (1985)	4.4
Scrooge (1970)	3.0	*Hope and Glory* (1987)	4.3
Women in Love (1970)	3.0	*Evil under the Sun* (1982)	4.0

*Britain/France; **Britain/West Germany; ***Britain/USA/India

Titles in bold indicate involvement by Goldcrest

be related to Ealing with its story of the impact of an American oil company on a small Scottish village.

Screen adaptations of Agatha Christie's mystery novels also established a popular formula that was repeated several times over the next decade and subsequently taken up by television in the *Murder, She Wrote* series starring British actress Angela Lansbury. The popularity of Agatha Christie would suggest a continued fascination with the lifestyle of the British upper class. This fascination has been evident in previous decades in a variety of genres including the historical/costume film, although as I have argued this often operated in a complex way. In their different forms, historical/costume films have featured significantly in discussion of British cinema in the 1980s and 1990s, not only in terms of their box-office success but also their status as texts that demonstrate qualities which have consistently proved to be eminently 'exportable'.

The Heritage Question

In the 1980s several historical/costume films were labelled 'heritage' by critics. Taken as a broad category that includes *Chariots of Fire, A Passage to India, A Room with a View* and *Henry V* (1989, directed by Kenneth Branagh), they are taken to represent the quintessentially 'English' film, despite their often international financial origins. This is largely due to their settings, adaptation from novels by writers such as E. M. Forster, and because of their predominantly British casts. The production of many of the first films to be associated with costume/heritage by the Merchant-Ivory company was another hallmark of the genre. While the debate launched by Higson (1993: 109–29) produced a fairly restrictive list of films that could be termed 'heritage', he has since acknowledged the possibility that this list could be expanded, perhaps including titles such as *Hope and Glory* (1987) to encompass films that broadly deal with issues of the 'national past' even though they are not based on works of 'classic' English literature (1996: 232–48). While I do not intend to redefine the genre or indeed suggest, as some critics have done, that it does not exist, I will consider the impact of films that can loosely be termed 'heritage' in America.[3] The films are interesting in this respect because of their British-centred subject matter and apparent deviation from the norms of blockbuster filmmaking. Their popularity was nevertheless apparent, as revealed by Table 8.1. This trend continued into the 1990s, the most successful in that decade being *Howards End* (1992), *The Remains of the Day* (1993), *Shadowlands* (1994), *The Madness of King George* (1994), *Mrs Brown* (1997), *Elizabeth* (1998) and *An Ideal Husband* (1999).[4] Many were international co-productions, attracting finance from Europe and America as well as creative input from all over the world. Yet they are still perceived to relate most fully to British themes and preoccupations, particularly class society.

Hipsky (1994) has argued that the appeal of 'heritage' films produced by the Merchant-Ivory production team lies in their conference of 'cultural capital' on professional-managerial audiences, much as 'highbrow' films were said to have earned loyalty from an educated clientele in the 1950s. In keeping with Higson's (1993) initial understanding of the function of the films' *mise-en-scène* as distracting attention from any critical or ironic perceptions of the class divisions that are integral to the source novels, Hipsky suggests that for middle-class Americans the films function as pure escapism:

> In many ways, these historical films function to efface the very social history they purport to portray; they provide North American viewers with a kind of sanitized, guilt-free nostalgia. It is, after all, the historical landscape of our trans-Atlantic cousins there on the screen, and while we are aware of empire and class hovering somewhere beyond the movies' immediate social landscape, they trouble us not, as they do not signify any dirty historical linen of our own. (Hipsky, 1994: 106)

He argues that even in *Howards End,* a film that would appear to offer more of a social critique than, say, *A Room with a View,* the portrayal of industrialist Henry Wilcox (Anthony Hopkins) 'humanizes' him far more than the novel – to such an extent that his function as a symbol of exploitative capitalism is forgotten by the end of the film. This interesting theory is to some extent supported by an examination of contemporary commentary, but I would argue that elements of 'social history' are not entirely 'effaced' by the films. The link with Forster's novel was an explicit feature of most American reviews of *A Room with a View,* for example, and several critics mentioned that while light-hearted in tone the film did not ignore questions of class; indeed, the film exposed 'Victorian sexual hypocrisy' and was 'an attack on the British class system'.[5] While the Merchant-Ivory films were frequently located in specifically British milieux, the fact that reviewers acknowledged comparison with films based on novels that dealt with class in an American context, such as *The Bostonians* (1984) or *The Age of Innocence* (1993), suggests that notions of class were not perceived as a purely British experience. Merchant-Ivory's adaptation of Henry James' *The Bostonians,* a film that 'sold $4 million worth of tickets at American theatres in 1984', was mentioned by several reviewers, serving as a reminder of the team's credentials at adapting 'classic' novels but also of their ability to translate the novels' acute awareness of social nuances.[6]

Hipsky's observations about the target audience for Merchant-Ivory pictures are supported by the initial marketing strategy employed by Cinecom, the US distributor and co-financer of *A Room with a View*. An analysis of the box-office performance of *A Room with a View* and subsequent 'heritage' films however indicates that they were popular with wider audiences. The marketing campaign for *A Room with a View* was aimed at 'highbrow' audiences, as Ismail Merchant explained, 'People have come to know our names, that we keep on making films of sensibility and quality and against the grain of the usual Hollywood movie. They know that at the least they'll get atmosphere and something thought-provoking'.[7] Consequently, Cinecom treated its release as 'special' product. As a small, independent company, Cinecom did not have much to spend on the film's exploitation, but made the most of a tie-in with the publishing firm Random House. A study guide was sent to high schools and colleges and the film was released selectively in major cities. It soon acquired a reputation, publicized by 'word-of-mouth', as a 'must-see' film. This strategy resulted in a less restrictive audience than had been predicted and the film 'crossed over' to reach a more extensive market. Cinecom's president, Amir Jacob, told *Variety*'s Lawrence Cohn that *A Room with a View* played on an unusually wide basis nationally.[8] This would support research into the accessibility of 'heritage' films to non-'highbrow' audiences in the United Kingdom (Monk, 1999). Although the film was therefore intended for a 'discerning' audience, clearly its appeal was more wide-reaching in both Britain and the United States.

The Remains of the Day was a heritage film that involved Anglo-American subject matter. Adapted from a novel by Kazuo Ishiguro, the film dealt with the international crisis of the late 1930s. It was based loosely on the 'Cliveden set' of aristocrats and politicians who supported the policy of 'appeasement' (Mowat, 1968: 592). The film is set in Darlington Hall, a large country house where a secret conference on Anglo-German relations was held. During the conference, the American delegate Lewis, played by Christopher Reeve, was the only diplomat to oppose appeasement of the Nazis. In the late 1950s (where the film begins and then proceeds to tell its story of the 1930s in flashback), Lewis returns and buys the country house. Along with the house, he obtains the services of Stevens (Anthony Hopkins), the butler of Lord Darlington, the Hall's former British occupant who has been discredited as a traitor. Lewis treats Stevens with kindness and courtesy that is clearly associated with post-war values and an American rejection of rigid social hierarchies (although Lewis does not object to having a butler). The moral force of the film therefore lies with the American character as a far-seeing diplomat who is contrasted with naïve British supporters of Hitler and the French Ambassador who fails to recognize the gravity of the international situation. In this way a film that ostensibly parades the values associated with English 'heritage' – the large country house; aristocrats and servants locked into an unyielding class system – offers a distinctly pro-American address. American ideas and characters are associated with modernity, insight and compassion.

The character of Lewis offers an outsider's perspective not only on the immediate international crisis but also of British social values, which are depicted as anachronistic. In a discussion of this aspect, one reviewer distinguished between Americans 'born to mobility' and 'the rigid British class system', implying that the film's delineation of class issues was clear but perceived as specifically British.[9] Other commentary concentrated on the frustrated romance between Stevens and Darlington Hall's former housekeeper (Emma Thompson) which was linked to their inability to put their personal happiness before their sense of duty to their master and, in particular, Stevens' unquestioning acceptance of his 'place' as a servant. Vincent Canby, writing in the *New York Times,* interpreted the entire film as a series of metaphors for Britain and its class system:

> Stevens is the proudly subservient, pre-World War II English working class. Darlington Hall is England. Stevens's fierce determination to serve, and the satisfaction it gives him, are the last, worn-out gasps of a feudal system that was supposed to have vanished centuries before.[10]

On the other hand, some reviewers compared the film to Scorsese's 1993 adaptation of Edith Wharton's novel *The Age of Innocence,* providing a convenient comparative framework that suggested class was far from a purely British experience.[11] The existence of class in America and its relation to money in New York society was a key theme of *The Age of Innocence.* Indeed, one review paired it with *The Remains of the Day,* observing that both films did justice to the social observations of their source novels, mainly by their focus on the point of view of a central character: Stevens (*The Remains of the Day*) and Archer (*The Age of Innocence*). While *The Remains of the Day* was praised as 'a model translation from one art to another', Scorsese's 'lavishingly beautiful' film was applauded for using its *mise-en-scène* to recreate 'all the seductive elegance of Archer's world; it is not pretty merely for the sake of being pretty but for the sake of luring us in as easily and inescapably as Archer'.[12] *The Age of Innocence* was set in the 1870s, a more distanced historical period than the 1930s setting of *The Remains of the Day.* While this might imply that for Americans class was something locked in the past, films set in the past do not necessarily prevent the drawing of contemporary parallels. This is indicated, for example, by the way the audience is encouraged to empathize with Archer's experience of the hypocrisy of the upper class. Indeed, two years later Amy Heckerling's *Clueless* (1995) took its inspiration from Jane Austen's

Emma for her comedic depiction of rich American teenagers. Her method was to transpose the structures and dilemmas evident in Austen's novel into a contemporary setting: she found no difficulty in locating this in American society. *The Remains of the Day* is arguably more aware than *The Age of Innocence* of historical shifts in class distinctions. Its flashback structure suggests that while class was all-pervasive in the 1930s, this was less pronounced after the Second World War, indicating a trajectory of social mobility rather than stasis. *The Remains of the Day* is therefore a case of a 'heritage' film offering an insight into the personal consequences of a rigid class society while at the same time suggesting that change is possible. While Hipsky's observation about American audiences dissociating themselves from the experience of class society is plausible, it must also be acknowledged that comparison with Scorsese's film (combined with a flashback narrative that permits a loosening of rigid class structures) meant that when *The Remains of the Day* was released, cross-cultural associations were identified as a significant framework of interpretation. Scorsese's uncharacteristic adoption of 'heritage' stylistics therefore provided *The Remains of the Day* with an interesting American equivalent, which emphasized that debates on class society were relevant to both countries.

Goldcrest and Film Finance in the 1980s

Eberts and Ilott (1990) have documented the involvement of Goldcrest, a British production company, in several key films of the 1980s, including two key 'heritage' films, *A Room With A View* and *Chariots of Fire*. Their account of an independent company that experienced great success with films such as *Chariots of Fire, Gandhi* and *The Killing Fields,* and incurred terrible losses with *Absolute Beginners* (1986) and *Revolution* (1986), is instructive on the strengths and limitations of British production during this period. Access to the American market was a core consideration in the company's transition from enterprising independent to major player in the international arena. In the early 1980s, the company was able to benefit from several key advantages which, in combination with good projects, resulted in Academy Awards and significant box-office takings. Founded by Jake Eberts, a Canadian living in London who had a banker's training, Goldcrest courted potential investors for film projects. Various methods were used including pre-selling to distributors; persuading investors to back films as a means of qualifying for tax shelter provisions known as 'capital allowances'; establishing film-development funds and making links with key American distributors. These included Fox (*Chariots of Fire*); Warners (*The Killing Fields*) and Columbia (*Gandhi* and *The Dresser*).

In the case of *Gandhi,* Goldcrest had to struggle for investors when Fox backed out of co-funding and distributing the film on the grounds that it was not commercial enough. Goldcrest and director Richard Attenborough eventually struck a deal with Columbia, whose distribution and advertising assisted the film's progress in the United States. In keeping with previous traditions of marketing British films, *Gandhi* was released at first in a few showcase cinemas in New York, Washington DC, Los Angeles and Toronto, but then as a wider release, 'a world event' in several countries simultaneously. The production team gave numerous interviews to the press, on radio and on television to promote the film. A lucrative television deal followed on the heels of excellent reviews and good initial box-office takings. *Gandhi* won eight Academy Awards and confirmed Goldcrest's position as a major film production company. The stark contrast between *Gandhi* and the fortunes of *The Emerald Forest,* a film developed in its first stages by Goldcrest but eventually financed and distributed by Embassy, an American independent distributor, underlines how important it was to obtain distribution through one of the majors. When *The Emerald Forest* was released in June 1985, it suffered from not having an astute marketing campaign behind it, nor access to key cinemas from which it could be showcased (Eberts and Ilott, 1990: 167).

Eberts and Ilott describe how, after the resignation of Eberts at the end of 1983, Goldcrest's fortunes declined. The favourable economic conditions that had assisted the company's rise were no longer prevailing, as more films were being made, creating intense market competition. Budgets and overhead costs rose, and exchange rates were no longer favourable. A series of disastrous investments in a small programme of big-budget films including *The Mission* and *Revolution* steered Goldcrest towards collapse in 1986. Internal squabbles and volatile relations with American companies also contributed to the company's demise. The history of Goldcrest illustrates how vulnerable British production companies were to external conditions. It also provides further evidence of the continued domination of the US market by the majors, a situation that did not alter in the 1990s.

British Films at the American Box-office in the 1990s

Table 8.2 gives an indication of the box-office performance of the top five British films in the United States each year during the 1990s. The nationalities primarily involved in each production have been indicated to illustrate the increasingly international dimensions of the film industry.[13]

The American careers of the films listed in Table 8.2 were in some cases impressive (*The Crying Game, Four Weddings and a Funeral, Bean, The Full*

Table 8.2 British Films at the US Box-office, 1990s

Year	Film	B/O $m	Year	Film	B/O $m
1992	The Crying Game (UK)	63	1996	Trainspotting (UK)	17
	Lawnmower Man (UK/US)	33		Secrets and Lies (UK/Fr)	6
	Howards End (UK/Japan)	18		Cold Comfort Farm (UK)	6
	Enchanted April (UK)	13		Jane Eyre (UK/US/Fr/It)	5
	Chaplin (UK/US)	9		Stealing Beauty (UK/It/Fr)	5
1993	Much Ado about Nothing (UK/US)	23	1997	Bean (UK/US)	45
	The Remains of the Day (UK/US)	19		The Full Monty (UK/US)	35
	Posse (UK/US)	14		Mrs Brown (UK/US/Ire)	8
	Shadowlands (UK)	14		The Wings of the Dove (UK/US)	8
	Orlando (UK/Russ/Fr/It/Neth)	5		Secrets and Lies (UK/Fr)	8
1994	Four Weddings and a Funeral (UK)	53	1998	Elizabeth (UK)	30
	Sirens (UK/Aust)	8		The Wings of the Dove (UK/US)	14
	Widow's Peak (UK)	6		Sliding Doors (UK/US)	12
	Princess Caraboo (UK/US)	3		The Governess (UK/Fr)	4
	Backbeat (UK)	2		Lock, Stock and Two Smoking Barrels (UK)	4
1995	The Madness of King George (UK)	15	1999	The World Is Not Enough (UK/US)	118
	The Englishman Who Went up a Hill and Came down a Mountain (UK)	11		Notting Hill (UK/US)	116
	Priest (UK)	4		Waking Ned (UK/Fr/US)	19
	Sense and Sensibility (UK/US)	4		An Ideal Husband (UK/US)	19
	Persuasion (UK/US/Fr)	4		Tea with Mussolini (UK/It)	14

Monty and *Notting Hill*), but large-scale success was experienced by a few films rather than across the board. As has been pointed out previously, real box-office success must be related to production costs, so that a film such as *Trainspotting,* that cost $3.5 million, earned a substantial amount in the United States, particularly considering its apparently 'parochial' address. There is not necessarily a correlation between high budgets and success at the American box-office, although of course the big-budget Bond movies such as *The World Is Not Enough* (budget $120 million) continue to be popular. What is more significant for the majority of British films is the marketing campaign, the number of prints available for distribution and the method of release. The profitability of *The Crying Game,* for example, can be related to the higher number of prints in circulation for its American release in comparison with the smaller number for its British release. Released in Britain with only twelve prints, the film earned an average of £169,000 per print. On the other hand, when Miramax released the film in America, 500 prints were available, earning an average of £798,000 per print (Watson, 2000: 84). Even with an increased number of prints, however, the method of distribution was also important. A 'sleeper' film such as *The Crying Game* became successful by being released selectively and then on a wider basis after 'word-of-mouth' advertising broadened its popularity.

Effective distribution has been a key to the success of British films, particularly by Miramax, the company that handled *The Crying Game, Enchanted April, Sirens, The Englishman Who Went Up a Hill and Came Down a Mountain, Priest, Trainspotting, Jane Eyre, Mrs Brown, The Wings of a Dove, Sliding Doors* and *An Ideal Husband.* Even though Miramax is a subsidiary of a larger American company (currently Disney), it has been influential in promoting British and foreign-language films such as *Il Postino* (1994) in the United States. As we shall see with the case study of *Trainspotting,* the film's presentation for US audiences was a key element of its unexpected success overseas. Gramercy, purchased by Polygram Filmed Entertainment in 1996, has been another company responsible for launching effective promotional campaigns for British films such as *Four Weddings and a Funeral, Bean, Elizabeth* and *Lock, Stock and Two Smoking Barrels.* Gramercy was established specifically 'to nurture and distribute films that are atypical of Hollywood's studios'.[14] Polygram Filmed Entertainment, a subsidiary of the record company controlled by Dutch electronics conglomerate Philips, financed many of the decade's biggest box-office successes. When Polygram absorbed Gramercy, it became a key distributor in the United States, responsible for many of Universal's films that had formerly been assigned to Gramercy.[15] Some critics have expressed concern about the extent to which Polygram has become enmeshed in a Hollywood-biased corporate network, particularly when Philips sold the company in 1998 to Seagram, a Canadian soft drinks company that controlled Universal (Watson, 2000: 83). On the other hand, access to American screens – cinemas, televisions or computers – can only be achieved by association with the 'majors' that dominate the market. A somewhat ironic twist occurred in 2000 when Seagram (and hence Universal) was bought up by and merged with Vivendi, a French media conglomerate, but at the time of this writing it is unclear what impact this will have on Polygram or Universal. What can be concluded, however, is that as long as specialized distribution subsidiaries continue to exist, British and foreign films will benefit from their marketing experience and from the assurance of adequate print generation, factors that have proved to be of key importance, especially for films such as *Four Weddings and a Funeral.*

The American release of *Four Weddings and a Funeral* followed a similar pattern to that adopted by Miramax for *The Crying Game.* After test screenings towards the end of 1993 in Secaucus, New Jersey, and Santa Monica, Gramercy decided to release *Four Weddings* in March 1994, before it had been released in the United Kingdom. No other romantic comedies were on the market to offer the film serious competition, so the company felt that it stood a good chance of success. Response to Hugh Grant was favourable in the test screenings, especially those held for editors of women's magazines. Since the film's opening coincided with the release of two other films starring Hugh Grant, *Sirens* and *Bitter Moon,* he was very much in the news (Plate 18). He was described as a 'peculiarly English character' possessing a 'careless schoolboy charm'.[16] Indeed, this 'peculiarly English' persona has been exploited in subsequent films. The film's popularity was built up from a limited first release, exhibited at only two screens in its first week. This was increased to five in its second, gaining ground to 240 in its fifth week and 721 in its seventh. By that time it had become a top-grossing film and went on to become a worldwide success (Roddick, 1995). It was even reported as being a box-office success in the South and Midwest of America. According to Thomas P. Pollock, Chairman of the MCA Motion Picture Group and head of Universal, the film was such a widespread success because of its traditional romantic formula.[17] Ed Koch of the *Manhattan Spirit* is representative of the most enthusiastic reviewers:

What a wonderful feeling it is to go to a movie and leave happy and smiling, with everyone talking about what a marvellous flick it was. That's what happened last Friday night after seeing *Four Weddings and a Funeral,* a superb British comedy. As for the plot, it is as though Oscar Wilde had come back to life and written the drollest, wittiest comedy of manners only in today's vernacular.[18]

While many critics similarly appreciated its gentle 'screwball' comedy, several objected to the casting of American actress Andie MacDowell as the romantic lead. This is interesting in view of the desire of many British film-makers to include American stars in the hope that their presence will enhance a film's popularity in the United States. Objections to MacDowell centred on her 'oddly mechanical' performance, considered to be 'stolid' in comparison with the 'rapier play' of the British actors.[19] Yet an American actress was essential in a film that centred on an Anglo-American 'special relationship' that operated much in the traditions of the screwball romantic comedy.

Writing in the *LA Weekly*, Elizabeth Pincus criticized the film's traditional (in the sense that marriage is the goal of most of the characters) 'anachronistic' attitudes, and 'feel-good' departure from British films with more radical intentions: 'It's a facile effort that relies on glib banter and the up-beat fantasy of a classless society'.[20] Another reviewer objected to its concentration on the affairs of the upper middle class: 'If an American made a movie like this about prosperous Harvard graduates, the audience would scream bloody murder. *Four Weddings and a Funeral* is less a cinematic triumph than a yardstick of critics' increasingly indiscriminate Anglophilia'.[21] These comments reveal the extent to which British films continued to be judged on their representation of class. In view of its contemporary setting, in comparison with opinions of 'heritage' films, the critique levelled against *Four Weddings* was more scathing. Arguably, *Four Weddings and a Funeral* contains aspects associated with the 'heritage' costume/historical films, particularly in its use of setting and concentration on the dilemmas of the rich and upper classes. The subsequent success of *Notting Hill* (1999) would suggest a continuum of 'Anglophilic' fascination. While this has been clearly expressed at the American box-office, critical discussion of these films reveals a more complex and ambivalent assimilation.

As well as effective distribution, the production of *Four Weddings and a Funeral* by Working Title, arguably the most successful British production company in the 1990s, was also significant. Working Title has been associated with many of the most notable subsequent film exports: *Bean*, *Elizabeth* and *Notting Hill*. When Universal absorbed Polygram, the association with Working Title was maintained, giving the company's films key access to US theatres. Working Title nevertheless maintains a firm interest in low-budget films, represented by the formation of a special division, WT2 producer (with Tiger Aspect Films, see below), of the Oscar-nominated *Billy Elliot* (2000). Adaptations of British bestselling novels is a feature of Working Title's most recent ventures, *Captain Corelli's Mandolin*, *Bridget Jones' Diary*, and *About a Boy*. The latter two films also star Hugh Grant, a British actor who has demonstrated consistent box-office appeal in the United States. In April 2001 *Bridget Jones' Diary* (2000) opened on 1,611 screens in the United States and grossed $10.7 million; by August this figure had increased to $71.5 million. While in five months *Notting Hill* earned more (opening on 2,747 screens at the end of May 1999 at a gross of $27.6 million, which accumulated to $116 million by October), it is nevertheless an impressive achievement.[22]

These commercially proven initiatives have led to optimistic comments in the press about the company's undoubted ability to produce films that demonstrate both indigenous and export appeal, inviting comparison with Alexander Korda and Michael Balcon.[23] Working Title established links with other companies, thereby facilitating access to Universal's exhibition outlets for producers such as Tiger Aspect, the British film and television company that was responsible for *Bean* and *Billy Elliot*. At the Cinema Expo International 2001, the annual cinema exhibitors' convention held in Amsterdam, Working Title's chief executives Tim Bevan and Eric Fellner were honoured as producers of the year in recognition of their status as being 'among the key, cutting-edge, dynamic players and companies in the motion picture industry'.[24]

Trainspotting in America

Heaven knows how the film will play here, where audiences get their fix of the British Isles through regular injections of Merchant Ivory. (*New Yorker*, 22 July 1996: 79)

A case study of *Trainspotting*, one of the more surprising successes of the 1990s, will provide further detail on the above points as well as a greater consideration of the role played by the films themselves when 'crossing over' to a different audience. *Trainspotting* was contrasted with Merchant-Ivory's 'heritage' films, seen as an exciting departure from other British films of the 1990s (Plate 19). Its appreciation by American critics and audiences can also be explained by Miramax's publicity campaign; the immediate context of its release in the summer of 1996; the response of critics and its 'stylish irreverence' that was likened to *A Hard Day's Night* (see below).[25]

Miramax handled the American release of *Trainspotting* in July 1996, after the film had been applauded at Cannes and was proving to be a box-office success in the United Kingdom. At first the pattern of release was fairly restricted and selective, earning $262,000 on its opening weekend on eight screens. By September, its earnings had risen to $14.52 million and by December to $16.47 million.[26] In terms of introducing risqué subject matter, Miramax was not worried about the film's drug connection. Mark Gill, Miramax's Marketing President, argued that it was a deterrent: 'If you're going to give heroin a look, this will be the movie to persuade you to look away'.[27] As we shall see, reviewers did not necessarily share this view, but it is significant that the company tried to de-emphasize the film's ambivalence about drug-taking at an early stage. Advertisements stressed that the film had received good reviews and that the film was 'massively entertaining', perhaps diverting attention away from its subject matter.[28] Indeed, Miramax took the lead from Polygram's British marketing campaign that instead emphasized the film's 'hipness'; its presentation of a serious subject in an exciting way that was aimed directly at the youth market (Street, 1998: 14). Tie-ins with HMV record stores for sales of the soundtrack compact disc publicized the film's distinctive monochrome poster with the main characters looking directly at the camera in assertive, confident poses. The soundtrack's combination of 'Brit-pop' music with classics by Iggy Pop and Lou Reed were considered to 'flaunt the flash, speed, and constant motion that intoxicates the movie'.[29] The music was very much a part of the film's overall narrative image: 'Lust for Life'.

The film was prepared carefully for the American market, not least because of the broad Scottish accents that were featured rather than downplayed. Indeed, the bold regionalism of *Trainspotting*'s appeal made the film appear distinctive and fresh. These associations were not, however, seen to be exclusive and parochial, as Harlan Kennedy observed: 'Boyle and writer John Hodge never characterize their story or their characters' dilemma as exclusively "Scottish". Drug addiction, after all, is a global franchise, and so are the petty crime, troubled love lives, and attempts by mixed-up youngsters to start life afresh'.[30] The same reviewer made the point that the character Sick Boy's 'trainspotter' obsession with James Bond also opened the film up to a more global address. To make the dialogue more accessible, forty lines were cut and dubbed from the first twenty minutes and Miramax provided a glossary and notes to explain some of the more obscure phrases. Care over the dialogue was influenced by the view that *The Commitments* (1991) and *Shallow Grave* (1994) were unintelligible to many US audiences, unlike the more successful *Gregory's Girl* (1981) and *Local Hero* (1983) that had been partially dubbed.[31] Information about the production team was made available to the press and Danny Boyle, John Hodge and Andrew Macdonald gave interviews in American newspapers and journals as the film was gaining notoriety. As with many 'cult' films, assimilation required audiences to do some work, playing on the intertextual possibilities offered by the soundtrack and within the film itself. In pre-publicity Miramax encouraged curiosity about the meaning of the title, a novelty that also preoccupied many reviewers concerning the extent to which 'trainspotting' was an entirely British pastime.[32]

The timing of *Trainspotting*'s release was of key importance in securing a 'space' in a market that was conducive to its reception. One reviewer in Chicago pointed out that 'as an edgy, artful piece of entertainment it beats any Hollywood release of the summer by miles'.[33] Many of Hollywood's summer 1996 releases were flops, including big-budget films such as *Matilda, Striptease, The Fan, Multiplicity* and *The Adventures of Pinocchio*. As *Entertainment Weekly* put it: 'This summer, movie-goers had either bad choices or no choices'.[34] In a survey of the summer's films *Trainspotting* was listed as an 'art hit', along with *Emma, Lone Star, Cold Comfort Farm* and *Welcome to the Dollhouse*.[35] The association of *Trainspotting* with a verve and vitality that was perceived to be lacking in Hollywood's offerings was reflected in the highly positive reviews the film received. Writing in the *New Yorker*, Anthony Lane observed, 'Boyle's brand of unwashed visionary cinema feels alarmingly new, and in a season of elephantine blockbusters anything this fast and rude is bound to gather admirers'.[36] Such comments set the tone for the film's reception, suggesting a powerful link between critics' opinions and the fate of selectively released art-house product.

Themes that were stressed in reviews were the film's stylistic freshness, its humour, ensemble acting and similarity to *A Hard Day's Night* (1964) and other films associated with experimentation. These elements were considered to be more important than the film's 'message' (or not) on drug-taking. Reviewers were both captivated and perplexed by the film's presentation of a dark subject in such a fresh and exuberant manner. Janet Maslin's view was typical of many critics' enthusiastic response that was nevertheless tempered with a hesitancy about the film's non-didactic approach: 'The stylish irreverence of *Trainspotting* is itself geared to the tourist trade, since it keeps a safely voyeuristic distance from the real dangers that go with its subject matter. Instead, it rocks to a throbbing beat and trains its jaundiced eye on some of the most loveable lowlifes ever to skulk across a screen'.[37] Given an 'R' rating, the film had two seconds cut and was considered to be dangerous by right-wing politicians including Republican presidential candidate Bob Dole. Capitol Records publicized the release of the *Trainspotting* soundtrack with a 'mock' campaign poster featuring Bob Dole wearing a large 'Iggy Pop for President' lapel badge. Dole's press secretary complained, commenting that 'Nothing better illustrates the need for corporate responsibility in the entertainment industry than this glib and whimsical advertisement for the soundtrack from a movie that glamorizes heroin abuse'.[38] Controversy of this nature assisted

Trainspotting's reputation as a 'must-see' film and consolidated its nonconformist 'youth' appeal.

A dominant strand of the American reception of *Trainspotting* was its comparison to Richard Lester's *A Hard Day's Night*. While other intertextual references were identified, including *A Clockwork Orange* (1971) and *Pulp Fiction* (1994), the Beatles' first film was by far the most frequently cited. Richard
Corliss of *Time* magazine predicted *Trainspotting*'s US success by acknowledging its similarity to *A Hard Day's Night*: 'It could also achieve the cult-hit
status of a certain 1964 movie, which was also about four British lads with
heavy Northern accents and anti-Establishment cheek and which also began
with the boys eluding their pursuers'.[39] The comparison even extended to the
production team, identified as unorthodox, ambitious and talented.[40] Interviews with Ewan McGregor highlighted his endorsement of the film's anti-
British commentary, associating him closely with his character, Renton. This
attitude also invited comparison with the Beatles' rejection of 'Establishment'
views in *A Hard Day's Night*. Appreciation of an irreverent comic attitude
even extended to McGregor's antipathy towards Hollywood, and to *Trainspotting*'s criticism of American tourists attending the Edinburgh festival.
These elements did not seem to alienate reviewers or audiences who were presented with them as integral aspects of the film's counter-cultural stance.

Just as Richard Lester experimented with film form in *A Hard Day's Night*,
Trainspotting also intrigued reviewers with its disregard for conventional realist traditions in favour of surrealism, fast-cutting and expressionist use of colour. *American Cinematographer* published a seven-page analysis of the work
of Brian Tufano, *Trainspotting*'s director of photography, likening his use of
colour to the work of Pedro Almodovar and Peter Greenaway, and also commenting on Danny Boyle's homage to the work of Quentin Tarantino.[41] For
one reviewer the evasion of Ken Loach-style realism turned *Trainspotting* into
a film that was primarily about upward social mobility:

> The boys shoot up and fall down in pleasure and sometimes they jump
> about Edinburgh chasing down streets like the Beatles in *A Hard Day's
> Night*, romping in and out of bars or just sitting around making pre-
> posterous jokes. . . . For all the scandalous goings-on, Renton's story is
> perhaps the most upbeat narrative of the season. The hero gets up and
> out: *Trainspotting* is a fable of upward mobility. It is also a shrewdly
> calculated and commercial piece of work.[42]

The association with *A Hard Day's Night* invested the film with a positive intertextual connection for American critics resulting, in this case, in an interpretation that endorses the ending when Renton ends up in London, having swin-

dled his friends out of a share of the money they have jointly stolen. This conflicted with reviews that attempted to privilege the drug theme and the friends' emotional and financial interdependence. Nevertheless, many agreed that the decision to opt for a mixture of realist and surrealist techniques to convey a subjective impression of addiction was extremely effective: 'Seeing this movie can make you feel as if you know what it's like to shoot junk'.[43]

British Comedies: *The Full Monty, Secrets and Lies, Bean* and *Notting Hill*

Several British comedies performed well at the American box-office in the 1990s. As we have already seen, *Four Weddings and a Funeral* was a highly regarded 'screwball' romantic comedy, released at a time when Hollywood was more concerned with making action blockbusters. In 1997 two very different comedies distinguished themselves as films that 'travelled well' to America: *The Full Monty* and *Bean*. Both were representative of different comic traditions. As with *Four Weddings and a Funeral*, the marketing of *The Full Monty* was crucial in establishing an audience for the film that grew after an initial campaign established its comic identity and narrative image. As a specialist subsidiary of Fox, Searchlight, the distributor of *The Full Monty*, was able to place the film beyond the art market. With its reputation for handling 'unusual' product, Searchlight drew on its experience in promoting German films for the exploitation of *The Full Monty*.[44] Once again, an appropriate campaign ensured that once the film gained a reputation as a 'must-see', it was booked more widely in cinemas throughout the United States. A successful screening at the Sundance Film Festival alerted Searchlight to its potential. After a 'world première' in Park City, Utah, the company arranged a series of Monday night test screenings in ten cities across the country. These areas were also the locations for 'target advertising'.[45] The score cards for the test screenings were high, and free showings followed in big cities, some of which were promoted by radio stations, newspapers and retail stores, particularly Ralph Lauren, retailer of polo shirts similar to those worn in the film. Much was made of the 'teaser' title, and Robert Carlyle and Mark Addy, the relatively unknown stars of the film, appeared on television on David Letterman's *The Late Show* and on Jay Leno's *The Tonight Show*.[46] Eventually, *The Full Monty* 'crossed over' from specialized theatres to the wider commercial arena, occasioning stunts including 'Full Monty' contests advertised in local HMV record stores.[47]

On its opening weekend the film took $244,375 from six screens. By September, it was on general release on 387 screens and had taken $2.91 million.[48] As well as this astute handling, *The Full Monty* benefited from reduced competition. When it was released in the United States in the summer of 1997, Hollywood produced a series of flops including *Father's Day, Conspiracy Theory* and *Speed 2*.[49] David Dinerstein, Senior Vice-President of Searchlight, observed that people were tired of summer blockbusters, perceiving 'something more real' in *The Full Monty*.[50] Although reviewers did not grant it the depth or sincerity of films directed by Mike Leigh or Ken Loach, it was well received as 'heart-warming fun with more serious undertones than you might have expected'.[51] The idea of a community combating unemployment by devising an ingenious money-making scheme harked back to the traditions of Ealing comedy. While advocating the 'self-help' approach to economic inequality ignored the underlying causes and failed to offer a long-term solution, the film was largely interpreted as another spin on the 'feel-good' comedy. As one critic observed, 'The serious comedy of British working-class manners is settling into a sweet but altogether too comfortable – and comforting – groove, its edges bevelled by the lure of the middle-brow export market'.[52]

On the other hand, Mike Leigh's *Secrets and Lies,* a comedy-drama with a less overtly 'feel-good' content, performed well in America, earning $8 million at the US box-office by 1997, nearly double its production cost of $4.5 million. The film's reputation was enhanced by being awarded the Palme d'Or at Cannes, an accolade that automatically placed it in a good position for the art market. Consequently, it opened the New York Film Festival in 1996, played on a selective basis in major cities and was nominated for an Academy Award. While Mike Leigh already had a 'small, passionate US following', *Secrets and Lies* was more widely popular than his pervious films.[53] One review compared Leigh's work, particularly his much-publicized improvisational technique with actors, to that of American independent film-maker John Cassavetes for its 'emotional rawness'.[54] While the British setting was acknowledged, the dilemmas facing the characters in *Secrets and Lies* were interpreted in the same review as 'universal': 'Everyone's had these family skirmishes and confrontations in their lives, and it's remarkable to see them recorded so accurately and painfully on film'. Similarly, *Time Magazine* identified the film's cross-cultural potential: 'It is easy to imagine dropping into a mall this fall and hearing America sob along with Cynthia'.[55] The enthusiastic reception of *Secrets and Lies* demonstrates the extent to which appreciation of British comedies existed on several levels in the American market. Reviewers made distinctions between them, usefully acknowledging their different chances of assimilation outside the art-house scene.

Bean, the other successful comedy of 1997, was quite different in its approach. Produced by Polygram, Tiger Aspect Films and Working Title, it was distributed in the United States by Gramercy. The star was Rowan Atkinson, already known to American audiences from Working Title's successful comedy *The Tall Guy* (1989); his role as the vicar in *Four Weddings and a Funeral* and on PBS Television in cult imports such as *Black Adder.* Atkinson's style of comedy was largely based on sight-gags performed by his character, Mr Bean, a clumsy, infuriatingly gawkish man who invariably causes havoc in any situation. As reviewers pointed out, the placement of Atkinson's character in an American setting for *Bean* appeared to be a deliberate attempt to introduce him to American audiences. Atkinson plays an incompetent attendant at the National Gallery who is sent to America by his angry managers who are forbidden to sack him. In America Mr Bean is mistaken for an art expert when he is charged with overseeing the delivery of a famous painting from Paris to Los Angeles. Much of the comedy arises from the incongruity of this situation – of someone who can almost pass as an expert because of his eccentric behaviour, occasioning a host of cross-cultural misunderstandings. Reviewers likened Atkinson's comedy to that of silent comedians, particularly Chaplin.[56] Not all American reviewers were amused. For example, Susan Wloszczna compared Atkinson unfavourably to Harpo Marx, describing 'Bean' as 'a witless twit'.[57] The non-verbal nature of the comedy was nevertheless conducive to worldwide success. *Bean* attracted large audiences in the United Kingdom, the United States, Australia, Japan and Germany.[58]

The success of *Four Weddings and A Funeral* prepared the way for *Notting Hill,* a romantic comedy starring Hugh Grant and Julia Roberts. The formula of the Anglo-American romance was repeated, but this time the setting was Notting Hill, a district of London, and the romance between an 'ordinary' travel bookseller William Thacker (Grant) and a major Hollywood star, Anna Scott (Roberts), who is in London to publicize her latest film. The progress of the romance is frustrated by her fame, the existence of an American boyfriend and an estrangement when she suspects that Thacker and his lodger have revealed her whereabouts to the press. By the end of the film, however, their differences are resolved and she chooses to stay in London. The film positions the non-achieving lifestyle of Thacker and his friends as superior to the self-denying consequences of Scott's worldwide, potentially ephemeral fame.

The casting of Roberts was a major reason for the huge box-office takings of *Notting Hill,* and most reviews declared her performance as her best to date. *Entertainment Weekly* observed that 'no other actress could pull off the role with such appeal and authority', while *Variety* compared her acting more than favourably to that of Andie MacDowell in *Four Weddings and a Funeral*: 'Roberts' American is a fully drawn character rather than a one-dimensional bolt-on, like Andie MacDowell'.[59] Many reviews appreciated the parallels between Roberts' own career and that of the fictional character she plays, caught in an incessant barrage of press conferences and tabloid comment: 'It comes as a bonus that this romantic comedy is one of the rare pictures of its type that actually is about something – the double-edged sword of celebrity'.[60] Intertextual reference was made in several reviews to Roberts' similarity to Audrey Hepburn, particularly in *Roman Holiday* (1953), the romantic comedy in which Hepburn plays a princess who falls in love with a reporter. She seeks an escape from the pressures of fame and like Scott, her salvation is the love and protection of an 'ordinary' man. As one reviewer declared: 'It [*Notting Hill*] takes an intrinsically democratic, American, *Roman Holiday*-style approach to celebrity: In a meritocracy, everyone's got a crack at capturing the heart of a royal personage'.[61] Grant was also appreciated as a star who had grown in stature and notoriety since *Four Weddings,* both on- and off-screen.

Yet despite its big budget and Hollywood star, as Murphy has observed, *Notting Hill* is 'more personal' than *Four Weddings* in the sense that 'the film makes cheekily few concessions to Hollywood. It is not just the way in which the film industry is represented as crass, cynical and superficial . . . it is the assurance with which a messy, unambitious, British lifestyle is shown as preferable to the gloss and glamour of Hollywood' (2000: 9). When Anna Scott becomes attracted to William Thacker (Grant), she is forced to confront the emptiness of her life, which is posited as materially satisfying but emotionally crippling. When Thacker finds himself in the midst of one of Anna's press conferences, his blissful ignorance of films and the film industry is used to ridicule that world of glitz, hype and glamour. He even appears to have an influence on her choice of roles, insinuating that literary adaptations might be more fulfilling than science fiction. At the beginning of the film, Anna Scott's latest starring role is in a science fiction blockbuster whereas by the end she is appearing in a 'heritage' adaptation of Henry James, filmed on location in London; it is as if the film is positing a set of norms associated with the British film industry rather than with Hollywood.

The characters who play William's friends are less aristocratic than in *Four Weddings,* perhaps indicating that the success of that film permitted its successor to be less obviously directed at the overseas market. As Murphy has commented: 'Despite the trendy location, *Notting Hill* offers a less obvious milieu to buy into for a non-British audience. The Britain of *Four Weddings* is inhabited by aristocratic bohemians and eccentrics, but *Notting Hill*'s gallery of determinedly non-achieving characters are not far removed from the struggling stoics of Mike Leigh's *Life Is Sweet* (1991)' (2000: 9–10). In this way *Notting Hill* represents an incidence of a major success easing the path of a variation on a formula, allowing that formula to contain indigenous elements while also demonstrating 'international' appeal. In their different ways, British variations of the comedy genre have therefore proved to be of particular interest to American distributors and audiences.

A Bigger Splash? Crossing the Pond, 2001

From this overview of the prevailing climate for British film exports, it will be apparent that while some films have been extremely successful, many continue to experience problems in getting access to American screentime. To export or not is, of course, a controversial subject, frequently at the heart of official discussions of the future of the British film industry.[62] The success of films such as *Chariots of Fire, A Room With A View, Four Weddings and a Funeral, Trainspotting, Notting Hill* and *Bean* are often taken as evidence that, handled with care, dollars will flow from the American market. This is certainly the case and these films have gone a long way to enhance the reputation of British films abroad. A film with a modest budget such as *Trainspotting* provides evidence that exportability need not necessarily be linked to a high budget or to a set of assumptions about non-specific 'international' address. *Trainspotting* is particularly interesting in this respect because its address could be described as both indigenous and cross-cultural. Films are consumed differently wherever they are exhibited. A study of the reception of *Trainspotting* in America illustrates that earlier films, especially *A Hard Day's Night,* paved the way for acceptance of a film that on first acquaintance might appear to be narrowly pitched. American assimilation of the 'heritage' films would also suggest that costume/historical subjects are absorbed and interpreted differently abroad. They were often reviewed in a critical context that privileged American frames of reference, most notably the linking of *The Remains of the Day* with *The Age of Innocence.* In their different ways, both films dealt with the subject of class in different national contexts, inviting cross-cultural comparison not only between films but also between nations.

British films continue to be inextricably bound up with American capital, leaving some commentators with an uneasy feeling that should this be withdrawn, 'our industry would effectively become a cottage industry overnight'.[63] Producers are seeking partnerships with American companies to ensure more effective distribution. Warner Brothers' co-production pact with Film Four, for example, has enabled Gillian Armstrong's *Charlotte Gray* to be produced for $20 million. Uberto Pasolini, producer of *The Full Monty,* has a 'first look' development partnership with 20th Century-Fox for his company Redgrave

Films. Increasingly, therefore, American and European partnerships characterize the contemporary film industry.[64]

In the American market, British films are part of a larger story of the place of independents and foreign films within the reconfigured 'global' Hollywood. As experienced by the Goldcrest executives in the 1980s, an increase in film production and expansion of new exhibition outlets (DVD and computers) has created intense competition for what is still a market controlled by a few major companies. Effective distribution was, and still is, the cornerstone of a film's profitability, as evidenced by several films discussed in this chapter. Anxiety over the problems experienced by British films funded with the Lottery franchises has placed emphasis on the key areas of distribution and exhibition in the United Kingdom and abroad. While method of release is clearly of paramount importance, timing is also crucial. Several examples discussed in this chapter attest to the benefits to be reaped from a careful assessment of the best date to release a British film overseas. *Gandhi, Four Weddings and a Funeral, Trainspotting* and *The Full Monty* were all released at times when their impact would be most effective. In all cases this involved the films' being perceived as different from standard Hollywood productions, appealing to a specialized audience in the first instance and then 'crossing over' to general release. The number of prints available on wider release is also crucial in ensuring that once a film has 'crossed over' demand can be satisfied at a pace that keeps up with word-of-mouth advertising. In 2000 British films made a more-than-respectable impression at the American box-office. Whether this can be sustained to produce 'a bigger splash' will depend on factors which, as this chapter has shown, are often beyond the control of individual producers.

Notes

1. The only non-European countries responsible for significant numbers of imports (indigenous and co-productions) were Australia (five in 1967–9 but thirty-six in 1987–9); Canada (sixteen in 1967–9 and fifty-five in 1987–9); Japan (ninety-three in 1967–9 and forty in 1987–9). Imports from Mexico had fallen from thirteen in 1967–9 to three in 1987–9. Imports from the United Kingdom were 209 in 1967–9 and 128 in 1987–9.
2. Table 8.1 compiled from 'All-time Film Rental Champs', in *Variety*, 15 Oct 1990: M-140-96. These figures are unlikely to have been adjusted for inflation so it is important to recognize that the sums earned by a film in 1974 are not equivalent to those earned a decade later.
3. The most significant writing on the heritage genre is Higson, 1993: 109–29; Higson, 1996: 232–48; Monk, 1994; J. Pidduck, 'Of women, windows and walks' in *Screen*, vol. 39, no. 4, 1998 and Church Gibson in Murphy ed., 2000: 115–24.
4. This list has been compiled from charts of box-office revenue of British films in the United States, as published in *The BFI Film and Television Handbooks* (London: British Film Institute, 1994–2001). See Table 8.2 on the box office performance of British films in the 1990s for further details.

5. *Boxoffice*, May 1986 and *Chicago Sun-Times*, 4 Apr 1986.

6. Figure for *The Bostonians* is quoted in the *New York Times*, 5 July 1986.

7. *New York Times*, 5 July 1986.

8. *Variety*, 24 June 1986.

9. Rita Kempley in the *Washington Post*, 5 Nov 1993.

10. *New York Times*, 5 Nov 1993: C1.

11. Roger Ebert in the *Chicago Sun-Times*, 11 May 1993. *The Age of Innocence* was released in September 1993 and *The Remains of the Day* in November 1993.

12. Caryn James in the *New York Times*, 14 Nov 1993: II: 13.

13. Table 8.2 has been complied from *The BFI Film and Television Handbooks*, 1994–2001. Unlike the previous *Variety* figures, these represent total box-office revenues rather than rental grosses. Like the rental figures, they have not been adjusted to take inflation into account, so a comparison of the figures for the earlier part of the decade does not necessarily equate with those from the end. Figures above 0.5 have been rounded up so that a film earning $62.5 million will be listed as having earned $63 million. The figures depend in part on when the film was released in each year, so caution again should be taken: these figures are a basic guide to popularity. The principal nationalities involved in each film have been compiled from *Sight and Sound* and the Internet Movie Database (www.imdb.com, accessed June 2001).

14. *New York Times*, 19 Apr 1994: C15.

15. *Screen International*, 23 Aug 1996: 16.

16. *New York*, 2 May 1994: 81; *Entertainment Weekly*, 25 Mar 1994.

17. *New York Times*, 19 Apr 1994: C15.

18. *Manhattan Spirit*, 31 Mar 1994: 17.

19. See for example the *New York Times*, 9 Mar 1994: C15; *Entertainment Weekly*, 25 Mar 1994; *New Republic*, 4 Apr 1994: 24.

20. *LA Weekly*, review, 11–17 Mar 1994: 25.

21. *New York*, 4 Apr 1994: 78.

22. Figures from Internet Movie Database.

23. *Observer Review*, 8 Apr 2001: 8.

24. *Screen International*, 11-24 May 2001: 6.

25. *New York Times*, 19 July 1996.

26. Figures from the Internet Movie Database.

27. Mark Gill, quoted in *People*, 22 July 1996.

28. See advertisement in *The Village Voice*, 10 Sept 1996: 72.

29. *Details*, Sept 1996: 184.

30. *Film Comment*, July–Aug 1996: 31.

31. *Independent on Sunday*, 26 May 1996: 8.

32. See for example *Pulse*, Aug 1996: 51, that describes *Trainspotting* as 'a typically British form of quiet desperation'.

33. *Chicago Reader*, 2 Aug 1996: 40.

34. *Entertainment Weekly*, 6 Sept 1996: 21.

35. *Entertainment Weekly*, 6 Sept 1996: 19.

36. *New Yorker*, 22 July 1996: 79.

37. *New York Times*, 19 July 1996.

38. Nelson Warfield, quoted in the *LA Times*, 1 Oct 1996.

39. *Time*, 15 July 1996: 64.

40. *Details*, Sept 1996: 182.

41. *American Cinematographer*, August 1996: 80–6.

42. *New York*, 12 Aug 1996.

43. *San Francisco Examiner*, 26 July 1996: D1.

44. *Guardian*, 27 Oct 1997: 5.

45. *LA Times*, 16 Sept 1997: section F1.
46. *New York Times*, 15 Sept 1997: D13.
47. *Film Journal International*, July 1997: 72 and *Time Out New York*, 18 Sept 1997.
48. Figures from the Internet Movie Database.
49. *New York Times*, 2 Sept 1997: C12.
50. Dinerstein quoted in the *LA Times*, 16 Sept 1997: F1.
51. *LA Times*, 13 Aug 1997: F5.
52. Ella Taylor in *LA Weekly*, 15 Aug 1997.
53. Richard Corliss in *Time Magazine*, 30 Sept 1996, vol. 148, no. 16.
54. *San Francisco Chronicle*, 4 Oct 1996.
55. Richard Corliss in *Time Magazine*, 30 Sept 1996, vol. 148, no. 16.
56. See for example review in *San Francisco Examiner*, 7 Nov 1997.
57. *USA Today*, 1 Dec 1998.
58. *BFI Film and Television Handbook*, 1999: 39.
59. *Entertainment Weekly*, no. 487, 28 May 1999: 116; *Variety*, 3 May 1999: 83.
60. *San Francisco Chronicle*, 28 May 1999.
61. *Entertainment Weekly*, no. 487, 28 May 1999: 115–16.
62. State policy is not the focus of this study but is obviously important in influencing the parameters of debate on exports as well as for much of the century encouraging companies' export drives. The present government is also interested in promoting American production in the United Kingdom.
63. Eddie Dyja in *BFI Film and Television Handbook*, 2001: 35.
64. *Screen International*, special edition on the United Kingdom, 20 Oct 2000: 12.

Conclusion

The study of 'transatlantic crossings' is a complex area that needs to be understood with reference to economic and cultural factors. With a home market that was dominated by Hollywood, and an acceptance of the premise that a successful national film industry must have an active export policy, British film producers could not isolate themselves from the imperatives of international competition. The decision whether to export a film was determined by complex, often contradictory factors. While many films were made with the British audience in mind, they nevertheless 'travelled' well overseas. Following Hollywood's model of 'transferability' and 'universalism', if a film was promoted for its 'international' qualities the expectation was that it would prosper at home and abroad. Often it was not the film itself that was of crucial importance but the financial circumstances of its production and chances of an American release. Overseas distribution often depended on the existence of an American partnership, such as that between Korda and United Artists or between Rank and Universal. While British films would have gained more screentime if they had been distributed more actively by vertically integrated 'majors', it is unlikely that United Artists and Universal would have handled so many if they had owned cinema chains. For them, the need to secure product was of paramount importance, and British films were looked on favourably because of their difference – sometimes referred to as 'quality' and 'prestige' – and production by the larger British companies. Given the chance, most British producers hoped for an American release, regardless of the film. In this way films which would not appear to be destined for export were submitted to the PCA and, if a distributor could be found, subject to publicity campaigns devised with American audiences in mind. It was this rather haphazard background that determined which British films found their way into American cinemas.

Once in the United States, British films were scrutinized by reviewers whose judgements were, as we have seen, extremely influential. Exhibitors located outside the larger cities usually did not have the opportunity to view the films before booking. Without being presented in blocks along with other films, British films that had received a bad press would not be high on exhibitors' booking targets. Whereas in Britain legislation ensured that a percentage of British films were distributed and exhibited, in America there was no quota to insist that they were screened. Adverse comments about accents being incomprehensible, a film's pace being too slow or its leading actors unknown were hardly an incentive for exhibitors who had fixed ideas about which films their patrons enjoyed most. As a country marked by regional and ethnic diversity, the US market was not homogenous. As we have seen, British films that were applauded in New York, Los Angeles and Chicago did not necessarily experience the same welcome in Atlanta, Denver or St Louis.

Despite these problems, enthusiastic reviews, combined with a specialized distribution strategy and targeted publicity campaign, were the most promising prerequisites for success. The successful 'roadshow' releases of several British films did much to enhance their reputation as 'dollar earners'. While the specific circumstances of United Artists' and Universal's handling of British films has been noted, it is clear that staff in both companies worked extremely hard to obtain bookings. Their publicity departments were also active in making the films more acceptable in America, revealing their uncertain identity but also their ability to achieve 'transferability'. The result of these efforts can be judged from the evidence of rental grosses and box-office performance, which frequently exceeded expectations. Many films did less well, but as the lists of films imported by America (see Appendix B) reveal, in numerical terms British films rated amongst the highest. As stressed in the introduction, 'success' is a relative measure, and one must be careful when discussing the performance of British films in the United States to distinguish between key variables including critical approbation, rental gross, box-office performance, producer's profit, Academy Awards and star recognition.

The films discussed in this book provide a basis for identifying factors which have been important in increasing a film's chances of 'success' or recognition in the United States. Apart from the economic incentives mentioned above, preoccupation with 'Britishness' is clearly a recurring theme, particularly if treated in a satiric, comedic manner. Historical costume films, represented by *Nell Gwyn* and *The Private Life of Henry VIII,* combine a fascination with British history and institutions with an appreciation of their satiric representation. This same tendency can be found in later films including Ealing comedies, *Monty Python* and the transatlantic success of *Bean.* In his study of the impact of British television in the United States, Jeffrey Miller (2000) has also identified patterns of cross-cultural assimilation, particularly of cultural artefacts that were different, such as the *Monty Python* series.[1] As well as being evident in historical costume films and comedy, 'Britishness', albeit configured with a different emphasis, is also a key element of the appeal of James Bond films. Writing about the 1930s, Reynolds observed a distinction between an 'Anglophile' cultural fascination with the British class system and an 'Anglophobe' political rejection of the idea that America might also be a class society (1981: 23). The popularity of 'heritage' films invites similar questions about American perceptions of class, either as a British experience or as one which relates to the United States. In their different ways, these films reveal how an issue which might not appear to be relevant to American experience is, in fact, closer to home than many would care to admit.

'Transferability' has also been assisted by an assumed 'special relationship' between Britain and the United States. This was more accentuated during periods when an Anglo-American alliance was in operation. During the Second World War national differences were subsumed by a common anti-fascist propaganda. Films such as *In Which We Serve* (1942) were presented as articulating a common goal, and patriotism was positive. In the later 1940s, Laurence Olivier's adaptations of Shakespeare, *Henry V* and *Hamlet,* were presented as the epitome of high culture, as educative art that was not interpreted as 'British' in a narrow or exclusive way. These eminently 'English' texts proved to be transferable beyond their initial 'highbrow' audiences, suggesting that national difference could only be a barrier when presented as such. In the 1960s, the James Bond films assumed a common transatlantic partnership that worked to destroy communist conspiracies. Romantic comedies including *The Ghost Goes West* and, more recently, *Four Weddings and a Funeral* and *Notting Hill,* also deployed the idea of the 'special relationship' as a narrational device. The exploration of similarities and differences between America and Britain was not, therefore, confined to critical discourse. Instead, it can be seen to work as an implicit and explicit framework in many of the films.

The popularity of British stars was another factor which increased the chances of a British film in the United States. While Hollywood stars undoubtedly dominated the polls, a few British stars gained a reputation and appeared in the lists compiled by the Audience Research Institute in the 1940s. The identity of British stars is somewhat complicated by the fact that many British actors had emigrated to Hollywood and appeared regularly in American films. This made accusations against the British accent as being 'unintelligible' less about the accent itself and more about the way it was enunciated in particular films. The overall presentation of a star was also significant: individual national identities could be subsumed by a generic identity or dominant 'narrative image' highlighted to publicize a picture. Once British stars such as James Mason had established personae, relevant publicity was devised. Once he was known for his sadistic roles in Gainsborough melodramas, particularly *The Man in Grey* (1943), posters advertising *The Wicked Lady* (1945) referred to him as 'That Mean Mason Man', assuming that audiences would remember the earlier picture. Stardom was not necessarily a key to success, however, as demonstrated by *The Red Shoes*. This film was hugely popular even though its star, Moira Shearer, was unknown. While *The Red Shoes* did not demonstrate the same level of engagement with notions of 'Britishness' discussed previously, it was exceptional in that it was able to draw on a 'dance craze' in America at the time of its release. While some patterns and trends can be discerned, it is therefore important to note the unpredictable nature of American reception as far as foreign films are concerned.

The export of films is a controversial subject. While it might be argued that money can be lost on trying to penetrate the American market, much can be gained from a positive experience, with, as I have argued, particularly conducive factors in operation. The recent experience of Working Title illustrates the benefits of combining transatlantic corporate synergy with films that do well at both the British and American box-office. David Aukin, former head of film at Channel Four, made the following observation:

> The conclusion I draw is that we can now make films for ourselves; that occasionally these films will 'travel'; that we need no longer feel overwhelmingly dependent on overseas markets to finance our films; and that we can remain true to our stories, to our casting and to our way of making films. The proviso is that the films must be made for a price that can be recouped from our own audiences. The paradox is that the truer we are to ourselves, the more likely we are to make films that will also appeal to the rest of the world. (Petrie, 1996: 3)

In the 1990s, with the international success of several films with 'indigenous' themes including *East Is East* (1999), a film which focused on conflicts within Anglo-Pakistani culture, this judgement would appear to be astute. It is interesting, however, that American reviews of the more celebrated films, such as *The Full Monty*, acknowledge that its representation is more 'feel good' than penetrating. On the other hand, the assimilation of *Trainspotting* indicates that 'feel good' can be combined with social comment in perhaps a more radical manner. It is unwise, however, to go down a route that strictly separates 'the indigenous' from 'the exportable'. As the cases discussed in this book demonstrate, in reality there is no easy distinction. In many respects looking for one is an exercise that obscures the realities of the international market.

Neither does it do justice to the films themselves, their ability to be 'transferable' and to be absorbed into different cultural contexts. Paradoxically, the greater the awareness of different cultural values and national experiences, the more acceptable their representation can be. Familiarity promises to broaden possibility and intensify cross-cultural exchange. As the experience of James Bond illustrates, *Goldfinger* was far easier to market than *Dr No*. Similarly, it took a careful publicity campaign to wean audiences away from their expectations of Universal horror films before Hammer horror could be understood as a specific adaptation of classic horror stories.

The study of the reception of British films abroad is therefore a key way of understanding what British cinema has meant to different audiences. This book has concentrated on the United States, but there are many other possibilities, including Canada and Australia, particularly as far as questions of past relations with the British empire and Commonwealth are concerned.[2] The extent to which British films were exhibited in the rest of Europe is also another potentially fascinating subject. This book aims to suggest productive lines of enquiry into researching questions of overseas reception. In so doing, we can present the history of British cinema from a new, more comparative and cross-cultural perspective, liberating the films from a narrow nationalist straitjacket as they travel all over the world.

Notes

1. Miller (2000: 130) links the appeal of Monty Python to college-age viewers, the series' surrealistic critique of institutions and its airing on public service broadcasting from 1974.
2. Michael Walsh is completing a study of British films in Australia and an AHRB-funded project based at Sheffield Hallam University is pursuing questions of 'the indigenous' and 'the exportable'.

Films Imported into the United States, 1927–1968

Year	British Imports	Total Imports	% British
1927	8	65	12.3
1928	35	192	18.2
1929	28	145	19.3
1930	30	86	34.9
1931	20	121	16.5
1932	31	196	15.8
1933	27	157	17.1
1934	43	181	23.8
1935	40	238	16.8
1936	39	240	16.3
1937	53	244	21.7
1938	44	319	13.7
1939	37	274	13.5
1940	53	211	25.1
1941	30	108	27.7
1942	22	47	46.8
1943	17	30	56.7
1944	22	40	55.0
1945	21	33	63.6
1946	24	91	26.4
1947	28	126	22.2
1948	33	109	30.3
1949	51	143	35.7
1950	47	239	19.6
1951	73	262	27.9
1952	45	209	21.5
1953	39	188	20.7
1954	52	152	34.2
1955	52	154	33.8
1956	46	221	20.8
1957	78	233	33.5

Year	British Imports	Total Imports	% British
1958	68	266	25.6
1959	37	246	15.0
1960	51	233	21.9
1961	54	331	16.3
1962	49	280	17.5
1963	44	297	14.8
1964	64	360	17.8
1965	60	300	20.0
1966	60	295	20.3
1967	63	284	22.1
1968	48	274	17.5

British Feature Films Imported by the United States, 1927–1967: Film Daily Year Book Listings[1]

British Imports: Title and Distributor (where available)

1927

The Cabaret Kid (Artlee)
Epic of Mount Everest
Flight across Africa
Living Buddah
Lost Tribe
Madame Pompadour (Paramount)
Tip Toes (Paramount)
Triumph of the Rat (Artlee)

1928

Battle of Coronel and Falkland Islands (Artlee)
Bolibar
The Bondsman (World Wide)
Case of Jonathan Drew (Artlee)
Confetti (First National)
Constant Nymph
Dawn (Columbia)
Downhill (World Wide)
Easy Virtue (World Wide)
Forbidden Love (Pathe)
Golden Dawn (Conquest)
Guns at Loos (New Era)
Honeymoon Abroad (World Wide)
Huntingtower (Paramount)

Looping the Loop (Br., Gm., Paramount)
Mlle. from Armentieres (MGM)
Moulin Rouge (World Wide),
Pawns of Passion (World Wide),
Q Ships (New Era),
Queen Was in the Parlour (Pathe),
The Rat (Aywon),
Robinson Crusoe (FBO),
Roses of Picardy (Excellent),
Shadow of Tragedy (5th Avenue Playhouse Group),
Shooting Stars (AmerAnglo),
Skirts (MGM),
The Somme (New Era),
South Sea Bubble (World Wide),
Tommy Atkins (World Wide),
The Vortex (AmerAnglo),
The Ware Case (First National),
When Fleet Meets Fleet (Hi-Mark),
Woman in the Night (World Wide),
Woman in White (World Wide),
Woman Tempted (Aywon),

1929

Battle of Mons (New Era)
The Betrayal (AmerAnglo)
Black Waters (Sono Art-World Wide)
Blackmail (Sono Art-World Wide)
The Bondman (Sono Art-World Wide)

Constant Nymph (Big Three Prod.)
Fanny Hawthorne (Excellent Pictures)
Filming of Golden Eagle (Capt,
C.W.R. Knight)
Honeymoon Abroad (Sono Art-
World Wide)
Kitty (Sono Art-World Wide)
Lady of the Lake (James Fitzpatrick)
Livingstone in Africa
Lost Tribe (Br/South Africa)
Moulin Rouge (Br/Fr., Sono Art-
World Wide)
Paradise (Ufa)
The Physician (Tiffany)
Piccadilly (Sono Art World-Wide)
Scarlet Daredevil (Br/Fr., Sono Art-
World Wide)
Shiraz (AmerAnglo)
Silver King (AmerAnglo)
Three Passions (United Artists)
Tommy Atkins (Sono Art World-
Wide)
Week End Wives (Sono Art-World
Wide)
Widecombe Fair (Sono Art-World
Wide)
Woman in the Night (Sono Art-
World Wide)
Woman in White (Sono Art-World
Wide),
Woman to Woman (Tiffany)
The Wrecker (Tiffany)

1930

After the Verdict (British New Era)
Atlantic (British International)
Bright Eyes (British International)
The Co-Optimists (New Era)
Crimson Circle (New Era)
Dark Red Roses (International Photo-
plays)
Drifters (Harold Auten)
Escape (RKO)

Escaped from Dartmoor (Harold Au-
ten)
Farmer's Wife (Ufa Eastern Division)
Flame of Love (British International)
Hate Ship (British International)
High Treason (Tiffany)
Juno and the Paycock (Harold Auten)
Loose Ends (British International)
Middle Watch (British International)
Murder (British International)
Mystery at the Villa (Harold Auten)
One Embarrassing Night (MGM)
Roses of Picardy (Excellent Pictures)
Sleeping Partners (British Interna-
tional)
Stampede (Pro Patria)
Suspense (British International)
Throw of the Dice (Hollywood Pic-
tures)
Two Worlds (British International)
Under the Greenwood Tree (British
International)
White Cargo (Harold Auten)
Would You Believe It? (Big Four)
Yellow Mask (British International)
Young Woodley (British International)

1931

Almost a Honeymoon (British Inter-
national)
Battle of Gallipoli (British Interna-
tional)
Children of Chance (British Interna-
tional)
Compromised (British International)
Dreyfus Case (Columbia)
Flying Fool (British International)
French Leave (Talking Picture Epics)
How He Lied to Her Husband (Brit-
ish International)
Jaws of Hell (Sono Art-World Wide)
Just for a Song (Sono Art-World
Wide)

Love Habit (British International)
Man from Chicago (Columbia)
Night Birds (British International)
Outsider (MGM)
Perfect Alibi (RKO)
Sherlock Holmes' Fatal Hour (First Division)
Should a Doctor Tell? (Regal)
Skin Game (British International)
The Speckled Band (First Division)
'W' Plan (RKO)

1932

Aren't We All (Paramount)
Avalanche (First Division)
Bachelor's Folly (World Wide)
Blame the Woman (Principal)
Boat from Shanghai (First Anglo)
Bridegroom for Two (Powers Pictures)
Condemned to Death (First Division)
Congress Dances (United Artists)
East of Shanghai (Powers)
Fascination (Powers)
Footsteps in the Night (Harold Auten)
Gable Mystery (Powers)
Her Strange Desire (Powers)
Hound of the Baskervilles (First Division)
Illegal (Warner Bros)
Keepers of Youth (Powers)
Limping Man (Powers)
Magic Night (United Artists)
Men Like These (Powers)
Michael and Mary (Universal)
Missing Rembrandt (First Division)
My Wife's Family (Powers)
Office Girl (RKO)
Reserved for Ladies (Paramount)
The Ringer (First Division)
Shadow Between (Powers)
Sign of the Four (World Wide)
Strictly Business (Powers)

Water Gypsies (Stanley Dist. Corp)
Why Saps Leave Home (Powers)
Woman in Bondage (Harold Auten)

1933

After the Ball (Fox)
Bitter Sweet (United Artists)
Blarney Kiss (Principal)
Charming Deceiver (Majestic)
City of Song (World Trade Exchange)
Criminal at Large (Helber)
F.P.1 (Fox)
Faithful Heart (Helber)
Fires of Fate (Powers)
Footsteps in the Night (Invincible)
Ghost Train (Gaumont-British – GB)
Good Companions (Fox)
The Ghoul (GB)
I Was a Spy (Fox)
Love in Morocco (GB)
Man They Couldn't Arrest (GB)
Man Who Won (Powers)
Night and Day (GB)
Outsider (MGM)
Perfect Understanding (United Artists)
Private Life of Henry VIII (United Artists)
Rome Express (Universal)
Sleepless Nights (Remington)
There Goes the Bride (GB)
Waltz Time (GB)
Wives Beware (Regent)
Yes Mr Brown (United Artists)

1934

Along Came Sally (GB)
Are You a Mason? (M.J. Kandel)
Ariane (Blue Ribbon)
Autumn Crocus (Harold Auten)
Blossom Time (B.I.P.)
Blue Danube (Mundus)

Broken Melody (Olympic Pictures)
Catherine the Great (United Artists)
Channel Crossing (GB)
Chu Chin Chow (GB)
The Church Mouse (Warner Bros)
Constant Nymph (Fox)
Crime of the Hill (B.I.P.)
Evensong (GB)
Evergreen (GB)
For Love or Money (British & Dominions)
Freedom of the Seas (B.I.P.)
Friday the 13th (GB)
The Great Defender (BIP)
Heart Song (Fox)
I Was a Spy (Fox)
It's a Boy (GB)
Jack Ahoy (GB)
Just Smith (GB)
Little Friend (GB)
Loyalties (Harold Auten)
Man of Aran (GB)
Man Who Changes His Name (DuWorld)
Nell Gwyn (United Artists)
No Funny Business (Principal)
On Secret Service (B.I.P.)
Orders Is Orders (GB)
Over Night (Mundus)
Power (GB)
Prince of Wales (GB)
Private Life of Don Juan (United Artists)
Runaway Queen (United Artists)
Scotland Yard Mystery (B.I.P.)
Sorrell and Son (United Artists)
Tell-Tale Heart (DuWorld)
The Wandering Jew (MGM)
Woman in Command (GB)
You Made Me Love You (Majestic)

1935

Abdul the Damned (Alliance)
Alias Bulldog Drummond (GB)
Bella Donna (Olympic Pictures)
Born for Glory (GB)
The Clairvoyant (GB)
Dance Band (Alliance)
The Dictator (GB)
Escape Me Never (United Artists)
Evergreen (GB)
First a Girl (GB)
Give Her a Ring (Alliance)
The Iron Duke (GB)
Jack Ahoy! (GB)
Java Head (First Division)
Lover Divine (GB)
Loves of a Dictator (GB)
The Man Who Knew Too Much (GB)
The Merry Monarch (Syndicate Exchange)
Mimi (First Division)
Mister Hobo (GB)
The Morals of Marcus (GB)
My Heart Is Calling (GB)
My Song for You (GB)
Old Curiosity Shop (Alliance)
The Passing of the Third Floor Back (GB)
Princess Charming (GB)
Red Wagon (Alliance)
Regal Cavalcade (Alliance)
Sanders of the River (United Artists)
Scandals of Paris (Regal)
Scarlet Pimpernel (United Artists)
Scotland Yard Mystery (Regal)
Scrooge (Paramount)
Secret Agent (Alliance)
Strauss' Great Waltz (Tom Arnold)
The 39 Steps (GB)
Transatlantic Tunnel (GB)

Unfinished Symphony (GB)
The Wandering Jew (Olympic)
Wolves of the Underworld (Regal)

1936

Accused (United Artists)
The Amateur Gentleman (United Artists)
An Old Spanish Custom (J. H. Hoffberg)
April Romance (MGM)
As You Like It (20th Century-Fox)
The Crimson Circle (DuWorld)
The Crouching Beast (Olympic)
East Meets West (GB)
Everything Is Thunder (GB)
Falling in Love (Times Pictures)
Gay Love (Marcy Exchange)
The Ghost Goes West (United Artists)
Girl from Maxims (J. H. Hoffberg)
I Stand Condemned (United Artists)
It's Love Again (GB)
King of the Damned (GB)
The Last Journey (Atlantic)
Life of Edward VII (GB)
Living Dangerously (GB)
The Man Who Lived Again (GB)
Mr Cohen Takes a Walk (Warners)
Mister Hobo (GB)
The Morals of Marcus (GB)
Murder in the Red Barn (Olympic)
Murder on the Setz (Globe Film Exchange)
Nine Days a Queen (GB)
Passing of the Third Floor Back (GB)
Peg of Old Drury (Paramount)
Rembrandt (United Artists)
Rhodes (GB)
Secret Agent (GB)
Seven Sinners (GB)
The Shadow (Globe)
Southern Maid (Alliance)

The Students' Romance (Alliance)
Things to Come (United Artists)
Trouble Ahead (Times Pictures)
Wanted Men (J.H. Hoffberg)
While London Sleeps (Ideal)

1937

April Romance (MGM)
Back Stage (GB)
The Beloved Vagabond (Columbia)
Broken Blossoms (Imperial)
Bulldog Drummond at Bay (Republic)
Dark Journey (United Artists)
Dinner at the Ritz (20th Century-Fox)
Doctor Syn (GB)
Dreaking Lips (United Artists)
Elephant Boy (United Artists)
Everybody Dance (GB)
Farewell Again (United Artists)
Fire over England (United Artists)
Forever Yours (Grand National)
Gangway (GB)
Glamorous Night (Republic)
Head over Heels in Love (GB)
Heart's Desire (GB)
Hideout in the Alps (Grand National)
High Treason (Olympic)
Juggernaut (Grand National)
King Solomon's Mines (GB)
The King's People (E.R. Conne)
Knight without Armour (United Artists),
Look Out for Love (GB)
Love from a Stranger (United Artists)
Man in the Mirror (Grand National)
Man of Affairs (GB)
Man Who Could Work Miracles (United Artists)
Men are Not Gods (United Artists)
Murder on Diamond Row (United Artists)

Non-Stop New York (GB)
Phantom Ship (Guaranteed Pictures)
River of Unrest (GB)
The Robber Symphony (Fortune)
Romance and Riches (Grand National)
Said O'Reilly to MacNab (GB)
Scotland Yard Commands (Grand National)
She Shall Have Music (Imperial)
Storm in a Teacup (United Artists)
Strangers on a Honeymoon (GB)
Talk of the Devil (GB)
The Tenth Man (GB)
Thunder in the City (Columbia)
The Two of Us (GB)
Two Who Dared (Grand National)
Victoria the Great (RKO Radio)
Week-End Millionaire (GB)
When Thief Meets Thief (United Artists)
Where There's a Will (GB)
Wings of the Morning (20th Century-Fox)
The Woman Alone (GB)
You're in the Army Now (GB)

1938

Action for Slander (United Artists)
The Beachcomber (Paramount)
The Citadel (Loew's)
A Clown Must Laugh (GB)
Crime Over London (GB)
Dangerous Secrets (Grand National)
Dark Sands (Record Pictures)
Divorce of Lady X (United Artists)
Drums (United Artists)
Edge of the World (Pax Films)
Emil (Olympic Pictures)
Forbidden Music (World)
Forbidden Territory (Hoffberg)
The Gaiety Girls (United Artists)

Girl in the Street (GB)
The Girl Thief (GB)
The Girl Was Young (GB)
He Loved an Actress (Grand National)
Hideout in the Alps (Grand National)
High Command (Grand National)
Invitation to the Waltz (Hoffberg)
The Lady Vanishes (GB)
Let's Make a Night of It (Universal)
Look Out for Love (GB)
Man With 100 Faces (GB)
Men of Ireland (Hoffberg)
Moonlight Sonata (Malmar)
Pygmalion (Loew's)
The Rat (RKO Radio)
Return of the Scarlet Pimpernel (United Artists)
Sailing Along (GB)
Sez O'Reilly to MacNab (GB)
The Show Goes On (GB)
Sixty Glorious Years (RKO Radio)
Song of Freedom (Treo Exchange)
South Riding (United Artists)
Strange Boarders (GB)
This'll Make You Whistle (C. & M. Pictures)
Three on a Week-End (GB)
To the Victor (GB)
Troopship (United Artists)
We're Going to Be Rich (20th Century-Fox)
Wife of General Ling (GB)
Yank at Oxford (Loew's)

1939

Black Limelight (Alliance)
Bombs over London (Film Alliance of the U.S.)
The Challenge (Film Alliance)
Climbing High (20th Century-Fox)
Clouds over Europe (Columbia)

Dead Men Tell No Tales (Alliance)
The Demon Barber of Fleet Street (Select)
Forbidden Territory (Hoffberg)
Four Feathers (United Artists)
The Frog (20th Century-Fox)
Goodbye, Mr Chips (MGM)
Housemaster (Alliance)
Inspector Hornleigh (20th Century-Fox)
Inspector Hornleigh on Holiday (20th Century-Fox)
Jamaica Inn (Paramount)
Just Like a Woman (Alliance)
The Mikado (Universal)
Mill on the Floss (Standard)
The Mutiny of the Elsinore (Regal)
North Sea Patrol (Alliance)
The Phantom Strikes (Monogram)
Prisoner of Corbal (Unity)
Prison without Bars (United Artists)
The Return of the Frog (Select)
Royal Divorce (Select)
School for Husbands (Hoffberg)
Second Bureau (Film Alliance)
Secret of Stamboul (Hoffberg)
Smiling Along (20th Century-Fox)
Stolen Life (Paramount)
This Man Is News (Paramount)
Torpedoed (Film Alliance)
Treachery on the High Seas (Film Alliance)
Two's Company (Times)
U-Boat 29 (Columbia)
The Ware Case (20th Century-Fox)
Wings over Africa (Merit)

1940

After Mein Kampf - ? (Crystal Pictures)
Among Human Wolves (Film Alliance)
Blackout (United Artists)
Blitzkrieg in the West France
Captain Moonlight (Atlas Film Exchange)
Chamber of Horrors (Monogram)
Design for Murder (World Pictures)
The Face at the Window (Arthur Ziehm)
The Face behind the Scar (Film Alliance)
False Rapture (Film Alliance)
French without Tears (Paramount)
The Fugitive (Universal)
Half a Sinner (Universal)
Haunted Honeymoon (Loew's)
Hell's Cargo (Film Alliance)
The Hidden Menace (Alliance)
The Human Monster (Monogram)
Inspector Hornleigh on Holiday (20th Century-Fox)
It's in the Air (B.S.B. Corp)
The Lambeth Walk (Loew's)
Larceny Street
Let George Do It (Film Alliance)
Lights out in Europe (Mayer & Burstyn)
The Lilac Domino (Select Attractions)
The Lion Has Wings (United Artists)
Lost on the Western Front (Standard Pictures)
Macushla (Transatlantic Films)
Mad Men of Europe (Columbia)
Mayerling to Sarajevo (Leo Films)
Missing People (Monogram)
Monkey into Man (World Pictures)
Mozart (Mozart Film)
Murder in the Night (Film Alliance)
The Mysterious Mr Reeder (Monogram)
Night Train (20th Century-Fox)
North Sea Patrol (Alliance)
One Night in Paris (Alliance)
The Outsider (Alliance)

Over the Moon (United Artists)
Pastor Hall (United Artists)
The Phantom Strikes (Monogram)
Secret Four (Monogram)
Sensation (Film Alliance)
Sidewalks of London (Paramount)
So This Is London (20th Century-Fox)
Song of the Road (Select)
Spies in the Air (Film Alliance)
Suicide Legion (Film Alliance)
They Came by Night (20th Century-Fox)
Torpedo Raider (Monogram)
Torso Murder Mystery (Arthur Ziehm)
21 Days Together (Columbia)
Who Is Guilty? (Monogram)

1941

Break the News (Monogram)
Chinese Den (Film Alliance)
Convoy (RKO Radio)
Dead Man's Shoes (Monogram)
Death at a Broadcast (Film Alliance)
Frightened Lady (Hoffberg)
The Girl in the News (20th Century-Fox)
A Girl Must Live (Universal)
House of Mystery (Monogram)
It Happened to One Man (RKO Radio)
Laburnum Grove (Anglo Films)
Mail Train (20th Century-Fox)
Major Barbara (United Artists)
Missing Ten Days (Columbia)
Murder at the Baskervilles (Astor)
Mystery of Room 13 (Alliance)
Pirate of the Seven Seas (Film Alliance)
Poison Pen (Republic)
The Prime Minister (Warners)

Proud Valley (Supreme Productions)
Queen of Crime (Film Alliance)
Quiet Wedding (Universal)
The Saint's Vacation (RKO)
Sons of the Sea (Warners)
The Stars Look Down (Loew's)
Target for Tonight (Warners)
The Terror (Alliance Films)
This England (World)
Three Cockeyed Sailors (United Artists)
The Voice in the Night (Columbia)

1942

The Avengers (Paramount)
Confessions of a Cheat (Gallic Films)
Continental Express (Monogram)
Death Cell (Monogram)
Flying Fortress (Warners)
In Which We Serve (United Artists)
The Invaders (Columbia)
Lady in Distress (Times Pictures)
Maxwell Archer, Detective (Monogram)
Mister V (United Artists)
One of Our Aircraft is Missing (United Artists)
The Playboy (Jewel)
The Remarkable Mr Kipps (20th Century-Fox)
Shadows of the Underworld (Monogram)
Ships with Wings (United Artists)
Sons of the Sea (Warners)
Suicide Squadron (Republic)
This Was Paris (Warners)
Tower of Terror (Monogram)
When Knights Were Bold (Fine Arts)
Wings and the Woman (RKO Radio)
The Young Mr Pitt (20th Century Fox)

1943

Adventure in Blackmail (English Films)
Alibi (Republic)
At Dawn We Die (Republic)
The Avengers (Paramount)
Coastal Command (RKO)
Desert Victory (20th Century-Fox)
The Great Mr Handel (Midfilm)
Jeannie (English Films)
Next of Kin (Universal)
The Saint Meets the Tiger (Republic)
The Shrine of Victory (20th Century-Fox)
Somewhere in France (United Artists)
Spitfire (RKO)
Squadron Leader X (RKO)
Suspected Person (PRC)
Tartu (MGM)
Terror House (PRC)

1944

The Amazing Mr Forrest (PRC)
Candlelight in Algeria (20th Century-Fox)
Castle of Crimes (PRC)
Champagne Charlie (AFE Corp)
Courageous Mr Penn (Hoffberg)
Dreaming (AFE Corp)
Escape to Danger (RKO)
Forty Eight Hours (AFE Corp)
Ghostly Inn (AFE Corp)
Men of the Sea (PRC)
Nine Men (AFE)
Return of the Vikings (AFE Corp)
Return to Yesterday (AFE Corp)
Room for Two (AFE Corp)
Saloon Bar (AFE Corp)
Secret Mission (English Films)
Shrine of Victory (20th Century-Fox)
They Came to a City (AFE Corp)

Thunder Rock (English Films)
Uncensored (20th Century-Fox)
Underground Guerillas (Columbia)
The Yellow Canary (RKO)

1945

Battle for Music (Four Continents)
Blithe Spirit (United Artists)
Burma Victory (Warner Bros)
Castle of Crimes (PRC)
Colonel Blimp (United Artists)
Dear Octopus (English Films)
Halfway House (A.F.E.)
Johnny in the Clouds (United Artists)
Love on the Dole (Four Continents)
The Man in Grey (Universal)
Mr Emmanuel (United Artists)
On Approval (English Films)
Painted Boats (A.F.E.)
The Randolph Family (English Films)
The Silver Fleet (PRC)
The Spell of Amy Nugent (PRC)
They Met in the Dark (English Films)
The True Glory (Columbia)
Vacation from Marriage (MGM)
The Way Ahead (20th Century-Fox)
You Can't Do Without Love (Columbia)

1946

Brief Encounter (Universal)
Caesar and Cleopatra (United Artists)
Dead of Night (Universal)
Frenzy (Four Continents)
The Gay Intruders (Four Continents)
Great Day (RKO)
Henry V (United Artists)
Hotel Reserve (RKO)
Johnny Frenchman (Universal)
Johnny in the Clouds (United Artists)
Journey Together (English Films)

Madonna of the Seven Moons (Universal)
The Man from Morocco (English Films)
The Man in Grey (Universal)
Murder in Reverse (Four Continents)
Notorious Gentleman (Universal)
The Raider (English Films)
The Seventh Veil (Universal)
Stairway to Heaven (Universal)
They Were Sisters (Universal)
Wanted for Murder (20th Century-Fox)
While Nero Fiddled (20th Century-Fox)
The Wicked Lady (Universal)
A Yank in London (20th Century-Fox)

1947

The Adventuress (Eagle Lion)
Bedelia (Eagle Lion)
Beware of Pity (Two Cities)
Black Narcissus (Universal)
Captain Boycott (Universal)
The Captive Heart (Universal)
Caravan (Eagle Lion)
Children on Trial (English Films)
Frieda (Universal)
The Girl on the Canal (Bell Pictures)
Great Expectations (Universal)
The Green Cockatoo (Devonshire)
Green for Danger (Eagle Lion)
Hungary Hill (Universal)
I Know Where I'm Going (Universal)
A Lady Surrenders (Universal)
The Magic Bow (Universal)
Meet Me at Dawn (20th Century-Fox)
Nicholas Nickleby (Universal)
Odd Man Out (Universal)
The Patient Vanishes (Film Classics)

San Demetrio, London (20th Century-Fox)
School for Danger (English Films)
So Well Remembered (RKO Radio)
The Tawny Pipit (Universal)
This Happy Breed (Universal)
The Upturned Glass (Universal)
The Years Between (Universal)

1948

An Ideal Husband (20th Century-Fox)
Anna Karenina (20th Century-Fox)
Bad Sister (Universal)
Blanche Fury (Eagle Lion)
The Brothers (Universal)
Champagne Charlie (Bell Pictures)
Code of Scotland Yard (Republic)
Corridor of Mirrors (Universal)
Dear Murderer (Universal)
Dulcimer Street (Universal)
The End of the River (Universal)
Escape (20th Century-Fox)
Hamlet (Universal)
Hatter's Castle (Paramount)
Her Man Gibney (Universal)
Holiday Camp (Universal)
I Became a Criminal (Warners)
Jassy (Universal)
Just William's Luck (United Artists)
Man of Evil (United Artists)
Meet Me at Dawn (20th Century-Fox)
Mine Own Executioner (20th Century-Fox)
Mr Perrin and Mr Traill (Eagle Lion)
The October Man (Eagle Lion)
One Night with You (Universal)
Piccadilly Incident (MGM)
The Plot to Kill Roosevelt (United Artists)
Quiet Week End (Distinguished)
Showtime (English Films)

The Smugglers (Eagle Lion)
So Evil My Love (Paramount)
Springtime (Four Continents)
Take My Life (Eagle Lion)

1949

Adam and Evelyn (U-I)
The Affairs of a Rogue (Columbia)
Against the Wind (Eagle Lion)
All over the Town (U-I)
The Amazing Mr Beecham (Eagle Lion)
The Blind Goddness (Rank)
The Blue Lagoon (U-I)
Broken Journey (Eagle Lion)
A Canterbury Tale (Eagle Lion)
Christopher Columbus (U-I)
Corridor of Mirrors (U-I)
Daybreak (U-I)
Dolwyn (London Films)
Easy Money (Eagle Lion)
Edward My Son (MGM)
The Facts of Love (Oxford Films)
The Fallen Idol (SRO)
Fame is the Spur (Oxford Films)
The Forbidden Secret (20th Century-Fox)
The Girl in the Painting (U-I)
Give Us This Day (Eagle Lion)
The Guinea Pig (Variety Film)
The Hasty Heart (Warners)
Her Man Gilbey (U-I)
It Always Rains on Sundays (Eagle Lion)
Magic Voice (Leo Cohen)
A Man about the House (20th Century-Fox)
Miranda (Eagle Lion)
My Brother Jonathan (Allied Artists)
My Brother's Keeper (Eagle Lion)
Once upon a Dream (Eagle Lion)
One Woman's Story (U-I)

Passport to Pimlico (Eagle Lion)
A Place of One's Own (Eagle Lion)
Quartet (Eagle Lion)
Saints and Sinners (Lopert)
Saraband (Eagle Lion)
Scott of the Antarctic (Eagle Lion)
Silent Dust (Monogram)
Sleeping Car to Trieste (Eagle Lion)
Snowbound (U-I)
Spring in Park Lane (Eagle Lion)
Temptation Harbor (Eagle Lion)
There Is No Escape (Screen Guild)
This Was a Woman (20th Century-Fox)
Tight Little Island (U-I)
Under Capricorn (Warners)
Waterloo Road (Eagle Lion)
The Weaker Sex (Eagle Lion)
Woman Hater (U-I)
The Woman in the Hall (Eagle Lion)

1950

The Astonished Heart (U-I)
The Black Rose (20th Century-Fox)
The Blue Lamp (Eagle Lion)
Bond Street (Stratford Pictures)
Conspirator (MGM)
The Dancing Years (Allied Artists)
Dear Mr Prohack (Pentagon Pictures)
Death in the Hand (Hoffberg)
For Them That Trespass (Monogram)
The Gay Lady (Eagle Lion)
Girl in a Million (Distinguished Films)
The Glass Mountain (Eagle Lion)
Good Time Girl (Film Classics)
The Great Manhunt (Columbia)
The Happiest Days of Your Life (London Films)
The Hidden Room (Eagle Lion)
Hue and Cry (Fine Arts Films)
If This Be Sin (United Artists)

Kind Hearts and Coronets (Eagle Lion)
Last Holiday (Stratford Pictures)
The Laughing Lady (Four Continents)
Madeleine (U-I)
Madness of the Heart (U-I)
Matter of Murder (Hoffberg)
The Miniver Story (MGM)
Mrs Fitzherbert (Stratford Pictures)
The Mudlark (20th Century-Fox)
Mystery at the Burlesque (Monogram)
Night and the City (20th Century-Fox)
No Room at the Inn (Stratford)
Paper Gallows (Eagle Lion Classics)
The Perfect Woman (Eagle Lion)
Pink String and Sealing Wax (Pentagon Pictures)
Prelude to Fame (U-I)
The Queen of Spades (Stratford)
The Rocking Horse Winner (U-I)
A Run for Your Money (U-I)
Seven Days to Noon (Mayer-Kingsley)
Silent Dust (Stratford)
The Silk Noose (Monogram)
Stage Fright (Warners)
The Third Man (Selznick Releasing Organization)
Third Time Lucky (Pentagon)
Treasure Island (RKO-Radio)
Trio (Paramount)
While the Sun Shines (Stratford)
The Winslow Boy (Eagle Lion)

1951

Another Shore (International Releasing)
Bad Lord Byron (International Releasing)
Beware of Pity (International Releasing)
Blackmailed (Bell Pictures)

Bless Them All (Gordon Films)
The Browning Version (U-I)
Cage of Gold (Ellis Films)
Canteen Follies (Arthur Davis Associates)
Captain Horatio Hornblower (Warners)
Chance of a Lifetime (Ballantine Pictures)
A Christmas Carol (United Artists)
Circle of Danger (Eagle Lion Classics)
The Clouded Yellow (Columbia)
Coming thru the Rye (Gordon Films)
Double Confession (Stratford Films)
Echo of Applause (Gordon Films)
The Galloping Major (Souvaine Selective)
The Golden Salamander (Eagle Lion)
Guilt Is my Shadow (Stratford)
Hangman's Holiday (International Releasing)
Happy Go Lovely (RKO-Radio)
Her Panelled Door (Souvaine Selective)
High Jinks in Society (Gordon Films)
Highly Dangerous (Lippert)
The History of Mr Polly (International Releasing)
Hotel Sahara (United Artists)
I Was a Dancer (Gordon Films)
I'll Never Forget You (20th Century-Fox)
The Inheritance (Fine Arts Films)
It Started at Midnight (Gordon Films)
Laughter in Paradise (Stratford)
The Lavender Hill Mob (U-I)
Lilli Marlene (RKO-Radio)
The Long Dark Hall (Eagle Lion)
The Magnet (U-I)
Man in the Dinghy (Snader Productions)
Man on the Run (Stratford)

Maniacs on Wheels (International Releasing)
Marry Me (Ellis Films)
Melody in the Sky (Gordon Films)
Men of the Sea (Astor)
Midnight Blonde (Arthur David)
Mister Drake's Duck (United Artists)
Murder without Crime (Stratford)
Naughty Arlette (United Artists)
No Highway in the Sky (20th Century-Fox)
No Orchids for Miss Blandish (Renown)
No Place for Jennifer (Stratford)
The Obsessed (United Artists)
Odette (Lopert)
Old Mother Riley, Headmistress (Gordon Films)
Old Mother Riley's Jungle Treasure (Gordon Films)
Oliver Twist (United Artists)
Operation Disaster (U-I)
Operation X (Columbia)
Pandora and the Flying Dutchman (MGM)
Penny Points to Paradise (Gordon Films)
Pool of London (U-I)
Portrait of Clare (Stratford)
Ray of Sunshine (Gordon Films)
The Reluctant Widow (Fine Arts Films)
Robinson-Turpin Flight (Republic)
Seven Days to Noon (Mayer-Kingsley)
Sin of Esther Waters (International Releasing)
Skimpy in the Navy (Gordon Films)
So Long at the Fair (Eagle Lion)
Tales of Hoffman (Lopert)
They Were Not Divided (United Artists)
Things Happen at Night (Gordon Films)

Third Time Lucky (International Releasing)
Tom Brown's Schooldays (United Artists)
Tony Draws a Horse (Fine Arts Films)
Young Scarface (Mayer-Kingsley)

1952

Another Man's Poison (United Artists)
Bad Lord Byron (Rank)
Bitter Springs (Rank)
Brady for the Parson (Mayer-Kingsley)
The Brave Don't Cry (Mayer-Kingsley)
Breaking the Sound Barrier (United Artists)
Cage of Gold (Rank)
Cloudburst (United Artists)
The Clouded Yellow (Columbia)
Encore (Paramount)
Gambler and the Lady (Lippert)
Hans Christian Andersen (Hoffberg)
High Treason (Rank)
The Hour of the 13 (MGM)
The Importance of Being Earnest (U-I)
Island Rescue (U-I)
Ivanhoe (MGM)
Lady Possessed (Republic)
The Magic Box (Rank)
Ma Bait (Lippert)
The Man in the White Suit (U-I)
Marry Me! (Rank)
Maytime in Mayfair (Realart)
Once a Sinner (Hoffberg)
Outpost in Malaya (United Artists)
Overnight Girl (Hoffberg)
The Promoter (U-I)
Scotland Yard Inspector (Lippert)
Secret Fright (Rank)
Secret People (Lippert)

The Small Black Room (Snader Productions)

The Spider and the Fly (Rank)

Stolen Face (Lippert)

The Story of Robin Hood (RKO-Radio)

The Stranger in England (U-I)

A Tale of Five Women (United Artists)

Train of Events (Rank)

Under the Red Sea (RKO-Radio)

Waterfront Women (Rank)

Where's Charley (Warners)

Whispering Smith vs. Scotland Yard (RKO-Radio)

White Corridors (Rank)

The Wild Heart (RKO-Radio)

Wings of Danger (Lippert)

The Woman in Question (Rank)

1953

The Assassin (United Artists)

Beggar's Opera (Warner Bros)

The Caretaker's Daughter (Beverly)

Crash of Silence (U-I)

The Cruel Sea (U-I)

Curtain Up (Fine Arts Films)

Desperate Moment (U-I)

Edge of Divorce (Meyer-Kingsley)

Five Angles on Murder (Columbia)

The Frightened Bride (Beverly)

The Gentle Gunman (U-I)

Ghost Ship (Lippert)

Gilbert and Sullivan (United Artists)

The Holly and the Ivy (Pacemaker)

Horror Maniacs (Hoffberg)

Horse's Mouth (Meyer-Kingsley)

Hundred Hour Hunt (Abner J. Greshler)

I Sing for You Alone (Hoffberg)

The Limping Man (Lippert)

Man in Hiding (United Artists)

Mr Denning Drives North (Carroll)

Murder on Monday (Mayer-Kingsley)

Murder Will Out (Kramer-Hyams)

My Heart Goes Crazy (United Artists)

Night without Stars (RKO)

Nothing to Lose (Mayer-Kingsley)

Passionate Sentry (Fine Arts Films)

Pickwick Papers (Mayer-Kingsley)

Project M. 7 (U-I)

A Queen Is Crowned (Mayer-Kingsley)

Scotch on the Rocks (Mayer-Kingsley)

The Slasher (Lippert)

So Little Time (MacDonald)

Something Money Can't Buy (U-I)

Strangler's Morgue (Hoffberg)

The Titfield Thunderbolt (U-I)

Trent's Last Case (Republic)

Twilight Women (Lippert)

Yellow Balloon (Allied Artists)

1954

Always a Bride (Universal)

An Inspector Calls (Associated Artists)

Angels One Five (Stratford)

Black Glove (Lippert)

The Black Pirates (Lippert)

Black 13 (20th Century-Fox)

Blackout (Lippert)

Both Sides of the Law (Universal)

Calling Scotland Yard (Paramount)

Crest of a Wave (MGM)

Deadly Game (Lippert)

The Detective (Columbia)

Devil's Harbor (20th Century-Fox)

The Diamond Wizard (United Artists)

The Fighting Pimpernel (Carroll)

The Final Test (Rank)

Genevieve (Universal)

The Golden Mask (United Artists)

The Heart of the Matter (Associated Artists)

Heat Wave (Lippert)
High and Dry (Universal)
Hobson's Choice (United Artists)
Intimate Relations (Carroll)
Lady Godiva Rides Again (Carroll)
The Kidnappers (United Artists)
Lovers, Happy Lovers! (A.F.E.)
Malta Story (United Artists)
Man with a Million (United Artists)
The Master Plan (Astor)
Mr Potts Goes to Moscow (Allied
  Artists)
Operation Manhunt (United Artists)
Paid to Kill (Lippert)
Personal Affair (United Artists)
Pickwick Papers (Meyer-Kingsley)
A Queen's Royal Tour (United Artists)
A Race for Life (Lippert)
River Beat (Lippert)
Romeo and Juliet (United Artists)
The Saint's Girl Friday (RKO Radio)
Scotch on the Rocks (Kingsley)
The Sleeping Tiger (Astor)
Terror Ship (Lippert)
Tonight's the Night (Allied Artists)
Trouble in the Glen (Republic)
Turn the Key Softly (Rank)
Twist of Fate (United Artists)
The Unholy Four (Lippert)
The Weak and the Wicked (Allied
  Artists)
West of Zanzibar (Universal)
White Fire (Lippert)
You Know What Sailors Are (United
  Artists)
Young Wives Tale (Allied Artists)

1955

The Adventures of Sadie (20th
  Century-Fox)
Alias John Preston (Associated Art-
  ists)

Animal Farm (Louis De Rochmont)
Appointment in London (Associated
  Artists)
The Beachcomber (United Artists)
The Belles of St. Trinian's (Associated
  Artists)
Break to Freedom (UA)
Case of the Red Monkey (Allied Art-
  ists)
Chance Meeting (Pacemaker Pictures)
The Colditz Story (Atlantic)
Court Martial (Kingsley International)
Cross Channel (Republic)
Cure for Love (Associated Artists)
The Dam Busters (Warners)
Dance, Little Lady (Trans-Lux)
A Day to Remember (Republic)
The Deep Blue Sea (20th Century-
  Fox)
The Divided Heart (Republic)
Doctor in the House (Republic)
Eight O'Clock Walk (Associated Art-
  ists)
The End of the Affair (Columbia)
Footsteps in the Fog (Columbia)
Four against Fate (Associated Artists)
Front Page Story (Associated Artists)
Fuss over Feathers (Associated Artists)
Game of Danger (Associated Artists)
The Good Die Young (United Artists)
The Green Buddha (Republic)
The Green Scarf (Associated Artists)
I Am a Camera (DCA)
Innocents in Paris (Tudor Pictures)
The Intruder (Associated Artists)
Lease of Life (IFE)
Let's Make Up (United Artists)
The Man Who Loved Redheads
  (United Artists)
The Master Plan (Astor)
Midnight Episode (Fine Arts)
The Night My Number Came Up
  (Continental)

Outlaw Safari (Majestic)
The Prisoner (Columbia)
The Purple Plain (United Artists)
Quentin Durward (MGM)
Roadhouse Girl (Astor)
The Sea Shall Not Have Them
(United Artists)
Shadow of the Eagle (United Artists)
Simba (Lippert)
The Square Ring (Republic)
The Teckman Mystery (Associated
Artists)
Three Cases of Murder (Associated
Artists)
To Paris with Love (Continental)
Trouble in Store (Republic)
Wicked Wife (Allied Artists)

1956

Above Us the Waves (Republic)
Anastasia (20th Century-Fox)
The Atomic Man (Allied Artists)
Blonde Sinner (Allied Artists)
The Brain Machine (RKO Radio)
Cash on Delivery (RKO Radio)
The Cockleshell Heroes (Columbia)
The Creeping Unknown (United Artists)
The Deadliest Sin (Allied Artists)
Doctor at Sea (Republic)
Dynamiters (Astor)
Finger of Guilt (RKO Radio)
Fire Maidens of Outer Space (Topaz)
Forbidden Cargo (Fine Arts)
The Gamma People (Columbia)
His Excellency (Joesph Brenner Associstes)
Invitation to the Dance (Loew's)
The Iron Petticoat (Loew's)
Joe MacBeth (Columbia)
A Kid for Two Farthings (Lopert)
The Ladykillers (Continental)

The Last Man to Hang (Columbia)
Let's Make Up (United Artists)
The Light Touch (Universal)
Lust for Life (Loew's)
Make Me an Offer (Dominant Pictures)
The Man Who Never Was (20th Century-Fox)
Men of Sherwood Forest (Astor)
Midnight Episode (Fine Arts)
Moby Dick (Warners)
Murder on Approval (RKO Radio)
1984 (Columbia)
Passport to Treason (Astor)
Postmark for Danger (RKO Radio)
Private's Progress (DCA)
Richard III (Lopert)
Satellite in the Sky (Warners)
The Ship That Died of Shame (Continental)
Simon and Laura (Universal)
Spin a Dark Web (Columbia)
Storm over the Nile (Columbia)
Suicide Mission (Columbia)
Track the Man Down (Republic)
23 Paces to Baker Street (20th Century-Fox)
The Way Out (RKO Radio)
Wee Geordie (George K. Arthur)

1957

Across the Bridge (RFDA)
The Admirable Crichton (Columbia)
An Alligator Named Daisy (RFDA)
As Long as They're Happy (RFDA)
The Baby and the Battleship (DCA)
Battle Hell (DCA)
Bermuda Affair (DCA)
The Black Tent (RFDA)
Black Tide (Astor)
Blue Peter (DCA)
The Bolshoi Ballet (RFDA)

Cast a Dark Shadow (DCA)

Cat Girl (American-Int.)

Checkpoint (RFDA)

The Colditz Story (DCA)

The Curse of Frankenstein (Warners)

Decision against Time (MGM)

Doctor at Large (Universal)

The End of the Road (DCA)

Enemy from Outer Space (United Artists)

Escapade (DCA)

The Fighting Wildcats (Republic)

Fire down Below (Columbia)

The Flesh Is Weak (DCA)

The French They are a Funny Race (Continental)

The Gentle Touch (RFDA)

The Green Man (DCA)

Heaven Knows Mr. Allison (20th Century-Fox)

Hell in Korea (DCA)

Hour of Decision (Astor)

How to Murder a Rich Uncle (Columbia)

Island in the Sun (20th Century-Fox)

It's Great to be Young (Fine Arts)

Jacqueline (RFDA)

John and Julie (DCA)

Journey to Freedom (Republic)

Lady of Vengeance (United Artists)

Let's Be Happy (Allied Artists)

The Little Hut (Loew's)

The Long Haul (Columbia)

Loser Takes All (DCA)

Man in the Road (Republic)

One Way Out (RFDA)

Operation Conspiracy (Republic)

Out of the Clouds (RFDA)

Panic in the Parlor (DCA)

Pickup Alley (Columbia)

The Pride and the Passion (United Artists)

The Prince and the Showgirl (Warners)

Pursuit of the Graf Spee (RFDA)

Raising a Riot (Continental)

Reach for the Sky (RFDA)

Rock around the World (American-International)

Saint Joan (United Artists)

The Ship Was Loaded (George K. Arthur)

The Silken Affair (DCA)

The Smallest Show on Earth (Times Film)

The Spanish Gardener (RFDA)

The Story of Esther Costello (Columbia)

Stowaway Girl (Paramount)

Stranger in Town (Astor)

Tears for Simon (Republic)

Teenage Bad Girl (DCA)

The Third Key (RFDA)

Thunder over Tangier (Republic)

Time Is My Enemy (Republic)

Time without Pity (Astor)

A Town Like Alice (RFDA)

Town on Trial (Columbia)

Triple Deception (RFDA)

Two Grooms for a Bride (20th Century-Fox)

Value for Money (RFDA)

The Weapon (Republic)

Wee Geordie (Times Film)

Wicked as they Come (Columbia)

Woman in a Dressing Gown (Warners)

X the Unknown (Warners)

Zarak (Columbia)

1958

All at Sea (MGM)

Another Time, Another Place (Paramount)

Blonde Blackmailer (Allied Artists)

Blood of the Vampire (Universal)

Blue Murder at St. Trinian's (Continental)

The Camp on Blood Island (Columbia)

Campbell's Kingdom (RFDA)

Chase a Crooked Shadow (Warners)

Contraband Spain (Stratford)

Count Five and Die (20th Century-Fox)

The Crawling Terror (Dominant)

Creatures from Another World (Dominant)

Cross-Up (United Artists)

Curse of the Demon (Columbia)

Dangerous Exile (RFDA)

Dangerous Youth (Warners)

Date with Disaster (Astor)

The Doctor's Dilemma (MGM)

Dunkirk (MGM)

Fiend without a Face (MGM)

Good Companions (Stratford)

The Gypsy and the Gentleman (RFDA)

The Haunted Strangler (MGM)

Hell Drivers (RFDA)

Henry V (RFDA)

High Flight (Columbia)

Horror of Dracula (Universal)

Horse's Mouth (United Artists)

Indiscreet (Warners)

The Inn of the Sixth Happiness (20th Century-Fox)

Intent to Kill (20th Century-Fox)

It's Great to Be Young (Fine Arts)

It's Never Too Late (Stratford)

The Key (Columbia)

Kill Me Tomorrow (Tudor)

Law and Disorder (Continental)

Lucky Jim (Kingsley International)

Mad Little Island (RFDA)

Mailbag Robbery (Tudor)

The Man Inside (Columbia)

Mark of the Hawk (Universal)

Murder Reported (Columbia)

Night Ambush (RFDA)

A Night to Remember (RFDA)

Now and Forever (Stratford)

One That Got Away (RFDA)

Orders to Kill (UMPO)

The Reluctant Debutante (MGM)

Revenge of Frankenstein (Columbia)

Robbery Under Arms (RFDA)

Rooney (RFDA)

Rx Murder (20th Century-Fox)

The Safecracker (MGM)

Scotland Yard Dragnet (Republic)

The Secret Place (RFDA)

She Played with Fire (Columbia)

The Sheriff of Fractured Jaw (20th Century-Fox)

The Silent Enemy (Universal)

The Snorkel (Columbia)

Steel Bayonet (United Artists)

The Strange Case of Dr. Manning (Republic)

Tale of Two Cities (RFDA)

Tank Force (Columbia)

Tom Thumb (MGM)

The Truth about Women (Continental)

The Whole Truth (Columbia)

Windom's Way (RFDA)

Your Past Is Showing (RFDA)

1959

Bad Girl (Valiant)

The Bandit of Zhobe (Columbia)

Breakout (Continental)

The Bridal Path (Kingsley-Union)

Carry On Sargeant (Governor)

The Circle (Kassler)

City after Midnight (RKO Radio)

A Cry from the Streets (Tudor)
The Devil's Disciple (United Artists)
Floods of Fear (Universal)
The Giant Behemoth (Allied Artists)
Gideon of Scotland Yard (Columbia)
Happy Is the Bride (Kassler)
Hidden Homicide (Republic)
Horrors of the Black Museum (American International)
The Hound of the Baskervilles (United Artists)
I Was Monty's Double (NTA)
It's a Wonderful World (Joseph Brenner)
Libel (MGM)
Look Back in Anger (Warners)
The Man Upstairs (Kingsley-Union)
The Man Who Could Cheat Death (Paramount)
The Mouse That Roared (Columbia)
The Mummy (Universal)
Nowhere to Go (MGM)
A Question of Adultery (NTA)
Room at the Top (Continental)
Sapphire (Universal)
The Scapegoat (MGM)
The Son of Robin Hood (20th Century-Fox)
Strange Affection (Joseph Brenner)
Three Men in a Boat (Valiant)
Tiger Bay (Continental)
The Two-Headed Spy (Columbia)
Web of Evidence (Allied Artists)
The Woman Hater (Columbia)
Yesterday's Enemy (Columbia)

1960

The Angry Silence (Valiant)
Another Sky (Harrison)
The Battle of the Sexes (Continental)
Behind the Mask (Show Corp. of America)

Bobbikins (20th Century-Fox)
The Boy Who Stole a Million (Paramount)
The Brides of Dracula (Universal)
The Captain's Table (20th Century-Fox)
Carry On Nurse (Governor)
Chance Meeting (Paramount)
Circus of Horrors (American Int.)
Conspiracy of Hearts (Paramount)
Cover Girl Killer (Fanfare)
The Day They Robbed the Bank of England (MGM)
Desert Attack (20th Century-Fox)
The Entertainer (Continental)
Expresso Bongo (Continental)
Flame over India (20th Century-Fox)
A French Mistress (Films-Around-the-World)
The Grass Is Greener (Universal)
The Green Carnation (Warwick)
Hand in Hand (Columbia)
Hell Is a City (Columbia)
I'm All Right Jack (Columbia)
In the Wake of a Stranger (Paramount)
Jack the Ripper (Paramount)
Jazz Boat (Columbia)
Kidnapped (Buena Vista)
Killers of Kilimanjaro (Columbia)
Man in a Cocked Hat (Show Corp. of America)
The Man Who Wouldn't Talk (Show Corp. of America)
More Deadly than the Male (Lester Schoenfeld)
Nature's Paradise (Fanfare)
Next to No Time (Show Corp. of America)
Once More, with Feeling (Columbia)
Oscar Wilde (Films-Around-the-World)
Please Turn Over (Columbia)

The Royal Ballet (Lopert)
S.O.S. Pacific (Universal)
The Shakedown (Universal)
Sink the Bismarck! (20th Century-Fox)
Sons and Lovers (20th Century-Fox)
The Stranglers of Bombay (Columbia)
Swiss Family Robinson (Buena Vista)
Tarzan the Magnificent (Paramount)
The 39 Steps (20th Century-Fox)
The Three Worlds of Gulliver (Columbia)
A Touch of Larceny (Paramount)
Tunes of Glory (Lopert)
The Village of the Damned (MGM)
The Wind Cannot Read (20th Century-Fox)

1961

The Anatomist (David Bader)
Beware of Children (American Int.)
Call Me Genius (Continental)
Carry On Constable (Governor Films)
The Curse of the Warewolf (Universal)
Dentist in the Chair (Ajay)
Doctor Blood's Coffin (United Artists)
Doctor in Love (Governor Films)
Double Bunk (Showcorporation)
Four Desperate Men (Continental)
Foxhold in Cairo (Paramount)
Gorgo (MGM)
The Green Helmet (MGM)
Greyfriar's Bobby (Buena Vista)
The Guns of Navarone (Columbia)
The Hand (American Int.)
House of Fright (American Int.)
Invasion Quartet (MGM)
The Kitchen (Kingsley Int.)
Konga (American Int.)
League of Gentlemen (Kingsley Int.)

Left, Right and Center (BCG Films)
The Long and the Short and the Tall (Continental)
Loss of Innocence (Columbia)
Man in the Moon (Trans-Lux)
The Mark (Continental)
The Millionairess (20th Century-Fox)
Mysterious Island (Columbia)
The Naked Edge (United Artists)
Never Take Candy from a Stranger (Sutton Pictures)
No Love for Johnnie (Embassy)
Passport to China (Columbia)
Portrait of a Sinner (American Int.)
The Pure Hell at St. Trinian's (Continental)
The Risk (Kingsley Int.)
The Roman Spring of Mrs. Stone (Warners)
Run across the River (Sutton Pictures)
Saturday Night and Sunday Morning (Continental)
Scream of Fear (Columbia)
The Secret Partner (MGM)
The Shadow of the Cat (Universal)
The Snake Woman (United Artists)
Stop Me Before I Kill! (Columbia)
Sword of Sherwood Forest (Columbia)
The Terror of the Tongs (Columbia)
Three on a Spree (United Artists)
Trouble in the Sky (Universal)
The Trunk (Columbia)
Two-Way Stretch (Showcorporation)
The Unstoppable Man (Sutton Pictures)
Upstairs and Downstairs (20th Century-Fox)
Vienna Waltzes (Hoffberg)
Watch Your Stern (Magna Pictures)
A Weekend with Lulu (Columbia)

1962

Billy Budd (Allied Artists)
Burn Witch Burn (American Int.)
Carry On Teacher (Governor Films)
Cash on Demand (Columbia)
A Coming-Out Party (Union)
The Concrete Jungle (Fanfare Films)
Damn the Defiant! (Columbia)
The Day the Earth Caught Fire (Universal)
Der Rosenkavalier (Rank Overseas)
Flame in the Streets (Atlantic Pictures)
The Frightened City (Allied Artists)
Guns of Darkness (Warners)
The Hellions (Columbia)
Horror Hotel (Trans-Lux)
I Like Money (20th Century-Fox)
I Thank a Fool (MGM)
In Search of the Castaways (Buena Vista)
Information Received (Universal)
Invitation to Murder (Atlantic Pictures)
A Kind of Loving (Governor)
Lolita (MGM)
The Loneliness of the Long Distance Runner (Continental)
Malaga (Warners)
A Matter of Who (Herts-Lion Int.)
Murder She Said (MGM)
Nearly a Nasty Accident (Universal)
Night Creatures (Universal)
Night of Passion (Astor)
No Place Like Homicide! (Embassy)
Only Two Can Play (Columbia)
Operation Snatch (Continental)
Payroll (Allied Artists)
Peeping Tom (Astor)
Phantom of the Opera (Universal)
The Pirates of Blood River (Columbia)
Ring-a-Ding Rhythm (Columbia)

Road to Hong Kong (United Artists)
Roomates (Herts Lion Int.)
Satan Never Sleeps (20th Century-Fox)
The Singer Not the Song (Warners)
A Taste of Honey (Continental)
The Valiant (United Artists)
Victim (Pathe-America)
Waltz of the Toreadors (Continental)
The War Lover (Columbia)
West End Jungle (Atlantic)
Whistle down the Wind (Pathe-America)
Wild for Kicks (Victoria Films)
Wonderful to Be Young! (Paramount)

1963

Billy Liar (Continental)
Call Me Bwana (United Artists)
Carry On Regardless (Governor)
Corridors of Blood (MGM)
Dr No (United Artists)
Fury at Smugglers Bay (Embassy)
Get On with It (Governor)
The Haunting (MGM)
Hellfire Club (Embassy)
Horror Hotel (Trans-Lux)
I Could Go On Singing (United Artists)
Journey into Nowhere (President)
Jungle Street Girls (Ajay)
Just for Fun! (Columbia)
Kiss of the Vampire (Universal)
The L-Shaped Room (Columbia)
Ladies Who Do (Continental)
Lawrence of Arabia (Columbia)
Lord of the Flies (Continental)
Macbeth (Prominent)
The Main Attraction (MGM)
The Maniac (Columbia)
The Mind Benders (American Int.)
Mouse on the Moon (Lopert)

Murder at the Gallop (MGM)
Mystery Submarine (Universal)
Never Let Go (Continental)
The Old Dark House (Columbia)
Paranoic (Universal)
The Password Is Courage (MGM)
Play It Cool (Allied Artists)
The Running Man (Columbia)
Siege of the Saxons (Columbia)
The Small World of Sammy Lee
(Seven Arts Assn.)
Stolen Hours (United Artists)
Summer Holiday (American Int.)
Sword of Lancelot (Universal)
Term of Trial (Warners)
This Sporting Life (Continental)
Tiara Tahiti (Zenith Int.)
Tom Jones (United Artists)
The Traitors (Universal)
The V.I.P.s (MGM)
The Wrong Arm of the Law (Continental)

1964

Becket (Paramount)
The Black Torment (Governor)
Bomb in the High Street (Hemisphere)
The Brain (Governor)
Carry On Spying (Governor)
The Chalk Garden (Universal)
Children of the Damned (MGM)
The Crimson Blade (Columbia)
Devil Doll (Associated Film)
Devil-Ship Pirates (Columbia)
Dr Crippen (Warners)
Doctor in Distress (Governor)
The Dream Maker (Universal)
The Earth Dies Screaming (20th
Century-Fox)
East of Sudan (Columbia)
Escape by Night (Allied Artists)
The Evil of Frankenstein (Universal)

The Eyes of Annie Jones (20th
Century-Fox)
The Finest Hours (Columbia)
From Russia with Love (United Artists)
Girl with Green Eyes (Lopert)
Goldfinger (United Artists)
The Guest (Janus)
Guns at Batasi (20th Century-Fox)
A Hard Day's Night (United Artists)
Hide and Seek (Universal)
The Horrible Dr Hichcock [sic]
(Sigma III)
The Horror of It All (20th Century-Fox)
A Jolly Bad Fellow (Continental)
Life in Danger (Allied Artists)
Man in the Middle (20th Century-Fox)
The Man Who Couldn't Walk (Taurus)
The Masque of the Red Death
(American Int.)
Master Spy (Allied Artists)
The Moon Spinners (Buena Vista)
Murder Ahoy (MGM)
Murder Most Foul (MGM)
Night Must Fall (MGM)
Night Train to Paris (20th Century-Fox)
Nightmare (Universal)
Nothing But the Best (Royal Films)
Psyche '59 (Columbia)
The Pumpkin Eater (Royal Films)
Rattle of a Simple Man (Continental)
Ring of Treason (Paramount)
Seance on a Wet Afternoon (Artixo)
The Servant (Landau Releasing)
A Shot in the Dark (United Artists)
Sing and Swing (Universal)
633 Squadron (United Artists)
Some People (American Int.)
Station Six-Sahara (Allied Artists)

The Swingin' Maiden (Columbia)
Tamahine (MGM)
The Third Secret (20th Century-Fox)
Tomorrow at Ten (Governor)
A Touch of Hell (Governor)
The Unearthly Stranger (American Int.)
Walk a Tightrope (Paramount)
Why Bother to Knock (Seven Arts)
Witchcraft (20th Century-Fox)
Woman of Straw (United Artists)
Young and Willing (Universal)
Zulu (Embassy)

1965

Agent 8¾ (Continental)
The Amorous Adventures of Moll Flanders (Paramount)
An Evening with the Royal Ballet (Sigma III)
A Boy Ten Feet Tall (Paramount)
The Brigand of Kandahar (Columbia)
Carry On Cleo (Governor)
Code 7 Victim 5 (Columbia)
Curse of the Fly (20th Century-Fox)
The Curse of the Mummy's Tomb (Columbia)
Curse of the Voodoo (Allied Artists)
Darling (Embassy)
Devils of Darkness (20th Century-Fox)
Die! Die! My Darling! (Columbia)
Die, Monster Die (American Int.)
Dr Terror's House of Horrors (Paramount)
Ferry Cross the Mesey (United Artists)
Go-Go Bibgreat! (Eldorado Pictures)
Go Go Mania (American Int.)
The Gorgon (Columbia)
Having a Wild Weekend (Warners)
Help! (Unied Artists)

A High Wind in Jamaica (20th Century-Fox)
A Home of Your Own (Cinema V)
Hysteria (MGM)
The Ipcress File (Universal)
Johnny Nobody (Medallion)
The Knack. . . and How to Get It (United Artists)
Life at the Top (Royal Films Int.)
The Little Ones (Columbia)
Lord Jim (Columbia)
Man in the Dark (Universal)
Masquerade (United Artists)
Mister Moses (United Artists)
The Nanny (20th Century-Fox)
One Way Pendulum (Lopert)
Operation Crossbw (MGM)
Operation Snafu (American Int.)
Repulsion (Royal Films)
Return from the Ashes (United Artists)
The Return of Mr Moto (20th Century-Fox)
Rotten to the Core (Cinema V)
Sands of the Kalahari (Paramount)
Seaside Swingers (Embassy)
The 2nd Best Secret Agent in the Whole Wide World (Embassy)
The Secret of Blood Island (Universal)
She (MGM)
Signpost to Murder (MGM)
The Skull (Paramount)
Spaceflight IC-I (20th Century-Fox)
The Spy Who Came in from the Cold (Paramount)
Swingers' Paradise (American Int.)
These Are the Damned (Columbia)
Those Magnificent Men in Their Flying Machines (20th Century-Fox)
Thunderball (United Artists)
Tomb of Ligeia (American Int.)
Underworld Informers (Continental)

War-Gods of the Deep (American Int.)
The Woman Who Wouldn't Die (Warners)
The Yellow Rolls Royce (MGM)
You Must Be Joking! (Columbia)

1966

Agent for H.A.R.M. (Universal)
Alfie (Paramount)
The Alphabet Murders (MGM)
Arabesque (Universal)
Arrivederci Baby! (Paramount)
Attempt to Kill (Schoenfeld)
Bang, Bang, You're Dead (American Int.)
Blues for Lovers (20th Century-Fox)
The Brides of Fu Manchu (Seven Arts)
Candidate for Murder (Schoenfeld)
Contest Girl (Continental)
Cul De Sac (Sigma III)
Death Trap (Schoenfeld)
Disk-O-Tek Holiday (Allied Artists)
Dr Who and the Daleks (Continental)
Dracula – Prince of Darkness (20th Century-Fox)
The Fighting Prince of Donegal (Buena Vista)
Funeral in Berlin (Paramount)
Georgy Girl (Columbia)
The Girl-Getters (American Int.)
Good Times, Wonderful Times (Rogosin Films)
Grand Prix (MGM)
Gypsy Girl (Continental)
The Heroes of Telemark (Columbia)
The Idol (Embassy)
Incident at Midnight (Schoenfeld)
It Happened Here (Lopert)
Judith (Paramount)
Kaleidoscope (Warners)
Khartoum (United Artists)

The Leather Boys (Allied Artists)
The Liquidator (MGM)
The Main Chance (Embassy)
A Man for All Seasons (Columbia)
McGuire, Go Home! (Continental)
Offbeat (Schoenfeld)
Othello (Warners)
Panic (Schoenfeld)
The Partner (Schoenfeld)
The Party's Over (Allied Artists)
The Plague of the Zombies (20th Century-Fox)
Promise Her Anything (Paramount)
The Psychopath (Paramount)
Rasputin – the Mad Monk (20th Century-Fox)
The Reptile (20th Century-Fox)
Ricochet (Schoenfeld)
Romeo and Juliet (Embassy)
The Share Out (Schoenfeld)
The She Beast (Eurpoix-Consolidated)
Solo for Sparrow (Schoenfeld)
The Spy with the Cold Nose (Embassy)
Stop the World – I Want to Get Off (Warners)
A Study in Terror (Columbia)
Traitor's Gate (Columbia)
Violent Moment (Schoenfeld)
Walk in the Shadow (Continental)
Where the Bullets Fly (Embassy)
Where the Spies Are (MGM)
Wild Affair (Goldstone Film Ent.)
The Wrong Box (Columbia)

1967

Accident (Cinema V)
After You, Comrade (Continental)
Berserk (Columbia)
Blast-Off (American-Int.)
Blood Fiend (Hemisphere)
Carnaby, M.D. (Continental)

Carry On Cabby (Governor)

Casino Royale (Columbia)

A Countess from Hong Kong (Universal)

Deadlier Than the Male (Universal)

The Deadly Affair (Columbia)

The Deadly Bees (Paramount)

The Devil's Daffodil (Goldstone Film Ent.)

The Devil's Own (20th Century-Fox)

The Dirty Dozen (MGM)

Doctor Dolittle (20th Century-Fox)

The Double (Schoenfeld)

Dutchman (Continental)

Eye of the Devil (MGM)

Fahrenheit 451 (Universal)

The Family Way (Warners-Seven Arts)

Far from the Madding Crowd (MGM)

Finders Keepers (United Artists)

Frankenstein Created Woman (20th Century-Fox)

The Frozen Dead (Warners-Seven Arts)

Goal! (Royal Films)

The Great British Train Robbery (Peppercorn-Wormser)

How I Won the War (United Artists)

Island of Terror (Universal)

Island of the Doomed (Allied Artists)

It (Warners-Seven Arts)

The Jokers (Universal)

A King's Story (Continental)

Love Is a Woman (Hemisphere)

The Malpas Mystery (Schoenfeld)

The Man Who Finally Died (Goldstone)

Marat/Sade (United Artists)

The Mikado (Warners-Seven Arts)

The Mummy's Shroud (20th Century-Fox)

The Naked Runner (Warners-Seven Arts)

Never Back Losers (Schoenfeld)

On the Run (Schoenfeld)

Our Mother's House (MGM)

Palaces of a Queen (Universal)

The Penthouse (Paramount)

Prehistoric Women (20th Century-Fox)

Privilege (Universal)

The Projected Man (Universal)

Psycho-Circus (American Int.)

Robbery (Embassy)

Sailor from Gibraltar (Lopert)

The Sea Pirate (Paramount)

Smashing Time (Paramount)

The Sorcerers (Allied Artists)

Terronauts (Embassy)

They Came from Beyond Space (Embassy)

To Sir, with Love (Columbia)

The Trap (Continental)

Two Weeks in September (Paramount)

Ulysees (Continental)

The Vulture (Paramount)

The War Game (Pathe Contemporary)

The Whisperers (United Artists)

Country of Origin of Imports	Number
1927	
Germany	38
Britain	8
France	5
Russia	4
Austria	2
Italy	2
China	1
Poland	1
Ireland	1
Africa	1
unknown	2
Total Imports	65
1928	
Germany	84
Britain	35
France	31
Russia	16
Sweden	7
Italy	6
Poland	4
Austria	2
Argentine	1
Canada	1
Czechoslovakia	1
Egypt	1
India	1
Norway	1
Syria	1
Total Imports	192
1929	
Germany	46
Britain	28
USSR	22
France	19
Italy	4

Australia	3
New Zealand	3
Austria	2
India	2
Turkey	2
Armenia	1
Brazil	1
China	1
Denmark	1
Egypt	1
Hungary	1
Japan	1
Norway	1
South Africa	1
Spain	1
Sweden	1
South Pole	1
World Tour[2]	1
Europe[2]	1
Total Imports	145
1930	
Britain	30
Germany	26
USSR	13
France	3
North Africa	3
South Pole	2
South Seas	2
Sweden	2
Alaska	1
Borneo	1
France/Italy	1
Italy	1
Japan	1
Total Imports	86
1931	
Germany	56
Britain	20
France	18

USSR	12	USSR	19
Italy	7	France	15
Sweden	3	Mexico	15
Arabia	1	Argentina	6
Central Africa	1	Sweden	5
Czechoslovakia	1	Hungary	4
Morocco	1	Palestine	4
Spain	1	Poland	4
Total Imports	**121**	Italy	3
		Ireland	2
1932		Puerto Rico	1
		Total Imports	**181**
Germany	105		
Britain	**31**	**1935**	
France	19		
USSR	17	Germany	90
Italy	9	**Britain**	**40**
Poland	8	France	20
Sweden	4	Mexico	17
Mexico	2	USSR	17
Hungary	1	Hungary	15
Total Imports	**196**	Spain	10
		Italy	9
1933		Argentina	5
		Sweden	5
Germany	62	Poland	4
Britain	**27**	Czechoslovakia	2
France	21	Bali	1
USSR	21	Morocco	1
Italy	6	Palestine	1
Mexico	5	Soudan	1
Poland	5	**Total Imports**	**238**
Hungary	4		
Spain	2	**1936**	
Iceland	1		
Norway	1	Germany	75
Sweden	1	**Britain**	**39**
Switzerland	1	Italy	29
Total Imports	**157**	Mexico	28
		France	16
1934		USSR	15
Germany	60	Hungary	13
Britain	**43**	Sweden	10

Poland	4	USSR	17
Spain	3	China	7
Czechoslovakia	2	Sweden	7
Argentina	1	Ireland	6
Austria	1	Finland	3
Central Asia	1	Greece	3
China	1	Austria	2
Mongolia	1	Spain	2
Palestine	1	Africa	1
Total Imports	**240**	Argentina	1
		Australia	1

1937

Bali	1
Bohemia	1
Japan	1
Ukrania	1
Total Imports	**319**

Germany	71
Britain	**53**
France	23
Hungary	18
Italy	17
USSR	14

1939

Poland	10
Sweden	10
Spain	9
Mexico	5
Austria	4
Argentina	2
Czechoslovakia	2
Armenia	1
Australia	1
Canada	1
Denmark	1
Japan	1
Switzerland	1
Total Imports	**244**

Germany	85
Britain	**37**
France	33
Mexico	22
Italy	18
USSR	15
Hungary	14
Sweden	10
Poland	7
Argentina	6
Czechoslovakia	6
Spain	4
China	3
Cuba	2
Ireland	2
Finland	2

1938

Germany	87
Britain	**44**
Mexico	35
France	30
Hungary	29
Italy	21
Poland	19

Australia	1
Denmark	1
Egypt	1
Greece	1
Holland	1
Norway	1
South Seas	1

Switzerland	1		Sweden	5
Total Imports	274		France	4
			Canada + Britain	1

1940

			China	1
Britain	53		Greece	1
Italy	44		Norway	1
Germany	35		Germany	1
France	27		**Total Imports**	47
Hungary	12			
Argentina	9		**1943**	
Sweden	9			
Spain	6		**Britain**	17
Mexico	4		USSR	11
Czechoslovakia	3		France	1
USSR	3		India	1
Australia	2		**Total Imports**	30
Cuba	2			
Ireland	2		**1944**	
Total Imports	211			
			Britain	22
			USSR	10

1941

			France	7
			Spain	1
Britain	30		**Total Imports**	40
Germany	24			
USSR	12		**1945**	
France	8			
Sweden	8		**Britain**	21
Spain	7		USSR	10
Italy	7		Switzerland	2
Argentina	5		**Total Imports**	33
Mexico	2			
Austria	1		**1946**	
China	1			
Czechoslovakia	1		Mexico	31
Ireland	1		**Britain**	24
Thailand	1		USSR	11
Total Imports	108		Austria	7
			France	6

1942

			Argentina	4
Britain	22		Italy	3
USSR	11		Australia	1
			Cuba	1
			Hungary	1

Sweden	1
Switzerland	1
Total Imports	**91**

1947

Mexico	36
Britain	**28**
Argentina	18
Italy	14
France	12
USSR	8
Austria	2
Canada	2
Belgium	1
Czechoslovakia	1
India	1
Palestine	1
Spain	1
Sweden	1
Total Imports	**126**

1948

Britain	**33**
France	33
Italy	15
USSR	9
Germany	7
Mexico	2
Argentina	1
Austria	1
British-Switzerland	1
Canada	1
Europe	1
Hungary	1
South America	1
Sweden	1
Switzerland-Germany	1
Switzerland	1
Total Imports	**109**

1949

Britain	**51**
Italy	31
Hungary	21
France	19
Sweden	7
Africa	2
Germany	2
Greece	2
Argentina	1
Australia	1
Canada	1
China	1
Denmark	1
Ireland	1
Poland	1
Spain	1
Total Imports	**143**

1950

Spain	62
Britain	**47**
Italy	33
France	32
Germany	26
Austria	9
USSR	6
Africa	3
Czechoslovakia	3
Ireland	4
Yugoslavia	2
Argentina	1
China	1
Cuba	1
Denmark	1
Hungary	1
India	1
Israel	1
Mexico	1

Philippines	1	Africa	5
Poland	1	Sweden	4
Sweden	1	Austria	3
Switzerland	1	Poland	2
Total Imports	239	Spain	2
		Argentina	1
1951		Canada	1
		Ceylon	1
Mexico	106	Egypt	1
Britain	73	India	1
Italy	26	Ireland	1
France	20	Israel	1
USSR	6	Japan	1
Germany	4	Lapland	1
Ireland	3	Latin America	1
Africa	2	Yugoslavia	1
Australia	2	**Total Imports**	209
Austria	2		
Czechoslovakia	2	**1953**	
Spain	2		
Sweden	2	Mexico	49
Canada	1	**Britain**	39
Cuba	1	Italy	36
Hawaii	1	Germany	31
Hungary	1	Spain	13
India	1	France	9
Japan	1	Austria	7
Korea	1	Australia	1
Latin America	1	Philippines	1
Puerto Rico	1	South Africa	1
Siam	1	Sweden	1
Switzerland	1	**Total Imports**	188
Yugoslavia	1		
Total Imports	262	**1954**	
		Britain	52
1952		Mexico	41
		Italy	20
Mexico	49	France	12
Britain	45	Germany	12
Germany	45	Austria	8
France	21	Denmark	2
Italy	15	Japan	2
USSR	7		

Greece	1		Austria	2
India	1		India	2
Spain	1		Arabia	1
Total Imports	**152**		Argentina	1
			Brazil	1

1955

		East Africa	1
Britain	**52**	Egypt	1
Italy	26	Greece	1
Germany	21	Israel	1
France	14	Japan	1
USSR	13	Monaco	1
Mexico	4	Morocco	1
Africa	3	North Africa	1
India	3	Pakistan	1
Japan	3	Portugal	1
Austria	2	Sweden	1
Israel	2	Switzerland	1
Sweden	2	West Africa	1
Australia	1	**Total Imports**	**221**
Brazil	1		

1957

Britain/Germany	1
Canada	1
Czechoslovakia	1
New Zealand	1
Poland	1
Spain	1
Switzerland	1
Total Imports	**154**

Britain	**78**		
Germany	42		
France	36		
Italy	31		
USSR	10		
Japan	8		
Austria	4		
Greece	3		
Copenhagen	2		

1956

			Mexico	2
Germany	79		Spain	2
Britain	**46**		Sweden	2
Italy	28		Africa	1
France	18		Australia	1
USSR	10		Brazil	1
Japan	5		Britain/Germany	1
Spain	4		Britain/Italy	1
Africa	3		Canada	1
Mexico	3		Europe/Africa	1
Yugoslavia	3		Finland	1
Australia	2		Ireland	1

Middle East	1		Sweden	3
Morocco	1		Africa	2
New Guinea	1		Ireland	2
North Africa/Italy	1		Argentina	1
Total Imports	233		Australia	1
			Denmark	1
1958			Greece	1
Germany	73		Holland	1
Britain	68		India	1
Italy	42		Israel	1
France	40		Japan	1
USSR	10		**Total Imports**	246
Austria	7			
Spain	6		**1960**	
India	3		Germany	65
Africa	2		**Britain**	51
Holland	2		Italy	50
Norway	2		France	21
Denmark	1		USSR	14
Finland	1		Japan	7
Greece	1		Sweden	4
Hong Kong	1		Austria	3
Hungary	1		Spain	3
Japan	1		Greece	2
South Africa	1		Ireland	2
South America	1		Yugoslavia	2
Thailand	1		Australia	1
West Africa	1		Brazil	1
Yugoslavia	1		China	1
Total Imports	266		Holland	1
			India	1
1959			Israel	1
Germany	64		Mexico	1
Italy	45		North Africa	1
Mexico	42		Switzerland	1
Britain	37		**Total Imports**	233
France	21			
USSR	11		**1961**	
Austria	5		Mexico	70
Japan	3		Italy	60
Spain	3		**Britain**	54

257

Germany	53
France	24
USSR	14
Spain	13
Hungary	8
Austria	7
Canada	6
Japan	5
Philippines	4
Denmark	2
Poland	2
Sweden	2
Africa	1
Australia	1
Czechoslovakia	1
Hong Kong	1
Ireland	1
Israel	1
New Guinea	1
Total Imports	331

1962

Mexico	54
Britain	49
Italy	47
Germany	35
France	28
USSR	13
Spain	12
Argentina	7
Austria	7
Greece	5
Japan	5
Sweden	4
Canada	2
Philippines	2
Brazil	1
Denmark	1
East Africa	1
Holland	1
Hong Kong	1
India	1

Ireland	1
Poland	1
Switzerland	1
Venezuela	1
Total Imports	280

1963

Italy	62
Mexico	57
Britain	44
France	35
Germany	22
Argentina	15
Spain	12
Austria	10
Japan	10
USSR	10
India	3
Greece	2
Israel	2
Philippines	2
Africa	1
Brazil	1
Canada	1
Cuba	1
Egypt	1
France/Italy	1
Japan/Sweden	1
Poland	1
Sweden	1
Switzerland	1
Yugoslavia	1
Total Imports	297

1964

Japan	82
Britain	64
Mexico	61
Italy	34
France	29
Germany	24

Argentina	12		Ireland	1
Austria	11		Portugal	1
USSR	10		Sweden	1
Spain	9		**Total Imports**	**300**
Sweden	5			
Puerto Rico	3		**1966**	
Africa	2		**Britain**	**60**
Canada	· 2		Mexico	60
Denmark	2		Germany	42
Greece	2		Italy	34
Yugoslavia	2		France	26
Columbia	1		Spain	16
Finland	1		USSR	16
Ireland	1		Czechoslovakia	5
Malaysia	1		Argentina	4
Philippines	1		Israel	4
Vietnam	1		Denmark	3
Total Imports	**360**		India	3
			Japan	3
1965			Philippines	3
Mexico	67		Africa	2
Britain	**60**		Brazil	2
Italy	46		Sweden	2
Germany	39		Yugoslavia	2
France	27		Canada	1
Japan	12		Holland	1
Spain	11		Hong Kong	1
Argentina	6		Ireland	1
Puerto Rico	4		Middle East/Europe	1
Africa	3		Poland	1
Brazil	3		Portugal	1
South Africa	3		Vietnam	1
Austria	2		**Total Imports**	**295**
Canada	2			
Greece	2		**1967**	
Israel	2		Mexico	75
Sweden	2		**Britain**	**63**
USSR	2		Italy	29
Britain/Ireland	1		Germany	26
Britain/Italy	1		Spain	25
Denmark	1		France	20
India	1			

USSR	5	Denmark	1
Argentina	4	Ecuador	1
Sweden	4	Hong Kong	1
Czechoslovakia	3	Israel	1
Greece	3	Italy/Spain	1
Algeria	2	Jamaica	1
Canada	2	Kenya	1
Canary Islands	2	Lebanon	1
Hungary	2	Poland	1
Japan	2	South America	1
Peru	2	West Africa	1
Yugoslavia	2	**Total Imports**	**284**
Africa	1		
Br/Fr/Japan/Gmy	1		

Note

1. The figures presented here have been compiled from *The Film Daily Year Book* (New York: Film Daily). They cover the years for which import lists were published. US distribution companies have been included, but for the early years this information was not always available. While the figures may not be completely comprehensive, they are the most accurate list available from contemporary sources.
2. It is not clear what these two groupings mean, but they have been included as in the original lists.

Archival Sources and Bibliography

Archival Sources

British Film Institute Library and Special Collections: Michael Balcon collection.
John Rylands Library, University of Manchester: Basil Dean and Robert Donat collections.
Public Record Office, Kew Gardens.
The Billy Rose Theatre Collection, New York Public Library.
Center for Motion Picture Study: the Margaret Herrick Library, Los Angeles: Production Code Administration special collection.
The Museum of Modern Art, New York.
The National Archives, Washington D.C.: US State Department and Department of Commerce Records.
The United Artists Archive, Madison, Wisconsin.
The Universal Studios and Warner Brothers archives, University of Southern California.

Bibliography

Allen, R. and Gomery, D. (1985) *Film History: Theory and Practice.* New York: Alfred A. Knopf.
American Institute of Public Opinion (1979) *Gallup Looks at the Movies: Audience Research Reports, 1940–50.* Wilmington, Delaware: Scholarly Resources.
Balcon, M. (1969) *Michael Balcon Presents . . . A Lifetime of Films.* London: Hutchinson.
Balio, T. (1976) *United Artists: The Company Built by the Stars.* Wisconsin: University of Wisconsin.
Balio, T. (1985) *The American Film Industry.* Wisconsin: University of Wisconsin.
Balio, T. (1987) *United Artists: The Company that Changed the Film Industry.* Wisconsin: University of Wisconsin.
Balio, T. (ed.) (1993) *Grand Design: Hollywood as a Modern Business Enterprise, 1930–39.* London: University of California Press.
Bamford, K. (1999) *Distorted Images: British National Identity and Film in the 1920s.* London: I.B. Tauris.
Barr, C. (1977) *Ealing Studios.* London and Devon: Cameron and Tayleur in association with David and Charles.
Bennett, T. and Woollacott, J. (1987) *Bond and Beyond: The Political Career of a Popular Hero.* London: Macmillan.
Bergfelder, T. (1997) 'Surface and Distraction: Style and Genre in Gainsborough's International Trajectory in the late 1920s and 1930s' in Cook, P. (ed.), *Gainsborough Pictures.* London: Cassell.

Bergfelder, T. (2000) 'The Nation Vanishes: European co-productions and Popular Genre formulae in the 1950s and 1960s' in Hjort, M. and Mackenzie, S. (eds.), *Cinema and Nation*. London: Routledge.

Bernstein, M. and Studlar, G. (eds.) (1997) *Visions of the East: Orientalism in Film*. London: I.B. Tauris.

Betts, E. (1960) *Inside Pictures*. London: Cresset Press.

Black, G. (1997) *The Catholic Crusade against the Movies, 1940–75*. Cambridge: Cambridge University Press.

Bourdieu, P. (1984) *Distinction: A Social Critique of the Judgement of Taste*. London: Routledge.

Burrows, J. (2002) 'Big Studio Production in the Pre-Quota Years' in Murphy, R. (ed.), *The British Cinema Book* (2nd ed.). London: British Film Institute.

Chapman, J. (1995) 'The Life of Colonel Blimp (1943) Reconsidered', *Historical Journal of Film, Radio and Television*, vol. 15, no. 2.

Chapman, J. (1999) *Licence to Thrill: A Cultural History of the James Bond Films*. London: I.B. Tauris.

Church Gibson, P. (2000) 'Fewer Weddings and More Funerals: Changes in the Heritage Film' in Murphy, R. (ed.) *British Cinema of the 90s*. London: British Film Institute.

Cook, P. (ed.) (1997) *Gainsborough Pictures*. London: Cassell.

Cormack, M. (1994) *Ideology and Cinematography in Hollywood, 1930–39*. London: Macmillan.

Crafton, D. (1997) *The Talkies: American Cinema's Transition to Sound, 1926–31*. London: University of California Press.

Davy, C. (ed.) (1938) *Footnotes to the Film*. London: Lovat Dickinson Ltd., Readers Union Ltd.

Dean, B. (1973) *Mind's Eye*. London: Hutchinson.

Dickinson, M. and Street, S. (1985) *Cinema and State: The Film Industry and the British Government, 1927–84*. London: British Film Institute.

The Distribution and Exhibition of Cinematograph Films: Report of a Committee of Enquiry, 1949. Cmd. 7839. HMSO.

Drazin, C. (1998) *The Finest Years: British Cinema of the 1940s*. London: André Deutsch.

Eberts, J. and Illot, T. (1990) *My Indecision is Final: The Rise and Fall of Goldcrest Films*. London: Faber and Faber.

Everson, W.K. (1975) 'Jessie Matthews', *Films in Review*, vol. 26, no. 10.

Film Daily Year Book (various). New York: Film Daily.

Finler, J. (1988) *The Hollywood Story*. New York: Crown.

Fraser, J. (1982) *America and the Patterns of Chivalry*. Cambridge: Cambridge University Press.

Glancy, H. M. (1999) *When Hollywood Loved Britain: The Hollywood 'British' Film, 1939–45*. Manchester: Manchester University Press.

Gomery, D. (1986) *The Hollywood Studio System*. London: Macmillan/British Film Institute.

Gomery, D. (1992) *Shared Pleasures: A History of Movie Presentation in the United States*. London: British Film Institute.

Guback, T. (1969) *The International Film Industry: Western Europe and America since 1945*. Bloomington: Indiana University Press.

Guzman, A. H. (1993) 'The Exhibition and Reception of European Films in the US during the 1920s', unpublished PhD Thesis, UCLA.

Haberski, Jr, R. J. (2001) *It's Only A Movie! Films and Critics in American Culture*. Lexington: University Press of Kentucky.

Handel, L. A. (1950) *Hollywood Looks at its Audience: A Report of Film Audience Research*. Urbana: University of Illinois Press.

Harding, J. (1997) *Ivor Novello: A Biography*. Wales Academic Press.

Harper, S. (1994) *Picturing the Past: The Rise and Fall of the British Costume Film*. London: British Film Institute.

Higson, A. (1993) 'Re-presenting the National Past: Nostalgia and Pastiche in the Heritage Film' in Friedman, L. (ed.), *British Cinema and Thatcherism: Fires Were Started*. London: UCL Press.

Higson, A. (1995) *Waving the Flag: Constructing a National Cinema in Britain*. Oxford: Oxford University Press.

Higson, A. (1996) 'The Heritage Film and British Cinema', in Higson, A. (ed.), *Dissolving Views: Key Writings on British Cinema*. London: Cassell.

Higson, A. (2000) 'The Limiting Imagination of National Cinema' in Hjort, M. and Mackensie, S. (eds.), *Cinema and Nation*. London: Routledge.

Higson, A. and Maltby, R. (eds.) (1999) *'Film Europe' and 'Film America': Cinema, Commerce and Cultural Exchange, 1920–39*. Exeter: Exeter University Press.

Hill, J. (1986) *Sex, Class and Realism*. London: British Film Institute.

Hjort, M. and Mackenzie, S. (eds.) (2000) *Cinema and Nation*. London: Routledge.

Hipsky, M. A. (1994) 'Anglophil(m)ia: Why Does America Watch Merchant-Ivory Movies?', *Journal of Popular Film and Television*, vol. 22, no. 3.

Hutchings, P. (1993) *Hammer and Beyond: The British Horror Film*. Manchester: Manchester University Press.

Jaikumar, P. (2001) '"Place" and the Modernist Redemption of Empire in *Black Narcissus*', *Cinema Journal*, vol. 40, no. 2.

Jarvie, I. (1992) *Hollywood's Overseas Campaign: The North Atlantic Movie Trade, 1920–50*. Cambridge: Cambridge University Press.

Kemp, P. (1997) 'Not for Peckham: Michael Balcon and Gainsborough's International Trajectory in the 1920s' in Cook, P. (ed.), *Gainsborough Studios*. London: Cassell.

Klingender, F.D. and Legg, S. (1937) *Money Behind the Screen*. London: Lawrence and Wishart.

Klinger, B. (1997) 'Film History Terminable and Interminable: Recovering the Past in Reception Studies', *Screen*, vol. 38, no. 2.

Koszarski, R. (1990) *An Evening's Entertainment: The Age of the Silent Feature Film, 1915–28*. New York: Charles Schribner.

Kulik, K. (1975) *Alexander Korda: The Man Who Could Work Miracles*. London: W.H. Allen.

Landy, M. (2000) 'The Other Side of Paradise: British Cinema from an American Perspective' in Ashby, J. and Higson, A. (eds.), *British Cinema, Past and Present*. London: Routledge.

Lane, J. (1994) 'Critical and Cultural Reception of the European Art Film in 1950s America: A Case Study of the Brattle Theatre', *Film and History*, vol. 24.

Low, R. (1971) *History of the British Film, 1918–29*. London: Allen & Unwin.

Low, R. (1985) *Film Making in 1930s Britain*. London: Allen & Unwin.

Macdonald, K. (1994) *Emeric Pressburger: The Life and Death of a Screenwriter*. London: Faber.

Macnab, G. (1993) *J. Arthur Rank and the British Film Industry*. London: Routledge.

Macnab, G. (2000) *Searching for Stars*. London: Cassell.

Maltby, R. (1996) 'Censorship and Self-Regulation' in Nowell-Smith, G. (ed.), *The Oxford History of World Cinema*. Oxford: Oxford University Press.

Marwick, A. (1980) *Class: Image and Reality in Britain, France and the USA since 1930*. Glasgow: Harper/Collins.

Massey, A. (2000) *Hollywood Beyond the Screen: Design and Material Culture*. Oxford: Berg.

May, L. (ed.) (1989) *Recasting America: Culture and Politics in the Age of the Cold War*. Chicago: University of Chicago.

Miller, J. S. (2000) *Something Completely Different: British Television and American Culture.* Minneapolis and London: University of Minnesota Press.

Monaco, P. (2001) *The Sixties: History of the American Cinema, Vol. 8.* New York: Charles Scribner's Sons.

Monk, C. (1994) 'Sex, Politics and the Past: Merchant-Ivory, the Heritage Film and Its Critics in the 1980s and 1990s', unpublished MA dissertation, Birkbeck, University of London.

Monk, C. (1999) 'Heritage Film and the British Cinema Audience in the 1990s', *Journal of Popular British Cinema*, no. 2.

Mowat, C. L. (1968) *Britain between the Wars.* London: Methuen.

Murphy, R. (1983) 'Rank's Attempt on the American Market' in Curran, J. and Porter, V. (eds.), *British Cinema History.* London: Weidenfeld and Nicolson.

Murphy, R. (1992) *Sixties British Cinema.* London: British Film Institute.

Murphy, R. (ed.) (2000) *British Cinema in the 90s.* London: British Film Institute.

Neale, S. and Smith, M. (eds.) (1998) *Contemporary Hollywood Cinema.* London: Routledge.

Neaverson, B. (1997) *The Beatles Movies.* London: Cassell.

Noble, P. (1951) *Ivor Novello: Man of the Theatre.* London: The Falcon Press.

Ogan, C. (1990) 'The Audience for Foreign Film in the US', *Journal of Communication,* vol. 40, no. 4.

Petrie, D. (ed.) (1996) *Inside Stories: Diaries of British Film-makers at Work.* London: British Film Institute.

Pirie, D. (1973) *A Heritage of Horror: The English Gothic Cinema, 1946–72.* New York: Avon Books.

Political and Economic Planning (1952). *The British Film Industry.* London: Author.

Pope, W. M. (1954) *Ivor: The Story of an Achievement.* London: Hutchinson.

Porter, V. (1997) 'Methodism versus the Market-place: The Rank Organization and British Cinema' in Murphy, R. (ed.), *The British Cinema Book.* London: British Film Institute.

Porter, V. (1998) 'Genre in Popular British Cinema', *Journal of Popular British Cinema,* no. 1.

Quinn, J. (2000) 'The British Historical Film', unpublished PhD Thesis, Sheffield Hallam University.

Reynolds, D. (1981) *The Creation of the Anglo-American Alliance.* London: Europa.

Richards, J. (1985) *The Age of the Dream Palace: British Cinema and Society, 1930–39.* London: Routledge Kegan Paul.

Richards, J. (1999) '*Things to Come* and Science Fiction in the 1930s' in Hunter, I. Q. (ed.), *British Science Fiction Cinema.* London: Routledge.

Riesman, D, Glazer, N. and Denney, R. (1953) *The Lonely Crowd: A Study of the Changing American Character.* New York: Doubleday Anchor Books.

Roddick, N. (1983) *A New Deal in Entertainment: Warner Brothers in the 1930s.* London: British Film Institute.

Roddick, N. (1995) 'Four Weddings and a Reckoning', *Sight and Sound,* vol. 5, no. 1.

Roud, R. (1956–57) 'Britain in America', *Sight and Sound,* vol. 26, no. 3.

Ryall, T. (2001) *Britain and the American Cinema.* London: Sage.

Said, E. W. (1985) *Orientalism: Western Conceptions of the Orient.* London: Routledge Kegan Paul).

Said, E. W. (1995). *Orientalism: Western Conceptions of the Orient.* London: Penguin.

Schatz, T. (1997) *Boom and Bust: American Cinema in the 1940s.* London: University of California Press.

Schickel, R. (1984) *D. W. Griffith and the Birth of Film.* London: Pavilion, Michael Joseph.

Sedgwick, J. (1996) 'Michael Balcon's Close Encounter with the American Market, 1934-36', *Historical Journal of Film, Radio and Television,* vol. 16, no. 3.

Sedgwick, J. (2000) *Popular Filmgoing in 1930s Britain: A Choice of Pleasures.* Exeter: University of Exeter Press.

Sklar, R. (1999) '"The Lost Audience": 1950s Spectatorship and Historical Reception Studies' in Stokes, M. and Maltby, R. (eds.), *Identifying Hollywood's Audiences*. London: British Film Institute.

Slide, A. (1998) *Banned in the USA: British Films in the United States and their Censorship, 1933–60*. London: I.B. Tauris.

Smythe, D. W., Lusk, P. B. and Lewis, C. A. (1953) 'Portrait of an Art-theatre Audience', *Quarterly of Radio and Television*, vol. 8, no. 1.

Staiger, J. (1992) *Interpreting Films: Studies in the Historical Reception of American Cinema*. Princeton, New Jersey: Princeton University Press.

Street, S. (1985) 'The Hays Office and the Defence of the British Market in the 1930s', *Historical Journal of Film, Radio and Television*, vol. 5, no. 1.

Street, S. (1986) 'Alexander Korda, Prudential Assurance and British Film Finance in the 1930s', *Historical Journal of Film, Radio and Television*, vol. 6, no. 2.

Street, S. (1997) *British National Cinema*. London: Routledge.

Street, S. (1998) 'Popular British Cinema?', *Journal of Popular British Cinema*, no. 1.

Street, S. (2000) 'Stepping Westward: The Distribution of British Feature Films in America, and the Case of *The Private Life of Henry VIII*' in Ashby, J. and Higson, A. (eds.), *British Cinema, Past and Present*. London: Routledge.

Street, S. (2002) '"Got to Dance My Way to Heaven": Jessie Matthews, Art Deco and the British Musical of the 1930s' in Conrich, I., and Tincknell, E. (eds.) *Musical Moments: Film and the Performance of Song and Dance*. Trowbridge: Flicks Books.

Swann, P. (2000) 'The British Culture Industries and the Mythology of the American Market', *Cinema Journal*, vol. 39, no. 4.

Telotte, J. P. (1999) *A Distant Technology: Science Fiction Film and the Machine Age*. Hanover and London: Wesleyan University Press.

Thompson, K. (1985) *Exporting Entertainment: America in the World Film Market, 1907–34*. London: British Film Institute.

Thompson, K. and Bordwell, D. (1994) *Film History: An Introduction*. New York: McGraw-Hill.

Thornton, M. (1975) *Jessie Matthews: A Biography*. St. Albans: Mayflower Press.

Thumim, J. (1992) *Celluloid Sisters: Women in Popular Cinema*. London: Macmillan.

Truffaut, F. (1978) *Hitchcock*. London: Paladin.

Turim, M. (1989) *Flashbacks in Film: Memory and History*. London: Routledge.

Vasey, R. (1997) *The World According to Hollywood, 1918–39*. Exeter: University of Exeter Press.

Walker, A. (1974) *Hollywood, England: The British Film Industry in the Sixties*. London: Michael Joseph.

Walsh, M. (1997) 'Fighting the American Invasion with Cricket, Roses, and Marmalade for Breakfast', *Velvet Light Trap*, no. 40.

Watson, N. (2000) 'Hollywood UK' in Murphy, R. (ed.), *British Cinema in the 90s*. London: British Film Institute.

Wilcox, H. (1967) *25,000 Sunsets*. London: Bodley Head.

Wilinksy, B. (1997) 'First and Finest: British Films on US Television in the Late 1940s', *The Velvet Light Trap*, no. 40.

Wilinsky, B. (2001) *Sure Seaters: The Emergence of Art House Cinema*. Minneapolis: University of Minnesota Press.

Williams, S. (1975) *Ivor*. London: Michael Joseph.

Index

Names and Subjects